The Perception of Stimulus Relations

Discrimination Learning and Transposition

THE CHILD PSYCHOLOGY SERIES

EXPERIMENTAL AND THEORETICAL ANALYSES OF CHILD BEHAVIOR

EDITOR
DAVID S. PALERMO
DEPARTMENT OF PSYCHOLOGY
THE PENNSYLVANIA STATE UNIVERSITY
UNIVERSITY PARK, PENNSYLVANIA

The Perception of Stimulus Relations: Discrimination Learning and Transposition, HAYNE W. REESE, 1968

THE PERCEPTION OF STIMULUS RELATIONS

Discrimination Learning and Transposition

HAYNE W. REESE

STATE UNIVERSITY OF NEW YORK
BUFFALO, NEW YORK

1968

ACADEMIC PRESS   New York and London

ACADEMIC PRESS INC.
111 Fifth Avenue, New York, New York 10003

United Kingdom Edition published by
ACADEMIC PRESS INC. (LONDON) LTD.
Berkeley Square House, London W.1

LIBRARY OF CONGRESS CATALOG CARD NUMBER: 68-18680

PRINTED IN THE UNITED STATES OF AMERICA

Preface

Most of the early experimental work on relation perception and transposition was conducted by German Gestalt psychologists. C. J. Warden and Rowley (1929) depreciated this work; but in a reply to the criticism, Perkins and Wheeler (1930) characterized the transposition data obtained by the first American investigators as "incidental" and "unsystematic." The epithets were not as "idle" as C. J. Warden and Winslow (1931) asserted, because the relational tests in the earlier American studies were usually incidental to the major purposes of the experimenters. However, the wealth of detail which the early journals permitted in the reports allows one to utilize the material. In fact, many of these early reports contained accounts of incidental observations that are directly relevant to topics reviewed here; in contrast, many of the more recently published reports have omitted relevant details, probably because of the modern editorial policies that greatly restrict page allotments.

Carter (1937) classified the studies of Watson and Watson (1921; see also Watson and Rayner, 1920), Lashley (1924), and Franz (1931) as transposition studies, but the classification was incorrect. The first study clearly involved simple stimulus generalization, and the last two involved interocular and bilateral transfer, which are probably also properly classified as simple stimulus generalization. Some other studies, however, are not so easily classifiable. These include studies of stimulus patterning or compounding, studies of depth perception and perceptual constancy, and certain "insight" studies. Studies of these kinds have been excluded from this review, except for a few examples used to further the theoretical analysis, because the literature on these phenomena is much too extensive to be included, and the phenomena themselves are too complex to be covered summarily. I have not included any material on such relations as "cause and effect" and "being married to," because these are conceptual rather than perceptual relations (see Vinacke, 1951) and they do not seem to be relevant to an analysis of the transposition problem.

I have tried to cover all of the transposition data, and have used secondary

v

sources for many of the foreign-language reports that have never been translated into English, and for the few English-language reports that were unavailable to me. The sources for these are given in the bibliography. The review covers about 250 studies of unidimensional transposition, from some 240 reports, and a large number of related studies. Any omissions were unintentional, with the exception of four Japanese studies (Sato, 1934; Sato, 1935; Sato, 1938; Yoshida, 1939) which were inadequately described in secondary sources. Perhaps they are covered in Sato's (1957) review of the Japanese studies of transposition; but this review, which was listed in Freeman's (1966) unpublished bibliography of transposition research, is also available only in Japanese. My bibliographic search ended in January, 1967.

Part of the material in Chapters 10 and 11 was presented at colloquia at the University of Western Ontario and the University of Texas early in 1966.

I am indebted to my research assistants Mr. Paul W. Blumenbaum, Miss Sheila R. Bob, Mr. Bernard Greenberg, Mr. Douglas F. Johnson, Mr. John B. Morganti, and Mr. Robert Tomkiewicz for aid in the bibliographic search, and to Professors David S. Palermo and Michael D. Zeiler, who read and criticized the draft. I am particularly indebted to the many investigators who provided me with preprints and other unpublished material, and who provided me with references to relevant work that I had overlooked. Finally, I am ineffably grateful to Nancy M. Reese for aid in the proofreading.

The bibliographic search was supported in part by Grant GB-252 from the National Science Foundation. The costs of preparing the manuscript were defrayed by a grant from the Graduate School of the State University of New York at Buffalo.

Buffalo, New York   HAYNE W. REESE
January, 1968

Contents

Part III: STUDIES OF MULTIDIMENSIONAL TRANSPOSITION

Part IV: THEORIES OF TRANSPOSITION

Chapter 11. Outline of a New Theory of Transposition

PART I

Introduction

CHAPTER 1

Introduction

The Problem of Relation Perception

Definition of "Relation"

The word "relation" is used to designate several kinds of connection between separable elements. It refers to (a) physical associations, for example, between two or more stimulus objects differing in a single dimension such as size, brightness, or position; (b) conceptual associations such as the associations between synonyms, between antonyms, between object and attribute, between whole and part, and between cause and effect (Cree Warden, 1933); and (c) connections resulting from special context such as the relation between "rabbit" and "corn" in the sentence, "The rabbit is eating the corn," and the relation between phrases connected by "if," "but," and other conjunctions. Relations such as identity and oddity can occur in all three categories. (L. G. Gotkin has developed a programmed series of "games" designed, in part, to teach children to understand some of these kinds of relations.[1])

Although there is vast literature on the perception of relations among stimuli, most writers who dealt with the problem failed to give a general definition of relation. They may have considered the concept to be a "primitive predicate" or "undefined term" that is incapable of being defined linguistically (Bergmann, 1957, p. 14), or a term about whose meaning there is such widespread agreement that no definition need be specified. Berlyne was a notable exception. Borrowing from the mathematical definition, he proposed that relation be defined as a set of "ordered pairs." An "ordered pair" is a pair of elements presented in a particular spatial or temporal order. It can be symbolized "aRb" to denote that "a stands in the relation R to b" or that the ordered pair $<a,b>$ is a member of the class of ordered pairs R (Berlyne, 1965, pp. 65–66).

According to Klüver: "Only logically is it possible to separate 'relations' and 'relata'" (Klüver, 1933, p. 343). But according to Loewenberg, it may

---

[1] The "games" have been published by Appleton-Century-Crofts under the trademark name, *Language Lotto.*

1

not be possible to separate them even logically: "Relations . . . having no reference to specific terms . . . have nothing to relate, and so cease to be relational" (Loewenberg, 1930, p. 319). John Locke seems to have been expressing the same idea when he wrote, two centuries earlier, that "a relation cannot be founded in nothing, or be the relation of nothing" (Locke, 1690, p. 101). Woodworth pointed out, however, that a "feeling of relation may exist without the feeling of any pair of terms" (Woodworth, 1908, p. 493).

Loewenberg (1930) suggested that actual relations are logically ineffable; when we speak of equality or causality, for example, we are no longer dealing with specific transactions between specific terms, but with logical forms or abstract concepts. There is a discrepancy between the relations known in specific contexts and the relations described independently of them, and to think of relations apart from any context is to falsify their experienced status, which is to be always a part of a context. From this point of view, Berlyne has defined not relations as experienced, but relations as they exist, since a relation is not experienced as a "set of ordered pairs."

(Loewenberg was arguing on logical grounds that the abstract concept of a relation has a meaning that is different from the relation as it is actually experienced. One is reminded of the controversy in classical psychology about whether wordless imagery can represent abstract meaning—is it possible to imagine "triangularity," for example, or must some specific kind of triangle be imagined in order to represent the abstract concept? Titchener [1909, pp. 14–19] briefly discussed this controversy, and gave references to the relevant works of the central figures.)

The dictionary definition seems to be adequate: A relation is any quality that can be predicated only of two or more things. However, Bergmann (1957, pp. 16–17) has pointed out that even though qualities that can be predicated about a single object must, by this kind of definition, be nonrelational, there are nonrelational predicates that are implicitly relational, in that their definitions contain relational predicates. As Bergmann said: "'Being married', for instance, is explicitly nonrelational since it requires only one subject, e.g., 'John is married'. 'Being married to', on the other hand, is a two-term predicate since it requires two subjects, e.g., 'John is married to Jean'. Yet the former can be defined in terms of the latter" (p. 17).

Berlyne (1965, pp. 66–68) distinguished between "natural relations" and "mediated relations," and seemed to include the nonrelational qualities that are implicitly relational in the second category. The distinction is based on whether or not an explanation of the perception of a relation requires the assumption that mediation occurred. Explanations of the perception of mediated relations require this assumption, but explanations of the perception of natural relations do not. There is a subtle but important point here that Berlyne apparently overlooked: The distinction is not based on the occurrence and nonoccurrence of mediation, but on the necessity and lack of necessity of assuming that mediation occurred. The point is that although it is not *necessary* to assume that mediation occurs in the perception of natural relations, it is *possible* that mediation occurs, at least in the perception of some natural relations.

HISTORICAL BACKGROUND

According to Bergmann's (1952) logical-positivistic analysis of the problem of relations in classical psychology, it was assumed in the classical theories of perception that physical processes in the object affect the sense organs, and physical processes aroused in the sense organs initiate a process in the central nervous system, the central process corresponding to the percept. The theory of reality then accepted was an "atomistic" ontology, in which the world was considered to consist only of punctiform elements or atoms. These elements were held to be nonrelational. As the British geologist H. B. Medlicott stated: "relations are immaterial, ultra-physical; the senses cannot touch them directly, and so no sensation of them can be recorded in the brain..." (1892, p. 24). Since relations were considered to have no external existence and therefore to be incapable of affecting the sense organs, the problem was to "reduce" the mental content corresponding to the perceived relation into elements which could not themselves be reduced. The method used to accomplish the reduction was usually introspective analysis. (See Bergmann [1952; 1955] for an explanation of the process and purpose of introspective reduction.) The perception of relations had to be either completely determined by the non-relational sensory elements, as James Mill (1829, Chapter III) suggested, or attributed to some contribution from within, some mental act that is itself an irreducible element, as in John Locke's analysis (1690, for example, p. 153).

Thomas Brown's (1860) position on relation perception is illustrative.[2] Brown was a Scot and worked for several years with Dugald Stewart, who was Thomas Reid's most distinguished disciple. However, Brown was closer to the tradition of the great British Associationists, John Locke, Bishop Berkeley, and David Hume, than to the Scottish school (see Boring, 1950, Chapters 10 and 11). In the *Lectures on the Philosophy of the Human Mind*,[3]

[2]Titchener (1909) briefly reviewed other relevant theories (pp. 184–187 and 301–305), and Bergmann (1952) gave an historical and a logical analysis of the problem of relations. According to William James, the "Sensationalists" denied the reality of relations *extra mentum*; the "Intellectualists" admitted their external existence but at the same time attributed knowledge of relations to a mental act (W. James, 1890, Vol. I, pp. 243–248). See also the comments of Spearman (1937a, pp. 214–236) and Bergmann (1954; 1956).

[3]The first edition of the *Lectures* was published in 1820, the year of Brown's death. The quotations given here are from the 1860 edition.

Brown said that relation perception results from an act of comparison; although there are " ... actual qualities in the objects themselves, the perception of which leads us afterwards to consider them as related, [there is] no actual quality in either of the objects that primarily and directly corresponds with the notion of the relation itself ... " (p. 28). Relations cannot be directly sensed, according to Brown, because there is no corresponding physical property to be sensed; but the mind "cannot regard a number of objects, without forming some comparison, and investing them consequently with a number of relations ... " (p. 28). (The idea was persistent. As late as 1916, Mary Calkins wrote that "there are no external physical stimuli ... of relational elements" [Calkins, 1916, p. 135].)

Bergmann (1952) maintained that in Brown's analysis some relations were both introspectively irreducible and "impressed from without," but it appears likely that Brown was unaware that his system included such relations. Perhaps Brown failed to recognize as relations the ones that are implicitly rather than explicitly relational.

According to Brown: "We have a capacity of conceiving objects, a capacity of feeling the relations of objects; and to those capacities all that is intellectual in our nature is reducible" (p. 337). The other mental acts or "faculties" that had previously been considered to be irreducible were actually "susceptible of still nicer analysis" (p. 213); and the phenomena "which are commonly ascribed to many distinct faculties, are truly referrable only to two—the capacity of simple suggestion ... and the capacity of relative suggestion ... " (p. 337). In simple suggestion: "Our perception or conception of one object excites ... the conception of some other object ... " (p. 214), and no notion of relation is involved (p. 288). Relative suggestion means " ... very nearly what is meant by the term *comparison*, when the will or intention which comparison seems necessarily to imply ... is excluded ... " (p. 288).

James McCosh, who Boring (1950) said was "one of the last of the old school of philosopher-psychologists" (p. 530), outlined a much more complicated system than Brown proposed. According to McCosh (1886), comparison is the mental faculty that discovers relations, but the relations have external existence: "The relations are in the things, and are as real as the things, only with a somewhat different kind of reality, a sort of dependent reality in the things. True, we only know individual things by the senses, but we know by contemplating them that they have relations" (p. 234; see also the entire *Book Third*, pp. 208–241, dealing with the "comparative powers"). Similarly, Lloyd Morgan (1903, Chapter XIII) believed that relations can be sensed, but can be *recognized* as relations only through a mental act of "reflection." (Werner [1948, pp. 220–222] expressed a similar position.) Herbert Spencer (1883), like McCosh, believed that relations have external existence: "there exist beyond consciousness, conditions of objective manifestation which are symbolized by relations as we conceive them" (p. 225); and William James also said that relations between objects exist "in rerum naturâ" (1890, Vol. I, p. 245).

The quotations in the preceding paragraph anticipate the later analysis outlined by Bergmann (1957), which has already been considered, but reflect not so much a change from the ontology accepted by the earlier philosopher-psychologists such as John Locke and Thomas Brown as a change in the interpretation of "existence." It had been believed that one can point at nonrelational, or absolute, qualities, but cannot point at relational qualities, and therefore that the absolute qualities exist, but the relational qualities do not. However, this view failed to distinguish between the "qualitied particular" and the "quality" itself (Bergmann, 1952), since one cannot point at even an *absolute* quality, but only at an object that exemplifies it. Since, furthermore, one can point at two objects that exemplify a natural relation, it must be held that natural relations exist in the same sense in which absolute qualities exist (Bergmann, 1957, p. 17).

In 1886, the German physicist-psychologist Ernst Mach adduced the transposition phenomenon as evidence for the existence of previously ignored elements, ontologically and introspectively irreducible sensations of form (see pp. 285–299 in the 1914 edition of Mach's treatise). Christian von Ehrenfels theorized in 1890 that these "form-qualities" are contributed by an act of the mind (see also von Ehrenfels, 1937). A similar position was expressed in 1940 by Raymond Wheeler, a Gestalt psychologist, who said: "The relations are not out there in the stimulus-pattern; the subject is not responding *to* relations, but *comprehends* the stimuli in relation to one another" (p. 185). Further: "Remember that the relationships were not out there between the lights, as relations to respond to. The animal perceived the relations *by his own act*. The relations pertained to his response, not to the lights" (pp. 188–189; Wheeler's italics in both quotations). This is not, however, the orthodox Gestalt position, in which form is assumed to be physically and psychologically emergent and to be irreducible. (On the concept of emergence, see Bergmann [1957] and Hempel and Oppenheim [1948, Part II].) Calkins (1926, pp. 137–138) emphasized that the "form-quality" or *Gestaltqualität* of von Ehrenfels is not the same as the *Gestalt* of Gestalt psychology, since the *Gestaltqualität* is an element (a "feeling of relation"), and the *Gestalt* is produced by a compound of elements. Koffka (1922, p. 536) also noted that these concepts are not equivalent, but did not specify how he considered them to differ.

The Gestalt psychologists have often written as though they alone recognized the importance and even the existence of form as a basic and fundamental perceptual phenomenon; but Boring (1927; 1930), Squires (1930), and Spearman (1937a; 1937b), among others, have argued against the claim of priority of the Gestalt school, pointing out that at least some of the

Structuralists recognized the phenomenon (see also the survey in Parsons, 1927, pp. 45–52). However, in Gestalt theory, as opposed to the classical theories, the proximal stimulation produced by real objects is not assumed to give rise to sensations that are organized in some way to yield the percepts. Rather, the neural excitation produced by the proximal stimulation is assumed to be organized in the nervous system without any intermediary sensations (Köhler, 1928). As Köhler (1928) pointed out, Rignano (1928) was inaccurate when he characterized Gestalt theory as a "sensationistic" theory, because there are no antecedent sensations in Gestalt theory; and Woodworth (1927) was inaccurate when he attributed to Gestalt theory the position that configurations pass "by some continuous flux into the organism," because according to Gestalt theory it is the proximal stimulation that is organized in the nervous system, not the distal stimulation.[4]

Contrary to Wheeler's position, the assumption in orthodox Gestalt theory is that configurations or "organizations" exist in the real world (see, for example, Koffka, 1915). It is also assumed that there is a correlation between the real world and the phenomenal field. The correlation is not assumed to be perfect, however, because although there is isomorphism between the object as perceived (the sensory experience) and the underlying psychophysiological structures or processes (Köhler, 1920), there is not always isomorphism between the perceived object and the real object (Köhler, 1928). The proximal stimulation produced by physically organized distal stimuli may be differently organized in the nervous system, as in the perception of illusions. In the Jastrow illusion, for example, two stimulus objects having one relation to each other, being equal in size, are perceived as having a different relation, the upper figure seeming to be smaller than the lower (the illusion is illustrated in Fig. 9–6a). Another example is Helmholtz's chessboard illusion, illustrated in Fig. 1–1. Relevant to the same point, Klüver (1933, p. 315) noted: "It is obvious that 'objective' relations are not necessarily relations 'reacted to'. . . . "

It should perhaps be pointed out that in classical psychology the concern was less with quantitative relations than with "conceptual" relations and "contextual" relations (for example, the relations between cause and effect and between terms connected by "if," "but," and the like.) The controversy was not about the possibility of relation perception, since it is obviously possible, at least in human observers. The controversy was about the ontological status of relations and about the kinds of elements needed to account for relation perception.

In the modern era of psychology, the controversy has been about whether an organism is more likely to respond to relations than to respond to

----

[4]In abstracting Rignano's paper, Helson (1928) remarked: "The author makes no reference to the literature except to his own works."

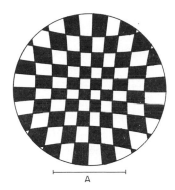

A

FIG. 1-1. The Helmholtz chessboard illusion. To see the illusion, the figure should be enlarged until line *A* is about eight inches long (20 cm). Fixate on the center of the enlarged figure with the eye at this distance from the center of the figure. The figure will appear to be a normal chessboard. (From von Helmholtz, 1910, Fig. 22, p. 181; also in D. Katz, 1945, Illustration 37, Plate 10, p. 14; Titchener, 1927, Fig. 42, p. 163.)

"absolute" qualities. The Gestalt school, as represented by Köhler, who was one of its chief spokesmen, admitted that responses to both absolute and relational qualities can occur, but believed that relational qualities are usually dominant (for example, Köhler, 1929, pp. 303–304). Similarly, Spence, who presented the best-articulated absolute theory of transposition, did not deny the possibility of responses to relations (for example, Spence, 1942, p. 270). The problem is therefore not only to determine whether organisms of a given species or age level can respond to relations, but also to determine under what conditions they do or do not respond to relations. The two problems are obviously related, but presenting them separately provides an opportunity to point out that there is no logical reason to expect that organisms of all species at all age levels will respond to relations. There are no logical grounds for denying the possibility of relation perception, as Bergmann (1957) pointed out; but having established the possibility that animals *may* respond to relations, logic has nothing further to do with the question of whether animals actually *do* respond to relations. Furthermore, to paraphrase Klüver,[5] it is one thing to determine whether or not a given animal is *capable* at all of responding to relations; it is another thing to find out whether or not the animal *tends* or prefers to respond to relations rather than to absolute properties.

The Transposition Problem

Ladd (1894, p. 355) used the term "transposition" in explaining the kind of phenomenon illustrated in Fig. 1–1; Okamoto (1962) used the term

[5] Klüver (1933, p. 328) was writing about abstraction in animals.

to refer to the "differentiation of language from the general to the particular in regard to the proper designation of objects" (Barclay, 1964). Campbell, Miller, and Diamond (1960) used the term to refer to change in the locus of stimulation (for example, from the second finger of the left hand to the third finger of the right hand). The literal meaning of "transposition" is change in spatial location, but the term has long been used to refer also to change in temporal position (see, for example, Verdon [1877], Douse [1878], and Gamble [1909, pp. 3, 131]. The term was also used in this sense in a report on the Fourteenth World Contract Bridge Team Championship [*Contract Bridge Bulletin*, 1966, Vol. 32, No. 7, p. 10]).

Probably under the influence of the Gestalt psychologists, transposition has come to refer to transfer based on relative "position" on any dimension, whether spatial, temporal, or attributive. The term "stepwise phenomenon" was used briefly to refer to this kind of transfer (for example, L. K. Frank, 1926; F. N. Jones, 1939a; F. N. Jones, 1939b; Koffka, 1922, pp. 540–545), but transposition has become the generally accepted term. Although it would be more proper to say that the experimenter *transposes* the stimuli and the subject *transfers* the response, the term "transposition" is now generally used to refer to both the change in the stimuli and the transfer of the response. A response that transfers to transposed stimuli is sometimes called a "relative" or "relational" response, but perhaps to avoid the interpretive element in these designations, many writers have preferred the term "transposition response." Since the use of the phrase "response to relations" implies a prejudgment of the interpretation of the transposition response, the phrase should be avoided in discussions of the empirical phenomenon.

(Gellert [1965] has used the term "transposition" in the sense which is etymologically more appropriate than the sense in which it has come to be used in studies of transfer. Her research was designed to determine which sides of an *en face* two-dimensional self-likeness children consider to refer to the right and left sides of their real body. The child can lateralize the drawing as though it were a mirror image, with pictured left directly opposite to real left, or as a photographic image, with pictured left diagonally across from real left. She found that with increasing age level, there were more diagonal designations, and she concluded that the age trend was probably a function of "learning to transpose points of view.")

It is easy to conceptualize position on a nonspatial dimension, as evidenced by the use of graphs with stimulus values on the baseline, but when the stimulus differences are not unidimensional, the simple spatial analogy breaks down. Multidimensional stimuli such as patterns and forms cannot be represented as points on a line, partly because there is more than one dimensional "line" involved, but also because a form depends on the relations among the elements it comprises at least as much as it depends on the elements themselves. Nevertheless, the Gestalt psychologists spoke of the transposition of forms (*Gestalten*), and even used transposability as one of the criteria of form perception. Von Ehrenfels considered transposition to be a necessary criterion, and Köhler considered it to be a sufficient but not necessary criterion (see Köhler, 1920, pp. 24–25).

Transposition, then, is a kind of transfer that appears to result from response to relations among stimuli or to patterns of stimulus qualities, rather than to the absolute qualities of the stimuli. It is exemplified by such phenomena as the recognition of a melody that has been transposed, in the musical sense, from one key to another; by the recognition of a shape or form after changes in color, size, or spatial orientation; and by the continuing choice of the larger of two stimulus objects after changes in their absolute sizes. Historically, the transposition phenomena were of interest because of their implications for the classical problem of relations. After Functionalism replaced classical Associationism, interest in the introspective reducibility of relations waned.[6] Nevertheless, the transposition phenomena continued to be important because of their apparent relevance to the problems of relation perception and form perception. It seemed obvious to many theorists that transposition responses are controlled by the stimulus relations and patterns, and not by the absolute properties of the stimuli. This interpretation, which for convenience can be designated the "relational hypothesis," has been fairly widely accepted, most notably by psychologists of the Gestalt school, but also by others (for example, Culbertson, 1963, p. 287). However, alternative interpretations of the transposition phenomena were suggested, and some, as already shown, were historically older than the "obvious" relational hypothesis. Transposition was a major experimental finding claimed as support for Gestalt theory (see, for example, Tolman, 1927); but this claim of support was challenged by such theorists as Spence (1937b), who attempted to explain transposition in terms of responses to absolute stimulus qualities, in order to show that it is not necessary to conclude that transposition demonstrates response to relations. More recently, still other alternative theories have been proposed, and have generated a renewed interest in transposition; but as will be shown in later chapters, none of these theories can account for all of the data obtained in the studies of transposition.

Critics of the relational hypothesis have used three kinds of argument against it. One of these arguments, which is logically invalid and can be dealt with summarily, is that the relational hypothesis is incorrect because alternative explanations work equally well. The argument is invalid, of

---

[6] The introspective analysis of relational judgments was still a topic of investigation as recently as 1923 (Bichowsky, 1923), and was a topic of discussion as recently as 1926 (Bichowsky, 1926; Lindworsky, p. 153 in the 1931 translation).

course, because there may be, at some level of analysis, more than one cause of a phenomenon, and because any or all of the proffered hypotheses could be wrong, since it is logically possible to deduce true conclusions from false premises (for example, Bergmann, 1957, pp. 29–35; M.R. Cohen and Nagel, 1934, pp. 269–272).

Another argument against the relational hypothesis denies the possibility of relation perception, at least in lower organisms. The argument is derived from the classical psychologies that are broadly designated as British Associationism, the relevant parts of which were examined in the preceding section. It assumes that relations do not exist in the real world external to the individual organism, and that the perception of relations is therefore a product of higher mental processes. However, if the first assumption is denied, the second is unnecessary, and the argument loses considerable force.

The third argument, which is mentioned here only to complete the introduction, is that the relational hypothesis fails to account for all of the findings of the studies of transposition. An evaluation of this argument requires a review of the findings, which is the major concern of this treatise, and requires a more detailed examination of relational theories, which include elaborations of the relational hypothesis. The evaluation, then, must be postponed to a later chapter.

Spearman (1937a) pointed out that the problem of relation perception "has been almost ignored by the great majority of psychologists" (p. 235); and if relation perception in general has been "almost ignored," transposition, as a special problem of relation perception, has received even less attention. Probably the major reason for this is that most psychologists are unfamiliar with the details of most of the relevant literature, and consequently believe that the problem has been solved, either by the Gestalt theorists or by the "absolute" theorists, depending on bias. The layman is unaware that there is any problem; he assumes that relations exist and can therefore be perceived directly, accounting for the general fact of transposition. However, this naive view fails to account for the detailed findings.

Stimulus Equivalence

Stevens has said that one of the pervasive problems in psychology is to identify stimuli that are functionally equivalent to one another (Stevens, 1951, p. 36). The purpose of transposition experiments, according to Klüver (1933), is to ascertain the range of stimulus equivalence. In the usual transposition experiment, the occurrence of transposition establishes that the stimuli are equivalent, even if the transposition response is preceded by hesitation, vacillation, or other intervening responses. (Woodworth and

Schlosberg [1954, p. 589] called the stimuli "nearly equivalent" in these cases.) If the percentage occurrence of transposition is well below 100 per cent, the stimuli are only "partially" equivalent; if it approaches or drops below the chance level, the stimuli are "nonequivalent." Zeiler (1963c; 1963d) argued that true nonequivalence would require random responses, presumably because absolute responses would indicate equivalence of the positive training stimulus and the test stimulus most similar to it.

Boring used sameness of response as the criterion of sameness of "meaning," extending Titchener's "context theory of meaning" (Boring, 1933, pp. 151–153, 221–238; Titchener, 1909, pp. 175–179). Stimulus equivalence is defined in the same way. Two stimuli are equivalent if one of them has the capacity to elicit a response that was never directly conditioned to it but was conditioned to the other one (for example, Hull, 1939; Hull 1942; Kjeldergaard and Horton, 1960; Klüver, 1933; Tolman, 1938). Hull (1939) identified as sources of stimulus equivalence (a) the presence of identical elements in stimulus compounds, (b) primary generalization, and (c) mediated generalization.

(a) When a response had been conditioned to a compound of stimulus elements, each element will tend to evoke the response, although when the element occurs in a new compound, its capacity to evoke the response is weakened, as Humphrey (1927) and Fraser (1948) demonstrated. The weakening has been attributed to "afferent neural interaction" (Hull, 1943) and to "stimulus interaction" (Spiker, 1963a).

(b) When a response has been conditioned to one stimulus, all other stimuli that are similar to the conditioned stimulus will tend to evoke the same response, presumably as a result of "primary stimulus generalization" (which is similar to Pavlov's [1927] concept of "irradiation").

(c) When two stimuli elicit the same response, and another response is later conditioned to one of them, the other stimulus also elicits the new response, as a result of mediation by the common response. Stimulus equivalence resulting from this mechanism is sometimes called "acquired equivalence."

Whether or not Hull's account is adequate is not under consideration here, but it does serve to emphasize that "stimulus equivalence" is not itself a theoretical concept, although it has sometimes been used as though it were. It is a descriptive or shorthand term meaning that the stimuli being tested arouse the same response.

Actually, stimuli have sometimes been considered to be equivalent even when the total pattern of responses is different, provided that the same terminal response is aroused (Klüver, 1933). Furthermore, stimuli have been said to be equivalent even when they arouse responses of different strengths. Gayton (1927) argued that since the performance level on the first transposition test is lower than on the training problem, the training and test situations are similar but not actually equivalent. (Other early investigators also discussed this drop in performance level [for example, Gulliksen, 1932a; F. N. Jones, 1939a; M. H. Lewis, 1930], but it has been ignored by the more recent investigators.) Grether and Wolfle (1936) and Jackson and Dominguez (1939) have also questioned the utility of the term. Jackson and Dominguez pointed out that the latencies of responses on the test trials are often longer than on the trials at the end of the training phase (see section entitled "Effect of Noticing Change in Stimuli from Training to Test," Chapter 5), and they argued that the increase in latency indicates that the test and training stimuli are not "equivalent" in Klüver's (1933) sense, even though the final responses to the stimuli are the same (see also Jackson, 1939; Jackson *et al.*, 1938). However, as already indicated, Klüver used only the terminal response, the instrumental act or differential response, as the basis for establishing equivalence (see Klüver, 1933, pp. 19–22). Klüver even pointed out that comparison behavior and the form of the "pulling in" response (the instrumental response) sometimes differed on training and test trials, yet he concluded that the stimuli were equivalent if the relational response eventually occurred. Changing the point of the criticism slightly, it might well be argued that "equivalence" in this sense is not a particularly good descriptive term.

Prokasy and Hall (1963) would presumably have agreed with Klüver. As they noted, Hiss and Thomas (1963), studying stimulus generalization in pigeons, found systematic increases in response latency with increasing differences between the training and test stimuli, yet the subjects continued to respond to the test stimuli (although at lower rates). Prokasy and Hall argued that if the subject detects a change in the external environment in the shift from the training to the test phase, responses such as the orienting reflex might occur, and these might alter or delay the conditioned response whether or not the critical attribute of the external event was perceived as having changed: " . . . a subject may detect environmental changes, which in turn affect other response characteristics, but this need not mean that for him the effective stimulus has been altered" (p. 320). That determination must be based on observation of the terminal response alone. However, this line of argument suggests that it is possible to arrive at the same terminal response by a different route when the external stimulus has indeed been perceived to be different, and makes stimulus equivalence a philosophical problem rather than a scientific one.

It might be a good idea to drop the term altogether, and to substitute terms such as "generalization" and "transposition," or if they seem to be inappropriate in a given case, to use the more general term, "transfer." The use of these terms would have some of the disadvantages of the use of "stimulus equivalence," but at least these terms do not imply *identity* of stimulus functions.

The term "transfer" refers to the "influence of previous experiences on current performance" (Underwood, 1949, p. 637), and refers to the *occurrence* of an influence rather than to the *source* or cause of the influence. "Generalization" refers to transfer along some stimulus continuum; "transposition" refers to transfer that apparently results from learning to respond to patterns or relations among stimuli rather than to stimulus elements. (Razran [1940] wanted to restrict the term "transposition" to transfer that is actually and not merely apparently based on responses to patterns or relations.)

The Transposition Paradigms

TWO-STIMULUS PROBLEMS

Most of the research has been concerned with transposition on visual and auditory dimensions, and with the transposition of unidimensional relations or multidimensional forms within these sensory modalities. The studies of unidimensional transposition fall into two broad categories, those using "two-stimulus" problems, and those using "intermediate-stimulus" problems. In typical two-stimulus transposition experiments, the subject first learns to choose one stimulus of a pair, and then is tested with a pair in which the relation between the stimuli is the same as in the training pair, but in which the absolute qualities of one or both of the stimuli differ from those of the training stimuli. For example, if the training stimuli had areas of two and four square inches, the test stimuli might have areas of four and eight square inches, a "one-step" change in the absolute areas preserving the 1 to 2 ratio of areas; or they might have areas of eight and sixteen square inches, a two-step change, and so forth (see Table 1-1).[7] A test with a one-step change in stimuli is called a "Near Test," and the tests beyond one step are called "Far Tests." ("Near" and "Far" have usually been used in a relative sense; the more precise usage adopted here has only a stylistic advantage over the more common usage.) The change can also be a fractional number of steps. In the example, a test with stimuli having areas of three and six square inches would be a one-half-step test, and a test with stimuli having areas of six and twelve square inches would be a one and one-half step test. To avoid confusion such tests are designated herein by the fractional number of steps, and the term "Near Test" is reserved to refer only to the one-step test. The use of the terms "Near" and "Far" in this context derives from the older use of the term "distance" in

---

[7]Kuenne (1946) credited S.T.S. Kendler (1943) with the introduction of the term "step," but Jackson used it in this sense at least three years earlier than Kendler (in Jackson and Jerome, 1940, p. 433), and the Gestalt psychologists used it in a similar sense even earlier (Koffka, 1922, pp. 540–545; Wheeler, 1929, p. 123). In the Gestaltist sense, however, step was sometimes synonymous with "relation," as in Koffka's (1935, p. 467) statement that a step is a "whole with two members between which there exists a gradient of potential."

TABLE 1-1

SAMPLE TWO-STIMULUS TRANSPOSITION PROBLEMS

Stimuli

Training pair	Test pair	Steps	Dimensional direction	Relative direction	Test stimulus chosen in:	
					Transposition response	Absolute response
3 vs 4 with 4 correct	2 vs 3	1	Downward	Negative	3	3
	1 vs 2	2	Downward	Negative	2	2
	4 vs 5	1	Upward	Positive	5	4
	5 vs 6	2	Upward	Positive	6	5
3 vs 4 with 3 correct	2 vs 3	1	Downward	Positive	2	3
	1 vs 2	2	Downward	Positive	1	2
	4 vs 5	1	Upward	Negative	4	4
	5 vs 6	2	Upward	Negative	5	5

denoting the position of an element in any series in which the elements grow progressively more different from the starting point. Stumpf seems to have been the first to use the term "distance" in this way (W. James, 1890, Vol. I, pp. 530–531).

If the larger stimulus in the example were the one the subject had learned to choose during training, then choice of the larger test stimulus would be a "transposition" response. Choice of the smaller one would be an "absolute" response, because the smaller test stimulus in the example is more similar to the correct training stimulus than the larger test stimulus is. The absolute response is presumed to be guided by the absolute qualities of the stimuli, rather than by the relational properties.

A distinction is made between transposition in the "positive" and "negative" directions. In the example, transposition would be in the positive direction, since the test stimuli are shifted from the training stimuli in the direction of the correct or positive training stimulus. If the subject were tested with stimuli having areas of one and two square inches, after training with stimuli having areas of two and four square inches, with the four-square-inch stimulus correct, transposition would be in the negative direction, since the test stimuli would be shifted in the direction of the incorrect or negative training stimulus (see Table 1–1). On tests in the negative direction, the absolute response and transposition response are identical, since the test stimulus that is more similar to the positive training stimulus is also the one that has the same relative position in the test pair as the positive training stimulus has in the training pair. Since the absolute response and transposition response are identical on a test in the negative direction, choice of the other stimulus is a "nontransposition-nonabsolute" response (sometimes called an "error" response).[8]

The direction of change along the stimulus continuum is designated as "upward" when the test stimuli have more of the quality being varied than the training stimuli, for example, when the test stimuli are larger or brighter than the training stimuli; and the direction is "downward" when the test stimuli have less of the quality than the training stimuli. Positive and negative transposition can be upward or downward, depending on the relative value of the positive training stimulus. Table 1-1 represents sample two-stimulus transposition problems, and illustrates the upward–downward and positive–negative directions of testing.

When a test includes stimulus values duplicating values used in training, these values should be represented by duplicate physical objects, rather than by the same objects, in order to minimize responses to irrelevant attributes of the objects. This control has not always been used. Zeiler and Paalberg (1964b) have pointed out that another procedural safeguard that should be used, but is often omitted, is to eliminate the experimenter from the situation while the subject is making a response, for example, by imposing a screen between the subject and the experimenter or by using some kind of automated apparatus. As C. J. Warden and Baar (1929) noted, this kind of control is required to prevent the "Clever Hans error" (see Katz, 1937, pp. 2–10).

INTERMEDIATE-STIMULUS PROBLEMS

In the other kind of unidimensional transposition problem, the intermediate-stimulus problem, three stimuli are presented during training, and the correct stimulus, relative to the other two stimuli, has an intermediate value on the stimulus continuum. Choice of the intermediate of three test stimuli is a transposition response, and choice of the test stimulus most similar to the positive training stimulus is an absolute response. Choice of the other test stimulus is a nontransposition-nonabsolute response. Transposition is always in the negative direction, since it must be in the direction of one of the two negative stimuli; but it can be upward or downward, and Near and Far transposition tests can be given.

FORM TRANSPOSITION

In typical studies of form transposition, the subject learns to choose

---

[8]It has sometimes been argued that the term "absolute response" should be reserved for response to the positive training stimulus when it is paired with the new stimulus on a one-step test in the positive direction, and avoidance of the negative training stimulus when it is paired with the new stimulus on a one-step test in the negative direction. This restricted meaning is not generally accepted, however, perhaps because it would limit the application of the term to one-step tests.

one of two multidimensional shapes or forms, and is then given tests in which the positive stimulus or the negative stimulus is modified in some way, or in which both stimuli are modified. There is no upward or downward or positive–negative direction of change, and it is doubtful that any useful meaning could be assigned to the "amount" of change. Instead, the interest is in the effect of various *kinds* of changes in the stimuli. The experiments have also been referred to as studies of "stimulus equivalence."

The discriminative cue in the training phase of the studies of form transposition has usually been visual form; but the transposition of melodies also belongs in this category, as Mach (1914, pp. 285–297) and the British Act Psychologist G. F. Stout (1918a) indicated. There have also been a few studies in which the discriminative cue was size or brightness, and in which an "irrelevant" dimension was changed on test trials, as, for example, when size was the discriminative cue in the training phase, and brightness was changed on the test trials, with size unchanged. (In the corresponding unidimensional transposition problem, size would be changed on the test trials, and brightness unchanged.)

Overview

It is an historical accident that transposition ever came to be distinguished from the other kinds of transfer. The circumstances were, first, the salient position of the relations problem in classical psychology, and, second, the revolt of the Gestalt psychologists and their precursors against classical Sensationalism and Associationism. It was almost inevitable that relation perception would be a dominant issue for the Gestalters, and the occurrence of transposition was readily available as an experimental demonstration of the validity of their theory.

Nowadays, few if any psychologists would deny on *a priori* grounds the possibility of relation perception, and some wonder why transposition continues to be considered separately from the other kinds of transfer. One reason is that even if relation perception is undeniably *possible*, it is still important to ask whether it is *usual*, and the transposition data are relevant to this question. The question has to do with the stimulus control of behavior, which is a pervasive problem in psychology. Furthermore, even though transposition is not yet completely understood, it is one of the most reliable kinds of transfer obtainable (given the appropriate testing conditions, which are specified in later chapters), and therefore it can be used as a vehicle for the study of other processes that are less amenable to experimental manipulation. (One such use is in the study of cognitive processes, as shown in Chapters 5 and 8.)

According to Lloyd Morgan, the primitive sensation of a relation is given, and it is fruitless for science to ask how it occurs (Morgan, 1903, p. 218). There is some evidence that there are receptor cells that respond to relative stimulation (see "Hebb," section entitled "Neural Theories," Chapter 9), but the major obstacle to scientific investigation of relation perception is that relational percepts are not directly observable by the investigator. Introspective reports (or more properly, verbal reports) might be accepted on the argument that when a person is asked to describe what he perceived, he is likely to report seeing a relation only if he actually experienced the perception of a relation, although he may fail to report seeing it when he actually did see it. When a relational percept is reported, it has not been proved that relation perception actually occurred, but the belief of the investigator that it occurred is strengthened. This argument can also be used as a basis for inferring relation perception in inarticulate subjects, by substituting for the verbal report some other appropriate response. The determination of which responses are appropriate is theoretical, and is considered in later chapters.

Finally, as shown in Chapter 11, the data on transposition have implications about the nature of discrimination learning and the nature of generalization, as well as implications about relation perception. The first task, then, is to discover what is known about transposition, and then to determine the implications of these facts. The first task is taken up in Parts II and III, and the implications are considered in Part IV.

PART II

Studies of Unidimensional Transposition

CHAPTER 2

Measurement

In studies of transpositon, there has usually been little interest in performance in the training phase of the experiment, beyond the bare fact of criterional performance. The major interest has been in performance in the testing phase, in which the occurrence of transposition is assessed. Although latency or some other response measure might be useful as a dependent variable, the usual measures are based on the frequency of choice of each test stimulus. There are several ways of assessing "choice," and informed selection of an appropriate measure involves theoretical and empirical considerations.

Theoretical Considerations

MEASURES

The most valid measure of transfer is based on performance on the first test trial, since this performance is uncontaminated by possible extinction or further learning that might occur if more than one test trial were given. However, this measure is relatively unstable, because only one response by each subject is observed, and the usual practice has been to give several test trials to obtain a more stable measure. Furthermore, Zeiler (1967) has pointed out that when only a single test trial is given, group data cannot represent the behavior of any one subject, because each subject has a score of either *zero* or *one*. However, it has long been recognized that group learning curves often do not faithfully reflect the learning curves of individual subjects (see, for example, Spence, 1956, pp. 59–61), and it is possible that group transposition scores might not faithfully reflect the combined-trial means of individual subjects. No one before Zeiler seems to have considered this possibility. Zeiler found little agreement between group curves and individual curves, but, as shown in a later section, re-analysis of the data of other studies indicates that other investigators have obtained substantial agreement between the two kinds of curves.

When several test trials are given, the most commonly used measure of transposition is the mean number of transposition responses on the combined test trials, or the percentage transposition on these trials. Other measures are the number of subjects who transpose "consistently" or "predominantly" on the combined test trials. Consistent transposition usually means that the subject transposes on every test trial (for example, Stevenson and Iscoe, 1955); but various criteria of predominance have been used, such as transposition on at least half of the test trials in the inter-mediate-stimulus problem (Rudel, 1960).

The rationale for the consistency and predominance measures is that the mean number of transposition responses includes "chance" transposition responses as well as "real" transposition responses. A subject responding at random would "transpose" on half of the trials in the two-stimulus problem, and his score would inflate the group mean, yielding an over-estimate of transposition. However, the consistency measure seems to be too strict, since it does not allow occasional chance errors.[1] The predominance measure, which does allow occasional errors, seems to be too imprecise. Two groups might differ considerably in consistency of transposition but not differ at all in predominance. If subjects with a strong tendency to transpose make fewer occasional errors than subjects with a weaker tendency, the predominance measure might fail to detect the difference. The consistency measure might detect the difference, but it would be possible to obtain no consistent transposition in either kind of subject.

REWARD CONTINGENCIES

The possibility of contamination by extinction or relearning when several test trials are given is perhaps a more serious problem than the problem of selecting a measure, since all of the measures based on multiple test trials might be invalid if contamination occurs. The problem is to manipulate the reward contingencies during testing in such a way that the likelihood of contamination is minimized. In some studies, only trans-position responses were rewarded; in other studies, all responses on the test trials were rewarded; and in a few studies, none of the test-trial responses were rewarded.

C. J. Warden and Rowley (1929) criticized the procedure of rewarding only transposition responses because further learning inflates the index of transposition. Perkins and Wheeler (1930) argued that this relearning effect ". . . seems entirely to be overestimated" (p. 46), but their documentation was weak. Admitting that the transposition test using this method is actually a relearning problem, it can still be argued that the speed of relearning provides an indirect measure of transposition since transposition would facilitate relearning. Zeiler (1963c, p. 519) criticized the procedure

---

[1]The chance errors might result from wandering attention, which is not uncommon in children late in an experimental session (for example, Shepard, 1957), or from a tendency to try out all objects in the situation, the "response-shift error" (for example, Harlow, 1959).

on other grounds, and in fact doubted the validity of using any multiple-trial method of testing; but his suggestion that only the data of the first test trial are valid seems to go too far, since the empirical evidence, which is summarized later, indicates that the different methods yield comparable data.

When all responses are rewarded during testing, the response tendency that produced the response on the first test trial is rewarded and strengthened, and should be more likely to control responses on subsequent test trials. If an "error" occurred on the first test trial, the probability that it would recur would be enhanced by the reward; if a transposition response occurred, the probability of its recurrence would be enhanced. Therefore, the method of rewarding all test-trial responses should, theoretically, give a relatively precise index of the strength of the response tendency that was dominant on the first test trial. This analysis is not accurate, however, for all of the theories. If relation perception is assumed not to occur at all, or if it is assumed that relation perception occurs on every trial, the analysis is accurate. However, if it is assumed that relation perception occurs only after the subject has compared the stimuli by successively observing first one stimulus and then the other, then it would be possible for absolute cues to determine the response on some trials, when the first stimulus observed elicits a response, and for relational cues to determine the response on other trials, when the stimulus observed first does not elicit a response but is followed by orientation toward the other stimulus and the perception of the relation. (These different conceptions are considered in detail in Part IV.)

The technique of rewarding none of the test-trial responses has seldom been used because of the possibility of extinction effects. It has been suggested that the use of an intermittent reinforcement schedule during training would minimize the extinction effects, allowing the use of the technique without disturbing the behavior previously established.[2] Furthermore, even without attempting to increase the resistance to extinction by giving partial reinforcement during training, the technique provides a valid, though indirect, measure of transposition, since the resistance to extinction should be positively correlated with the strength of the tendency to transpose.

SUMMARY

It seems obvious that theoretical considerations do not dictate a choice of any one of the alternative measures, and the only practical limitation

[2]Personal communication from an anonymous consulting editor of *Child Development*, 1963. The technique seems to have been used with children only in G. R. Thompson's (1965) doctoral dissertation and in a series of studies by Zeiler and his colleagues (see Zeiler, 1967).

is on the use of the first measure, which requires a large sample size because only the first test trial provides data. Therefore, the only basis for choice among the multiple-trial measures, aside from personal bias, is empirical, and requires a comparison of studies using the different measures. The relevant comparisons are summarized in the next section, dealing first with two-stimulus problems and then with intermediate-stimulus problems.

Empirical Considerations

TWO-STIMULUS PROBLEMS

First Test Trial versus All Test Trials

In the reports of several studies of two-stimulus transposition, separate data have been given for the first test trial and for combined test trials. (These data are summarized in Tables 2-1 and 2-2.) The studies with different reward contingencies on test trials are considered separately below, although in the two studies providing data on the effects of different reward contingencies only slightly more transposition was obtained when transposition responses alone were rewarded than when all test-trial responses were rewarded. Gayton (1927) gave rats 30-trial tests, and obtained about 68 per cent transposition when only transposition responses were rewarded, and about 60 per cent when all test-trial responses

TABLE 2–1

COMPARISON OF MEASURES (TWO-STIMULUS PROBLEMS)

Percentage transposition on first test trial and on combined test trials with only transposition responses rewarded

Study	Subjects	Percentage transposition		No. of test trials
		Trial 1	All trials	
McGrade (1958)	Children	79	89	5
McGrade (1958)	Children[a]	96	96	5
Stevenson and Iscoe (1955)	Children	66	70	5
Stevenson et al. (1955a)	Children	73	83	5
Stevenson and Langford (1957)	Children	75	Unspecified	—
Terrell (1959)	Children	100 [b]	100 [b]	4
Terrell et al. (1959)	Children	100[b]	100[b]	4
Stevenson and Weiss (1955)	Adults	64	Unspecified	—
Baker and Lawrence (1951)	Rats	80	60	10
R. Thompson (1955)	Rats	70	72	12
Hadley (1927)	Guinea pigs	80	88	10

[a]Blind children and blindfolded sighted children.

[b]Approximate. In Terrell's (1959) study, "virtually all Ss responded correctly on the transposition test" (pp. 706–707). In the study by Terrell et al., all but one S transposed on every trial.

were rewarded. Hadley (1927) tested guinea pigs, and obtained 88 per cent transposition on the first 10 test trials when only transposition responses were rewarded, and 82 per cent transposition when all test-trial responses were rewarded.

Transposition Responses Rewarded. When only transposition responses are rewarded, and when there is almost perfect transposition in the group on the first test trial, there can be little or no further increase in transposition over the combined test trials because of the ceiling effect, but no *decline* in transposition has been found in children under these conditions (McGrade, 1958, blind and blindfolded subjects; Terrell, 1959; Terrell, Durkin, and Wiesley, 1959). When there is less transposition on the first trial, there is generally a slight increase in transposition over as few as five test trials. Testing children, Stevenson and Iscoe (1955) found an increase from about 66 per cent transposition to about 70 per cent; Stevenson, Iscoe, and McConnell (1955a) obtained an increase from 73 to 83 per cent; and McGrade (1958) obtained an increase from 79 to 89 per cent. Stevenson and Weiss (1955), testing college students in a four-stimulus problem with an extreme or intermediate stimulus correct (in subgroups), found an increase from about 64 per cent (combining the various groups) to a higher but unspecified level. ("The discrimination was learned so rapidly on the test trials that after the initial trial, differences between the groups quickly disappeared" [p. 286].) Stevenson and Langford (1957) obtained this kind of rapid learning in children. (Shirai [1954, footnote, p. 26] reported that in a pilot study with 25 human adults, all subjects responded on three test trials in the same way they responded on the first test trial. However, the reward contingency was not specified.)

The increase in transposition from the first test trial to the combined test trials has been obtained in guinea pigs (Hadley, 1927) and rats (R. Thompson, 1955), but as shown in Table 2-1 the opposite trend has also been obtained in rats (Baker and Lawrence, 1951).

All Responses Rewarded. Studies in which all test-trial responses were rewarded have yielded inconsistent data. Alberts and Ehrenfreund (1951) and Marsh and Sherman (1966) found less transposition in preschoolers on the first test trial than on 10 test trials, and I. M. L. Hunter (1952a, Experiments I and II) obtained the same effect with two combined test trials (see Table 2-2). McKee and Riley (1962) obtained the increase in first-grade children, and D. E. Gould (1963) and Riley and McKee (1963) obtained the increase in older children and college students. Sherman (1966) obtained the increase in nine groups of children, no change in one group, and a decrease in 11 groups. Corbascio (1964) and Riley, McKee, and Hadley (1964) found essentially equal transposition on the first test trial and on 10 test trials combined; M. S. Scott (1966) obtained about the same amount of transposition on the first test trial as on five test trials; and

TABLE 2–2

COMPARISON OF MEASURES (TWO-STIMULUS PROBLEMS)

Percentage transposition on first test trial and on combined test trials with
all test-trial responses rewarded

Study	Subjects	Percentage transposition		No. of test trials	Problem difficulty[a]
		Trial 1	All trials		
Alberts and Ehrenfreund (1951)[b]	Children	64	81	10	Easy
Corbascio (1964)	Children	86	89	10	Easy
I. M. L. Hunter (1952a, Exp. I and II)	Children	84	92	2	Irrelevant[c]
Jackson and Dominquez (1939)	Children	50	40	3	Easy[d]
Jackson et al. (1938, Exp. IV)	Children	83	83	3	Easy
Marsh and Sherman (1966)[b] (Exp. I)	Children	39	54	10	Easy
Marsh and Sherman (1966)[b] (Exp. II)	Children	13	25	10	Easy
McKee and Riley (1962) (pitch)	Children	50	65	10	Hard
McKee and Riley (1962) (loudness)	Children	81	86	10	Easy
Riley et al. (1964) (pitch)	Children	69	72	10	Hard
Riley et al. (1964) (loudness)	Children	92[e]	93[e]	10	Easy
M. S. Scott (1966)[b]	Retardates	81	77	5	Irrelevant[c]
Sherman (1966)[bf] (9 groups)	Children	67	77	10	Irrelevant[c]
Sherman (1966)[bf] (11 groups)	Children	86	77	10	Irrelevant[c]
Sherman and Strunk (1964)[bg]	Children	83	76	10	Easy
Shirai (1951)	Children	92[e]	92[e]	3	?
Zeiler (1966a) (1.4 to 1 ratio)	Children	69	69	10	Hard
Zeiler (1966a) 2 to 1 ratio)	Children	94	87	10	Easy
Riley and McKee (1963) (pitch)	Children and adults	65	73	10	Hard
Riley and McKee (1963) (loudness)	Children and adults	94[e]	93[e]	10	Easy
Gould (1963)[b]	Adults	30	38	10	Easy
Heyman (1951)[b]	Rats	72	75	10	Hard
T. S. Kendler (1950)	Rats	64	74	10	Hard
Maltzman (1949, Exp. I)	Rats	27	32	10	Easy
Riley et al.[h] (3 groups)	Rats	56	81	20	—
Riley et al.[h] (5 groups)	Rats	83	70	20	—
Hadley (1927)	Guinea pigs	50	82	10	Hard
Campbell and Kral (1958)	Parakeets	83	76	20	Hard

[a] Difficulty determined by ratio of stimulus areas in size discriminations, and by trials to criterion in brightness discriminations.

[b] All experimental conditions combined.

[c] Because multiple-problem training given.

[d] The stimuli were four dimensional, with all four dimensions relevant; this usually reduces problem difficulty.

[e] Could be a ceiling effect.

[f] Includes data from four experiments and two pilot studies.

[g] Trial-l data omitted from published report, but given by Sherman (1966, Table 1, p. 18).

[h] Riley et al. (1960; 1963).

Jackson, Stonex, Lane, and Dominguez (1938, Experiment IV) and Shirai (1951) obtained the same amount on the first test trial as on three test trials combined. Zeiler (1966a) found slightly more transposition on the first test trial than on 10 combined trials, and Zeiler (1965b) obtained the same effect in a three-stimulus problem with the largest or smallest stimulus correct (in subgroups). Jackson and Dominguez (1939) and Sherman and Strunk (1964) obtained even larger decreases.

The data for infrahuman subjects are also inconsistent when all test-trial responses are rewarded. Hadley (1927) obtained the increase in guinea pigs, and Maltzman (1949) obtained it in rats. Chisum (1965) obtained the increase in rats tested at one-half step, and obtained a slight decrease and then the increase in rats tested at one and one-half steps (see Fig. 2-1). Riley and co-workers (Riley, Goggin, and Wright, 1963; Riley, Ring, and Thomas, 1960) obtained the increase in three groups of rats, averaging 56 per cent transposition on the first trial and 81 per cent on 20 combined trials; and T. S. Kendler (1950) also obtained the increase in rats. However, Heyman (1951) found virtually no change, and five groups of rats in the Riley studies exhibited a decreasing trend, averaging 83 per cent on the first trial and 70 per cent on 20 combined trials. Campbell and Kral (1958) obtained the decrease in parakeets.

Summary. The data indicate, not surprisingly, that when only transposition responses are rewarded, there is usually less transposition on the first

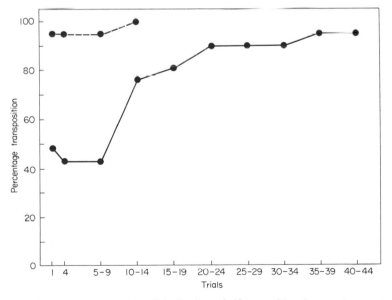

FIG. 2-1. Transposition over test trials: (- - -) one-half step and (——) one and one-half steps. (Drawn from Chisum, 1965, Table 2, p. 420.)

test trial than on combined test trials, presumably because further learning occurs during the test phase. The cause of the decline obtained in the Baker and Lawrence study is not known. The data from the studies in which all test-trial responses were rewarded indicate that there is usually less transposition on the first test trial than on the combined trials, but there is sometimes more. Campbell and Kral (1958) implied that a drop in the performance level after the first test trial reflects a disturbance resulting from the shift in stimuli, but the effect should actually be to reduce the performance level from the end of training to the beginning of testing, and not necessarily from the first test trial to subsequent test trials (see section entitled "Effect of Noticing Change in Stimuli from Training to Test," Chapter 5). Furthermore, the hypothesis fails to explain why there is usually an increase. The data of Riley and co-workers suggest that whether transposition increases or decreases after the first test trial is related to the level of transposition on the first test trial. The median percentage transposition on the first test trial of the combined studies in Table 2-2 is 70.5 per cent. In 12 of the 16 studies in which the increase was obtained, the percentage transposition on the first test trial was less than the median; in the other 4, it was greater than the median. In 10 of the other 12 studies, the percentage transposition on the first test trial was greater than the median; in the other two (one obtaining the decrease and one obtaining no change), it was less than the median. This difference is highly significant statistically ($\chi^2 = 7.15$, with Yates' correction; $df = 1$; $p < .01$). It can be concluded, therefore, that if the level of transposition on the first test trial is relatively low, transposition usually increases over subsequent trials; if it is relatively high, transposition usually decreases or remains high over the subsequent trials.

Changes across Blocks of Test Trials (All Responses Rewarded)

It might be argued that no valid conclusion can be obtained from comparisons of first-trial data with combined-trial data, because on the first trial "percentage transposition" is a percentage of subjects, and on combined trials it is a percentage of responses. However, unquestionably valid comparisons can be made between measures of transposition in blocks of equal numbers of test trials, and these data have been given in a few reports. The question is whether the percentage transposition tends to change systematically over test trials when all responses are rewarded on the test trials.

G. R. Thompson (1965) found a decrease in transposition with repeated testing in mentally retarded subjects. In normal children, Zeiler (1966a) obtained an increase, but Alberts and Ehrenfreund (1951) and Rudel (1958) obtained no change (in combined groups). Hadley (1927) obtained a slight increase in guinea pigs. Maltzman (1949) and T. S. Kendler (1950) reported an increase in rats from the first five test trials to the second five; but in a study similar to Kendler's, except that partial steps were used in testing, Ehrenfreund (1952) found no consistent change in transposition with continued testing. Comparing the performance on Trials 1 to 5 and 16 to 20 in Ehrenfreund's study, there was an increase in transposition in three groups, a drop in four groups, and no change in one group. Ehrenfreund obtained less transposition than Kendler, and some variation in procedure might account for the difference in results, but what the variation might be is not known. Also testing rats, Heyman (1951) obtained essentially no change from the first five test trials to the second five, and Gayton (1927) obtained no change on tests repeated after retraining. Gulliksen (1932b) said that in his work with rats, he often found that transposition decreased over test trials. In the study he was probably referring to (Gulliksen, 1932a), 30-trial tests were given, and there was no appreciable difference in transposition on a test whether it was given first or second. Transposition averaged 73 per cent on first administrations and averaged 71 per cent on second administrations. (Apparently Gulliksen was referring in the 1932b paper to changes within tests, but, if so, the relevant data were not reported in the 1932a paper.) Gulliksen believed that the rats notice the change in stimuli from the training phase to the test phase, and that this eventually changes the behavior. However, it is not clear why he believed that the effect of noticing the change would not immediately affect behavior. (Compare with the discussion above of Campbell and Kral's similar hypothesis.)

Riley et al. (1960) obtained the increase in transposition over test trials in rats when the discrimination was between similar brightnesses, and was therefore a difficult discrimination; but they obtained a decrease when the discrimination was between distinctive brightnesses, and was therefore an easy discrimination. However, problem difficulty was also varied by using contiguous cues in one condition and noncontiguous cues in another condition. Separating the cues made the discrimination more difficult, but the direction of the change in transposition was not related to this source of problem difficulty. The data of another study by Riley and his colleagues (Riley et al., 1963) suggest that problem difficulty determined by cue separation has an effect opposite to the effect of problem difficulty determined by stimulus similarity. The effects varied somewhat with amount of training, but there seem to have been increases in transposition when the cues were contiguous and easily comparable, and decreases when the cues were noncontiguous and comparable only with difficulty.[3]

[3]Increasing the difficulty of a discrimination problem seems to increase responsiveness to irrelevant cues (Mackintosh, 1965a), and might therefore increase the probability that the subject will learn about both relative and absolute properties of the stimuli; but this effect of problem difficulty seems to be unrelated to the apparent effect on the change in transposition over test trials.

Chisum (1965) tested rats at one-half step and at one and one-half steps, and obtained a considerable increase in transposition over trials on the more distant test (see Fig. 2-1). The problem was of intermediate difficulty, compared with the "easy" and "hard" problems used by Riley *et al.* in 1960; but it was considerably more difficult than both of the problems used by Riley *et al.* in 1963, judging from the numbers of trials required to reach the training criterion. Table 2-3 summarizes the data of other relevant studies. It can be seen that, although the findings of some of the studies are ambiguous, there is enough contradictory evidence to warrant rejection of the hypothesis that problem difficulty *per se* is the effective variable.

The amount of transposition in the first block of test trials in the studies in Table 2-3 was not significantly related to the direction of the change over blocks. The percentage transposition in the first block was less than the median (71.5 per cent) in 45 per cent of the groups with an increase over blocks, and in 56 per cent of the groups with a decrease or no change.

Washburn and Abbott (1912) tested one rabbit twice, with interspersed

TABLE 2–3

CHANGE IN TWO-STIMULUS TRANSPOSITION OVER TEST TRIALS IN EASY AND DIFFICULT PROBLEMS[a]

(All test-trial responses rewarded)

Study	Subjects	Problem difficulty[b]	Direction of change in transposition	
			Trial 1 to all trials	First to last block
Ehrenfreund (1952)	Rats	Easy	—	No change
Gulliksen (1932a)	Rats	Easy	—	No change
I. M. Maltzman (1949, Exp. I)	Rats	Easy	Increase	Increase
Alberts and Ehrenfreund (1951)	Children	Easy	Increase	No change[c]
Zeiler (1966a) (2 to 1 ratio)	Children	Easy	Decrease	Increase
Gayton (1927)	Rats	Hard	—	No change
Heyman (1951)	Rats	Hard	No change	No change
T. S. Kendler (1950)	Rats	Hard	Increase	Increase
Hadley (1927)	Guinea pigs	Hard	Increase	Increase
Rudel (1958)	Children	Hard	—	No change
G. R. Thompson (1965)	Children	Hard	—	Decrease
Zeiler (1966a) (1.4 to 1 ratio)	Children	Hard	No change	Increase

[a]See also Fig. 2–1.

[b]See Footnote *a*, Table 2–2.

[c]Riley *et al.* (1960) and Zeiler (1966a) noted that Alberts and Ehrenfreund obtained an increase, but I found it too small to be of interest (.38 of a response more transposition on Trials 6–10 than on Trials 1–5).

retraining trials, and obtained less transposition in the second administration (Series 35, 100 per cent transposition; Series 37, 73 per cent transposition). However, there was also a steady decline in performance on the interspersed training trials, suggesting that extraneous variables brought about the decline in transposition.

Conclusion. Until the sources are identified, it will not be possible to predict whether a rise or fall in transposition will occur over test trials, and the interpretation of the absolute levels of transposition obtained will be to some extent ambiguous.[4] The relative levels of transposition can be interpreted with less ambiguity, because in five of the eight studies in which there was some change in the amount of transposition over blocks of test trials, and in which all test-trial responses were rewarded, there was little or no change in the rank orders of experimental conditions with continued testing (T. S. Kendler, 1950; Riley *et al.*, 1960; Riley *et al.*, 1963; G. R. Thompson, 1965; Zeiler, 1966a); in a sixth study (Chisum, 1965), there was no change over the first nine test trials (see Fig. 2-1). One of the other two studies (Hadley, 1927) included so few subjects that a meaningful determination of the rank orders of conditions could not be made, and the other (Maltzman, 1949) obtained marked changes in the rank orders of conditions. The trends relating transposition to independent variables were essentially the same in the first-trial data as in the data for combined trials in 18 experiments (Baker and Lawrence, 1951; Heyman, 1951; I. M. L. Hunter, 1952a, Experiments I and II; Jackson and Dominguez, 1939; Jackson *et al.*, 1938, Experiment IV; P. Johnson and Bailey, 1966; McGrade, 1958; Marsh and Sherman, 1966; Riley and McKee, 1963; Riley *et al.*, 1964; Rudel, 1958 [apparently also included in Rudel's report abstracted in 1954]; Sherman, 1966; Sherman and Strunk, 1964; Shirai, 1951; Stevenson *et al.*, 1955a; R. Thompson, 1955; Zeiler, 1966a). Different trends were obtained with first-trial data and combined-trial data in 10 studies (Alberts and Ehrenfreund, 1951; Corbascio, 1964; D. E. Gould, 1963; Hadley, 1927; T. S. Kendler, 1950; McKee and Riley, 1962; Maltzman, 1949; Riley *et al.*, 1960; Riley *et al.*, 1963; Stevenson and Iscoe, 1955). However, the last group of studies includes some in which there was striking agreement in *parts* of the data (for example, D. E. Gould, 1963).[5]

[4]H. James (1953) developed a theory of transposition based on Helson's concept of the adaptation level, and was able to predict the increase in transposition over test trials. However, the theory cannot predict the decrease that is sometimes obtained. (The theory is discussed in Chapter 8.)

[5]Stevenson and Weiss (1955) and Stevenson and Langford (1957) did not report enough data to permit a conclusion to be drawn about the point under consideration. The data of Campbell and Kral (1958) are not relevant, since all subjects were given the same treatment. The data of Terrell (1959) and Terrell *et al.* (1959) are irrelevant because transposition did not vary with experimental conditions.

"Consistency" of Transposition

The data of several studies show that the percentage of subjects transposing "consistently" is less than the percentage of subjects transposing on the first test trial, whether only transposition responses are rewarded (Stevenson and Iscoe, 1954; Stevenson and Iscoe, 1955; Stevenson *et al.*, 1955a) or all test-trial responses are rewarded (I. M. L. Hunter, 1952a, Experiment I; McGrade, 1958; Shirai, 1951).

H. E. Jones and Dunn (1932) found that the percentage of subjects transposing consistently on combined test trials was less than the percentage of transposition responses on these trials. The published report did not specify what the reward contingency was during the test trials, but the description of the apparatus suggests that either transposition responses alone were rewarded or no responses were rewarded. The group averaged 54 per cent transposition, but the closeness of this average to the chance level does not mean that the subjects responded at random. Table 2-4 presents the percentage of subjects transposing from zero to four times on the four test trials, and the percentage of each score expected on a chance basis. It seems clear from an inspection of the data that chance did not determine the responses.

TABLE 2–4

"Chance" and Obtained Transposition Scores in the Jones and Dunn Study[a]

Percentage of subjects making each score

Score	Chance	Obtained (first experiment)	Obtained (second experiment)
4	6.25	18.7	19.4
3	18.75	27.5	24.2
2	50.00	18.7	27.4
1	18.75	17.5	17.7
0	6.25	17.5	11.3

[a]Based on H. E. Jones and Dunn (1932, Table 3, p. 8). The "second experiment" (N = 62) was a replication of the first experiment (N = 80), but the subjects in the second experiment had also served in the first. The average amount of transposition was 53.1 per cent in the first experiment and 55.6 per cent in the second.

In three studies in which only transposition responses were rewarded, there was less consistent transposition than overall transposition (Stevenson and Iscoe, 1955; Stevenson *et al.*, 1955a; Terrell, 1958).[6] The same result was

[6]In the combined groups in a study by McGrade (1958), 76 per cent of the subjects transposed consistently, and there was 93 per cent transposition on the first five test trials. However, the consistency measure was apparently not over only the first five trials but over all trials to a learning criterion.

obtained in three other studies, rewarding all test-trial responses (R. E. Cole, Dent, Eguchi, Fujii, and Johnson, 1964; Ross, Hetherington, and Wray, 1965[7]; Shirai, 1951). Given the overall percentage transposition, the percentage of subjects transposing consistently, and the number of test trials, it is possible to estimate the overall transposition by the subjects who did not transpose consistently. The last column in Table 2-5 gives these estimates for the last six studies. (The 42 per cent estimated for the Shirai study is very close to the 36 per cent actually obtained.) It can be seen that in all

TABLE 2–5

AVERAGE TRANSPOSITION COMPARED WITH CONSISTENT TRANSPOSITION
(Two-stimulus problems)

Study	No. of test trials	Overall trans-position (%)	Consistent trans-position (%)	Av. transposition by inconsistent subjects
R. E. Cole et al. (1964)	10	85	72[a]	55
Ross et al. (1965)[b]	4	75	64	32
Shirai (1951)	3	92	87	42
Stevenson and Iscoe (1955)				
One-step test	5	72[c]	40	27
Two-step test	5	76[c]	33	32
Four-step test	5	62[c]	21	26
Stevenson et al. (1955a)	5	83[c]	63[c]	27
Terrell (1958)	4	96	88	27

[a]Transposed on at least 9 of the 10 test trials.
[b]The data given here were not included in the published report but were sent to me by Dr. Ross.
[c]Estimated from curves.

but the study by Cole et al., the "inconsistent" subjects transposed at less than the chance level. Presumably, the inconsistent group generally includes a subgroup of subjects who give absolute responses consistently or predominantly, a second subgroup of subjects who transpose predominantly but not consistently, and a third subgroup giving consistent position responses or responding at random (with respect to the manipulated cues). It would be primarily the last subgroup which *spuriously* inflates the overall transposition measure; but, except in the study by Cole et al., the first subgroup must have been the largest of the three in order to yield the below-chance average obtained by the combined inconsistent subjects.

In two of the three studies reporting enough data to allow a determination to be made, the effects of independent variables on consistent transposition

[7]The published report did not include these data; they were sent to me by Dr. Ross.

were less similar to the effects on other combined-trial measures than to the effects on first-trial transposition (Stevenson and Iscoe, 1955; Stevenson *et al.*, 1955a). In the third study (Stevenson and Iscoe, 1954), the other combined-trial measure was trials to criterion, and it is not surprising that the consistency measure was closely related to it.

INTERMEDIATE-STIMULUS PROBLEMS

First Test Trial versus All Test Trials

In intermediate-stimulus problems with only transposition responses rewarded during testing, children transpose relatively more on combined test trials than on the first test trial (Baumeister, Beedle, and Hawkins, 1964; Martin and Blum, 1961; Price, 1960, Experiments I and II; Stevenson and Bitterman, 1955; Whitman, 1965). The same result is generally obtained when all test-trial responses are rewarded (Beaty, 1966; Gonzalez and Ross, 1958; Rudel, 1957 [included in Rudel, 1954]; Rudel, 1960) and when no test trials are rewarded (Caron, 1966, see Table 3-21; Caron, 1967, see Table 2-6). However, Zeiler (1956b) and Zeiler and Paalberg (1964b) obtained about the same amount of transposition on 10 test trials as on the

TABLE 2–6
COMPARISON OF MEASURES IN CARON'S STUDY [a]

Group	Distance (steps)	Percentage transposition		
		Trial 1	6 trials	Predominant[b]
Nonverbal young	1	62	63	62
	3	7	13	4
	6	29	47	46
Nonverbal old	1	56	73	81
	3	29	33	25
	6	32	52	46
Verbal young	1	56	88	89
	3	39	52	46
	6	54	72	75
Verbal old	1	81	95	89
	3	50	70	71
	6	68	83	86

[a] From Caron (1967).
[b] At least four transposition responses on the six test trials.

first test trial, and in the one study providing relevant data on human adults, Zeiler and Lang (1966a) found that the response that occurred on the first test trial was maintained over five test trials by "almost all" of the subjects. All test-trial responses were rewarded in the last three studies.

Table 2-7 compares first-trial and six-trial data from my own studies (Reese, 1961; Reese, 1962a; Reese, 1964b; Reese, 1966; Reese and Fiero, 1964). As in the studies already considered, there was generally more transposition on the combined trials than on the first trial; but when all test-trial responses were rewarded, the difference between the two indices of transposition averaged only 3.3 percentage points, not a particularly impressive change. In the four groups with only transposition responses rewarded, the average increase was 25.5 percentage points.

When the interest is in the nature of the relation between transposition and independent variables, rather than in the absolute level of transposition, it makes little or no difference which measure is used. In all of the above studies, similar trends were obtained with first-trial data and combined-trial data, and Zeiler (1965a) obtained the same result in pigeons.[8]

There seems to be no increase in transposition over blocks of test trials in the intermediate-stimulus problem, but this conclusion is tentative because it is based on only two studies with children (Rudel, 1957; Rudel, 1960) and one with chimpanzees. In the study with chimpanzees, which involved transposition of intermediate position, Spence (1939b, Problem 1) found no increase in transposition from the first to the second administration of the test setting (53.3 per cent vs 56.7 per cent transposition). (The problem was rather complex; and the study is discussed in detail in the section entitled "Multiple-Problem Training," Chapter 3.)

Other Measures

Table 2-7 gives the percentage transposition obtained with different measures in my studies (some of the data are previously unpublished). Table 2-8 gives the rank-order correlation coefficients between the measures. Examination of the data in these tables confirms the suggestion that the measures are essentially interchangeable when the interest is in treatment effects rather than in the absolute level of transposition.

GROUP VERSUS INDIVIDUAL DATA

Zeiler and Salten (1966, Experiment 1) studied the effects of distance, delay, and stimulus similarity on intermediate-size transposition in children. An intermittent reinforcement schedule was used during training, and retraining trials were interspersed among the test trials. The group data on the effects of the three experimental variables were in essential agreement with the data of previous studies (see appropriate sections in Chapters 3 and 4), but the curves of individual children did not agree with the group

[8]In addition, however, Zeiler (1965a) found that the reward contingency was not irrelevant; pigeons gave predominantly absolute responses when tested under an extinction condition, but gave absolute responses and then random responses when tested under a reinforcement condition (variable-interval reinforcement for all test-trial responses).

TABLE 2–7

COMPARISON OF MEASURES IN THE REESE STUDIES[a]

Study	Group	Sample size	Percentage transposition			
			Con-sistent	Pre-dominant	Trial 1	Over-all
Reese (1961)	Concept near	6	16.7	66.7	33.3	52.8
	Concept middle	6	0.0	16.7	0.0	25.0
	Concept far	6	16.7	16.7	16.7	22.2
	No-concept near	7	28.6	42.9	57.1	54.8
	No-concept middle	7	0.0	0.0	0.0	4.8
	No-concept far	6	0.0	0.0	0.0	13.9
Reese (1962a)	2 to 1 near	10	40.0	60.0	60.0	73.3
	2 to 1 far	10	0.0	40.0	10.0	51.7
	1.3 to 1 near	11	72.7	90.9	81.8	89.4
	1.3 to 1 far	10	0.0	40.0	10.0	51.7
Reese (1964b)	2 to 1 concept near young	25	12.0	28.0	20.0	27.3
	2 to 1 concept near old	7	85.7	85.7	85.7	85.7
	2 to 1 no-concept near young	22	27.3	40.9	40.9	44.7
	2 to 1 no-concept near old	1	100.0	100.0	100.0	100.0
	2 to 1 questionable near young	9	11.1	33.3	22.2	21.1
	2 to 1 questionable near old	0	—	—	—	—
	2 to 1 concept far young	20	0.0	10.0	10.0	11.7
	2 to 1 concept far old	7	0.0	14.3	0.0	11.9
	2 to 1 no-concept far young	20	5.0	5.0	15.0	24.2
	2 to 1 no-concept far old	0	—	—	—	—
	2 to 1 questionable far young	10	0.0	0.0	20.0	16.7
	2 to 1 questionable far old	0	—	—	—	—
	1.3 to 1 concept near young	14	57.1	85.7	92.9	83.3
	1.3 to 1concept near old	16	87.5	100.0	93.8	97.9
	1.3 to 1 no-concept near young	4	50.0	100.0	75.0	91.7
	1.3 to 1 no-concept near old	5	80.0	80.0	80.0	80.0
	1.3 to 1 questionable near young	0	—	—	—	—
	1.3 to 1 questionable near old	7	28.6	71.4	57.1	61.9
	1.3 to 1 concept far young	13	30.8	38.5	30.8	39.7
	1.3 to 1 concept far old	17	0.0	17.6	0.0	20.5
	1.3 to 1 no-concept far young	10	10.0	10.0	20.0	23.3
	1.3 to 1 no-concept far old	2	0.0	0.0	0.0	0.0
	1.3 to 1 questionable far young	1	0.0	0.0	0.0	33.3
	1.3 to 1 questionable far old	0	—	—	—	—
Reese (1966)	I near	14	21.4	71.4	57.1	64.3
	I far	14	0.0	14.3	31.0	21.4
	II near	14	28.6	85.7	71.4	75.0
	II far	14	0.0	14.3	28.6	38.1
	III near	13	0.0	15.4	38.5	34.6
	III far	14	0.0	7.1	0.0	17.9
Reese and Fiero (1964)	5/5 near	15	46.7	46.7	46.7	52.2
	5/5 far	14	14.3	14.3	14.3	15.5
	9/10 near	12	25.0	33.3	25.0	33.3
	9/10 far	12	8.3	25.0	8.3	25.8
	14/15 near	14	21.4	42.9	28.6	40.5
	14/15 far	14	14.3	21.4	14.3	20.2

curves. For example, the gradient of transposition in the group declined with increasing distance, but this gradient was representative of only 3 of the 20 children tested. Zeiler and Gardner (1966a) and Zeiler and Salten (1966, Experiment 2) also found that the group data were representative of only a few subjects.

TABLE 2–8

SPEARMAN RANK-ORDER CORRELATION COEFFICIENTS BETWEEN MEASURES IN THE REESE STUDIES[a,b]

Study	Measure	Consistent	Predominant	Trial 1
Reese (1961)	Predominant	.800	—	—
	Trial 1	.986	.857	—
	Overall	.786	.914	.829
Reese (1962a)	Predominant	1.000	—	—
	Trial 1	1.000	1.000	—
	Overall	1.000	1.000	1.000
Reese (1964b)	Predominant	.750	—	—
	Trial 1	.876	.669	—
	Overall	.762	.603	.650
Reese (1966)	Predominant	.871	—	—
	Trial 1	.857	.986	—
	Overall	.857	.900	.829
Reese and Fiero (1964)	Predominant	.757	—	—
	Trial 1	.943	.814	
	Overall	.757	1.000	.814

[a]Based on Table 2–7.

[b]The correlation coefficients in the 1964b study increased by an average of .064 when the two groups with $N = 1$ were omitted. The treatment groups were rank-ordered within each study separately, and separately on each measure.

Zeiler and Salten classified the individual curves into four types: flat gradients showing uniform transposition, flat gradients showing uniform absolute responses, declining gradients of transposition, and gradients showing inconsistent responses. I reexamined the data of the individual children in my own studies of transposition (Reese, 1961; Reese, 1962a; Reese, 1964b; Reese, 1966; Reese and Fiero, 1964), and classified the individual curves into seven types, since the four identified by Zeiler and Salten seemed to be inadequate. I included the two uniform patterns (uniform transposition and uniform absolute responses) and the pattern

Footnote for Table 2–7

[a]Consistent indicates 100 per cent on the 6 test trials. Predominant indicates at least 4 transposition responses. Part of the data given here are previously unreported. Only the data for the first test given are included. The table includes the data of subjects who were eliminated at random to equalize the cell frequencies for the statistical analyses in the published reports. All test-trial responses rewarded except in 1962a study, in which only transposition responses rewarded.

of declining transposition, and added a pattern of increasing absolute responses since group data show that absolute responses increase in frequency as transposition declines in frequency. I also added a category including both the declining transposition gradient and the gradient of increasing absolute responses. This category includes only the subjects whose curves for both transposition and absolute responses are consistent with the group curves, and the percentage of subjects in this category provides the most strict test of the agreement between individual data and group data. I added a pattern of random responses, since my impression has been that a fairly large number of subjects give position responses on test trials, yielding a "random" pattern with respect to the stimulus objects. Finally, I included a miscellaneous category of "Other patterns." Table 2-9

TABLE 2–9

CLASSIFICATION OF TRANSPOSITION-TEST CURVES OF INDIVIDUAL SUBJECTS[a]

(Combined samples from Reese studies)

Pattern	No. of subjects	Percentage
(1) Decreasing transposition	222	49.0
(2) Increasing absolute	229	50.6
(3) Both gradients	201	44.4
(4) Uniform transposition	39	8.6
(5) Uniform absolute	53	11.7
(6) Random	34	7.5
(7) Other patterns	105	23.2
Total sample	453	100.0

[a] Patterns 1, 2, and 3 overlap (201 Ss); and Patterns 2 and 7 overlap (28 Ss). The samples are from Reese (1961; 1962a; 1964b; 1966) and Reese and Fiero (1964). Subjects whose data were omitted (at random) from the published reports to yield proportional cell frequencies for the statistical analyses are included here. The data given here were omitted from the previous reports.

presents the number and percentage of subjects from the combined studies falling into each of the seven categories. A large percentage (44 per cent) fell into the category showing both the decline in transposition with distance and the increase in absolute responses, indicating that the agreement between the group curves and the individual curves was quite good.

Table 2-10 presents the data from my 1961 study (also included in Table 2-9). This was my only study in which tests at more than two distances were given. About 34 per cent of the subjects fell into the third category, which required consistency of decline in transposition and increase in absolute responses over three distances (one, two, and three steps).

Whitman (1965) trained children on the intermediate-size problem and gave tests at three and six steps. The transposition data of individual subjects were reported in an appendix to his thesis, but because individual frequencies of absolute responses were omitted, I could classify the individual curves into only five categories, as shown in Table 2-11. Examination of these data shows that agreement between the individual curves and the group curves improved with increasing age level, and tended to vary with pretraining conditions. The "no-pretraining" condition was closely similar to the standard method of training; the "perceptual" condition was designed to focus the child's attention on the size dimension; and the "verbal" condition was designed to elicit verbal labels for the sizes. (The study is discussed in detail in the section entitled "Concept Knowledge," Chapter 5.)

TABLE 2–10

CLASSIFICATION OF TRANSPOSITION-TEST CURVES OF INDIVIDUAL SUBJECTS[a,b]

Pattern	No. of subjects	Percentage
(1) Decreasing transposition	17	44.7
(2) Increasing absolute	17	44.7
(3) Both gradients	13	34.2
(4) Uniform transposition	1	2.6
(5) Uniform absolute	6	15.8
(6) Random	2	5.3
(7) Other patterns	12	31.6
Total sample	38	100.0

[a] From 1961 study by Reese.
[b] See footnote to Table 2–9.

Individual data were reported in three studies of intermediate-size transposition in subhuman primates. Gonzalez, Gentry, and Bitterman (1954) found that four chimpanzees averaged more transposition downward than upward. Three of the four chimpanzees showed this pattern. Gentry, Overall, and Brown (1959) found no difference between mean transposition downward and upward in monkeys. Seven of the eight subjects transposed about equally in both directions (having scores differing by no more than one response out of 12 responses on each test). In the third study, Brown, Overall, and Gentry (1959) obtained more half-step transposition upward than downward in a group of monkeys. Eight of the nine subjects exhibited this pattern. On one-step tests, the group means indicated a predominance of absolute responses in both directions. All but one subject gave at least 90 per cent absolute responses on both tests, and the other gave 100 per cent absolute responses in the downward test and 83 per cent in the upward test.

TABLE 2–11
SUMMARY OF WHITMAN'S (1965) DATA FOR INDIVIDUAL SUBJECTS
Percentage of subjects in each pattern category[a]

Age level (years)	Pretraining condition	Category				
		C	?	G	RG	Other
3	No pretraining	30	10	30	30	0
	Perceptual	40	30	10	10	10
	Verbal	30	40	20	10	0
	All conditions	33	27	20	17	3
4	No pretraining	30	70	0	0	0
	Perceptual	60	10	0	30	0
	Verbal	90	0	0	10	0
	All conditions	60	27	0	13	0
5	No pretraining	40^b	10	20^b	10	20
	Perceptual	90	0	10	0	0
	Verbal	90	0	0	10	0
	All conditions	73	3	10	7	7
All ages	No pretraining	33	30	17	13	7
	Perceptual	63	13	7	13	3
	Verbal	70	13	7	10	0
	All conditions	56	19	10	12	3

[a]Ten children per subgroup. C indicates individual curve of same shape as group curve and with both scores within 20 per cent of group means; ? indicates same shape and within 30 per cent of group means; G indicates decreasing transposition with increasing distance; and RG indicates reverse of G. See text for explanation of pretraining conditions.
[b]Group curve showed slight decrease; G indicates steep decrease.

Data from two-stimulus problems are also available. Kuenne (1946) reported the data of individual children in a study of the distance effect in the two-stimulus problem. The means of the various subgroups and the patterns of responses of individual subjects are given in Table 2-12. (Only five categories are used because in two-stimulus problems, the first two categories listed in Table 2-9 are identical to the third category.) The patterns of about 77 per cent of the subjects were consistent with the direction of the subgroup trends. However, a more strict criterion of agreement between the individual patterns and the group means is to require that the scores of the subject deviate no more than some fixed amount from the group means. Using a maximum allowable deviation of 10 per cent (one response in Kuenne's study), the scores of 64 per cent of the subjects were consistent with the subgroup means. There was, then, striking agreement between the group data and the individual data.

The data of Jackson and Jerome (1943), like those of Whitman for the

TABLE 2–12
GROUP DATA AND INDIVIDUAL DATA
(Kuenne, 1946)

		Group data[a]		Individual data: pattern					
MA level	Sample size	Near Test	Far Test	Consistent trans-position	Consistent absolute	Trans-position gradient	Random	Other	Consistent with group[b]
				Near Test Given First					
3	4	95	50	0	0	4^c	0	0	4
4	6	83	68	2	0	3^c	0	1	1
5	6	100	68	2	0	4^c	0	0	2
6	7	100	99	7^c	0	0	0	0	7
				Far Test Given First					
3	3	90	50	0	0	3^c	0	0	2
4	5	62	62	0	0	3	0	2	0
5	6	100	88	4^c	0	2^c	0	0	5
6	7	100	100	7^c	0	0	0	0	7

[a]Mean percentage transposition.

[b]This column gives the number of subjects whose scores were both within 10 per cent (one response) of the subgroup means.

[c]General trend predicted from direction of subgroup means. Note that the pattern predicted for the MA4 subgroup given the Far Test first is not in the table, and that both consistent and decreasing transposition have been marked for the MA5 subgroup given the Far Test first.

intermediate-stimulus problem, demonstrate that the procedure used can influence the variability among the subjects. Groups of gifted children and dull children were given a transposition test after various kinds of discrimination training. In groups tested after simultaneous discrimination training, the modal pattern of transposition responses was exhibited by 75 per cent of the gifted children and 75 per cent of the dull children. In groups tested after a kind of successive discrimination training (response withheld until after both stimuli had been presented), the modal pattern was exhibited by 67 per cent of the gifted children and 42 per cent of the dull children. In groups tested after standard successive discrimination training, the modal pattern was exhibited by 25 per cent of the gifted children and 17 per cent of the dull children. The total numbers of different patterns exhibited, combining the groups of children, were 4 after simultaneous discrimination training, 7 after the modified successive discrimination training, and 15 after the standard successive discrimination training. In an earlier study, Jackson and Jerome (1940) obtained consistent transposition in all subjects given simultaneous discrimination training, and obtained consistent absolute responses in 58 per cent of subjects given standard successive discrimination training. There were a total of four different response patterns in the group given the successive discrimination training.

In a study by Jackson and Dominguez (1939) on transposition as a function of overtraining, eight subjects exhibited six different patterns of responses. The stimuli were four dimensional, and data reported by Jackson (1939) on the same eight subjects suggest that there were marked individual differences in the dimensions and combinations of dimensions responded to, perhaps accounting for the extreme variability obtained by Jackson and Dominguez.

In a study of stimulus generalization, Landau (1966) found that the mean performance curve of preschool children was representative of the gradients of 13 of the 14 children tested, but the group curve of college students was markedly different from many of the individual curves. Posttest questioning indicated that the college students had a variety of "hypotheses" about the nature of the conditioned stimulus, but most of the children had the same "hypothesis." These data suggest that at least one of the factors determining the variability among individual curves is related to variability of verbal mediating processes. It may be that the variability of these processes is influenced by the procedure used during training, as well as the age of the subjects.

Data are available from four studies of two-stimulus transposition in rats. F. N. Jones (1939b) reported individual data for 28 rats given a transposition test twice, with 20 trials per test and with 100 retraining trials between the tests. The group averaged 70.5 per cent transposition on the first test and 72.5 per cent on the second test. Sixteen of the subjects changed no more than 10 percentage points from the first to the second test (plus or minus two responses), and 10 subjects changed no more than 10 percentage points *and* were within 15 percentage points of both group means. Hebb (1937b) used a similar kind of design, with 10-trial tests and 10 retraining trials between the tests. Of 28 rats, 17 changed no more than 10 percentage points from the first to the second test, and 11 changed no more than 10 percentage points *and* were within 15 percentage points of both group means. (The frequencies in Hebb's study are for combined size- and brightness-transposition groups.)

Heyman (1951) gave tests at one-half step, one step, and one and one-half steps; and Flory (1938) gave tests at from two-thirds of a step to two and one-half steps, varying somewhat with different ratios of stimulus areas. Both investigators reported the data of individual subjects in appendices to their theses, and I classified these data into the five categories used for Kuenne's data. Of 30 rats in the Heyman study, 77 per cent had decreasing gradients, 7 per cent transposed consistently, 3 per cent responded at random, and the other 13 per cent fell into the miscellaneous category. Of 18 rats in the Flory study, 61 per cent exhibited the gradient, 17 per cent transposed consistently, and the other 22 per cent fell into the miscellaneous category. (Ten of Flory's subjects were given each test twice. Six of these exhibited the gradient on both pairs of tests. The other four made up the 22 per cent of the total sample in the miscellaneous category. All four exhibited one decreasing gradient; three responded at random on the other pair of tests, and the fourth transposed consistently on the other pair of tests.)

With the more strict criterion of agreement (deviation of no more than 10 per cent—one response—from the group means), 43 per cent of Heyman's subjects were consistent with the group as a whole. However, only one subject with a decreasing gradient had more than one score that deviated more than 10 per cent from the group mean, and only one had any score that deviated more than 20 per cent from the group mean. (The subgroup sizes were too small in Flory's study to permit a meaningful application of this criterion.)

Perkins and Wheeler (1930) obtained fairly good agreement between group curves and individual curves in goldfish. (See the discussion of these data in the section entitled "Disruptive Effects of the Tests," Chapter 4.)

It seems clearly apparent that the findings of Zeiler and Salten need not discourage the use of group data, although these findings might discourage the use of certain training procedures. The data of Whitman (1965) and of Jackson and Jerome (1943) demonstrate that certain experimental conditions can affect the variability of the subjects, and a comparison of the data of Zeiler and Salten with the data of my studies suggests that the reinforcement schedule used also has an effect. The procedures of Zeiler and Salten's study differed in two major ways from the procedures of my studies. Zeiler and Salten used an intermittent-reinforcement schedule during training, and I used continuous reinforcement. Zeiler and Salten gave retraining trials among the test trials, and I did not. Sato and Nishijima (1955) reported that the average amount of intermediate-size transposition in children was the same with and without interspersed retraining trials. This finding suggests that the critical procedural difference between the Zeiler and Salten study and my studies was the difference in reinforcement schedules. Apparently intermittent reinforcement during training increases the variability of human subjects on the transposition test.

Although, in general, group transposition data seem to represent fairly accurately the performance of individual subjects, there are many discrepancies. Ideally, therefore, one would examine only the individual data, but there are two major considerations which lead one to prefer to use group data in spite of the discrepancies. One is that the independent variable under investigation may have a relatively weak effect, and may not produce clearly unambiguous changes in the curves of individual subjects. The second is that errors of measurement and other chance fluctuations in an individual curve may obscure treatment effects. The advantages of using group data are, first, that examination of the differences between group means may indicate that an effect, however weak, has been obtained, and, second, that statistical analysis may indicate that the obtained effect is not attributable to errors of measurement and other chance fluctuations among individual subjects.

Conclusions

There is relatively more intermediate-stimulus transposition on combined test trials than on the first test trial, whether all responses are rewarded or only transposition responses are rewarded (the increase is greater in the latter case than in the former), and the trends relating transposition to independent variables are similar whichever measure of transposition is used. In the two-stimulus problem, however, first-trial transposition is usually but not always less than transposition on combined trials (the inconsistency in the data is greater when all responses are rewarded than when only transposition responses are rewarded), and the trends relating transposition to independent variables may be different when different measures are used. The consistency of results among the studies of intermediate-stimulus transposition and the inconsistency among the studies of two-stimulus transposition may be spurious products of the numbers of experiments involved in the comparisons, since there are many more two-stimulus experiments than intermediate-stimulus experiments providing relevant data. However, the difference may reflect the greater number of different possible methods of solving the two-stimulus problem than of solving the intermediate-stimulus problem, on the assumption that different methods of solution would yield different amounts of transposition.

Measures of the consistency of transposition and the predominance of transposition have sometimes been found to be more sensitive to experimental manipulations than other measures of transposition, but are not widely used, perhaps because part of the raw data is ignored.

One question about transposition is whether it occurs at all. Given an affirmative answer, a second question is about the strength of the tendency to transpose. All measures of transposition are relevant to the first question. The trial-1 measure, consistency measure, and predominance measure can provide data relevant to the second question for the group of subjects as a whole, but not for individual subjects. The mean score on combined trials is relevant to the second question, but is inflated by chance transposition responses, resulting, for example, from position habits; and if only transposition responses are rewarded during the test, it is further inflated by the occurrence of learning. If no responses are rewarded on the test trials, the mean amount of transposition is reduced by extinction effects. Therefore, the best procedure, when the interest is in the absolute level of transposition and multiple test trials are given, is to reward all test-trial responses.

When the interest is in the nature of the relation between transposition and independent variables, rather than in the absolute level of transposition, it makes little or no difference which measure is used; but probably the best solution to the problem of selecting an appropriate measure is to beg the question by reporting analyses of the first-trial data and of the data of at least one combined-trial measure.

CHAPTER 3

Training Variables

The effects of variables that are manipulated during the training phase of transposition experiments are considered in this chapter. For convenience, the chapter is divided into two sections, one section dealing with variables related to the stimuli and one section dealing with variables related to training procedures. Even with this arrangement, each section is somewhat more heterogeneous in content than might be desired.

Stimulus Variables

STIMULUS SIMILARITY

Köhler (1918) suggested that human adults will not transpose when stimulus differences are large, which implies that they will transpose when stimulus differences are small. Extending the prediction over the range of degrees of stimulus similarity and over the range of species and age levels of subjects, it might be expected that transposition will increase as stimulus similarity increases. Köhler might not have agreed with these extensions, but Gundlach and Herington (1933, pp. 203–204) explicitly predicted this effect of stimulus similarity.

Two-Stimulus Problems

Spence (1937b, Experiment II) seemed to obtain less transposition in chimpanzees as stimulus similarity increased, contrary to the expected trend, but the number of subjects was small (four subjects were trained and tested with a 2 to 1 ratio of stimulus areas, and only two subjects with a 1.6 to 1 ratio). In another study, Spence (1938) trained chimpanzees with stimuli having a ratio of areas of 1.6 to 1, 2.0 to 1, 2.6 to 1, or 4.0 to 1, and gave a transposition test with stimuli having a ratio of 1.6 to 1. The subjects trained with distinctive stimuli (the two larger ratios) transposed at the chance level, but those trained with similar stimuli (the two smaller ratios) transposed almost perfectly. Ohtsuka (1937) also confirmed the prediction.

Monkeys gave relational responses when the differences between brightnesses were small, and gave absolute responses when the differences were large. (Ohtsuka apparently obtained similar effects in 1939 and 1942.)

When extremely large stimulus differences are used, relatively little transposition is obtained. Using a black-gray-white series, Takei (1927) and Taylor (1932a) obtained a predominance of absolute responses in chicks, Spigel (1963) obtained only 58 per cent transposition in turtles, and Kuroda (1933) obtained "a poor percentage of relative choice" in tortoises (Shirai, 1951, p. 20). Using somewhat less distinctive stimuli, Gayton (1927) obtained little transposition in rats, and Wesman and Eisenberg (1941) obtained little in human adults.

Harrison and Nissen (1941) found that chimpanzees transposed spatial position only when the positions were relatively close together, indicating that increasing "similarity" of positions increased transposition. Delayed-response problems were used, with the stimulus settings shown in Table 3-1. The first trial of each problem was an information trial, on which the subject watched the experimenter bait one of two visually undifferentiated containers. The second trial was a test trial, given after a 20-second delay during which the containers were concealed from the subject and were shifted to the test positions. Transposition responses averaged 70 per cent on problems with five-inch separations between the containers, but averaged only 33 per cent on problems with fifteen-inch separations

TABLE 3-1
THE HARRISON AND NISSEN (1941) DESIGN

Problem	Trial	Stimulus positions[a]			
		a	b c d e		f
1	Baiting trial		b *c*		
	Test trial		c d		
2	Baiting trial		*d* e		
	Test trial		c d		
3	Baiting trial	a	*b*		
	Test trial		b e		
4	Baiting trial		*e*		f
	Test trial		b e		

[a]The distance from a to b and from e to f was 15 inches; the distance from b to c, c to d, and d to e was 5 inches. The italicized position on the first trial was baited.

R. Thompson (1955) obtained the predicted effect of stimulus similarity in rats, but the effect was relatively weak; Flory (1938, 1939) and Riley *et al.* (1960) found no effect of stimulus similarity on transposition in rats. (Riley *et al.* obtained no effect on overall transposition, but there was an effect on the change in transposition over test trials [see section entitled "Changes across Blocks of Test Trials (All Responses Rewarded)," Chapter 2].)

There have been only eight studies of the effect of stimulus similarity on two-stimulus transposition in human subjects (D. E. Gould, 1963; Jackson *et al.*, 1938, Experiment IV; Line, 1931; Motoyoshi, 1948; Riley and McKee, 1963; Sato, 1936; M. S. Scott, 1966; Zeiler, 1966a), and two of these (by Motoyoshi and by Sato) are unavailable in English. According to Shirai (1951, p. 20), Sato obtained the predicted effect in children, but Motoyoshi obtained no effect of stimulus similarity. Of the six studies published in English, three included only the Near transposition test (Gould; Jackson *et al.*; Riley and McKee), and a fourth (Line) apparently included only the Near Test. (Line only summarized his transposition studies, and the procedures used must be inferred from his description of the results.) Jackson *et al.* found that children transposed equally well with 2 to 1 and 4 to 1 ratios of stimulus areas, but Line obtained increasing transposition of brightness as the brightnesses became more similar. Riley and McKee obtained increasing transposition of pitch as the pitches became more similar.

McKee and Riley (1962) found more transposition of loudness than pitch, with some evidence that the loudnesses were more similar than the pitches. Subjects were asked to tell whether in each of 10 successive pairs of tones the two members of the pair were the same or different. On half of the trials the tones were identical, and on half they were different. The mean number of correct responses was significantly less for tones differing in loudness than for tones differing in pitch (7.0 vs 9.8). However, Riley and McKee (1963) and Riley *et al.* (1964) also obtained more transposition of loudness than pitch, as shown in Table 3-2, and reported evidence that the difference is not attributable to differences in the similarity of the stimuli. In the study by Riley and McKee, adult subjects rated the difference

TABLE 3–2

THE DATA OF THE RILEY AND MCKEE STUDIES

Study	Dimension	Trial-1 transposition (%)
McKee and Riley (1962)	Pitch	50.0
	Loudness	81.2
Riley and McKee (1963)	Pitch (low similarity)	62.5
	(moderate similarity)	65.0
	(high similarity)	70.8
	Loudness	94.2
Riley *et al.* (1964)	Pitch	68.8
	Loudness	92.5

between "moderately similar" pitches and the difference between loud-nesses, using a method similar to the psychophysical method of single stimuli (Stevens, 1951, p. 43). The pitch interval was consistently judged to be smaller than the loudness interval. In the study by Riley *et al.* (1964), the initial discrimination between pitches was found to be much harder to learn than the initial discrimination between loudnesses, implying that the pitches were more similar than the loudnesses. This difference was also obtained by McKee and Riley.

McKee and Riley suggested that children may have verbal labels for loudnesses but not for pitches. If so, the learning data could be explained by the "acquired distinctiveness of cues," and the transposition data could be explained by the "acquired equivalence of cues" (see for example, Reese, 1962b; Reese, 1963a). The acquired distinctiveness of the stimuli used during training would facilitate the learning of the loudness discrimi-nation, and the acquired equivalence of the training and test stimuli would facilitate transposition of loudness. The latter mechanism could yield more transposition of loudness, relative to transposition of pitch, even if the pitches were psychophysically somewhat more similar than the loudnesses were. However, the data of Riley, McKee, Bell, and Schwartz (1967) were not consistent with this explanation. Children were instructed to choose on a test trial either the same absolute tone or the same relative tone as had been presented on the previous trial. In general, the children were more accurate in identifying the relative tone than in identifying the absolute tone, regardless of whether the stimuli differed in loudness or pitch, and regardless of whether the test tones were identical to the standard tones or were transposed one step. These data indicate that the children under-stood the verbal references to relative pitch differences.

In an alternative interpretation, McKee and Riley referred to Stevens's (1957) distinction between "prothetic" and "metathetic" dimensions. A prothetic dimension is one for which the relevant question is "How much?"; a metathetic dimension is one for which the relevant question is "What kind?" or "Where?" A prothetic dimension is represented by an additive process at the physiological level; progress along the dimension results from adding excitation to excitation. A metathetic dimension is represented by a substitutive process; progress is achieved by substituting one excita-tion for another, for example, by changing the locus of excitation. More transposition would presumably be expected on a prothetic dimension than on a metathetic dimension, but Lindworsky (1931, pp. 160–161) may have erred when he said that "qualitative nuances" are not transposable at all. Loudness is a prothetic dimension and pitch is a metathetic dimension; therefore, there should be more transposition of loudness than pitch.

Riley *et al.* (1964) have reported data that seem to be consistent with this explanation. In a pretraining task, it was found that children learned to order stimuli differing in loudness more rapidly than they learned to order stimuli differing in pitch. The children were also given a discrimination-learning problem and a transposition test. More transposition of loudness than of pitch was obtained, suggesting that the ease of ordering is related to the probability of transposition. Furthermore, children who quickly learned to order the pitches in the pretraining task learned the pitch discrimination significantly more rapidly than children who were slower in the pretraining task, and also transposed more (77 per cent vs 44 per cent, significant at the .10 level). (Riley [1965a] has summarized the data of the series of experiments on auditory transposition, and has suggested that the studies are relevant to the problem of "establishing differences between sense dimensions.")

Zeiler (1966a) obtained more transposition with a 2 to 1 ratio of stimulus areas than with a 1.4 to 1 ratio, especially on Far Tests (see Table 3-3). He suggested that when discrimination is easy (2 to 1 ratio), the stimulus differences are perceived immediately, and the relational characteristic stands out and is learned, leading to a high level of transposition. When discrimination is difficult, however, the subject must attend closely to the individual components, and the absolute stimulus properties are learned. Transposition is controlled by stimulus generalization in the latter case, and is less than when controlled by relation perception.

The difference between loudness and pitch transposition (Table 3-2) is consistent with Zeiler's suggestions, but one might question the validity

TABLE 3–3

DATA RELEVANT TO ZEILER'S HYPOTHESIS
ABOUT STIMULUS SIMILARITY

Study	Area ratio of stimuli	Percentage transposition			
		1 step	2 steps	3 steps	4 steps
Zeiler (1966a)	1.4 to 1	78	85	61	54
	2 to 1	85	84	90	89
R. C. Johnson and Zara (1960)[a]	2.6 to 1	80	55	52	—
Sherman and Strunk (1964)[a]	2.6 to 1	68	73	40	—
Sherman (1966) (Exp. 1)[a]	2.6 to 1	90	—	63	—

[a] Data are for groups given "standard" training.

of using this interdimensional comparison as supporting evidence. M. S. Scott (1966) obtained apparently contradictory data in mentally retarded subjects. There was less transposition at one step with stimuli having a ratio of 8 to 1 than with stimuli having a ratio of 2 to 1, but the stimulus ratio had no effect on transposition at four steps. However, the stimuli on the tests had a ratio of 2 to 1 regardless of what the training ratio was, and the shift from the 8 to 1 training ratio to the 2 to 1 test ratio could have reduced transposition quite apart from any other effects of training with the 8 to 1 ratio. Data obtained by R. C. Johnson and Zara (1960), Sherman and Strunk (1964), and Sherman (1966) contradict Zeiler's hypothesis, since these investigators used a 2.6 to 1 ratio, but obtained considerably less transposition than Zeiler obtained with the 2 to 1 ratio, rather than more as his interpretation would predict (see Table 3-3; see also Table 4-6). It might be argued than when the stimulus differences are too great, the relation is no longer obvious, accounting for the discrepancy. (This argument has been suggested in another context, and is discussed in the section entitled "Gestalt Theory," Chapter 8.) However, Johnson and Zara and Sherman and Strunk tested only "nonverbal" children and all of Zeiler's subjects were "verbal," suggesting that Zeiler's interpretation might be modified in the following way: The young child who possesses the required concepts can use them only if the stimulus differences are large, perhaps because small stimulus differences do not arouse the conceptual responses (see section entitled "Concept Knowledge," Chapter 5).

D. E. Gould (1963) studied the effect of stimulus similarity on two-stimulus transposition in human adults, and found that transposition increased as the stimuli became increasingly similar.

Data reported by McGrade (1958) can be interpreted as further evidence that stimulus similarity has an effect on transposition. The subjects were required to feel each stimulus on every trial before making a choice. Sighted children who were blindfolded throughout the experimental session and blind children learned the initial discrimination much more slowly than sighted children who were permitted to see the stimuli as well as to feel them (20.0 and 13.1 vs 3.4 trials to criterion, excluding criterional trials). The blindfolded children and the blind children transposed much more than the sighted children (96 and 95 per cent vs 79 per cent transposition on the first test trial), even though more of the sighted children verbalized the problem solution (92 per cent vs 86 and 71 per cent). If the slower initial learning of the subjects who were required to respond solely on the basis of tactual cues, in comparison with the subjects who could respond to visual cues, is taken to reflect greater similarity of the tactual cues than of the visual cues, as seems reasonable, then the transposition data reflect effects of different degrees of stimulus similarity. M. Wilson (1964) found less inter-problem improvement in the performance of rhesus monkeys on tactual problems than on visual problems, which is consistent with the suggestion that tactual cues are more similar than visual cues are.

Intermediate-Stimulus Problems

Using the intermediate-size problem, Zeiler (1965a) and Zeiler and Price

(1965) found that either absolute responses or random responses pre-dominated in pigeons on transposition tests, and there was no effect of stimulus similarity. In normal children, there is more intermediate-size transposition on the Near Test with similar stimuli than with distinctive stimuli when the children are tested immediately after training (Reese, 1962a; Reese, 1964b; Rudel, 1957), but there is no effect of stimulus similarity when the test is delayed (Rudel, 1957). In brain-damaged children the effect is obtained with both immediate and delayed testing (Rudel, 1960). On the combined trials of a three-step Far Test, the stimulus-similarity effect was found in preschool children but not kindergarten children in one study (Reese, 1962a), and the effect was obtained in both younger children (four to six years old) and older children (six to eight years old) at this distance in another study (Reese, 1964b). These combined-trial data were not altogether consistent with the first-trial data, which indicated that stimulus similarity had an effect on Near Test transposition, but not on transposition at three steps (see Table 2-7).

Zeiler obtained considerably more intermediate-stimulus transposition in a study with stimuli that were highly similar (1.4 to 1 ratio of areas) than in another study with distinctive stimuli (2.0 to 1 and 2.8 to 1 area ratios).[1] In the first study transposition predominated at one step, but in the second it predominated only at one-half step (the half-step test was not given in the first study). Zeiler and Gardner (1966b) replicated these results, using ratios of 1.4 to 1 and 2.0 to 1; and Zeiler and Salten (1966, Experiment 1) and Zeiler and Lang (1966b) obtained essentially similar findings. Zeiler and Gardner (1966a) obtained decreasing transposition at one, two, and three steps with decreasing stimulus similarity, using ratios of 1.2 to 1, 1.4 to 1, and 1.7 to 1 (see Table 3-4; see also discussion of these studies in section entitled "Distance," Chapter 4).

Rudel (1957) suggested that rather than stimulus similarity *per se*, the difficulty of the learning problem is the relevant variable. The data of Ross *et al.* (1965) are relevant to this point, but not conclusive. In normal subjects and mentally retarded subjects, delay of reward increased the difficulty of discrimination learning, but it tended to increase transposition in the normal subjects and to reduce transposition in the mentally retarded subjects. However, neither effect on transposition was statistically significant. Furthermore, Zeiler and Lang (1966a) found that the use of a correctional procedure made the intermediate-size problem easier for college students to learn, but produced no more transposition than the use of a noncor-rectional procedure. They also found that the three-stimulus intermediate-

---

[1]Zeiler (1963c, pp. 523–524) summarized the results. In both studies symmetrical stimulus sets were used in both the training and test phases. A "symmetrical" set of three stimuli is one in which the intermediate stimulus is midway between the other two stimuli on a psycho-physical scale.

TABLE 3-4
ZEILER'S DATA ON STIMULUS SIMILARITY
IN THE INTERMEDIATE-SIZE PROBLEM

Study	Area ratio	Percentage transposition						
		$\frac{1}{2}$ step	1 step	$1\frac{1}{2}$ steps	2 steps	3 steps	4 steps	5 steps
Zeiler and Gardner (1966a)	1.2 to 1	—	86	—	67	66	—	—
Zeiler (1963c)	1.4 to 1	—	75	—	14	17	25	17
Zeiler and Gardner (1966a)	1.4 to 1	—	61	—	50	53	—	—
Zeiler and Gardner (1966b)	1.4 to 1	—	69	—	31	25	19	25
Zeiler and Lang (1966b)[a]	1.4 to 1	—	75	—	25	12	38	—
Zeiler and Salten (1966)	1.4 to 1	—	66	—	49	40	44	—
Zeiler and Gardner (1966a)	1.7 to 1	—	61	—	36	39	—	—
Zeiler (1963c)	2 to 1	83	25	4	—		—	—
Zeiler and Gardner (1966b)	2 to 1	75	42	8	—	—	—	—
Zeiler and Lang (1966b)[a]	2 to 1	—	38	—	0	12	12	—
Zeiler and Salten (1966)	2 to 1	89	50	—	50	43	—	—

[a]Immediate test only.

size problem was easier than a five-stimulus intermediate-size problem, but there was no difference in transposition on the two problems.

Conclusion

In both animal and human subjects, increasing stimulus similarity generally increases two-stimulus transposition on the Near Test. No relevant data have been reported on Far Test transposition in animals, and the Far Test data for human subjects are inconsistent. It may be that the effect is reversed in young "verbal" children, not because of a reduction of transposition with similar stimuli, but because of an enhancement of transposition with distinctive stimuli. The young child may be able to utilize the verbal concept to mediate the transposition response only when the stimulus differences are large, perhaps because small stimulus differences fail to arouse the conceptual response.

In children, increasing stimulus similarity increases intermediate-stimulus transposition on the Near Test, but probably has less effect on transposition on Far Tests. Stimulus similarity appears to have no effect on intermediate-stimulus transposition in pigeons.

ASYMMETRICAL STIMULUS SETS

One of the methodological problems in research on transposition is concerned with the selection of the stimuli to be used. In most studies it is desirable to select the stimuli in such a way that they form a series in which the ease of discriminating between two adjacent stimuli is the same for all pairs of adjacent stimuli. According to Weber's law, this kind of series is obtained when the ratio of the stimulus values on the dimension being varied is the same in all of the stimulus pairs (see Stevens, 1951, p. 35, for example). Using stimuli differing in size, a constant ratio of areas yields an approximation to the desired series; but some investigators used series of stimuli differing on a linear dimension, with a constant increment rather than a constant ratio. Such series are asymmetrical, with decreasing discriminability between adjacent stimuli rather than constant discriminability, and these series are generally avoided.

Zeiler (1963a; 1963b; 1963c), however, has deliberately used asymmetrical stimulus sets to test his adaptation level theory of performance in the intermediate-size problem (see section entitled "Adaptation Level Theories," Chapter 8). He has predicted and obtained all four types of responses possible in the intermediate-stimulus problem (transposition responses, absolute responses, nontransposition-nonabsolute responses, and random responses). However, the data are less convincing for the random response than for the others. One finding which Zeiler did not predict, but which could have been predicted by changing the values of certain constants in his theoretical equations, was an obtained increase in transposition with increasing similarity between the training and test sets of stimuli (Zeiler, 1963a, Experiment 3). Subjects were trained on Stimuli 1, 2, and 8 of a series with a constant area ratio, and tested on 1, 2, and 3; 1, 2, and 4; 1, 2, and 5; or 1, 2, and 6. The percentage transposition for the four respective test sets was 33, 60, 70, and 80 per cent. There was concomitantly a progressive decrease in the nontransposition-nonabsolute response, which could also have been predicted (see Zeiler, 1963b, p. 527), but this response was predominant only on the test with Stimuli 1, 2, and 3. Riley, Sherman, and McKee (1966) attempted to replicate this last result, but without success. They obtained a predominance of transposition responses with Stimuli 1, 2, and 3, after training on 1, 2, and 8. Zeiler has reported that he also has not always been able to replicate this finding (1966b; 1967).

The increase in transposition obtained by Zeiler with increasing similarity between the training and test sets, in terms of amount of asymmetry, suggests that the transposition might have been a function of the probability of discriminating between the sets, or of noticing the change in stimuli (see section entitled "Generalization Theory," Chapter 9). However, Zeiler (1963c) has suggested that it may reflect a developing inattentiveness to the extreme stimulus. Asymmetrical stimulus sets may effectively consist of two "important" stimuli and one relatively "unimportant" stimulus, according to Zeiler.

Effect of Absolute Stimulus Components

Whether or not a subject can learn about absolute and relative stimulus properties at the same time is a question of theoretical significance. (For example, the theory outlined in Chapter 11 requires the assumption that such learning is possible.) Studies in which transposition occurred at less than the perfect level suggest a positive answer, but are generally ambiguous because it is often not necessary to assume that relational learning occurred at all in order to account for the obtained trends (see Chapter 9). However, the designs of a few studies, reviewed in this section, permit more unambiguous inferences to be drawn.

Grice (1948; 1951) reported evidence apparently indicating that absolute stimulus preferences and aversions established in rats in preliminary training affect the speed of subsequent simultaneous discrimination learning. This kind of finding would contradict the notion that the subject *must* learn to respond to some relation in order to solve discrimination problems (but as Grice [1948] noted, it would not necessarily contradict the notion that the subject *can* learn to respond to relations, since the possibility of relational learning was not tested). However, Mackintosh (1965a, p. 128; 1965b) has demonstrated that Grice's experimental situation could have actually involved the successive learning of two simultaneous brightness discriminations, and could have involved relational learning. Table 3-5 shows the designs used by Grice and Mackintosh. In the "absolute-constant" conditions, the reward contingency of the stimulus object used in Stage 1 was retained in Stage 2; and in the "absolute-reversal" conditions, the reward contingency of this stimulus was reversed in Stage 2. In the "relation-constant" conditions, the same direction of brightness relation was positive in both stages; and in the "relation-reversal" conditions, the reward contingency of this relation was reversed in Stage 2. As shown in the last two columns of Table 3-5, Mackintosh (1965b) replicated Grice's (1948; 1951) results, but the data of the four additional conditions used by Mackintosh show clearly that relation reversal was more important than absolute reversal. The combined data of the three studies are given in Table 3-6, where it can be seen that absolute reversal was not completely ineffective. Therefore, the relational quality was the predominant stimulus, but the absolute quality also exerted an influence on behavior.

The effect obtained by Grice in rats was obtained by Spence (1941) in chimpanzees. Three chimpanzees were given tests with two stimulus objects to assess initial preferences, and were then given successive presentations of these two stimuli, both rewarded, and a new stimulus that was not rewarded. Finally, a second preference test was given with the first two stimuli. As shown in Table 3-7, the training reversed the initial preferences. A fourth subject was given a preference test with six

TABLE 3–5

THE DESIGNS AND DATA OF THE GRICE (1948; 1951) AND MACKINTOSH (1965c) STUDIES[a]

Study	Condition Absolute	Condition Relation	Stage 1 S^+ S^-		Stage 1 Positive relation	Stage 2 S^+ S^-		Stage 2 Positive relation	Stage-2 performance Correct on trials 1–20 (%)	Stage-2 performance Trials to criterion
Grice (1948)	Constant	Constant	8	X	B	8	5	B	64^b	30
	Reversal	Constant	5	X	B	8	5	B	62^b	72
Grice (1951)	Constant	Constant	X	8	D	5	8	D	82^c	—^{d}
	Reversal	Constant	X	5	D	5	8	D	61^c	—^{d}
Mackintosh	Constant	Constant	8	X	B	8	5	B	56	46
(1965b)	Reversal	Reversal	8	X	B	5	8	D	35	137
	Constant	Reversal	5	X	B	5	8	D	32	138
	Reversal	Constant	5	X	B	8	5	B	74	54
	Constant	Constant	X	8	D	5	8	D	75	16
	Reversal	Reversal	X	8	D	8	5	B	26	185
	Constant	Reversal	X	5	D	8	5	B	38	160
	Reversal	Constant	X	5	D	5	8	D	70	30

[a] In Grice's studies, X indicates black card; in Mackintosh's study, X indicates brown door. In all 3 studies, 8 indicates white circle with 8-cm diam., and 5 indicates white circle with 5-cm diam. B indicates brighter; D indicates dimmer.

[b] Estimated from Grice's Fig. 2 (1948, p. 639).

[c] Estimated from Grice's Fig. 1 (1951, p. 152).

[d] Not reported. Mean errors through criterion were 3.7 for first group and 11.7 for second group.

stimulus squares differing in area, then it was given a training series with an intermediate stimulus nonreinforced and each of the other five stimuli reinforced, and finally it was given a second preference test series with

TABLE 3–6

SUMMARY OF GRICE (1948; 1951) AND MACKINTOSH (1965c) DATA[a]

Stage-2 performance

Measure	Reward contingency of absolute stimulus	Reward contingency of relation Constant	Reward contingency of relation Reversal
Per cent correct (trials 1–20)	Constant	69	35
	Reversal	67	30
Trials to criterion	Constant	30.7	149.0
	Reversal	52.0	161.0

[a] See text for explanation of symbols. The table gives means of unweighted means.

TABLE 3–7

THE SPENCE (1941) DESIGN AND DATA FOR THE FIRST THREE SUBJECTS [a]

Subject	Variable	Preference series		Training series (choices forced)			Test series	
		A	B	$A^{|}$	B^+	C^-	A	B
1	Stimulus area (cm²)	256	160	256	160	100	256	160
	Frequency of choice	5	25	50	50	50	10	0
2	Stimulus area (cm²)	160	256	160	256	409	160	256
	Frequency of choice	2	18	40	40	60	6	4
3	Stimulus area (cm²)	202	303	202	303	455	202	303
	Frequency of choice	9	11	30	30	60	10	0

[a] After the first test series, the training series and then the test series were repeated, with similar results. The third subject was also tested on 303 vs 455 before and after training, with similar results.

all six stimuli. The training affected preferences, as shown in Table 3-8. According to Spence, the intermediate stimulus acquired an inhibitory tendency, as a result of the nonreinforcement, and the inhibitory tendency generalized to the other stimuli. The amount of generalization decreased as the distance from the intermediate stimulus increased, and therefore preferences for stimuli adjacent to the intermediate stimulus were weakened more than preferences for stimuli more remote from the intermediate stimulus

The data for the first three subjects can be interpreted as reflecting the development of relational preferences, if it is assumed that the subjects compared each positive stimulus with the trace of the negative stimulus. (The duration of the intertrial interval used was not reported, but it might be noted that the assumption would be more reasonable with a short intertrial interval than with a long one.) However, this interpretation cannot account for the data of the fourth subject, which was

TABLE 3–8

TASK AND DATA FOR SPENCE'S FOURTH SUBJECT[a]

Series	Stimulus					
	60	90	135	202	303	455
Preference	.30	.59	.76	.80	.40	.18
Test [b]	1.00	.80	.10	.20	.40	.40

[a] During the training series, the 135-cm² stimulus was presented 50 times without reinforcement, and every other stimulus was presented 10 times with reinforcement. High score = high preference.

[b] Values estimated from Spence's Fig. 1 (1941, p. 228).

given training with the negative stimulus in the middle of the range of positive stimuli.

In a study of conditional discrimination in chimpanzees, Nissen (1942) varied brightness within problems and size between problems, then re-paired the stimuli to form new problems with size the discriminative cue within problems and brightness the discriminative cue between problems (see Table 3-9). On the new problems, the subjects at first chose the previously positive stimulus, even though the relevant relational cue (brightness difference) had been eliminated within problems. The absolute stimulus

TABLE 3–9
THE NISSEN (1942) DESIGN[a]

	Stimulus combinations			
	Problem 1		Problem 2	
Problem	+	−	+	−
Training I	BL	WL	WS	BS
Training II	BS	BL	WL	WS
Transposition	BS'	BL'	WL'	WS'

[a]Counterbalancing is not represented in the table. In the transposition test S' and L' were different in area from S and L of the training problems: S indicates small, L indicates large, W indicates white, and B indicates black.

properties obviously must have determined the response. Three of the subjects were subsequently given a transposition test with size the dis-criminative cue within problems and brightness the discriminative cue between problems. The absolute sizes were different from the sizes originally used, but the brightnesses were the same. All three subjects transposed, but the average amount of transposition (89 per cent) was probably inflated by relearning since only transposition responses were rewarded. The numbers of transposition test trials were 16, 33, and 39 for the three subjects; and there could therefore have been a marked effect of relearning.

I. M. L. Hunter (1953b) also showed that absolute properties can determine the response. Rats were trained to criterion on a size discrimination with stimuli A and B of a series, and were then given a 10-trial transposition test with stimuli B and C. Responses to B were rewarded during training, and responses to both test stimuli were rewarded. Any animal that did not transpose on at least 9 to the 10 test trials was retrained on the initial dis-crimination, then tested again; the process of retraining and testing con-tinued until the animal transposed on at least 9 of the 10 test trials. Hunter reported that one rat out of 15 met the transposition criterion on the first test, three never met this criterion, and the other 11 required up to 195 retraining trials.

In the next phase of the study, the rats were given discrimination training on two problems. In one problem, stimulus B (the absolute stimulus) was paired with a new stimulus, X; and in the other problem, stimulus C (the transposition stimulus) was paired with the new stimulus. For one group of subjects, the new stimulus was correct in both problems; for the other subjects, the new stimulus was incorrect in both problems. The design is outlined in Table 3-10. Relational theory predicts equally good performance on the two problems regardless of which stimulus is correct. The relational cues in these problems (the difference between B and X and between C and X) are not the same as the relational cue in the original training problem, and therefore there is no basis for transfer to either problem. Absolute theory, however, predicts that since the reaction–evocation potential of stimulus C is greater than that of stimulus B, as demonstrated by the occurrence of transposition in the first phase of the study, the new problem requiring choice of C should be easier than the new one requiring choice of B, and the new problem requiring avoidance of C should be harder than the one requiring avoidance of B. As indicated in the last column of Table 3-10, which gives the mean numbers of correct responses on these problems, the predictions of the absolute theory were confirmed.

TABLE 3–10
HUNTER'S DESIGN AND TRANSFER DATA[a]

Condition		Stimuli	Means no. of correct responses in Phase II
Phase I			
	Training	A^- vs B^+	—
	Test	B^+ vs C^+	—
Phase II			
	Group A	B^+ vs X^-	9.8
		C^+ vs X^-	14.8
	Group B	B^- vs X^+	16.4
		C^- vs X^+	10.6

[a]I.M.L. Hunter (1953b). See text for explanation of symbols.

The results of a study by Lawrence and DeRivera (1954) were inconsistent with absolute theory, but absolute components apparently had an effect on performance. Rats were trained with stimulus cards on each of which two shades of gray were presented. The lower half of each card was constant (Gray No. 4), and the top half was lighter (No. 1, 2, or 3) or darker (No. 5, 6, or 7) than the bottom half. On test trials, the bottom half could be any shade except 4, and the top half could be any shade that was lighter or darker than the bottom half. With a one-unit separation between the upper and lower brightnesses, the more similar the top half was to the neutral value, 4, the fewer were the relational responses; and the more similar the bottom half was to 4, the more were the relational responses (see Table 3-11). These trends also appeared with a two-unit separation, but were indeterminate with a three-unit separation because only three combinations were possible with the three-unit separation. It is readily apparent that the subjects learned something about the absolute brightness 4, and that D. J. Lewis (1963, p. 196) was in error when he inferred that the subjects tended to change from a relational to an absolute basis of responding when the relation was "difficult" (one-unit separation).

TABLE 3–11

PERCENTAGE RELATIONAL RESPONSES IN THE LAWRENCE AND DERIVERA STUDY[a,b]

Difference between top and bottom halves	Bottom half of card[c]	Top half of card[c]				Mean
		0	1	2	3	
1	1	50	—	91	—	
	2	—	55	—	95	
	3	—	—	45	—	
						87
2	1	—	95	—	100	
	2	91	—	—	—	
	3	—	68	—	—	
						83
3	1	—	—	100	—	
	2	—	91	—	—	
	3	82	—	—	—	
						65
Mean		74	77	79	98	

[a] As a function of the difference between the top and bottom halves of the test cards and the difference between each half and the neutral value (Gray No. 4).

[b] Differences are in steps. All other combinations are impossible, since 4 cannot appear in the bottom half and no half can be more than three steps from the other half.

[c] Distance (in steps) from Gray No. 4.

Maier (1939) found that the equivalence reactions of rats trained to respond to one of two forms were not always opposite to those of rats trained to respond to the other form. There were, in fact, many discrepancies in the equivalence reactions of these subgroups, and Maier concluded that absolute stimulus properties as well as relational properties influence stimulus equivalence.

P. Johnson and Bailey (1966) used stimuli similar to the ones used by Lawrence and DeRivera, and studied the effects of varying the method of presentation. Essentially, the stimuli were presented simultaneously in

Group I, and successively in Groups II and III. In Group II, two grays were presented one at a time, with only one presentation of each on each trial; in Group III, the two grays were visible only successively, but could be inspected an unlimited number of times on each trial. For the presentation of the stimuli to Group III, one gray was mounted on one side of a card and the other was mounted on the other side. The card was fixed in position with one edge extending toward the subject, so that the location of, say, the medium gray was invariant (always on left or always on right). Each stimulus consisted of two grays, one a medium gray and the other lighter or darker than the medium gray. The spatial or temporal position of the medium gray was constant for all stimuli (for example, always on bottom for Group I, always second for Group II, always on left side for Group III, but these positions were reversed for half of the subjects).

On test trials the spatial or temporal position of the medium gray was reversed from its position during training. Ignoring the medium gray would yield an "absolute" response; a "relational" response would be a reversal of the response to a given pair (for example, shifting from left for light gray over medium gray during training—lighter on top—to right for medium gray over light gray during testing—darker on top—and the opposite shift from dark gray over medium gray to medium gray over dark gray).

It was found that Group I learned the initial problem with fewer errors than Group III, and Group III learned with fewer errors than Group II. On the test trials there were more relational responses than absolute responses, more relational responses in Group III than in Group I, and more in Group I than in Group II. The superiority of Group I over Groups II and III in original learning is in line with the findings of other studies of simultaneous and successive discrimination learning; but the superiority of Group III over Group II, and the greater frequency of relational responses in Group III than in the other groups is surprising, even though Johnson and Bailey predicted that Group III would give more relational responses than Group II. They reasoned that the multiple inspections possible in Group III should increase the opportunity for "forming impressions of the relational properties of the stimulus" (1966, p. 366), and the limited inspection possible in Group II should reduce the saliency of the relational properties. However, it seems more reasonable to expect that Group III would learn to ignore the side of the card containing the constant stimulus and would learn to respond to the absolute value of the variable stimulus on the other side, especially since there were only two variable stimuli. The results indicated that this strategy was used by only about 14 per cent of the subjects.

Berman (1963; also reported by Berman and Graham, 1964) studied the second-trial choices of children in a two-stimulus size discrimination problem and reported the data given in Table 3-12. The data can be interpreted as indicating that if the Trial-1 response was rewarded, both the two-year-olds and the four-year-olds chose the same relative size on Trial 2 as on Trial 1 (*B* in the *A-B* pair, *C* in the *B-C* pair); if the Trial-1 response was not rewarded, the older children switched to the other relative size (*A* in the *A-B* pair, *B* in the *B-C* pair), and the younger children switched to the other absolute size (*A* in the *A-B* pair, *C* in the *B-C* pair). The older children, according to this interpretation, responded to relations; but the responses could have been verbally mediated, since the four-year-old child is likely to know the concepts required in the two-stimulus problem (see section entitled "Concept Knowledge," Chapter 5). The younger children could have been responding to the relation following reward and to the absolute qualities following nonreward; but their data can also be interpreted as indicating absolute responses following both Trial-1 outcomes. The choices

TABLE 3–12
TRIAL-2 DATA OF THE BERMAN STUDY[a]

		Trial-2 response (%)			
		A vs *B*		*B* vs *C*	
Trial-1 outcome	Age level (years)	*A*	*B*	*B*	*C*
Reward	2	25	75	17	83
	4	42	58	25	75
Nonreward	2	54	46	21	79
	4	58	42	71	29

[a] *B* designates the stimulus chosen on Trial 1, on which it was presented with *A*; *C* relative to *B* was the same as *B* relative to *A*.

of *A* and *B* in the *A-B* pair could be based on absolute qualities, and the choice of *C* in the *B-C* pair could reflect a tendency to approach novel stimuli. New stimuli are novel in the sense that the subject has not seen them before in the experimental context; there is some evidence that children (and monkeys) have a tendency to approach novel stimuli of this kind (see Reese, 1963b, p. 130; Reese, 1964a, pp. 324–331). Fantz (1964) has shown that even young infants prefer novel stimuli to familiar ones, spending progressively less time fixating familiar material and more time fixating new material. (See also Berlyne, 1966.)

Conclusion

The data reviewed in this section demonstrate that subjects can learn about the absolute properties of stimuli whether or not they learn anything about relative properties.

Procedural Variables

Four quite disparate variables are considered in this section. They have in common only two properties, that they are manipulated during the training phase and that they are related to the procedure of the experiment. They are (a) the amount of training given, (b) the kind of reward used, (c) the number of problems given, and (d) the manner of presenting the stimuli.

AMOUNT OF ORIGINAL TRAINING

Two-Stimulus Problems

Gulliksen (1936) and F. N. Jones (1939b) found that overtraining produced an insignificant increase in two-stimulus transposition in rats, but Riley et al. (1963) obtained larger increases in transposition after overtraining, especially when the cues were not contiguous with one another (see Table 3-13). I. M. L. Hunter's (1952b; 1953b) data also indicate that overtraining increases transposition in rats. (The relevant data of I. M. L. Hunter's 1953b study are included in Table 3-13. The data of the 1952b study were for individual rats, given various amounts and kinds of training, and are too complicated to summarize in the table.)

According to Shirai (1951, p. 21), the increase was obtained by H. Keller and Takemasa (1933) and Takemasa (1934) in chickens, and by Kafka (1931) and Ohtsuka (1937; 1939; 1942) in monkeys; and a decrease was obtained by Kuroda (1933) in the tortoise.

Jackson concluded from a series of studies of two-stimulus transposition in children that, as overtraining increases, three stages of response occur. The first stage is characterized by unstable relational responses, the second by stable relational responses, and the third by stable absolute responses (Jackson and Dominguez, 1939; Jackson and Jerome, 1940; Jackson and Jerome, 1943; Jackson et al., 1938). A great amount of overtraining is required to reach the third stage, according to Jackson, but practice is important only in proportion to the degree of motivation of the subject. With inadequate motivation, practice yields little or no additional learning in children (Jackson and Dominguez, 1939). Jackson assumed that overtraining increases stimulus differentiation, reducing generalization (Jackson et al., 1938).

The findings of Jackson et al. (1938) are inconclusive because of small sample sizes, but suggest that there is a decrease in transposition with increasing overtraining (see Table 3-13). However, in the Jackson and Jerome studies (1940; 1943), there was possibly a tendency for transposition to increase with overtraining in groups given standard simultaneous discrimination training, although almost all of the subjects in these group

TABLE 3–13

EFFECT OF OVERTRAINING ON TRANSPOSITION IN TWO-STIMULUS PROBLEMS

Study	Subjects	Learning criterion	No. of over-training trials	No. of test trials	Trans-position (%)
Gulliksen (1936)	Rats	10/10	0	10	74
		30/30	0	10	78
F. N. Jones (1939b)	Rats	10/10	0	20	71
			100	20	73
Riley et al. (1963)	Rats	18/20[a]	0	20	80[b]
			60	20	86[b]
			0	20	55[c]
			60	20	70[c]
I. M. L. Hunter (1953b)	Rats	68/75	0	10	7[d]
			Variable[e]	10	80[d]
Jackson et al. (1938)					
Experiment II	Children[f]	4/5	5	1	100
			10	1	67
			20	1	33
Experiment III	Children[f]	4/5	5	1	100
			10	1	100
			20	1	67
Experiment IV	Children[f]	4/5	30	1[g]	88
			100	1[g]	75

[a] It was also required that the last 10 responses be correct, and that the subject meet the criterion twice.

[b] Problem with "contiguous" cues.

[c] Problem with "noncontiguous" cues.

[d] Percentage of subjects transposing consistently (at least 90 per cent transposition).

[e] If the subject did not transpose at least 90 per cent on the first test, it was given additional training trials and transposition tests until it achieved this criterion of transposition.

[f] Three subjects per group in Experiments II and III, six per group in Experiment IV.

[g] The same percentages were obtained on three combined test trials.

transposed after each amount of overtraining. In a group trained on one kind of successive discrimination problem (one response, choice withheld until after both stimuli had been presented), overtraining increased transposition; but in a group trained on another kind of successive problem (two responses, one to each stimulus as it was presented), overtraining reduced transposition. The data of Jackson and Dominquez (1939), presented in Table 3-14, suggest that overtraining may reduce transposition in most subjects, but may increase transposition in some; and the direction of the effect may be related to motivational variables.

Razran (1940) obtained evidence corroborating Jackson's data. Human adults were trained on a pattern discrimination, with test trials interspersed among the training trials. In eight successive experimental sessions,

TABLE 3–13 (*continued*)

Study	Subjects	Learning criterion	No. of over-training trials	No. of test trials	Trans-position (%)
Jackson and Jerome	Children	—[h]	30[i]	1	100
(1940)			50[i]	1	100
			90[i]	4	100
			50[j]	1	42
			90[j]	4	23
Jackson and Jerome	Children[k]	—[h]	10[i]	2	88
(1943)			40[i]	2	98
			100[i]	4	98
			10[j]	2	58
			40[j]	2	44
			100[j]	4	42
			10[l]	2	60
			40[l]	2	90
			100[l]	4	95
I. M. L. Hunter (1952a)	Children	9/10	10	1	85
Exp. II			30	1	100
I. M. L. Hunter (unpublished)		?	10	6	43
			30	6	86
R. E. Cole *et al.* (1964)	Children	[h]	30	10	73
			45	10	92
			60	10	92
Stevenson and Iscoe	Children	4/4	0	1	53
(1954)		10/10	0	1	66

[h] No training was given prior to the trials listed in the overtraining column.

[i] Simultaneous discrimination training.

[j] Successive discrimination training (two responses).

[k] The data given here are for gifted and dull groups combined.

[l] Successive discrimination training (one response).

transposition averaged 38, 50, 56, 64, 67, 66, 52, and 44 per cent. Unfortunately, the exact point at which the decline began is indeterminate because the numbers of training trials were not constant across subjects and sessions. According to Shirai (1951, p. 21), Sato (1936) obtained the same trend in children, and Takagi (1935a; 1935b; 1937) obtained it in tomtits.

M. S. Scott (1966) obtained no significant effect of overtraining on transposition in mentally retarded subjects. The subjects were tested on one- and four-step tests, given in counterbalanced order with retraining between tests; Scott reported that order of tests had no effect on transposition. I. M. L. Hunter (1952a, Experiment II) found more transposition in children on a test given after 30 overtraining trials than on one given

TABLE 3–14

PERCENTAGE TRANSPOSITION IN THE JACKSON AND DOMINGUEZ (1939) STUDY[a]

Group	Subject	Motivation	Number of overtraining trials							
			25	50	75	100	125	150	175	200
Control	1	Good	33	100	100	100	100	100	100	100
	2	Good	67	67	67	100	100	100	100	100
	3	Poor	100	100	0	0	0	0	0	0
Experimental	1	Good								100
	2	Good								40
	3	Good								0
	4	Fair								0
	5	Poor								0

[a]Control subjects were given 25 overtraining trials and 3 test trials per day for 8 days. Experimental subjects were given the 8 days of overtraining, and then 5 test trials. Motivation was rated by observers (see Jackson and Dominguez, 1939, Table 1).

after 10 overtraining trials, and referred to an unpublished study in which he obtained the same effect on a five-step transposition test. R. E. Cole *et al.* (1964) also found that overtraining increased Near Test transposition; Stevenson and Iscoe (1954), using a three-stimulus problem with the largest or smallest stimulus correct (in subgroups), obtained the same effect.

H. E. Jones and Dunn (1932) gave only six training trials on each of a series of problems, and found a significant positive correlation between transposition and the discrimination learning score, suggesting that the frequency of transposition is also related to the amount of original learning at low levels of training. However, the experiment was repeated with 62 of the original 80 subjects, and in the replication the percentage transposition was 55.6 per cent, only a slight increase from the 53.1 per cent transposition on the original tests. Table 2-4 gives the percentage of subjects obtaining each of the possible transposition scores. These data suggest that the increase in transposition resulted from fewer subjects giving consistent absolute responses on the second test, and more giving "chance-level" responses.

Intermediate-Stimulus Problems

Reese and Fiero (1964) found that overtraining had no significant effect on transposition in children in the intermediate-size problem, but the amount of overtraining was small. Zeiler (1965b) found that overtraining did not increase transposition in children in the three-stimulus problem, whether the largest, smallest, or middle-sized stimulus was correct. The comparison in Zeiler's study was within subjects. Each child was trained to criterion, given a transposition test, and then retrained to criterion on the original discrimination. On the following day, the child was again retrained to criterion on the original discrimination, and then given a second transposition test. There was no significant change in the amount of transposition from the first to the second test.

Conclusion

Moderate overtraining increases transposition in the two-stimulus problem, in both human and infrahuman subjects; but prolonged over-training may reduce transposition in human subjects. In the intermediate-size problem, moderate overtraining apparently has no effect on transposition. Prolonged overtraining has never been given in intermediate-stimulus problems.

REWARD

Terrell and Kennedy (1957) obtained significantly more two-stimulus transposition in children when candy was used as a reward than when non-consumables were used. Terrell (1958) obtained the same kind of effect, although not at a statistically significant level. In a later study by Terrell (1959) and one by Terrell et al. (1959) the relationship was indeterminate, since virtually all subjects transposed on every trial.

The reward variable has not been investigated in infrahuman subjects and has not been investigated in the intermediate-stimulus problem in human subjects.

MULTIPLE-PROBLEM TRAINING

Studies of the effects of "multiple-problem training" on transposition are reviewed in this section. In these studies subjects were trained with more than one set of stimuli, differing on the same dimension in all sets, and were then given transposition tests.

Position Discriminations

Sadovinkova (1923) gave multiple-problem training to songbirds, using spatial or position discriminations requiring choice of fixed relative positions. Yerkes (1934) and Spence (1939b) used the same kind of problems with chimpanzees, and W. Brown and Whittell (1923) and Wong and Brown (1923) used similar ones with college students. The method used in these studies was developed by Yerkes (see Yerkes, 1916a; Yerkes, 1916b; and the review by Spence, 1939b). Unfortunately, no comparable single-problem transposition data are available to allow an assessment of the effect of the multiple-problem training.

Two-Stimulus Problems

In his experiments on weight transposition in monkeys, Klüver (1933) gave a kind of multiple-problem training. He used a constant negative stimulus but changed the positive stimulus to increase the stimulus difference until the problem became easy for the monkeys to solve. Comparative data are unavailable to determine the effect of this procedure on transposition in monkeys, but it could reduce positive transposition in tests with two previously positive stimuli, since the data suggested that the monkeys had learned to select an absolute stimulus as well as a relative one. The monkeys "compared" the weights, by alternately pulling the strings attached to the weights, on only 59 per cent of the trials on the last two days of training, but gave correct responses on 98 per cent of the trials on these two days. The correct stimulus must have been recognized by "absolute feel," to use Klüver's phrase, on virtually all of the noncomparison trials. Klüver reported that comparison behavior during testing was the same as during training. Positive transposition was somewhat less frequent than negative transposition (positive upward, 79 per cent, downward, 79 per cent; negative upward, 98 per cent, downward, 87 per cent), but this is often true even when standard training procedures are used.

H. M. Johnson (1916) gave a monkey a series of problems, each followed by a transposition test. Width of striae (coarseness) was the relevant dimension in all problems. In some problems the positive stimulus remained constant in value and the negative stimulus varied (always with narrower stripes than the positive stimulus), and in other problems the negative stimulus remained constant and the positive stimulus varied (always with wider stripes than the negative stimulus). Transposition increased over problems, presumably because of the multiple-problem training.

Takei (1927) trained and tested chicks with brightness, then size, then form, and found little transposition with any dimension. There was more transposition of size than brightness, but there was less transposition of form than brightness, suggesting that no preference for a relational basis of learning developed with the multiple training. (See also the discussion of the Coburn [1914] study in the section entitled "Phylogenetic Comparisons," Chapter 5.)

Lawrence and DeRivera (1954) trained rats on a successive discrimination problem, using stimulus cards on each of which two shades of gray were presented. The lower half of each card was a neutral gray (Gray No. 4), and the upper half was a lighter gray (No. 1, 2, or 3) or a darker gray (No. 5,

6, or 7). The apparatus was a two-choice jumping stand, and on any one trial the subject was confronted by two doors containing identical stimulus cards. In the first phase of the study the subjects learned to jump left when Card 7/4 (No. 7 on top, No. 4 on bottom) was presented, and right when Card 1/4 was presented. In the second phase, a set of six cards was used, and the subjects learned to jump left when the upper half was darker than the lower half (Cards 5/4, 6/4, and 7/4) and right when the upper half was lighter than the lower half (Cards 1/4, 2/4, and 3/4). In the test phase, 24 new combinations were presented, as shown in Table 3-15; all responses were rewarded. Table 3-15 also gives the percentage of relational responses to each stimulus (left jump if top darker, right if top lighter). Absolute theory predicts correctly for only 8 of the 24 discriminations (1/2, 1/3, 2/3, 4/5, 6/5, 7/5, 7/6, and 6/7), but relational theory predicts correctly for all but 4 (4/5, 5/6, 5/7, and 6/7). Furthermore, in a second test phase, the subjects were given 50 trials on a successive discrimination between Cards 3/3 (right jump) and 5/5 (left jump), and performance remained at the chance level, in line with relational theory but contrary to absolute theory. These findings are consistent with the conclusion that multiple-problem training enhances the probability of relational learning. (Other data from this study are discussed in the section entitled "Effects of Absolute Stimulus Components," this chapter.)

P. Johnson and Bailey (1966) used the same kind of stimuli as Lawrence and DeRivera, but presented them in different ways (see above-mentioned section) and tested human subjects. The subjects were given one, two, or three training problems. The multiple-problem training increased relational responding in college students, but not in kindergarten children or fourth-grade children.

TABLE 3–15

The Lawrence and DeRivera Test Stimuli and the
Percentage Relational Responses Obtained on Test Trials[a]

Bottom half of stimulus card	Top half of stimulus card						
	1	2	3	4	5	6	7
1	—	73	82	91			
2	91	—	64	91	91		
3	100	82	—	73	91	100	
4				—			
5		100	100	27	—	91	100
6			91	91	45	—	100
7				73	55	18	—

[a] For cells above the diagonal, the relational response was to the left window; for cells below the diagonal, the relational response was to the right window.

R. C. Johnson and Zara (1960) gave one group of children training on a problem with Stimuli 3 and 4 of a size series, and gave multiple-problem training to a second group, using Stimuli 1 and 2 for one problem and 3 and 4 for the other problem. The larger stimulus (designated by a higher number) was correct in both problems. After reaching criterion, the children were given transposition tests with Stimuli 4 and 5, 5 and 6, or 6 and 7. The group given multiple-problem training transposed significantly more than the single-problem group, and in fact transposed almost perfectly on all three tests. Sherman and Strunk (1964) obtained essentially the same results in a replication of this study; but Sherman told me that they had great difficulty in replicating the effect (personal communication, 1966).

Sherman (1966) studied the effect in a series of experiments designed to test various alternative explanations of the phenomenon. A control group was given single-problem training with Stimuli 3 and 4 of a series varying in size. A second group was given training on the same problem, and was also given presentations of Stimuli 1 and 2 of the series, not as a learning problem but as an opportunity to become familiar with two additional sizes. A third group was given multiple-problem training with Stimuli 1 and 2 in one problem and 3 and 4 in the other. A fourth group was given training on two problems, one with Stimuli 3 and 4 and the other with stimuli differing in brightness rather than size. A fifth group was given the same learning problems as the fourth group, and in addition the same kind of familiarization experience with Stimuli 1 and 2 as given to the second group. The group differences in transposition were not statistically significant in any one of the four experiments Sherman conducted (not all including all five treatments), but the combined probabilities indicated that multiple-problem training produced significantly more transposition than single-problem training, and significantly more than the fifth treatment. (Sherman did not report combined probabilities for the other comparisons.) The major problem in demonstrating facilitation was that the levels of transposition were extremely high in all groups.

Sherman also examined the effects of two other kinds of multiple-problem training, both with three problems. In one condition, the stimuli were 1 vs 4, 2 vs 4, and 3 vs 4, with 4 correct in all three problems; in the other condition, the stimuli were 1 vs 2, 2 vs 3, and 3 vs 4, with the larger correct in each problem. The first kind of series was significantly easier to learn than the second kind, but the second kind produced somewhat more transposition on the first trial of a three-step test (40 per cent vs 20 per cent), although not on 10 combined test trials (57 per cent vs 56 per cent). It remains to be explained why these kinds of multiple-problem training produced so much less transposition than is produced by two-problem training.

M. S. Scott (1966) studied the effects of multiple-problem training on transposition in mentally retarded subjects. As shown in Table 3-16, Group

TABLE 3–16
THE DESIGN OF M. S. SCOTT'S (1966) STUDY[a]

Group	Stimulus pairs in training phase	Stimulus ratio	Description	Group data[b]
A	1 vs 2	2 to 1	Same as used by Johnson and	
	3 vs 4	2 to 1	Zara	81
B	1 vs 4	8 to 1	Same absolute stimulus correct in	
	3 vs 4	2 to 1	both pairs	44
C	1 vs 4	8 to 1	Control for use of 2 stimulus	
	2 vs 3	2 to 1	ratios	31
D	1 vs 2	2 to 1	Control	25
E	1 vs 4	8 to 1	Control	38

[a]The group designations and stimulus designations are not the same as Scott's. Counterbalancing subgroups are not indicated here (see Scott's Tables 1 and 2, pp. 10–11). In Groups A, B, and C, the same direction of relation was correct in both pairs.

[b]Percentage of subjects transposing perfectly on both tests (five trials per test).

A was given the same kind of multiple-problem training as given by Johnson and Zara. Group B was given training with the same absolute stimulus correct in both training pairs, and with the same direction of relation correct in both pairs; but this procedure required that the stimulus ratio in one pair be four times greater than in the other pair. Group C was used as a control to check on the effect of training with different ratios in the two pairs, but without a constant absolute stimulus correct. Groups D and E were single-problem control groups, one with the smaller stimulus ratio and the other with the larger one. The ratio between the test stimuli was 2 to 1 for all five groups. On a one-step test, Group A transposed more than Groups B, C, and D, which did not differ significantly from one another; and Group D transposed more than Group E. On a four-step test, there were no significant differences among the groups. The percentages of subjects transposing perfectly on both tests were consistent with the mean-transposition data (see last column of Table 3-16).

In the Terrell studies (Terrell, 1958; Terrell, 1959; Terrell et al., 1959; Terrell and Kennedy, 1957), the subjects were trained on three problems simultaneously. The problems differed only in the shape of the stimuli used (cones, cubes, and cylinders), and required choice of the same relative size in each problem. In two of the studies (Terrell, 1959; Terrell et al., 1959), virtually all subjects transposed on every trial. In the other two, the amount of transposition was large (96 per cent in Terrell, 1958; 75 per cent in Terrell and Kennedy, 1957). I. M. L. Hunter (1952a) obtained 83 to 100 per cent transposition following multiple-problem training.

Wesman and Eisenberg (1941) trained and tested college students on eight two-stimulus problems. In one experiment, the group observed a subject being trained, and was given a single one-step test trial immediately after the subject reached criterion on each problem. In another experiment, the subjects were trained and tested individually. The problems were given in a fixed order in the first experiment, and were given in counterbalanced order in the second experiment. Table 3-17 gives the percentage of subjects transposing on each problem, as a function of the order of the problems. The absolute amounts of transposition were low, but when it is considered that the stimuli in each problem differed markedly from each other on the dimension manipulated, the amounts of transposition obtained become relatively high (see section entitled "Stimulus Similarity," this chapter, for further data on this point). It can be seen in Table 3-17 that the amount of

TABLE 3-17
ORDER EFFECT IN THE WESMAN AND EISENBERG (1941) STUDY

| | Percentage transposition | |
Order	Experiment I[a]	Experiment II[a]
1	63	45
2	62	55
3	66	55
4	71	55
5	75	55
6	74	55
7	74	65
8	70	65

[a] Experiment I was the group study; Experiment II was the individual study. Order and stimulus set were confounded in Experiment I, but not in Experiment II.

transposition increased from the first problems to the last ones, indicating that the multiple-problem training increased transposition.

The eight problems in the Wesman and Eisenberg study can be divided into four pairs, each pair with a different relevant dimension. Table 3-18 presents the percentage of subjects transposing on the two problems of each pair. In the group experiment, there was more transposition in each pair on Problem B, the problem given second, than on Problem A; but there was no difference between Problems A and B of each pair in the individual study, in which Problems A and B were given in counterbalanced order. These data, then, bolster the conclusion that multiple-problem training increased transposition.

Stevenson and Iscoe (1954) trained children to choose one of three stimuli (largest or smallest), then to choose the same relative size in a one-step transposition test, and finally to choose the same relative size in a second

TABLE 3–18

ORDER EFFECT IN THE WESMAN AND EISENBERG STUDY FOR EACH DIMENSION
SEPARATELY

Dimension	Experiment I[a]		Experiment II[a]	
	Problem A	Problem B	Problem A	Problem B
Size	63	75	55	65
Color[b]	62	70	55	55
Number[c]	66	74	50	50
Completeness[d]	71	74	60	60

[a] In Experiment I, Problem A was given before Problem B; in Experiment II, the order of the problems was counterbalanced, providing a rough control for comparison with Experiment I.

[b] Brightness for Problem A; color for Problem B.

[c] Two, four, and six of hearts for Problem A; eight, six, and four of diamonds for Problem B.

[d] Circles with different amounts of arc blocked out for Problem A; squares with different amounts of corner blocked out for Problem B.

transposition test one step from the original stimuli and two steps from the stimuli of the first transposition test (see Table 3-19). Transposition on the second test was greater than on the first, in line with the other data on the effect of multiple-problem training, but the first test was in the positive direction and the second was in the negative direction, which could have been the effective variable (see section entitled "Effect of Direction of Transposition Test," Chapter 4).

H. E. Jones and Dunn (1932) used four sets of stimuli, differing in area, form, brightness, or color. Each subject was given six training trials and

TABLE 3–19

THE STEVENSON AND ISCOE (1954) DESIGN[a]

Group	Phase	Stimuli				
		1	2	3	4	5
Large	1		S−	S−	S+	
	2			S−	S−	S+
	3	S−	S−	S+		
Small	1		S+	S−	S−	
	2	S+	S−	S−		
	3			S+	S	S−

[a] Subjects were trained to criterion in each phase.

one test trial with each set. For 62 of the original 80 subjects, the entire procedure was repeated after an interval of at least eight days. The data, which are summarized in Table 2-4, provide no evidence that the multiple-problem training might have increased transposition.

Intermediate-Stimulus Problems

Spence (1942) trained chimpanzees on an intermediate-size problem, then after testing for transposition at one step, he trained the subjects to criterion on the one-step problem, and then tested for transposition with the stimuli of the original training problem. As shown in Table 3-20, there was more transposition on the second test than on the first one. Spence suggested that the "reversal training" might have led to a "different basis of response than an absolute one." Ebel and Werboff (1966) used the same kind of design with dogs as subjects, and added a third transposition test after retraining on the original discrimination. Transposition increased significantly over the three tests, but absolute responses were predominant as in Spence's study. McCulloch (1935) used the same kind of design with rats, but with "relative discrimination" problems (the relative discrimination problem is discussed in Chapter 6). There were fewer errors on the second test than on the first one, again indicating that reversal training increases transposition.

Gentry et al. (1959) gave monkeys a kind of multiple-problem training with intermediate-size problems. On Problem 1, Stimuli 1, 5, and 9 of a

TABLE 3-20
DESIGN AND DATA OF SPENCE (1942) STUDY[a]

		Percentage responses			
Condition	Stimuli	Absolute	Transposition	Nontransposition-nonabsolute	Predominant transposition[b]
Training	1,2,3	—	—	—	—
Test (10-min delay)	2,3,4	86.6	12.2	1.2	0
Test (24-hr delay)	2,3,4	73.3	23.3	3.4	17
Retraining to criterion	1,2,3	—	—	—	—
Test (24-hr delay)	2,3,4	75.5	18.9	5.6	17
Training to criterion	2,3,4	—	—	—	—
Test (10-min delay)	1,2,3	61.1	38.9	0.0	50
Test (24-hr delay)	1,2,3	64.4	35.6	0.0	33
Test[c]	2,3,4	43.3	53.3	3.3	50
Test[c]	3,4,5	100.0	0.0	0.0	0

[a] All test-trial responses were rewarded.

[b] Predominant indicates at least 8 transposition responses on 15 trials.

[c] Only two of the six subjects were given these tests.

size series were used; and on Problem 2, Stimuli 3, 5, and 7 were used. Stimulus 5 was positive in both problems. On transposition tests the stimuli were shifted one-half step upward or downward from the stimuli of the second training problem, the one-half-step shift reflecting a change in area of 1.15 to 1. Transposition averaged about 74 per cent.

W. L. Brown et al. (1959) used the same design except that the preliminary training with Stimuli 1, 5, and 9 was omitted. Transposition averaged only 58 per cent at one-half step (again a 1.15 to 1 change in area). This percentage is inflated, furthermore, because there was an absolute preference for one of the stimuli, which was chosen 75 per cent of the time, and was the largest in one test set and intermediate in the other test set. After being retrained on the original discrimination, the subjects were given one-step tests in the upward and downward directions. On these tests there was even less transposition than on the half-step tests: 98 per cent of the responses were absolute.

Brown et al. speculated that they obtained less transposition than Gentry et al. because of a difference in the age or amount of experimental sophistication of the subjects used in the two studies. Gentry et al. used five-year-old monkeys with more than three years of experience in psychological experiments, and Brown et al. used four-year-old monkeys with less previous experience (the amount was not specified exactly). However, it seems more likely that the critical condition was the omission of the preliminary problem in the study by Brown et al., and that the comparison of results illustrates the effect of multiple-problem training. An alternative explanation is possible, since it has been shown that training on an easy discrimination facilitates later learning of a difficult discrimination (for example, Barnett and Cantor, 1957; Pavlov, 1927, pp. 121–123; Spiker, 1959), presumably through the development of appropriate observing responses (Spiker, 1959; Sutherland, 1964a) or a "set to discriminate" (G. N. Cantor, 1962), or through minimizing failure and hence frustration during the early stages of learning (Spiker, 1959).

Wolfle (1937) gave rats "special training" involving a shift from a 16 to 1 ratio of brightness to a 4 to 1 ratio, but it was not comparable to the procedure used by Gentry et al., because the special training followed the first transposition test, and was followed by further training on the original discrimination.

Gonzalez et al. (1954) used the same design as Gentry et al. (1959), and obtained one-half-step transposition in chimpanzees (the half-step shift was a 1.15 to 1 change in areas). Absolute stimulus preferences unrelated to training appeared to interfere with transposition in the chimpanzees, but this phenomenon was not found in monkeys by Gentry et al., although it was found in monkeys by Brown et al., who omitted the preliminary training problem.

In a partially completed study, Zeiler (personal communication, 1966) obtained no evidence that multiple-problem training has any effect on inter-mediate-size transposition in pigeons.

Zeiler (1967) reported that he was unsuccessful in his attempts to demon-strate the effect of multiple-problem training in children, using intermediate-size problems: "Many children could not learn the multiple training set problem at all, and the single-training-set control groups transposed so much that no significant increase could be demonstrated with two training sets" (p. 140). Zeiler and Paalberg (1964b) were also unable to demonstrate the multiple-problem training effect in children, even though the level of transposition in the single-problem control groups was low (about 15 per cent transposition on 10 test trials). Gonzalez and Ross (1958), however, obtained the effect with intermediate-size problems. Following training with two sets of stimuli each five steps from the test set, and with the middle-sized stimulus correct in both training sets, 73 per cent of the children transposed on the first test trial, considerably more than in two closely similar studies using single-problem training and testing at five steps (8 per cent in Stevenson and Bitterman, 1955; 17 per cent in Zeiler, 1963d).

Caron (1966) compared the kinds of multiple-problem training used by Johnson and Zara and by Gonzalez and Ross. A "Multiple" group was trained with Stimuli 1, 2, and 3 of a series in one problem and with 4, 5, and 6 in the other problem, and was tested with Stimuli 7, 8, and 9. A "Range" group was trained with 1, 2, and 3 and with 7, 8, and 9, and was tested with 4, 5, and 6. The Multiple condition is like the condition used by Johnson and Zara, and the Range condition is like the condition used by Gonzalez and Ross. The subjects learned the two problems in the Range condition more rapidly than the two in the Multiple condition. Beaty (1966) obtained the same effect with a 10-step separation in the Range condition. The stimulus sets in the Range problems were six steps apart in Caron's study, and were presumably so widely separated in both studies that there was little generalization between sets. The separation between the Multiple problems was three steps in Caron's study and one step in Beaty's study. These separations were presumably small enough to permit generalization. On switching from the first training problem to the second one, then, there would be a weaker tendency to give absolute responses in the Range condition than in the Multiple condition. In order to solve the second problem, the subjects in the Range condition would need to over-come only a weak habit, but the subjects in the Multiple condition would need to overcome a strong habit. (In communicating with Dr. Caron, I "postdicted" random responses on the first few trials after each switch in the Range group and absolute responses in the Multiple group. He replied that absolute responses actually occurred in both groups, but agreed that the tendency to choose on an absolute basis was probably weaker in the Range group than in the Multiple group [Caron, personal communication, 1966].)

The Range groups transposed more than the Multiple groups, as shown in Table 3-21. In order to provide further information about the cause of the group differences, Caron ran a new group in a "Range Control" condition. This group was trained with Stimuli 1, 2, and 3 and with 7, 8, and 9, and was tested with 10, 11, and 12. The training problems were the same as the ones given the Range group, but the test was more like the test given the Multiple group in that the test stimuli in the Range Control and Multiple conditions were beyond the range of training stimuli rather than being included in the range of training stimuli. As shown in Table 3-21, the Range Control group transposed more than the Multiple group but less than the Range group.

On the basis of these data, Caron suggested that the effect of multiple-problem training on transposition is enhanced when the distance between the two training sets of stimuli is increased, and is enhanced when the test set is included in the range of training stimuli.

In a study by Stevenson and Bitterman (1955), subjects were given a Near Test and a five-step Far Test, in counterbalanced order, and only transposition responses were rewarded. The group given the Far Test

TABLE 3-21
THE CARON (1966) AND BEATY (1966) DATA[a]

Training condition	Trials to criterion	Percentage transposition		
		Trial 1	10 trials	Consistent[b]
Caron				
Multiple[c]	6.2[d]	26	40	32
Range[c]	5.2[d]	59	68	66
Range control[e]	—	—	55	—
Beaty				
Single problem	28	0	23	—
Multiple[c]	61	20	36	—
Multiple[f]	52	10	31	—
Range[c]	34	70	77	—
Range[f]	27	90	91	—

[a] See text for explanation of conditions.

[b] Transposed on at least seven trials. Percentages derived from Caron's Table 4 (p. 306). On page 310, Caron gave the percentages as 28 and 61. These included 15 Ss randomly omitted to obtain equal cell frequencies (Caron, personal communication, 1966).

[c] Problems given consecutively.

[d] Sets to criterion.

[e] Data omitted from published report, but sent to me by Dr. Caron (personal communication, 1966).

[f] Problems given concurrently.

first was similar to the Range group in Caron's (1966) study, in that both groups had two widely separated intermediate-size problems; the group given the Near Test first was similar to the Multiple group in Caron's study, in that both groups were given two problems with fairly little separation between the stimulus sets. However, Stevenson and Bitterman gave only six trials on the second "problem" (the first transposition test, with differential reinforcement), and Caron trained his groups to criterion on both problems. Stevenson and Bitterman's groups transposed less on the second test than on the first one. Stevenson and Bitterman concluded that no "generalized intermediate preference" had developed. (Actually, they were considering only their "Range" group, apparently because they expected that the development of a generalized intermediate preference would require training with the same relation correct in widely separated stimulus sets.) Presumably, not enough trials were given on the second "problem" to generate the multiple-problem training effect.

Whitman (1965) compared the effects of three kinds of pretraining on intermediate-size transposition in three-, four-, and five-year-old children. During pretraining, the children were shown 12 sets of cards, one set at a time, depicting figures differing in size. In a "no-pretraining" condition, the subjects were told to look at the set of cards presented; in a "perceptual pretraining" condition, the subjects were told to look at *each* card in the set presented; and in a "verbal pretraining" condition, the experimenter gave the names of the sizes of the figures ("large," "small," "middle-sized"), and tried to get the subject to verbalize these labels. In the last two conditions, the subject was trained to choose the middle-sized figure on each of the last two sets of cards, depicting triangles (one, two, and three inches high in one set; four, five, and six inches high in the other set). During this discrimination training, the subjects in the verbal pretraining condition were told after each correct response that the middle-sized one was correct, and that the large and small ones were incorrect, the experimenter pointing to each one in turn. In the perceptual pretraining condition, the experimenter pointed to the figures in the same way, but did not verbally label the sizes.

After the pretraining, the subjects were trained to choose the middle-sized of three boxes, and then were given three- and six-step transposition tests, with only transposition responses rewarded and with ten trials on each test. Table 3-22 gives the percentages of transposition on the first trial and on combined test trials. The four- and five-year-old groups did not differ significantly from each other, and transposed more than the three-year-olds. The groups given the perceptual pretraining and verbal pretraining conditions were not significantly different from each other, and transposed more than the group given the no-pretraining condition.

The "transposition" scores are relearning scores, since only transposition

TABLE 3–22

PERCENTAGE TRANSPOSITION IN THE WHITMAN (1965) STUDY

Pretraining condition	CA	First test trial		All test trials	
		3 steps	6 steps	3 steps	6 steps
No pretraining	3	20	0	42	46
	4	40	40	75	71
	5	60	40	84	67
Perceptual	3	40	20	75	75
	4	80	40	75	88
	5	60	20	91	90
Verbal	3	40	40	73	70
	4	40	80	93	96
	5	100	100	94	97

responses were rewarded during each of the tests, and the extremely high levels of the scores indicate that the relearning was rapid. The rapidity of the relearning could be attributed to the effects of a learning set in the perceptual and verbal pretraining groups, since they were given the two problems with triangles and the one with boxes before the transposition tests. There is evidence that the learning set can be acquired even when only one preliminary problem is learned (Reese, 1965a). However, it could also be attributed to the enhanced probability of transposition resulting from the multiple-problem training. The learning-set interpretation is weak, because even the no-pretraining group transposed at a high level relative to the levels that were obtained in other studies testing children of comparable age at comparable distances and rewarding only transposition responses. Reese (1962a) obtained 57 per cent transposition at three steps in five-year-olds; and Stevenson and Bitterman (1955) obtained 49 per cent transposition at five steps in four- and five-year-olds. Whitman's four- and five-year-olds averaged 80 per cent transposition at three steps and 69 per cent at six steps. Whitman's no-pretraining group was given experience with figures differing in size, and this experience could have resulted in directing attention to the size dimension. Therefore, the data of this group are not necessarily inconsistent with the interpretation of the data of the other groups as reflecting effects of multiple-problem training.

Zeiler and Paalberg (1964a) studied the effect of multiple-problem training on intermediate-size transposition in human adults. When the stimulus sets of the two training problems were one-half step apart, there was no more transposition on the test than was obtained after single-problem training (averaging 50 per cent transposition); but when the training sets were one full step apart, almost all of the subjects transposed on the test. Tentatively, the reason the multiple-problem training effect was not obtained with the half-step difference between training sets was that the subjects failed to notice that the two problems had different stimuli. If this were so, then in effect these subjects received single-problem training. Two considerations support this suggestion. First, the ratio of the stimulus areas was 2 to 1, and the half-step change was therefore by a ratio of only 1.4 to 1, which is a relatively small change. Second, and perhaps more convincing, there was a considerable amount of transposition between the half-step problems, as would be expected if the change were unnoticed (see section entitled "Effect of Noticing Change in Stimuli from Training to Test," Chapter 5); but there was absolute transfer between the full-step problems, as would be expected in college students if the change were noticed (see the discussion of the Zeiler [1964b] data in the section entitled "Distance," Chapter 4). Therefore, it is suggested that the multiple-problem training effect was obtained only in the subjects who were aware that they were given two different training problems.

Zeiler and Paalberg (1964b) obtained evidence that tends to corroborate this interpretation. One group of children was trained with Stimuli 1, 3, and 5 and 3, 5, and 7, and another group was trained with 2, 4, and 6 and 3, 5, and 7. The first group did not transpose between training problems, but the second group did. On a 10-trial test with Stimuli 5, 7, and 9, the first group averaged about 26 per cent transposition, and the second group averaged 17 per cent transposition. A control group given single-problem training with 3, 5, and 7, averaged 16 per cent transposition, virtually the same percentage as the second experimental group. (The first group combines Zeiler and Paalberg's Groups 1 and 2, the second group combines their Groups 5 and 6, and the control group in their Group 11.)

Conclusion

When multiple-problem training is given, with the stimuli differing on the same dimension in each problem and with the same direction of relation correct in each problem, there is generally more transposition than when single-problem training is given.

OPPORTUNITY FOR COMPARISON

According to Fröbes and Spearman, relation perception usually requires no comparison of stimuli by the observer, but rather occurs immediately, in the sense that no mediating process is required (Fröbes, 1923; Spearman, 1923, Chapters 5 and 6, especially pp. 63 and 86; see also Spearman, 1937a, pp. 215–222). More commonly, however, it was assumed that relation perception requires an act of comparison (for example, Boring, 1933, p. 95; T. Brown, 1860, p. 288; von Ehrenfels, 1890; Koffka, 1922, p. 545; Ladd, 1894, p. 302; Lashley, 1926; Locke, 1690, p. 156; Lotze, 1886, pp. 40–41).

John Locke believed that comparison is necessary for relation perception, and that subhuman animals are deficient in the ability to compare: "How far brutes partake in this faculty is not easy to determine; I imagine they have it not in any great degree..." (Locke, 1690, pp. 146–147).[2] Stout (1918b, pp. 172–173) agreed that animals are deficient in comparison, but he believed that the perception of some relations is not dependent upon comparison, and that animals would not be deficient in the perception of these relations. Stout also said that Lloyd Morgan, "in agreement with Locke, formulates his result in the denial that animals perceive relations. This is at least a misleading way of stating the case; unless we put an artificial restriction on the meaning of the term relation..." (p. 173). However, Morgan actually said that relative qualities can be sensed, but that it is only through reflection that they are identified as relations. The sensations have their origin in the "transitions of consciousness" that result from focusing on first one object and then the other (Morgan, 1903, Chapter XIII, pp. 217–240). Animals—and young children—can sense these transitions, but cannot perceive relations, because the faculty of reflection has not developed (Chapter XIV, pp. 241–261). The distinction between sensing the relative qualities and perceiving the relations is a distinction between an "undefined marginal awareness and a well-defined focal idea," between "passing on in consciousness from impression to impression and reflectively directing the attention to the nature of the transitions between them," and between "the naïve reception of a sequence of experiences and the beginnings of introspection" (p. 242).

Angell (1908, pp. 177–178) was also convinced that comparison is necessary for relation perception, but he believed that the essential factor was the movement of the eyes; "... the *vital meaning* of all space relations is simply a given amount and direction of movement." Mach (1914, pp. 127–130) agreed; but Külpe (1909, pp. 351–373) and Lindworsky (1931, pp. 107–109) believed that these movements are relatively unimportant in the perception of spatial relations.

Rudel (1959) concluded that response to an *absolute* stimulus also depends upon the opportunity for comparison of stimuli during training, and suggested that comparison is equally important during testing if the absolute response is to be maintained. According to Lindworsky (1931, p. 240), the perception of "absolute" size is actually based on the discrimination of relative sizes. Boring (1933) wrote: "In strict logic size has meaning only relativistically; nevertheless size may be 'absolute' psychologically when the perception includes no conscious comparison" (p. 95).

[2]Thomas Jefferson (1782, p. 194) wrote of Negroes: "In general, their existence appears to participate more of sensation than reflection." He probably had in mind John Locke's analysis of these faculties, and apparently based his conclusion on observation rather than on bigotry.

Nissen (1953) cited a personal communication from Spence which seemed to say that comparison is necessary in the "transverse patterning" problem (see Fig. 3–1). The subject must look at one object and then the other; and if the trace of Stimulus 1 combines with the perception of Stimulus 2, the subject approaches; but if the trace of Stimulus 2 combines with the perception of Stimulus 1, the subject does not approach. Nissen noted the similarity of this mechanism to the act of comparison assumed by Lashley (1926) to be required for relation perception. (However, North *et al.* [1958] showed that rats can solve a conditional discrimination problem by learning to respond to specific stimulus compounds, and need not respond on the basis of a configuration of the positive and negative compounds.)

It has also been argued (Lashley, 1942; Lashley and Wade, 1946) that comparison is necessary for discrimination learning, but that it is not necessary that two objects be directly compared, since one object can be compared with the memory trace of the other object (see also W. James, 1890, Vol. I, pp. 494–502). Similarly, Ananiev (1957) has asserted that "In [the process of discrimination], individual (simultaneous or consecutive) sensations are linked with each other and become the source of a complex intellectual process, namely comparison.... The material basis of the process of discrimination is the discriminatory (differentiating) activity of the cerebral cortex" (p. 136).

According to Muenzinger (1938), Tolman (1926) was the first investigator to suggest a relation between comparison behavior, or "vicarious trial and error," and efficiency of discrimination learning (see Tolman, 1926, pp. 366–367). However, in 1907 Yerkes (pp. 234–235) at least implied that there is a relation, and Dennis and Russell (1939) pointed out that other investigators had also observed the relation before Tolman. There is a correlation between comparison behavior or vicarious trial and error and successful discrimination learning (for example, in sea lions, Schusterman, 1965; in the bottlenose porpoise, Kellogg and Rice, 1963; Kellogg and Rice, 1964; in the dancing mouse, Yerkes, 1907, pp. 130–132 and 234–236; in rats, Dennis, 1930; Geier, Levin, and Tolman, 1941; Hoge and Stocking, 1912; Lashley, 1912; Lashley 1920; Muenzinger, 1938; Tolman, 1939 [see also Tolman, 1938, pp. 27–34]; in monkeys, Galt, 1939; Klüver, 1933; and in children, Gellermann, 1933a; Gellermann, 1933b; White and Plum, 1964[3]). The correlation is not perfect, however, and there is some evidence that in the later stages of training, comparison is un-

---

[3] Penney also obtained this effect in children, in a study published in 1963 (Penney, personal communication, 1965; the published version did not report this finding). Rieber (1965) obtained corroborative evidence, in a study testing fourth-grade children. Response latencies increased on the trial immediately preceding the criterional run, presumably indicating that the subjects were scrutinizing the stimuli more carefully than on the previous trials. See also Zaporozhets (1955).

necessary, or is at least less necessary than in earlier stages (Davenport, 1959; Davenport, 1962; Davenport, 1963; Ettlinger, 1960b, Experiment I; I. M. L. Hunter, 1952b; Klüver, 1933; Muenzinger, 1938; Penney, 1963; Schuster-man, 1965; Tolman, 1938; Tolman, 1939; White and Plum, 1964; Yerkes, 1907, pp. 131 and 235; see also Goss and Wischner, 1956; Mowrer, 1960b, pp. 212–213). In these later stages, the subject responds to the absolute properties of the correct stimulus. Hadley (1927) observed comparison behavior in a guinea pig, and reported that "as discrimination grew more perfect this 'comparison' behavior gave way to what one might call 'direct recognition'" (p. 204). However, he also reported that the other 10 guinea pigs tested did not show this kind of behavior and that they seemed to learn no more slowly than the one that did. (Spence [1960, footnote 7, p. 387] presented an equation that predicts that the amount of vicarious trial and error will decrease as discrimination learning progresses.)

"Vicarious trial and error" is the same as "comparison behavior," but is not the same as "comparison." Vicarious trial and error is observable behavior; comparison is a covert or implicit process. However, comparison results from vicarious trial and error (Hull, 1952, p. 93), even though the vicarious trial and error may result from conflict (Goss and Wischner, 1956). The point is that vicarious trial and error and comparison behavior should not imply any necessary will or intention to compare.

If restricting the direct comparison of stimuli interferes with relation perception, then it should interfere with discrimination and reduce trans-position. Teplov and Borisova (1957) found that pitch discrimination was considerably worse when the presentations of the stimuli were separated by a two-minute interval than when they were separated by an interval of one and one-half to two seconds. Since the two-minute intervals were "normally occupied by conversation between subject and experimenter" (p. 150), the finding seems to indicate that reducing the opportunity for comparison increased the difficulty of discrimination. Unfortunately, however, the investigators used different methods with the different inter-stimulus intervals. With the short intervals, the psychophysical method of constant stimuli (Kurtz, 1965, pp. 298–300) was used in one condition and a modification of this method was used in another condition. With the two-minute interval, the method that was used did not correspond to any of the classical psychophysical methods, although it was most like the method of successive categories (Kurtz, 1965, pp. 354–358). It is well known that different methods can yield different results in psychophysical work; therefore, it would be incautious to offer the Teplov and Borisova findings as conclusive. Bachem (1954), however, obtained a similar result using the same method for all intervals. I. M. L. Hunter (1952b; 1953b, p. 496) obtained evidence that the absence of vicarious trial and error or com-parison behavior reduces transposition in rats. The data of these studies agree with the prediction. Calvin (1955) obtained an opposite effect, testing young children on what he called "configurational" and "nonconfigurational" problems. In the configurational problem the stimuli were contiguous to one another, and in the nonconfigurational problem the stimuli were separated from one another. The nonconfigurational problem was learned more rapidly than the configurational problem. However, on the configurational problem the stimuli were separated from the response loci, and on the nonconfigurational problem the stimuli were contiguous with the response loci. The results could be attributable to the difference between the problems in the amount of separation between the stimulus and response loci. (There is ample evidence to justify this explanation [see Reese, 1964a, p. 323].)

The opportunity for comparison can be restricted by presenting the stimuli successively instead of simultaneously, but two methods of successive presentation have been used. In the "go–no-go" successive discrimination problem, which is also identified as a "differential conditioning" problem, the subject learns to approach one stimulus and to avoid another (or to withhold response). This kind of successive task is like the simultaneous discrimination problem except that only one stimulus is presented on each trial in the successive task, leading to other differences which are discussed later. In the "standard" successive discrimination problem, only one stimulus is presented on each trial, and the subject learns a different response to each stimulus. (The problem can also be identified as a paired-associates task.) This kind of successive discrimination problem can be analyzed as a conditional discrimination problem with position the discriminative cue and color (for example) the conditional cue (Nissen, 1950); but Spence (1952) classified the successive task as a patterning problem, involving response to cue–position compounds, rather than as a conditional discrimination. Warren (1960) also distinguished between the successive discrimination problem and the conditional discrimination problem, which he designated as "sign-differentiated positional" and "sign-differentiated object" problems.

According to Spence's (1952) analysis, there are three possible kinds of effective stimulus in discrimination situations. In the two-stimulus simultaneous discrimination problem (Fig 3-1A) and the go-no-go successive discrimination problem (Fig. 3-1B), the effective stimulus is a single component or element. In the standard successive discrimination problem (Fig. 3-1C), the effective stimulus is a cue–position pattern or compound; in the conditional discrimination problem (Fig. 3-1D), the effective stimulus is a cue–cue relation or "transverse pattern." The transverse patterning problem described by Spence involves three different stimuli presented in pairs (Fig. 3-1E). The usual conditional discrimination problem involves only two stimuli with variation of some background cue, but both the

(A) Two-Stimulus Simultaneous Discrimination Problem.

	Left		Right			Left		Right
	$\triangle^+$	vs	$\circ^-$	and		$\circ^-$	vs	$\triangle^+$

(B) Two-Stimulus Go–No-Go Successive Discrimination Problem.

	Left		Right			Left		Right
	——	$\triangle^+$	——	and		——	$\circ^-$	——

(C) Standard Two-Stimulus Successive Discrimination Problem.

	Left		Right			Left		Right
	$\triangle^+$	vs	$\triangle^-$	and		$\circ^-$	vs	$\circ^+$

(D) Conditional Discrimination Problem

		Left		Right			Left		Right
1.		$\wedge^+$	vs	$\circ^-$	and		$\circ^-$	vs	$\triangle^+$
2.		$\blacktriangle^-$	vs	$\bullet^+$	and		$\bullet^+$	vs	$\blacktriangle^-$

(E) Transverse Patterning Problem.

		Left		Right			Left		Right
1.		$\triangle^+$	vs	$\circ^-$	and		$\circ^-$	vs	$\triangle^-$
2.		$\circ^+$	vs	$\square^-$	and		$\square^-$	vs	$\circ^+$
3.		$\square^+$	vs	$\triangle^-$	and		$\triangle^-$	vs	$\square^+$

FIG. 3-1. Sample discrimination problems. See text for explanations.

transverse patterning problem and the conditional discrimination problem must be solved on the basis of transverse or cue–cue patterns according to Spence. Eimas and Doan (1965) noted that the conditional discrimination problem is more similar to the standard successive discrimination problem, which requires response to cue-position patterns, than it is to the transverse patterning problem. The argument is that the two cues in the conditional discrimination problem and in the standard successive discrimination problem are spatially overlapping, whereas in the transverse patterning problem the two cues present on any one trial are spatially separated (Eimas, personal communication, 1965).

In the standard successive discrimination problem the discriminative cue on a given trial is position of response unit, but in the conditional discrimination the discriminative cue is the difference between the stimulus objects, and position is an irrelevant cue. (Positional cues are also irrelevant in the simultaneous problem.)

A group of monkeys tested by Warren (1960) solved the conditional discrimination more rapidly than standard successive discrimination, probably because the monkeys had previously been subjects in learning-set studies, in which position habits were presumably eliminated. A tendency to ignore positional cues would facilitate conditional discrimination learning and interfere with successive discrimination learning (see also Shepp, 1962).

Since the opportunity to compare stimuli is restricted in successive discrimination problems, (a) successive discrimination problems should be solved more slowly than simultaneous discrimination problems and (b) there should be less transposition following successive discrimination training than following simultaneous discrimination training. Since the analysis also implies that the basis of solution of successive discrimination problems should be different from the basis of solution of simultaneous discrimination problems, (c) there should be little transfer between the two kinds of problem even when the same stimulus objects are used in both. Data relevant to these three predictions are reviewed below. (It should be noted, however, that I have attempted an exhaustive review of only the transposition data. The literature related to the other two predictions is much too extensive to be covered completely here.)

Ease of Solution

The go-no-go successive discrimination problem was used in all the studies reviewed in this section. The problem can be solved, even with a relatively long interval between stimulus presentations (Hanson, 1961; Honig, 1962; Maltzman, 1949, Experiment I), but it has generally been found to be more difficult than the simultaneous discrimination problem (Baker and Lawrence, 1951; North and Jeeves, 1956; Riley *et al.*, 1963; and perhaps Moody, 1929), especially when highly similar stimuli are used (MacCaslin, 1954; Riley *et al.*, 1960; Sutherland, Mackintosh, and Mackintosh, 1963). However, contradictory data have been reported by Grice (1949) and Maltzman (1949, Experiment II), who obtained no difference in speed of learning.

Although the data suggest that successive discrimination learning is generally harder than simultaneous discrimination learning, there is a problem in interpreting the data, because of differences in the definitions of "errors" and of "trials." In the simultaneous problem, an error is a choice of the incorrect stimulus; but in the successive problem, an error is (a) a response latency less than the median when the negative stimulus is presented, and (b) a latency greater than the median when the positive stimulus is presented. (An error in the successive problem can also be defined as a choice of the incorrect stimulus, regardless of latency.) In the simultaneous problem a trial is the presentation of the two stimuli simultaneously, and in the successive problem a trial is the presentation of one stimulus. If the numbers of presentations of the positive and negative stimuli in the successive problem are equal, as is usually the case, there is positive reinforcement on 50 per cent of the trials and nonreinforcement on 50 per cent throughout training. In the simultaneous problem, however, the percentage of reinforced trials increases as learning progresses (unless forced runs to the negative stimulus are given, but this is usually not done). Baker and Lawrence considered this difference between the two kinds of problem to be the major objection to the comparison of the groups in their study.

Transfer between Successive and Simultaneous Discriminations with Same Stimuli

As in the preceding section, the successive discrimination used in all of the studies reviewed here was the go–no-go problem. The same stimuli were used in successive and simultaneous discriminations. North and Jeeves (1956) obtained little transfer between successive and simultaneous discriminations in the first two phases of their experiment, in which the tasks were given successively. The apparatus was a four-unit maze; and in a final phase of the study, the two kinds of problem were given concurrently for eight runs, with successive discriminations at two of the choice points and simultaneous discriminations at the other two in each run. In this phase, the subjects gave 89 per cent correct responses on the successive discriminations and 91 per cent correct on the simultaneous discriminations.

Riley et al. (1960) obtained less than perfect transfer from successive discrimination to simultaneous discrimination. However, high levels of transfer from successive to simultaneous discriminations were obtained by Grice (1949) and D. H. Cohen (1963); high levels of transfer from simultaneous to successive discriminations were obtained by Riekel (1922), Stavsky and Pattie (1930), Grice (1949), Webb (1950), Goldberg and Clark (1955), and Schmerler (1965).

S. J. Lachman (1956) found that the amount of transfer depended upon which stimulus was initially correct. The stimuli differed in brightness. In the "successive" task, the positive or negative stimulus was presented in one window and the other window was not illuminated, but since the dark (unilluminated) window differed from the discriminative stimuli in brightness, the "successive" task actually consisted of two simultaneous discriminations. In one of these discriminations, one stimulus was correct and the other was incorrect; in the other discrimination, neither stimulus was correct. If rats respond to relations, then Lachman's successive task was actually a simultaneous discrimination with intermittent reinforcement of the correct relational response. For one group of subjects, a bright light was correct; for another group, a dim light was correct. Relative to the unilluminated window, however, both of the discriminative stimuli were "brighter." When the rats were shifted to a simultaneous discrimination with both discriminative stimuli present on each trial, the group with the bright light correct gave 94 per cent correct responses, and the group with the dim light correct gave only 24 per cent correct responses (first 10 transfer trials, with differential reinforcement). Since both groups tended to choose the brighter light on these trials, it can be concluded that relational learning occurred during the training phase.

S. J. Lachman and Taylor (1963) used the same apparatus and design as S. J. Lachman (1956), except that responses to the negative stimulus were punished with electric shock and the dimmer light was positive for all subjects. The maximum numbers of responses to the positive and negative stimuli in the group trained with simultaneous stimulus presentations were determined, and these numbers of presentations of each stimulus were given to the successive group, followed by 42 "test" trials with simultaneous stimulus presentation. On these test trials, responses to the positive stimulus were rewarded, but responses to the negative stimulus were not punished.

The simultaneous group required a mean of about 129 trials to reach a criterion of 42 consecutive correct responses. On the 42 test trials given to the successive group, there was an average of 28.4 correct responses (about 68 per cent correct). Lachman and Taylor interpreted this to mean that learning was impeded by the lack of opportunity for relational learning; but they also noted that the number of correct responses on the test trials was significantly greater than chance, that the mean response latency on the last 28 trials with successive stimulus presentations was more than ten times longer when the negative stimulus was presented than when the positive stimulus was presented, and that the successive group achieved the learning criterion after a mean of only 16.3 additional trials with simultaneous stimulus presentations. Furthermore, they observed that "Responses to the darkened chamber ... occurred *very rarely* and only at the beginning of training ..." (p. 129, their italics).

These data are not consistent with an assumption that only relational learning occurred in the successive group. In the first place, the correct relation would be "brighter" in the successive group, since the lighted window is compared with a dark window, and responses to this relation would have been intermittently reinforced during training. However, intermittent reinforcement should increase resistance to extinction, and therefore retard reversal learning, yet the successive group required only about 58 trials (including the 42 test trials) to achieve the learning criterion with the "dimmer" relation correct (with simultaneous stimulus presentations). This number of trials does not seem to be excessive, and is less than half the number of trials required by the simultaneous group for original learning.

In the second place, the longer latencies on trials with the negative stimulus than on trials with the positive stimulus is inexplicable on the relational assumption. The relation would presumably be more difficult to perceive when the positive stimulus was presented, since the difference between the positive stimulus (three foot-candles) and the dark window was less than the difference between the negative stimulus (fifteen foot-candles) and the dark window.

There are also, however, objections to an assumption that only absolute learning occurred. The most telling argument is that almost no responses to the dark window occurred after the first few trials, even when the negative stimulus was the alternative choice.

Assuming that both absolute and relational learning occurred would account for the data. Relational learning would account for the lack of responses to the dark window, and absolute learning would account for the latency data. The response to the positive stimulus would be determined by a "relational" habit and an "absolute" habit, but the response to the negative stimulus would be determined by the relational habit and a generalized absolute habit which would be weaker than the conditioned absolute habit. On the simultaneous test trials, the absolute habit is correct, and the relational habit is incorrect, but having one correct habit would facilitate reversal, compared with having none correct.

The assumption that absolute as well as relational learning occurred would not be contradictory to the conclusion based on the S. J. Lachman (1956) results, since on even the first 10 trials with the simultaneous stimulus presentations, with the dimmer light correct, Lachman found that 24 per cent of the responses were correct. If only the relation determined the responses, this percentage should probably have been much smaller.

In summary, it appears that there is generally a high level of transfer between the successive and simultaneous discriminations when the same stimuli are used in both problems. The transfer seems to be usually based on absolute stimulus qualities, but may sometimes be based on relational qualities when the stimulus dimension has not been carefully chosen.

Transposition following Successive Discrimination Training

Go-No-Go Successive Discrimination. Maltzman (1949, Experiment II) obtained equal transposition in rats on a test with simultaneous stimulus presentations following simultaneous and successive discrimination training. (Absolute responses predominated in both conditions.) However, Baker and Lawrence (1951) obtained more transposition in rats after simultaneous discrimination training than after successive discrimination training, and D. H. Cohen (1963) obtained the same effect in pigeons. The transposition test in both the Baker and Lawrence study and the Cohen study was a simultaneous discrimination, perhaps favoring the groups trained on the simultaneous discrimination because, as R. Thompson (1955) suggested, the kind of receptor-orienting habit learned in the one-choice go-no-go successive discrimination may be inappropriate in a two-choice transposition test.

Riley *et al.* (1960) used an apparatus that almost guaranteed that simultaneous and successive groups would acquire different orienting responses (see Fig. 3-2). One group of rats, Group NC (for noncomparison), was given successive discrimination training and then a simultaneous discrimination transposition test. A second group, Group NCC (for noncomparison control), was given successive discrimination training and then a simultaneous discrimination test with the same stimuli as used in the successive discrimination problem. A third group, Group C

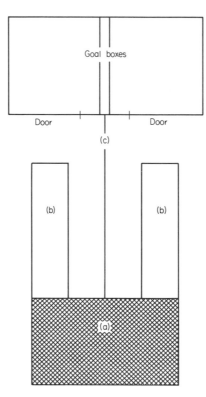

FIG. 3-2. Apparatus used by Riley *et al.* in 1960: (a) starting box, (b) runways, and (c) removable opaque barrier. The subject cannot see the stimuli from the starting box and can jump to only the nearer stimulus. To jump to the other stimulus, the subject must reenter the starting box and go to the other runway. With the barrier removed, the subject can see both stimuli from either runway. With the barrier in place, the subject can see only one stimulus and must reenter the starting box and go to the other runway in order to see the other stimulus. (After Riley *et al.*, 1960, Fig. 1, p. 416.)

(comparison), was given simultaneous discrimination training and then a simultaneous discrimination transposition test. There was no control group for comparison with Group C.

In the second task, the performance of Group NCC dropped below the criterional level attained at the end of the first task, and was inferior to the second-task performance of Group C. Group C transposed more than Group NC, as shown in Fig. 3-3. Group NC was inferior throughout testing to Group NCC, but the differences were not statistically significant.

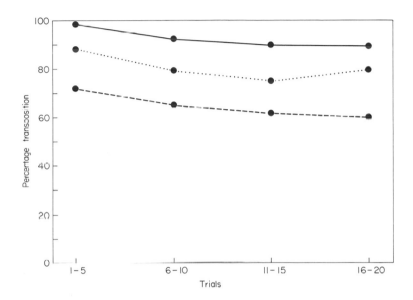

FIG. 3-3 Test-trial data of Riley *et al.* (1960): (——) C, (···) NCC, and (- - -), NC. Groups trained and tested with highly distinctive stimuli. (After Riley *et al.*, 1960, Fig. 3, p. 418).

Inspection of Fig. 3-3 indicates that the differences between the curves of Group NC and Group NCC were of about the same order of magnitude as the differences between the curve of Group C and the level of perfect transfer. Perfect transfer would be expected in a simultaneous discrimination training group given a simultaneous discrimination "transfer" test with no change in the stimuli. Such a group would serve as a control for comparison with Group C. Therefore, Group NC, relative to its control group (Group NCC), transposed as much as Group C, relative to its hypothetical control group. Restricting the opportunity for comparison during training interfered with transfer to a task on which comparison was possible, but there was no additional interference with transposition.

Baker and Lawrence did not run a control group, but other evidence suggests that if they had, it would have exhibited a high level of transfer, and the relative amount of transposition in the successive group would still have been less than that in the simultaneous group. Baker and Lawrence tried to minimize the possibility that the groups would acquire different receptor-orienting habits, by the design of the apparatus and by random alternation of the left–right position of the successive stimuli to induce the same kind of "search" behavior as in the simultaneous group (see Baker and Lawrence, 1951, p. 381).

In a study by R. Thompson (1955), subjects learned two simultaneous discrimination problems concurrently, but one group could compare the members of each dimension (for example, large vs small, dark vs light) and one group could not (for example, large vs light, dark vs small). The comparison group transposed slightly more than the noncomparison group, suggesting that relation perception occurred more often in the first group than in the second group. The transposition tests were comparison problems, and the change in type of problem could have reduced the performance level in the noncomparison group. However, both of the problems required the same kind of gross receptor-orienting response, and therefore the difference in transposition supports the conclusion that the difference obtained by Baker and Lawrence is at least not entirely attributable to a change in the kind of orienting response required.

Riley et al. (1963) used an apparatus similar to the one used earlier by Riley et al. (1960) (see Fig. 3-2), but with a modification that changed the nature of the problem. In the apparatus used in the earlier study, the stimuli could be separated by a barrier that made direct comparison of the stimuli impossible. With this barrier in place, the problem was successive discrimination, since only one stimulus could be seen on any one trial. In the apparatus used in the later study, the barrier was smaller, and comparison was not impossible, although the ease of comparison was less than it would be with the barrier removed. The purpose of the later study was to examine the effect of cue separation on transposition. In one condition the cues were contiguous, touching each other on the inner edge; in the other condition, the cues were 4.25 inches apart and were further separated by the barrier, extending one inch into the choice compartment, and a glass panel extending three inches farther into the choice compartment. The barrier and panel made it necessary for the subject to turn away from one stimulus in order to approach the other stimulus. The cue separation during the transposition test was the same as during training. There was more transposition in the contiguous-stimulus condition than in the separated-stimulus condition. Riley et al. (1963) suggested that in the contiguous-stimulus condition the subject learns to respond to the difference between the two stimuli, but in the separated-stimulus condition the subject learns to respond to this difference and to the relation of each stimulus to the background. However, the reduction of the opportunity for comparison in the separated-stimulus condition would presumably interfere with the perception of the relation between the discriminative stimuli, accounting for the reduction in transposition, and it is not necessary to assume perception of the relation of stimulus to ground, although the fact that the assumption is unnecessary does not, of course, mean that it is false.

Mackintosh's (1965b) analysis of the Grice (1948; 1951) studies (reviewed in section entitled "Effect of Absolute Stimulus Components," this chapter) and my analysis of the S. J. Lachman (1956) and S. J. Lachman and Taylor (1963) studies (described above), suggest that Baker and Lawrence's subjects in the successive discrimination condition could also have learned to respond to brightness relations. Grice and Mackintosh gave rats presentations of a single stimulus, with or without reward, and then gave the subjects discrimination training in which this stimulus was paired with a new one. The stimuli were white circles differing in size, and the location of the stimulus in the first phase of the experiment was varied between the left and right positions. The background of the response unit that was unused on a given trial in the first stage was darker than the stimulus circle used, and therefore, as Mackintosh pointed out, the subjects could have learned during this stage to respond to a particular brightness relation rather than a particular absolute size. Mackintosh's data (summarized in Table 3-5) supported this analysis of the situation. In line with this analysis, Lashley (1938b) reported that some rats trained to respond to the size of white figures presented on a black ground transferred the response to stimuli differing in brightness.

Baker and Lawrence also used as stimuli white circles differing in size, and varied their left–right positions in the successive discrimination condition. The smaller circle was positive during training, but since both circles were brighter than the background, the subjects could have learned to respond to the "brighter" side, with intermittent reinforcement of this response. In the simultaneous discrimination group, the rewarded response would be to the "dimmer" side, since the smaller circle was presumably dimmer than the larger one. On the transposition test, which was downward in the positive direction, the transposition response would be to the "dimmer" side. As already indicated, the simultaneous discrimination group transposed more than the successive discrimination group. Furthermore, the successive discrimination group transposed somewhat less than the chance level on the first 10 trials (43 per cent, with differential reinforcement).

Honig (1962) found that after successive discrimination training in the two-stimulus problem, pigeons transposed at one step in both the positive and negative directions, but gave absolute responses on Far Tests. After simultaneous discrimination training, pigeons gave absolute responses on all tests except at one step in the negative direction, where they tended to avoid the negative training stimulus and to choose the new stimulus (yielding another kind of "absolute" response). The outcome on the test in the positive direction is consistent with the predictions derived for the Baker and Lawrence study, but the outcome on the test in the negative direction is not. Honig concluded, however, that the data would be consistent with Spence's (1937b) theory if the stipulation were added that the subject be required to extinguish the response to the negative stimulus rather than required only to develop a preference for the positive stimulus.

Robert Rudolph (cited by Riley, 1965b, pp. 308–310) confirmed Honig's results in a series of experiments using the same procedures as Honig. However, Honig had tested for transposition and generalization in the same subjects, and Rudolph speculated that the single-stimulus generalization tests might have affected the performance on the transposition tests in the group trained with simultaneous stimulus presentations. To test this hypothesis, Rudolph used different groups to assess transposition and generalization. The group trained with successive stimulus presentations transposed, as in Honig's study, but the group trained with simultaneous stimulus presentations also transposed, contrary to Honig's finding. D. H. Cohen (1963) obtained similar results in pigeons. Riley (1965b) suggested that "transposition following simultaneous training occurs because the animal responds to the relationship and . . . it occurs following successive training because of a peak shift . . ." (p. 310).

In Honig's study, the amounts of transposition obtained could be predicted from the obtained generalization gradients. However, in Rudolph's study, the amounts of transposition were not predictable from the generalization gradients. In a partially completed study, Zeiler (personal communication, 1966) obtained results that agree with Rudolph's.

Although Terrace (1964) did not mention the problem of transposition, his data suggest that "transposition probably will not occur in lower organisms unless the organism has made a considerable number of errors during training trials" (R. E. Cole et al., 1964, p. 359), in agreement with Honig's conclusion. Terrace found that when generalization tests were given to pigeons after discrimination training, the peak of the generalization gradient shifted away from the negative stimulus only if errors occurred during training. When few or no errors occurred, in fact, there were *more* responses to stimuli in the direction of the negative stimulus on the continuum than to ones in the direction of the positive stimulus. When a large number of errors occurred, the shift away from the negative stimulus was obtained. Terrace suggested that when few errors occur, the negative stimulus is neutral; but when the number of errors is large, the response to the negative stimulus is extinguished, and the negative stimulus becomes aversive.

R. E. Cole et al. (1964), however, found that children who made virtually no errors during training, tended to transpose on a Near Test, even though none could verbalize the basis for solving the problem. I. M. L. Hunter (1953b) reported the same behavior in 2 of 12 subjects tested in a previous experiment (I. M. L. Hunter, 1952a, Experiment III). Cole *et al.* concluded that although Spence's (1937b; 1942) theory is valid for infrahuman subjects, it is not completely adequate to explain transposition in human subjects. It should be noted, however, that all of the subjects tested by Cole *et al.* possessed the required verbal concepts, as determined by a posttest inquiry, and could have responded on a verbal basis without being able to report that they had done so. In support of this suggestion, it has been demonstrated that even college students sometimes fail to report verbalizations upon inquiry (Bugelski and Scharlock, 1952). Furthermore, Cole *et al.* gave no Far Test, and since the area ratio of the stimuli was only 1.6 to 1, it is possible that the subjects failed to notice that the stimuli had been changed.

Sherman (1966) attempted to determine, in a series of experiments, why multiple-problem training facilitates transposition in preschool children, but was thwarted because the control groups transposed at such high levels that almost no facilitating effect of multiple-problem training could be demonstrated. The apparatus permitted the subject to see the two stimuli simultaneously. In an attempt to reduce the level of transposition in the control condition, Sherman modified the apparatus in such a way that the subject could see only one stimulus at a time and had to turn his head to see the other stimulus. Learning was somewhat more rapid with the modified apparatus than with the one that permitted direct comparison, but there was somewhat less transposition with the modified apparatus (see Table 3-23). Line (1931) also found that increasing the separation between the stimuli reduced transposition. (Line referred to this as an effect of "distance"; but it is not to be confused with the "distance effect," which results from increasing separation on the stimulus dimension rather than increasing separation on the spatial dimension.)

TABLE 3-23
DATA FROM THE SHERMAN STUDIES[a]

Training condition	Stimulus exposure	Performance measure	
		Trials to criterion	Transposition (%)
Single problem	Simultaneous	12.5	87
	Successive	9.7	60
Multiple problem	Simultaneous	15.5	93
	Successive	13.9	80

[a]The data are from Sherman's (1966) Experiments 2 and 4, which were the only ones with comparable age groups receiving both kinds of training. Transposition is on the first trial of a three-step test.

Standard Successive Discrimination. Margery G. Cutsforth (1933)[4] gave chicks a successive discrimination problem in a multiple maze with three choice points, each with three choices. The problem required learning to select the dimmest of three lights at the first choice point, the intermediate brightness at the second choice point, and the brightest light at the third choice point. The three brightnesses were the same at all choice points, and therefore the location of the choice point was a conditional cue. The design differed from the standard successive problem only in that brightness rather than position was the discriminative cue, and location rather than color was the conditional cue. (A similar design has been used successfully with rats [Rose, 1931; Rose, 1939; Tolman, 1934].) One group learned the sequence of responses as in the usual multiple-maze problem; a second group learned Choice 3 to criterion, then learned Choices 2 and 3 as in a multiple-maze problem, and finally learned all three choices as in a multiple-maze problem. A third group learned Choices 1 and 2 as in a multiple-maze problem, and was then given Choices 1, 2, and 3 with all Choice 3 responses rewarded. The first two groups learned equally rapidly, and the third group gave mostly position responses at Choice 3, with a slight preference for the intermediate brightness. (Repeating the previously correct choice was the most common error in all three groups.) These findings indicate that the problem was not solved on the basis of the relational progression; but on transposition tests with the brightnesses reduced by a constant ratio, performance was almost as good as at the end of training, indicating either that relative rather than absolute stimulus values were discriminated, or that the subjects failed to perceive the change in absolute stimulus values (see section entitled "Generalization Theory," Chapter 9).

Cutsforth gave three "stages" of transposition test: The reduction of brightnesses from training to Stage I was 4 to 1; from Stage I to Stage II, 2 to 1; and from Stage II to Stage III, 2 to 1. Performance was somewhat better at Stage III than at Stage II, reversing the usual distance effect, but the stages were given to all subjects in sequential order, which could have increased transposition on the later tests (see section entitled "Multiple Tests," Chapter 4). It is also possible that the more distant tests were analogous to the extreme tests used by Rudel (1958) with children, since Rudel also obtained more transposition on extremely distant tests than on less distant tests (see section entitled "Distance," Chapter 4).

[4]Margery G. Cutsforth was probably the same investigator as "M. G. Cutsworth (Kansas)," who was cited in Ruckmick's (1930) summary of the fifth annual meeting of the Midwestern Psychological Association, but the study may have been different from the one cited here. Ruckmick reported only that "M. G. Cutsworth (Kansas) studied the successive brightness discrimination of chicks and found that 85% of the group learned the problem completely, making choices in terms of the relations of the total brightness-situation rather than in terms of isolated elements and absolute brightness" (p. 651).

Two studies, both by Jackson and Jerome (1940; 1943), dealt with transposition in children after simultaneous and successive training. The simultaneous method was used on the test trials in both studies. There was more transposition after simultaneous training than after successive training in which the subject was required to respond to each stimulus as it was presented. (The subject indicated his response by putting a ticket in one of three boxes, the left box if the positive stimulus was on the left, the right box if it was on the right, and the middle box if the negative stimulus was presented.) Virtually all subjects in the simultaneous group transposed after various amounts of overtraining, but the frequency of transposition was less in the successive group and decreased with increasing amounts of overtraining. After successive training in which the subject was to respond only to the correct stimulus, using the same method of response as in the simultaneous condition, there was as much transposition as in the simultaneous condition.

Rieber (1965) used a similar kind of problem, presenting three stimuli one at a time in different positions, and requiring the subject to withhold response until after all three stimuli had been presented. Under conditions in which the response reinstated one or more of the stimuli, a group given the successive problem was inferior in performance to a group given standard simultaneous discrimination training. However, when the stimuli were not visible again until the next trial started, the successive group was superior to the simultaneous group. Rieber did not assess the effects of these procedures on transposition.

Buss (1953) used a successive training technique with college students, requiring a different response ("vec" or "non-vec") to each stimulus, and found no evidence of transposition. Talland (1957), however, argued that the responses used in the Buss study required "exclusive" categorizing, and therefore favored neither an absolute nor a relational basis of discrimination. Talland assumed that (a) in a universe divided into two "inclusive" categories, a relational criterion of discrimination will be adopted in preference to an absolute one, whether the categories are relational or absolute; and (b) when a concept is formed within an exclusive category, a relational criterion will not be more readily available than an absolute one. (He further assumed that inclusive relational categories are established more easily than exclusive categories, and inclusive absolute categories less easily, but the assumption was not verified by the data, and is not crucial to the issue under consideration anyway.) Although the assumptions seem to be gratuitous, they were confirmed, since relational responses occurred when the responses were inclusive ("vec" and "bix" or "bix" and "bixer") but not when they were exclusive ("vec" and "non-vec").

Analyzed from Talland's point of view, both of the successive training methods used in the Jackson and Jerome studies seem to require exclusive categorizing. Basically, the subject is required to designate the stimulus presented as "correct" or "incorrect" (in the two-choice method, "correct" means choice of one or the other end box, depending on the position of the stimulus, and "incorrect" means choice of the middle box; in the one-response method, "correct" means choice of one of two boxes, depending on the position of the stimulus, and "incorrect" means no response). Talland's assumptions would, then, account for the lack of transposition in the two-response group, but would also lead to the prediction of no transposition in the one-response group. However, the one-response method was identical to the simultaneous-presentation method except for the duration of the delay between stimulus exposures. There was presumably some slight delay even in the simultaneous condition, as the subject shifted his attention from one stimulus to the other, but it was surely less than in the one-response successive condition, in which the delay between stimulus exposures was one second. The delay in both conditions was probably short enough that the subject could easily and accurately compare the second stimulus with the trace of the first, but if comparison is the essential condition for relational learning (and transposition), then it might be expected that comparison would also occur in the two-response method. However, the delay between stimulus exposures in the two-response method was five seconds, which could be too long for accurate comparison of the second stimulus with the trace of the first, preventing or retarding relational learning, and reducing transposition.

In summary, the opportunity to compare stimuli during training seems to increase transposition, although there are contradictory data. Whether or not the comparison behavior yields relation perception is not known, but relation perception seems to be possible in rats (S. J. Lachman, 1956; S. J. Lachman and Taylor, 1963). The Honig (1962) and Terrace (1964) data suggest that pigeons transpose only if the tendency to respond to the negative stimulus is extinguished, implying that transposition in pigeons is based on stimulus generalization rather than relation perception. The data of R. E. Cole et al. (1964), however, indicate that children may transpose even if they never respond to the negative stimulus during training, implying that transposition in children may be based on relation perception rather than stimulus generalization.

CHAPTER 4

Test Variables

The variables considered in this chapter are ones that are specifically introduced on transposition *tests*. The variables could have been subdivided into "stimulus variables" ("distance" and "direction") and "procedural variables" ("delay" and perhaps "multiple tests" and "disruptive effects") as in Chapter 3, but the sections seemed to be short enough to make the division unnecessary.

Disruptive Effects of the Tests

In several studies of transposition, trials with the original discriminanda were interspersed among test trials, in order to maintain the original discrimination through the testing phase. In most of these studies, the performance level on the interspersed training trials was below the initial criterional level, attained before any test trials were given (see Table 4-1).[1] Perkins and Wheeler (1930), testing goldfish, found that about half of the subjects showed this drop in discriminative performance, and half did not. H. M. Johnson (1916) obtained the disruption in the single Indian gamecock that solved the initial discrimination. Gayton (1927) found no consistent effect in rats; but McCulloch (1935), Hebb (1937b), F. N. Jones (1939b), Heyman (1951), and Lawrence and DeRivera (1954) obtained the effect in rats. Maier (1939) obtained the disruption in rats on only a small percentage of the interspersed blocks of retraining trials; but when it did occur, it was about three times more likely to follow a test pair that was behaviorally nonequivalent to the training pair than to follow a pair that was behaviorally equivalent to the training pair.

Washburn and Abbott (1912) obtained the disruption in the rabbit, Hadley (1927) obtained it in guinea pigs, and W. L. Brown *et al.* (1959)

[1]Gentry *et al.* (1959), Gonzalez *et al.* (1954), Gulliksen (1932a), Hebb (1938), Meyer (1964b), Riley (1958), M. S. Scott (1966), Spence (1937b), and Towe (1954) used relevant procedures, but did not report relevant data; and it is impossible to determine what the effect was in studies by Coburn (1914) and Nissen (1942).

TABLE 4–1
DISRUPTING EFFECT OF THE TESTS ON INTERSPERSED
RETRAINING TRIALS

Study	Training criterion	Performance change
W. L. Brown et al. (1959)	16/18	Drop (?)
Caron (1967)	a	Drop
Gayton (1927)	80% (group average)	No consistent effect
Hadley (1927)	20/20 or 29/30	Drop
Hebb (1937b)	20/20 (but not all Ss met criterion)	Drop
Heyman (1951)	18/20	Drop
H. M. Johnson (1916)	?	Drop
F. N. Jones (1939b)	10/10	Drop
Klüver (1933)	Varied but generally higher	
Weight	than in more recent studies	Drop
Sound		Drop
Size		No effect
Brightness		No effect
Color		No effect
Lawrence and DeRivera (1954)	9/10 on Problem 1, then 6/6 to new training sets	Drop
Maier (1939)	30/30	Drop
McCulloch (1935)	23/24	Drop
Perkins and Wheeler (1930)	Final level attained varied	Half of Ss: drop Other half: increase or no change
Rowley and Bolles (1935)	23/30	No effect
G. R. Thompson (1965)	15/15	60% of Ss: drop 40%: increase or no change
Washburn and Abbott (1912)	20/20 (e.g., Series 34–36)	Drop
Zeiler (1965b)	5/5	Drop
Zeiler and Price (1965)	Continuous reinforcement: 10/10 Variable interval:2 successive days with 95% R$^+$ (45 periods/day)	Drop
Zeiler and Salten (1966)	20/20 to 25/25	No change

[a] 3/3 with guided responses, using boxes as stimuli, then 5/5 using paper squares as stimuli.

appear to have obtained it in monkeys.[2] Klüver (1933) obtained the effect in monkeys on weight and auditory discriminations, but obtained no effect on size, brightness, or color discriminations.

[2] Two statements in the report by W. L. Brown et al. (1959) imply that there was a disruption in performance. After four days of testing, with interspersed training trials, the subjects were retrained on the original discrimination, to a criterion of 16 correct responses in 18 trials. A correctional procedure was used (implying that some errors occurred), but the criterion "was quickly reached" (p. 594) (also implying some errors).

Rowley and Bolles (1935) obtained no effect on the performance level of white mice, but only irrelevant dimensions were changed on the tests that were interspersed among the training trials.

Zeiler and Price (1965) found that after variable-interval reinforcement during training, there was less disruption of performance in pigeons on interspersed training trials than after continuous reinforcement during training. However, the reinforcement schedules were confounded with "trials" procedures: The variable-interval reinforcement was given with free-responding trials, and the continuous reinforcement was given with discrete trials. Zeiler and Salten (1966) used the intermittent reinforcement procedure in two experiments with children, and found no disruption of performance on retraining trials. Using continuous reinforcement procedures, Zeiler (1965b) and Caron (1967) obtained the disruption in children, and G. R. Thompson (1965) obtained it in mental retardates.

The performance level on the transposition test is also usually lower than the criterional level of the training phase, even on the Near Test. (The studies that provide the evidence for this conclusion are not listed, because the list would include almost all of the transposition studies.) This drop, and the disruption of performance on training trials interspersed among the test trials, might be in a sense spurious. Learning curves typically become negatively accelerated as the subject approaches the criterional level, perhaps because the subject reaches a temporary stage characterized by an asymptote below the criterional level. Subjects in this subcriterional stage might by chance attain a criterional level of performance. Having apparently learned the discrimination, these subjects would be shifted immediately to the test trials. On the test trials, and on subsequent retraining trials, these subjects would probably revert to the subcriterional level that had actually been achieved, producing the apparent drop in performance level. (This possible explanation was suggested to me informally by Dr. Fred Stollnitz in 1965.)

Inspection of Table 4-1 provides no evidence that the effect was obtained more often when less stringent criteria of learning were used. On the assumption that a less stringent criterion is more likely to be attained briefly by chance than more stringent criteria, the data fail to support the suggested explanation. Furthermore, Reese and Fiero (1964) found that six-year-old and seven-year-old children attained criteria of 5 consecutive correct responses, 9 correct of 10 consecutive responses, and 14 correct of 15 consecutive responses with equal numbers of errors. These data suggest that subjects infrequently reach even a low criterion of learning by chance.

The disruptions can be attributed to interfering effects produced by the shifting of the absolute magnitudes of the stimuli. The shift might disrupt attentional processes, or arouse emotional reactions that in turn generate interfering responses, or produce the interference in some other way.

Perkins and Wheeler (1930) offered a Gestaltist account of the drop that is obtained on the first transposition test: "To be sure, transpositions frequently disturb the animal, doubtless *because the total effect of the change is noticed; the summated brightness or size or form is altered*" (p. 47, their italics). They added: "On the other hand, there are many cases in which transpositions result in no decrement, and even in further progress at once" (p. 47). They offered no documentation for the latter assertion; and in their own curves for individual subjects there were 16 cases with a drop in performance, 3 with no change, and only 2 with an increase, considering only the first transposition test given each subject. (I have excluded from this analysis their "Group II-A" because the first test did not involve transposition and their "Group IV" because the tests are not separable.) In both cases of increase, transposition was positive and downward, and since the learning data indicated a preference for the dimmer intensity, it is likely that the transposition scores were inflated by pre-experimentally acquired preferences. (All 13 subjects with the dimmer intensity correct performed at above the chance level from the beginning of training. With the brighter intensity correct, three subjects began above the chance level, one began at the chance level, and two began below the chance level. With three lights present, the intermediate brightness was preferred.)

Delay

Data on the effects of delay between the end of the training phase and the beginning of the testing phase are summarized in Table 4-2 and are discussed below.

Two-Stimulus Problems

Köhler (1918) reported that chickens transposed less when testing immediately followed training than when it was delayed; and Takemasa (1934) apparently obtained the same effect. H. M. Johnson (1916) found no effect of a 24-hour delay in the single Indian gamecock that solved the initial discrimination. Transposition averaged 35 per cent on two immediate tests and 30 per cent on two delayed tests. D. H. Cohen (1963) found that delay had no statistically significant effect on transposition in pigeons; but the obtained trends suggest that delays up to 5 minutes reduced transposition, a 10-minute delay facilitated transposition (after simultaneous discrimination training), and delays of 30 minutes and 24 hours reduced transposition. R. Thompson (1955) found that delay enhanced transposition in rats, especially when the within-pair stimulus differences were large. Gayton (1927) found no effect of delay on transposition in rats; but the tests with no delay were given after the delayed tests, with all of the tests interspersed among training trials, and the additional learning could have obscured the expected decrease in transposition with immediate testing. However, Flory (1938) also found that delay had no effect on transposition in rats, and Ohtsuka (1937) reported that the interval between training and test had "no pronounced effect" on transposition in monkeys. (Insufficient details of procedure were given in the available report of the last study to allow an evaluation of the finding. Adams [1937] also varied the delay interval, but the available report does not indicate whether delay affected transposition.) Warren (1964) found that delay had no effect on transposition in cats trained to choose one or the other extreme stimulus in a three-stimulus set.

Line (1931) found that delay enhanced transposition in children; and Sato (1936), Stevenson, Langford, and Reese (1955b), and Stevenson and Langford (1957) also obtained the effect in children. Wohlwill (1957) obtained evidence suggesting that a one-minute delay enhanced transposition in college students. D. E. Gould (1963) found that four-minute and ten-minute delays increased transposition in college students when the stimuli were similar but not when they were distinctively different.

INTERMEDIATE-STIMULUS PROBLEMS

There have been only three studies of the effect of delayed testing on transposition in the intermediate-stimulus problem in infrahuman subjects. In one, Spence (1942) found somewhat more transposition in chimpanzees when testing was delayed 24 hours than when testing was delayed 10 minutes, but the effect was weak and the absolute response predominated in all tests. (As Zeiler [1963c] noted, this was the first study of intermediate-size transposition using a simultaneous discrimination procedure.) In the second relevant study, Warren (1964) obtained essentially the same results in cats. In the third study, Ebel and Werboff (1966) obtained significantly more transposition in dogs after a 24-hour delay than after a 10-minute delay, but absolute responses were predominant on all tests.

Rudel (1957) found more Near Test transposition in children after a 3-hour delay than immediately after training when the stimuli in the series were relatively easily discriminated (3 to 1 ratio of stimulus areas), but delay had no effect when the stimuli were highly similar (1.5 to 1 ratio). The transposition response was predominant in the latter case with both immediate and delayed testing, suggesting that delay failed to enhance transposition because of a ceiling effect. Zeiler and Lang (1966b) partially replicated this finding, using a 24-hour delay. However, there was clearly no ceiling effect with the more similar stimuli; on two- to four-step Far Tests, absolute responses predominated in both the immediate-testing

TABLE 4–2
EFFECT OF DELAYED TESTING ON TRANSPOSITION

Study	Subjects	Length of delay	Effect[a]
	Two-Stimulus Problems		
Köhler (1918)	Chickens	b	Increase
Takemasa (1934)	Chickens	?	Increase
H. M. Johnson (1916)	Gamecock	24 hr	No effect
D. H. Cohen (1963)[c]	Pigeons	5 min	Decrease
		10 min	Increase
		30 min	Decrease
		24 hr	Decrease
Adams (1937)	Rats	Varied	d
Flory (1938)	Rats	24 hr	No effect
Gayton (1927)	Rats	24 hr	No effect[e]
R. Thompson (1955)	Rats	24 hr	Increase
Warren (1964)	Cats	24 hr	No effect
Ohtsuka (1937)	Monkeys	?	No effect[g]
Line (1931)	Children	?	Increase
Sato (1936)	Children	?	Increase
Stevenson and Langford (1957) 1–4 steps	Children	24 hr	Increase
Stevenson et al. (1955b)	Children	24 hr	Increase
D. E. Gould (1963)			
Similar stimuli	Adults	4 and 10 min	Increase
Distinctive stimuli	Adults	4 and 10 min	No effect
Wohlwill (1957)	Adults	1 min	Increase

[a] Delayed transposition relative to immediate transposition (or relative to transposition after short delay).

[b] Apparently delays of several minutes, 18 hours, and longer durations were used (see Köhler, 1918, pp. 19–27 [p. 222 in the translation]).

[c] Trends not statistically significant.

[d] No relevant data given in available secondary source.

[e] Immediate tests given after delayed tests and after further training.

[f] Three-stimulus problems with extreme stimulus correct.

[g] No pronounced effect, according to secondary source.

and delayed-testing conditions, and with both levels of stimulus similarity. Zeiler and Salten (1966, Experiment 1) trained children on the intermediate-size problem with intermittent reinforcement for correct choices. A 24-hour delay increased transposition at one step, and had no effect at two to four steps, with both a 1.4 to 1 ratio of stimulus areas and a 2 to 1 ratio. The average amount of transposition was about 50 per cent on the Far Tests.

Rudel (1960) replicated with brain-damaged (cerebral-palsied) children

TABLE 4–2 (*continued*)

Study	Subjects	Length of delay	Effect[a]
	Intermediate-Stimulus Problems		
Warren (1964)	Cats	24 hr	Increase
Ebel and Werboff (1966)	Dogs	24 hr	Increase
Spence (1942)	Chimpanzees	24 hr	Increase
Rudel (1957)			
Similar stimuli	Children	3 hr	No effect
Distinctive stimuli	Children	3 hr	Increase
Zeiler and Lang (1966b)			
Similar stimuli 1 step	Children	24 hr	No effect
2–4 steps	Children	24 hr	No effect
Distinctive stimuli 1 step	Children	24 hr	Increase
2–4 steps	Children	24 hr	No effect
Zeiler and Salten (1966)			
Similar stimuli 1 step	Children	24 hr	Increase
2–4 steps	Children	24 hr	No effect
Distinctive stimuli 1 step	Children	24 hr	Increase
2–4 steps	Children	24 hr	No effect
Rudel (1960)			
Similar stimuli	*h*	3 hr	No effect
Distinctive stimuli	*h*	3 hr	Increase
Distinctive stimuli	Mongoloids	3 hr	No effect
Stevenson and Weiss (1955) 2 steps	Adults	10 min	Increase
		24 hr	No effect

[h] Brain-damaged children.

the results she obtained with normal children (Rudel, 1957), but found no effect of delay in mongoloid children.

Using a four-stimulus problem with an extreme or intermediate stimulus correct (in subgroups), Stevenson and Weiss (1955) found more transposition in college students after a 10-minute delay than immediately after training and after a 24-hour delay, and found no difference between the latter two conditions.

CONCLUSION

Delay generally increases transposition in human subjects, and may increase transposition in animals. Delay seems to increase transposition when it reduces the likelihood that the subject will notice that the stimulus materials have been changed. If this probability is already low, delay has little or no effect on transposition. There may also be a limit to the effect of delay at the other extreme. It may be possible to devise situations in which the probability of noticing the change is so great even after a delay that delay can have little or no effect on transposition. For example, D. E. Gould (1963) varied the similarity of pitches in two-stimulus discrimination problems, and found that 88 per cent of a group of 144 college students learned with no more than one error. Even the most difficult problem was solved with an average of only 1.6 errors. Delay did not affect transposition with the most distinctively different pitches—in fact, transposition averaged only 22 per cent after the longest delay (10 minutes)—but with the more similar pitches, or perhaps more accurately, with the less distinctively different pitches, transposition increased with delay. Over all conditions, transposition occurred with greater than chance frequencies only with the 10-minute delay and with the less distinctively different pitches.

In the other studies in which stimulus similarity was varied, delay increased transposition with distinctive stimuli (except in severely mentally retarded subjects), and had no effect on transposition with similar stimuli (except in the Zeiler and Salten study). These results are consistent with the discriminability explanation, since the "distinctive" stimuli in these studies were probably more like the "similar" stimuli of Gould's study than like the distinctive stimuli of her study.

The effect of delay in two-stimulus problems is independent of the distance of the test stimuli from the training stimuli, at least within the range that has been studied (one to four steps). In intermediate-stimulus problems, however, delay enhances only Near Test transposition (except in adults). This difference in effects is consistent with the generalization that the probability of noticing the change in stimuli can be so high that delay cannot reduce it. (The rationale for this conclusion is given in Chapter 11.)

D. E. Gould (1963) gave psychophysical discrimination problems with the training and transposition-test stimuli, requiring the subjects to identify the stimulus that was common to the two sets, or to judge whether particular pairs were identical to each other or were different from each other. Delay had no effect on the accuracy of the judgments involving the most distinctive stimuli, and reduced the accuracy of the judgments involving the less distinctive stimuli, as required by the explanation outlined above. Gould had predicted that the transposition function would fall between the two psychophysical functions if the discriminability explanation were correct, and this prediction was not confirmed. The shapes of the gradients were as predicted, but the absolute levels were not. However, the failure to confirm the prediction is not necessarily contradictory to the discriminability hypothesis. Different groups of subjects were used in the transposition work and the psychophysical work, and presumably these groups had different sets. It is well known that under a set to learn, subjects will generalize to stimuli that under a psychophysical set would be easily discriminated. It is of course disappointing that the attempt to derive predictions from the discriminability functions was not successful, but the hypothesis remains tenable until contradictory evidence is obtained with set controlled.

Distance

The "distance effect" is a decrease in transposition responses with increasing separation between the training and test sets of stimuli on the stimulus dimension that is being manipulated. As already noted, transposing from the training stimuli to one-step test stimuli has produced a drop in the performance level in almost every study of transposition. Even bigger drops were usually obtained when the stimuli were changed more than one step. Most of the exceptions were in studies of children who possessed verbal concepts of the relations involved (for example, Jackson and Jerome, 1940), or in studies utilizing some experimental condition that has been shown to increase transposition (for example, Lawrence and DeRivera, 1954).

TWO-STIMULUS PROBLEMS

Klüver (1933) included Far Tests in his extensive studies of two-stimulus transposition in monkeys, but the Far Tests were given after a long series of other tests, and this procedure often increases the frequency of transposition (see section entitled "Multiple Tests," this chapter). Nevertheless, both monkeys given Far Tests of size transposition responded at the chance level (see Table 4-3). On a Far Test of brightness transposition, the only subject tested transposed, but less than at one-half step. Spence (1937b) obtained less size transposition in chimpanzees on Far Tests (one and one-half and two steps) than on the Near Test, and Kleshchov (1933) obtained the distance effect in dogs (see section entitled "Phylogenetic Comparisons," Chapter 5).

Several studies demonstrated the distance effect in rats (see Table 4-3). In all of these studies except those of Flory (1938), Ehrenfreund (1952), and Meyer (1964b), the minimum frequency of transposition responses was at or above the chance level, and absolute responses never predominated. The data of the Flory study are summarized in Table 4-4, where it can be seen that the exception occurred in only one group, and on a Far Test. In Ehrenfreund's study, absolute responses predominated at one step, where the test set included the positive training stimulus, choice of which is an absolute response. Meyer obtained greater-than-chance positive transposition, but less-than-chance negative transposition. Honig (1962) obtained absolute responses in pigeons (see below), but the only other studies in which absolute responses were predominant over transposition responses on the Near Test were ones in which markedly distinctive stimuli were used (see section entitled "Stimulus Similarity," Chapter 3).

TABLE 4-3

THE DISTANCE EFFECT IN ANIMALS: TWO-STIMULUS PROBLEMS

Species	Study	Dimension	Direction of test	Percentage transposition										
				1/3 step	1/2 step	2/3 step	1 step	1 1/3 steps	1 1/2 steps	2 steps	2 1/2 steps	3 steps	4 steps	5 steps
Monkey	Klüver (1933)	Size	Positive up	—	—	—	57	—	—	—	48	—	—	—
			Negative down	—	—	—	95	—	—	—	—	—	48	—
		Brightness	Positive down	—	90	—	64	—	72	78	—	—	—	—
Chimpanzee	Spence (1937b)	Size	Positive up	—	—	—	88	—	80	40	—	—	—	—
			Positive down	—	—	—	55	—	—	—	—	—	—	—
Rat	Flory (1938)[a]	Size												
	Gulliksen (1932a)	Size	Positive up	—	—	—	83	—	—	55	—	—	—	—
			Negative up	—	—	—	78	—	—	—	—	—	—	—
			Positive down	—	95	—	62	—	—	—	—	—	—	—
			Negative down	—	—	—	65	—	—	—	—	—	—	—
	Lashley (1938b)[b]	Size												
	Maier (1939)	Size	Positive down	98	—	80	56	—	49	—	—	—	—	—
			Negative down	92	—	60	52	—	51	—	—	—	—	—
	Meyer (1964b)[c]	Size	Positive up	—	89	—	89	—	56	—	—	—	—	—
			Negative up	—	44	—	33	—	22	—	—	—	—	—
	Enhenfreund (1952)	Brightness	Positive up	83	—	87	26	42	—	—	—	—	—	—
			Positive down	90	—	80	44	58	—	—	—	—	—	—
	Heyman (1951)	Brightness	Positive up	—	89	89	78	—	58	—	—	—	—	—
	T. S. Kendler (1950)	Brightness	Positive up	—	—	—	83	—	—	76	—	67	75	81
			Positive down	—	—	—	80	—	—	70	—	67	67	—
	Riley (1958)[d]	Brightness	Positive up	—	—	—	92	—	—	—	—	—	—	—
Dog	Kleshchov (1933)[e]	Pitch												
Pigeon	D. H. Cohen (1963)	Brightness	Positive up	—	—	—	63	—	—	40	—	—	—	—
	Honig (1962)[f]	Color	Positive up	—	—	—	—	—	—	—	—	—	—	69

[a] See Table 4-4.
[b] Distance effect reported (pp. 167, 170), but no data given.
[c] Groups I and II only, and only data for tests with relation same as during training.
[d] Only groups with background constant.
[e] See section entitled "Phylogenetic Comparisons" (subsection entitled "Dogs"), Chapter 5.
[f] See Table 4-5.

TABLE 4-4
THE FLORY (1938) DATA ON THE DISTANCE EFFECT[a]

Group	Sample size	Ratio of stimulus areas	Direction of test[b]	Distance (steps)	Transposition (%)
A	2	2.25 to 1	Upward	1	95
				$2\frac{1}{2}$	60
B	4	2.25 to 1	Downward	1	58
				$2\frac{1}{2}$	32
C	4	3.38 to 1	Upward	1	86
				$1\frac{1}{3}$	74
D	2	3.38 to 1	Downward	1	90
				$1\frac{1}{3}$	70
E	2	3.38 to 1	Downward	$\frac{2}{3}$	80
				1	75
F	2	5.06 to 1	Upward	$\frac{3}{4}$	100
				1	90

[a] The 1939 paper by Flory reported the same study.
[b] All tests were in positive direction.

Okano (1957) reported that rats that did not transpose tended to give position responses. If this finding were typical, it would explain why the frequency of transposition responses seldom drops below the chance level. The evidence from other sources suggests that rats often do revert to position habits when visual discriminations break down (for example, Mowrer, 1960a, pp. 413–414).

T. S. Kendler (1950) tested rats at one through five steps, and found that transposition decreased with increasing distance up to three steps, but increased thereafter. Spence's (1937b) theory predicted a decrease in transposition leading to a predominance of absolute responses, followed by a rise to the chance level, but Kendler's curves never dropped below the chance level and terminated well above the chance level. Riley (1958) noted that the reason for this increase in transposition at great distances "... is not clear, but one possibility is that the voltage changes that were introduced [in Kendler's experiment] changed the wave length of the light. This in turn might influence brightness discrimination" (footnote 1, p. 2).

D. H. Cohen (1963) found that pigeons transposed at one step but not at two steps. (These distances are approximate.) Honig (1962) also found that pigeons transposed only at one step, after successive discrimination training; but he obtained different results in pigeons given simultaneous discrimination training. The "simultaneous" group gave absolute responses at all distances in the positive direction, and avoided the originally negative stimulus at one step in the negative direction. However, they transposed at two, three, and four steps in the negative direction (see Table 4-5). The avoidance of the originally negative stimulus on the one-step test in the negative direction is a kind of "absolute response" (see footnote 8, Chapter 1); on Far Tests in the negative direction, transposition and absolute responses are identical. Therefore, the data of the "simultaneous" group indicate that only absolute responses occurred after simultaneous discrimination training.

Kuenne (1946) obtained more transposition in children on the Near Test than on a five-step Far Test, and Sherman (1966, Experiment 1) obtained more at one step than at three steps. Stevenson *et al.* (1955b), Stevenson and Langford (1957), R. C. Johnson and Zara (1960), and Sherman and Strunk (1964) also obtained the distance effect, each using the Near Test and several Far Tests at up to four steps (see Table 4-6). The gradient relating transposition to distance was monotonic and decreasing in the last four studies. Alberts and Ehrenfreund (1951), testing at one to five steps, obtained the decreasing gradient in three-year-old children, but obtained a high flat gradient in an older group of children, who were 4.5 to 5.5 years old. Stevenson *et al.*, Stevenson and Langford, Johnson and Zara, and Sherman and Strunk tested three- and four-year-olds, perhaps resolving any apparent discrepancy from the findings of Alberts and Ehrenfreund.

TABLE 4-5
HONIG'S DATA ON THE DISTANCE EFFECT IN PIGEONS[a]

Direction of test	Distance (steps)	Successive discrimination group Number of responses[b]			Simultaneous discrimination group Number of responses[b]		
		A	B	A − B	A	B	A − B
Positive down	5	10	15	−5	10	25	−15
	4	5	30	−25	10	25	−15
	3	15	65	−50	10	35	−25
	2	25	170	−145	10	75	−65
	1	185	45	+140	50	100	−50
(Training)	0	125	5	—	145	0	—
Negative up	1	5	0	+5	30	60	−30
	2	0	0	0	70	10	+60
	3	0	0	0	25	20	+5
	4	0	0	0	15	0	+15

[a]*A* indicates transposition response; *B* indicates nontransposition-nonabsolute response on test in negative direction and indicates absolute response on test in positive direction. If *A* − *B* is positive, transposition occurred; if it is negative, transposition did not occur. Free-responding technique was used.

[b]Estimated (to nearest 5) from Honig's Figs. 3 and 4 (1962, pp. 243–244).

TABLE 4-6

THE DISTANCE EFFECT IN HUMAN SUBJECTS: TWO-STIMULUS PROBLEMS[a]

Study	Age range (months)	Training criterion	Area ratio	Percentage transposition					
				1 step	2 steps	3 steps	4 steps	5 steps	6 steps
Alberts and Ehrenfreund (1951)[b]	36–47	9/10	2 to 1	100	78	—	60	57	—
Alberts and Ehrenfreund (1951)[b]	55–55	9/10	2 to 1	—	93	—	85	95	—
R. C. Johnson and Zara (1960)[b,c]	39–60	14/15	2.6 to 1	30	55	52	—	—	—
Kuenne (1946)[b]	30–59	9/10	1.8 to 1	31	—	—	—	59	—
Kuenne (1946)[b]	60–70	9/10	1.8 to 1	100	—	—	—	89	—
Rudel (1958)[b]									
Positive direction	21–45	9/10	1.5 to 1	75	55	53	62	90	90
Negative direction	21–45	9/10	1.5 to 1	76	70	72	85	87	88
Sherman (1966)[b,c] Exp. 1	36–47	7/7	2.6 to 1	90	—	63	—	—	—
Exp. 2	36–47	7/7	2.6 to 1	—	—	83	—	—	—
Exp. 3	30–42	10/10	2.6 to 1	—	—	66	—	—	—
Exp. 4	36–47	7/7	2.6 to 1	—	—	55	—	—	—
Sherman and Strunk (1964)[b,c]	35–55	7/7	2.6 to 1	68	73	40	—	—	—
Stevenson and Iscoe (1955)[d]	Retarded	9/10	2 to 1	67	67	—	64	—	—
Stevenson and Langford (1957)[d]									
Delayed test	36–47	9/10	2 to 1	100	100	80	50	—	—
Immediate test	36–47	9/10	2 to 1	90	70	50	50	—	—
G. R. Thompson (1965)[b]	Retarded	15/15	2 to 1	51	49	—	—	—	—
Zeiler (1966a)[d]	48–71	5/5	1.4 to 1	78	85	61	54	—	—
	48–71	5/5	2 to 1	85	84	90	89	—	—
Unweighted means				82	73	64	58	80	89

[a] M. S. Scott (1966) and Stevenson et al. (1955b) did not report group means, but reported that the distance effect was significant, testing at one to four steps.

[b] Ten test trials.   [c] Control groups only.   [d] One test trial.

111

Zeiler (1966a) obtained the decreasing gradient in four- and five-year-olds, using a 1.4 to 1 ratio of stimulus areas, but he obtained the high flat gradient using a 2 to 1 ratio of areas. Alberts and Ehrenfreund (1951), Stevenson *et al.* (1955b), and Stevenson and Langford (1957) used a 2 to 1 ratio, and R. C. Johnson and Zara (1960) and Sherman and Strunk (1964) used a 1.6 to 1 ratio, suggesting that the decreasing gradient is obtained in younger children regardless of stimulus similarity, and is obtained in older children with similar stimuli but not with distinctive stimuli (see Table 4-6). The effect of stimulus similarity is discussed more fully in Chapter 3 (see section entitled "Stimulus Similarity").

Stevenson and Iscoe (1955) also obtained a flat gradient, testing mentally retarded subjects at one, two, and four steps, and using both first-trial data and the data of the first five test trials. Less transposition was obtained on the Near Test than in 10 other studies using the same ratio of stimulus areas (2 to 1) (Alberts and Ehrenfreund, 1951; I. M. L. Hunter, 1952a, Experiment II; Jackson *et al.*, 1938, Experiment IV; Stevenson *et al.*, 1955a; Stevenson and Langford, 1957, Terrell, 1958; Terrell, 1959; Terrell and Kennedy, 1957; Terrell *et al.*, 1959; Zeiler, 1966a), and less was obtained than in one other study using a similar ratio (Kuenne, 1946, 1.8 to 1 ratio). On the Far Tests, Stevenson and Iscoe obtained about the same amount of transposition as was obtained in two of the three other studies in which two- and four-step tests were given (Alberts and Ehrenfreund, 1951, younger group; Stevenson and Langford, 1957), but they obtained less transposition than was obtained in the third relevant study (Zeiler, 1966a) (see Table 4-6). Although there were procedural differences among the studies, and these comparisons are therefore not strictly valid, it appears that Stevenson and Iscoe obtained a flat gradient because the frequency of transposition on the Near Test was depressed, rather than because the frequency was elevated on the Far Tests. G. R. Thompson (1965) obtained the same kind of effect in mental defectives.

The relatively low level of transposition on the Near Test is, then, the phenomenon to be explained in Stevenson and Iscoe's study; and it may be attributable to the intellectual level of the subjects, who were mentally retarded. In the other studies cited, the subjects were mentally normal. However, M. S. Scott (1966) also tested mentally retarded subjects and obtained the distance effect on the first test trial and on five combined test trials. Furthermore, the evidence on the effect of intellectual level on transposition indicates that the effect is usually weak (see section entitled "Intelligence," Chapter 5).

Stevenson and Iscoe rewarded only transposition responses, and continued testing until the subjects met a learning criterion. The median number of trials through criterion on the transposition test increased significantly with increasing distance, indicating that a distance effect was obtained, but appeared only after the first few test trials.

Testing children at one through six steps in both the positive direction and the negative direction, Rudel (1958) obtained gradients similar to the ones obtained by T. S. Kendler (1950) in rats. Rudel's curves dropped from one through three steps and then rose, and by five or six steps the curves had reached a higher level than at one step. Cutsforth (1933) appears to have obtained a similar effect in chicks (see section entitled "Opportunity for Comparison," Chapter 3).

Table 4-6 includes the percentage transposition in the positive direction obtained by Rudel, and data for comparable groups from other studies. (Rudel's gradient of transposition in the negative direction is discussed later in this chapter, in the section entitled "Effect of Direction of Transposition Test.") The greatest discrepancy in results occurred at five steps, where Rudel obtained considerably more transposition than was obtained in the two other studies testing young children at this distance (Alberts and Ehrenfreund, 1951, younger group; Kuenne, 1946, younger group). The procedures were similar except that in the latter two studies (a) the test was delayed 24 hours and in Rudel's study the test was immediate, and (b) stimulus similarity was less than in Rudel's study (2 to 1 and 1.8 to 1 vs 1.5 to 1 area ratios). The delay could be expected to facilitate transposition at five steps or at worst to have no detrimental effect on transposition (see Stevenson and Langford [1957], who did not, however, test beyond four steps). Therefore the difference in delay cannot account for the difference in results. Greater stimulus similarity could be expected to produce more transposition (see section entitled "Stimulus Similarity," Chapter 3), but it should have produced more at all distances in Rudel's study than in Alberts and Ehrenfreund's and Kuenne's studies, and not more only at five steps. As can be seen in Table 4-6, this effect was not obtained; therefore, there is as yet no satisfactory explanation of the discrepancy in results.

In all of these studies with children, the frequency of transposition never dropped below the chance level. (Okano [1957], however, found that "infants" who did not transpose shifted to absolute responses.)

Razran (1938a) studied the transposition of musical intervals in human adults and obtained a distance effect. As shown in Table 4-7, there was more transposition when the test stimuli were one octave from the training pair than when the difference was two octaves.

Shirai (1954) trained human adults on three two-stimulus size discriminations, and gave a one-trial transposition test after each problem. The test after the first problem was at one step; the test after the second problem was at one step, but with the brightness of the transposition stimulus altered;

TABLE 4–7
TRANSPOSITION OF MUSICAL INTERVALS (RAZRAN, 1938a)

Interval	Test[a]		Mean transposition (%)
	Octave	Key	
Same	One lower	Same	60.4
Same	One lower	Different	50.1
Same	One higher	Same	64.8
Same	One higher	Different	59.8
Same	Two higher	Same	44.8
Same	Two higher	Different	41.5
Different	Same[b]	—	39.3
Different	Same[c]	—	28.8

[a] The description of the test condition is relative to the training condition.
[b] One note in common with training pair.
[c] No note in common with training pair.

and the test after the third problem was at two steps, but with the brightnesses of both stimuli altered. Transposition averaged 50, 30, and 50 per cent on the three respective tests. Comparison of the first and third percentages suggests that there was no distance effect, but the confounding of distance with order of tests and with the treatment of the irrelevant brightness dimension makes it impossible to generalize this result.

INTERMEDIATE-STIMULUS PROBLEMS

Transposition in Animals

Zeiler's (1965a) study with pigeons was the first in which subprimates learned the intermediate-size problem when the stimuli were presented simultaneously. However, earlier studies had obtained simultaneous discrimination learning of intermediate *brightness* in goldfish (Perkins, 1931; Perkins and Wheeler, 1930) and chicks (M. H. Lewis, 1930), and had obtained successive intermediate-brightness learning in pigeons (Hanson, 1961). Intermediate-brightness learning had also been obtained in rats (Wolfle, 1937), and intermediate-size learning had been obtained in doves (C. J. Warden and Rowley, 1929; C. J. Warden and Winslow, 1931), using the "absolute" discrimination method, in which the stimuli are presented two at a time (see Chapter 6).

On transposition tests with all responses nonreinforced, Zeiler (1965a) and Zeiler and Price (1965) found consistent absolute stimulus preferences in pigeons at all distances studied (from one-half to four steps); on tests with all responses reinforced, Zeiler (1965a) obtained absolute responses at first and random responses later in testing.

Testing monkeys in the intermediate-size problem, W. L. Brown *et al.* (1959) found significant transposition at one-half step and consistent absolute responses at one full step. (See, however, the discussion of this study in the section entitled "Multiple-Problem Training," Chapter 3). Spence (1942) found more transposition in chimpanzees at one step than at two steps, but absolute responses predominated on both tests.

Transposition in Children

Table 4-8 summarizes the data on the distance effect on intermediate-stimulus transposition in human subjects. Stevenson and Bitterman (1955) found significantly more transposition in children at one step than at five steps; Price (1960), Reese (1962a; 1964b; 1966), and Reese and Fiero (1964) found significantly more at one step than at three steps; Reese (1961) found significantly more at one step than at two and three steps; and Zeiler and Lang (1966b) and Zeiler and Salten (1966, Experiment 1) found significantly more at one step than at two, three, and four steps. Zeiler and Paalberg (1964b) found that children transposed at one-half step, but not at one step, nor at one and one-half and two steps. There was no difference in transposition at the latter three distances. Reese (1961) found no difference in transposition at two and three steps; Zeiler and Lang (1966b) found no difference at two to four steps; and Whitman (1965) found no difference at three and six steps. (The Whitman study is discussed in detail in the section entitled "Multiple-Problem Training," Chapter 3). Caron (1967) obtained significantly more transposition at six steps than at three steps, failing to replicate Whitman's result; but there was significantly less transposition at these distances than at one step, replicating the trend obtained by Rudel in the two-stimulus problem. Both Rudel and Caron obtained a decrease in transposition at a moderate distance and an increase at an extreme distance.

Baumeister *et al.* (1964) obtained no significant distance effect on transposition in normal and mentally retarded children who were trained on a task requiring choice of the intermediate or largest stimulus (in subgroups). The published report did not give the data for the separate subgroups, but Table 4-9 reports these data (kindly supplied by Dr. Baumeister). Since only transposition responses were rewarded on test trials, the data for combined test trials may be inflated by the effects of relearning. On the first test trial, transposition occurred only in the subgroup with the largest stimulus correct. The average mental age of the children in this subgroup was about eight years, and since eight-year-olds generally know the relevant size concepts (see section entitled "Concept Knowledge," Chapter 5), it may be that most of the transposition responses in this subgroup were mediated by the conceptual response. This would explain the lack of a distance effect in this subgroup. The

TABLE 4-8

THE DISTANCE EFFECT ON INTERMEDIATE-STIMULUS TRANSPOSITION IN HUMAN SUBJECTS

Study	Age level (years)	Dimension	Stimulus ratio	No. of test trials	Percentage transposition							
					$\frac{1}{2}$ step	1 step	$1\frac{1}{2}$ steps	2 steps	3 steps	4 steps	5 steps	6 steps
Baumeister et al. (1964)[a]	Retarded	Size	2 to 1	—	—	—	—	—	—	—	—	—
Caron (1967)	3.8–4.8	Size	1.8 to 1	6	—	80	—	—	42	—	—	63
Price (1960)[b] Exp. I	c	Weight	2 to 1	12	—	38	—	27	27	—	—	—
Reese (1961) Verbal	3.6–5.3	Size	1.6 to 1	6	—	48	—	27	22	—	—	—
Nonverbal	3.6–5.3	Size	1.6 to 1	6	—	57	—	12	8	—	—	—
Reese (1962a) Younger	5.0–6.0	Size	1.3 to 1	6	—	73	—	—	57	—	—	—
Older	6.0–6.8	Size	1.3 to 1	6	—	88	—	—	55	—	—	—
Younger	5.0–6.0	Size	2 to 1	6	—	67	—	—	28	—	—	—
Older	6.0–6.8	Size	2 to 1	6	—	72	—	—	62	—	—	—
Reese (1964b) Middle verbal	4.2–6.0	Size	1.3 to 1	6	—	82	—	—	35	—	—	—
Middle nonverbal	4.0–6.4	Size	1.3 to 1	6	—	70	—	—	17	—	—	—
Old verbal	6.0–7.6	Size	1.3 to 1	6	—	87	—	—	22	—	—	—
Young verbal	3.2–3.9	Size	2 to 1	6	—	50	—	—	25	—	—	—
Young nonverbal	2.9–3.8	Size	2 to 1	6	—	38	—	—	25	—	—	—
Middle verbal	4.2–5.9	Size	2 to 1	6	—	47	—	—	15	—	—	—
Middle nonverbal	3.8–6.6	Size	2 to 1	6	—	57	—	—	18	—	—	—
Old verbal	6.0–7.4	Size	2 to 1	6	—	52	—	—	15	—	—	—
Reese (1966)[b] Younger	2.8–3.6	Size	2 to 1	6	—	31	—	—	25	—	—	—
Older	3.7–5.3	Size	2 to 1	6	—	42	—	—	19	—	—	—
Reese and Fiero (1964)												
Criterion 5/5	6.3–7.9	Size	2 to 1	6	—	72	—	—	15	—	—	—
9/10	6.3–7.9	Size	2 to 1	6	—	53	—	—	13	—	—	—
14/15	6.3–7.9	Size	2 to 1	6	—	62	—	—	20	—	—	—
Stevenson and Bitterman (1955)	4–6	Size	1.4 to 1	6	—	66	—	—	—	—	49	—

Study	Age	Dimension	Ratio	No.								
Stevenson and Weiss (1955)[d]	Adult	Size	Varied	1	—	80	—	53	—	—	—	—
Whitman (1965)[b]	3.2–3.9	Size	1.4 to 1	10	—	—	—	—	42	—	—	46
	4.1–4.9	Size	1.4 to 1	10	—	—	—	—	75	—	—	71
	5.0–5.9	Size	1.4 to 1	10	—	—	—	—	84	—	—	67
Zeiler (1963c; 1963d)	4–5	Size	1.4 to 1	1	—	75	—	14	17	25	17	—
Zeiler (1963c)	4–5	Size	2 to 1	1	83	25	4	—	—	—	—	—
Zeiler (1964b)[e] Simultaneous	Adult	Size	1.4 to 1	1	—	12	—	38	62	81	94	—
Successive	Adult	Size	1.4 to 1	1	—	—	—	0	6	6	12	—
Zeiler (1965b)	5–6	Size	1.4 to 1	10	—	52	—	24	28	—	—	—
Zeiler (1965b)[f]	5–6	Size	1.4 to 1	10	—	89	—	84	86	—	—	—
Zeiler and Gardner (1966a)	5–7	Size	1.2 to 1	4	—	86	—	67	66	—	—	—
		Size	1.4 to 1	4	—	61	—	50	53	—	—	—
		Size	1.7 to 1	4	—	61	—	36	39	—	—	—
Zeiler and Gardner (1966b)	7–8	Size	1.4 to 1	1	84	69	—	31	25	19	25	—
	7–8	Size	2 to 1	1	—	31	6	—	—	—	—	—
Zeiler and Lang (1966a)	Adult	Size	1.4 to 1	1	—	40	—	—	—	85	—	—
Zeiler and Lang (1966b) Immediate	4–5	Size	1.4 to 1	1	—	75	—	25	12	38	—	—
Delayed	4–5	Size	1.4 to 1	1	—	50	—	38	0	25	—	—
Immediate	4–5	Size	2 to 1	1	—	38	—	0	12	12	—	—
Delayed	4–5	Size	2 to 1	1	—	88	—	0	12	12	—	—
Zeiler and Paalberg (1964a)[b]	Adult	Size	2 to 1	1	—	—	56	44	—	—	—	—
Zeiler and Paalberg (1964b)[b]	3.9–5.9	Size	2 to 1	1	83	25	17	17	—	—	—	—
Zeiler and Salten (1966) Exp. 1	5–7	Size	1.4 to 1	8	—	66	—	49	40	44	—	—
Exp. 1	5–7	Size	2 to 1	8	89	50	—	50	43	—	—	—

[a] See Table 4-9 for data.
[b] Only groups with standard training.
[c] Kindergarten and first grade.
[d] Four-stimulus problems with extreme or intermediate stimulus correct (in subgroups). Separate data not reported.
[e] Five-stimulus problems with middle-sized correct.
[f] Three-stimulus problems with extreme stimulus correct.

117

TABLE 4-9
PERCENTAGE TRANSPOSITION IN THE STUDY
BY BAUMEISTER *ET AL.*

IQ	S^{+a}	Trial 1		6 trials	
		Near	Far	Near	Far
Normal	L	80	80	87	88
Retarded	L	60	50	88	83
Normal	M	20	20	67	68
Retarded	M	30	30	63	53

[a]L indicates largest stimulus, and M indicates middle-sized stimulus.

low level of transposition in the other subgroup on both tests is consistent with part of the data of Reese and Fiero (1964) for a group comparable in age to the normal subjects tested by Baumeister *et al.*; but Reese and Fiero obtained this effect when the training criterion was 14 correct of 15 consecutive responses, and not when it was five consecutive correct responses. Baumeister *et al.* used the latter criterion. The cause of the low level of Near Test transposition of intermediate size in the study by Baumeister *et al*, is not apparent, since both they and Reese and Fiero used a 2 to 1 ratio of stimulus areas, and used highly similar procedures.

Absolute Responses in Children

Stevenson and Bitterman (1955), Price (1960), Reese (1962a), and Whitman (1965) rewarded only transposition responses, and found that the transposition response was generally at least as strong as the absolute response over combined trials on the Far Test. Reese (1961; 1964b) and Reese and Fiero (1964) rewarded all test-trial responses, and found a predominance of transposition responses only on the Near Test. There was a predominance of absolute responses on the Far Test except in three-year-olds, who gave the nontransposition-nonabsolute response slightly more often than the absolute response (Reese, 1964b). Reese (1966) obtained the same effects in groups trained and tested under "standard" conditions. (The complete experiment is discussed in the section entitled "Concept Knowledge," Chapter 5.) In older preschoolers, the transposition response predominated on the Near Test, and the absolute response predominated on the Far Test; but in younger preschoolers, the absolute response predominated on the Near Test, and the nontransposition-nonabsolute response predominated on the Far Test. The relevant findings of my studies are summarized in Table 4-10.

Zeiler ran a series of studies in which each subject was given a single

TABLE 4-10
PREDOMINANT RESPONSE ON NEAR AND FAR TESTS
All test-trial responses rewarded (Reese studies)[a]

CA range (mo.)	Study	Near Test	Far Test
34–43	Reese (1966)	A	N
35–47	Reese (1964b)	A	N
43–64	Reese (1961)	T	A
44–63	Reese (1966)	T	A
50–72	Reese (1964b)	T	A
72–91	Reese (1964b)	T	A
76–95	Reese and Fiero (1964)	T	A

[a]T indicates transposition response; A indicates absolute response; N indicates non-transposition-nonabsolute response. Three-step Far Test.

one-trial test. Using stimuli with a 1.4 to 1 ratio of areas, and testing at one through five steps, he obtained the same distance effects as Reese (1961; 1964b) and Reese and Fiero (1964) (Zeiler, 1963d; also given in the 1963c report). Transposition responses were predominant on the Near Test, and absolute responses were predominant on the Far Tests. Using a 2 to 1 ratio of stimulus areas, and testing at half-step intervals, Zeiler (1963c) obtained a predominance of transposition responses only at one half step. Absolute responses predominated at greater distances (except when the area ratio in the test set was different from the area ratio in the training set). The results of these two studies by Zeiler suggest that the distance effect on absolute responses is related to stimulus similarity. Zeiler and Gardner (1966b) reported data confirming the relation. The first-trial data reported by Reese (1965c) are also in line with Zeiler's findings. On the Near Test, transposition responses clearly predominated when a 1.3 to 1 ratio was used, but the absolute response was generally predominant when 1.6 to 1 and 2 to 1 ratios were used. The data of Zeiler and Lang (1966b) also confirm Zeiler's findings. With a 1.4 to 1 ratio, transposition responses predominated at one step and absolute responses predominated at two, three, and four steps; and with a 2 to 1 ratio, absolute responses predominated on all four tests (except that transposition responses also predominated on the Near Test with the 2 to 1 ratio when the test was delayed 24 hours).

Sato and Nishijima (1955) apparently obtained transposition in children at one-half step (Experiments 2 and 2a) and absolute responses at one step (Experiments 1 and 1a). Kuenne (1948) also obtained a predominance of absolute responses (60 per cent) at one step in children. The available reports did not give the stimulus ratio.

Nontransposition-Nonabsolute Responses in Children

Zeiler (1963d) obtained an increase in the nontransposition-non-absolute response with increasing distance, using highly similar stimuli (1.4 to 1 area ratio), but he (1963c) found no such distance effect using highly distinctive stimuli (2 to 1 ratio). These trends, based on data for a single test trial, were also apparent in the first-trial data reported by Reese (1965c). The distance effect on the nontransposition-nonabsolute response was obtained with highly similar and moderately similar stimuli (1.3 to 1 and 1.6 to 1 ratios); but with more distinctive stimuli (2 to 1 ratio), the distance effect was obtained in only one of four groups. Zeiler and Lang (1966b) failed to confirm the finding, but only 12 per cent of the responses were nontransposition-nonabsolute responses.[3]

The data on the nontransposition-nonabsolute response over multiple test trials are more complex. Reese (1961; 1962a; 1964b; 1966) obtained the increase in this response with increasing distance in young children (about three to five years old), using distinctive and moderately similar stimuli (2 to 1 and 1.6 to 1 ratios), but obtained the opposite effect in older children (six to seven years old). With highly similar stimuli (1.3 to 1 ratio), Reese (1964b) obtained no effect in young children who lacked the concept of middle-sizedness, and obtained the opposite distance effect in ones who knew the concept and in older children. Reese (1962a) obtained the increase in six-year-olds, but obtained no effect in five-year-olds. (The relevant data are summarized in Table 4-11.)

Using first-trial data, Zeiler (1963d) found that the nontransposition-nonabsolute response became more frequent than the transposition response, although it remained much less frequent than the absolute response. Reese (1965c) obtained the same finding in three of the four groups showing the distance effect (the exception was with a 1.3 to 1 ratio). Using the data of all test trials, Reese obtained this finding in six of the ten groups showing the distance effect on this kind of response (see Table 4-11). These data suggest that the increase in the nontransposition-nonabsolute response with increasing distance is not entirely attributable to an increase in the number of subjects responding at random. If it reflected only random responding, then the frequency of this kind of response would never be greater than the frequency of transposition responses. It appears, therefore, that with increasing distance, most subjects shift to an absolute basis of responding, but some shift to another systematic basis (other than position).

[3]Zeiler and Gardner (1966b) found no relation between stimulus similarity and this distance effect, but only 3 of 176 subjects gave the nontransposition-nonabsolute response at all. Zeiler (1965b) obtained *no* responses of this kind in 118 children, using a small ratio of stimulus areas; Caron (1967) obtained almost none in 288 children.

TABLE 4-11

THE DISTANCE EFFECT ON NONTRANSPOSITION-NONABSOLUTE RESPONSES

Summary of Reese studies[a]

Study	Age of subjects (years)	Area ratio of stimuli	Group	Percentage responses		Distance effect	Transposition on Far Test
				Near	Far[b]		
Reese (1964b)	3	2 to 1	C[c]	10.0	16.7	Yes	25.0
	3	2 to 1	NC[c]	33:3	43:3	Yes	25.0
Reese (1966)[d]	3	2 to 1	—	26.1	42.9	Yes	25.0
	4	2 to 1	—	20.2	29.8	Yes	19.0
Reese (1964b)	4 and 5	2 to 1	C	13.3	16.7	Yes	15.0
	4 and 5	2 to 1	NC	23.3	25.0	Yes	18.3
Reese (1962a)	5	2 to 1		13.3	20.0	Yes	28.3
	6	2 to 1	—	11.7	8.3	Opposite	61.7
Reese (1964b)	6	2 to 1	C	16.7	11.7	Opposite	15.0
Reese and Fiero (1964)	6 and 7	2 to 1	C	8.1	5.0	Opposite	16.4
Reese (1961)	4	1.6 to 1	C	18.3	21.7	Yes	21.7
	4	1.6 to 1	NC	15.0	30.0	Yes	8.3
Reese (1964b)	4 and 5	1.3 to 1	C	8.3	5.0	Opposite	35.0
	4 and 5	1.3 to 1	NC	13.3	13.3	No	16.7
Reese (1962a)	5	1.3 to 1	—	18.3	18.3	No	56.7
	6	1.3 to 1	—	6.7	10.0	Yes	55.0
Reese (1964b)	6 and 7	1.3 to 1	C	3.3	0.0	Opposite	21.7

[a]There were six trials on each test.
[b]Three-step test.
[c]C indicates possessed concept of middle-sizedness; NC indicates lacked this concept.
[d]Only groups given standard training.

Transposition in Human Adults

Zeiler (1964b) trained human adults on a five-stimulus intermediate-size problem, with either simultaneous or successive stimulus presentations, and tested for transposition at from one-half step to five steps. On the first test trial, almost all of the subjects trained with the successive method gave absolute responses at all distances. The subjects trained with simultaneous stimulus presentations, however, transposed at one-half step, but exhibited a reversed distance effect on the tests from one step to five steps. Absolute responses predominated at one step but declined in frequency with increasing distance, and transposition responses increased in frequency with increasing distance. The absolute response became less frequent than transposition responses between two and three steps. Posttest questioning indicated that only 10 of the 128 subjects in the successive group were aware that the intermediate stimulus had been the positive training stimulus, but all of the subjects in the simultaneous group were aware of this relation. Zeiler's conclusion was that absolute learning occurred in the successive group, and that both absolute and relational learning occurred in the simultaneous group. He was particularly impressed by finding that virtually all of the subjects in the latter group shifted responses after a single nonreinforcement. The response of these subjects on the first test trial was not rewarded; on the second test trial, about 96 per cent of the group exhibited a changed basis of responding, shifting either from absolute on Trial 1 to relative on Trial 2 or from relative to absolute.

Zeiler and Lang (1966a) confirmed the reversed distance effect in human adults, and found that the trend was the same with the three-stimulus intermediate-size problem as with the five-stimulus intermediate-size problem, and was the same when a noncorrectional procedure was used as when a correctional procedure was used. (Zeiler [1964b] used a correctional procedure.) Transposition averaged 40 per cent at one step, and 85 per cent at four steps.

Zeiler and Paalberg (1964a) obtained contradictory evidence. Human adults trained on the three-stimulus intermediate-size problem averaged 56 per cent transposition at one-and-one-half steps and 44 per cent transposition at two steps.

Using a four-stimulus problem with an extreme or an intermediate stimulus correct (in subgroups), Stevenson and Weiss (1955) found more transposition in college students at one step than at two steps. However, Zeiler (1965b) and Zeiler and Gardner (1966a), using a three-stimulus problem with the middle-sized stimulus or an extreme stimulus correct, obtained this effect only when the middle-sized stimulus was correct. When an extreme stimulus was correct, the subjects transposed at a high level at all distances studied (one, two, and three steps).

CONCLUSION

In two-stimulus problems, performance drops from training to test, even when a Near Test is given. Transposition decreases with increasing distance, except that it apparently increases again at extreme distances. How much it increases is not well established. Absolute responses do not predominate at any distance, except under unusual testing conditions.

In intermediate-stimulus problems the performance level on the Near Test is lower than the performance level at the end of training. Transposition does not occur beyond one step in children, and does not occur beyond one-half step in infrahuman subjects, except under unusual testing conditions and as a result of mediation. Absolute responses tend to predominate when transposition does not occur. When relatively similar stimuli are used, there is a distance effect on the nontransposition-nonabsolute response on the first test trial. The response becomes more frequent than the transposition response on the first trial of tests at extreme distances, but it remains less frequent than the absolute response at all distances. This distance effect is not obtained with highly distinctive stimuli, and is probably not obtained over repeated test trials.

Effect of Direction of Transposition Test

A "positive" transposition test includes stimuli that are shifted on the stimulus continuum in the direction of the positive training stimulus, and a "negative" transposition test includes stimuli that are shifted in the direction of the negative training stimulus. The shift is "upward" if the test stimuli are more intense than the training stimuli, and it is "downward" if the test stimuli are less intense than the training stimuli. On a positive transposition test, the transposition response and the absolute response conflict; but on a negative transposition test, these responses are identical. Therefore, there should be more negative transposition than positive transposition. A greater frequency of negative transposition than positive transposition could also be explained by assuming a tendency to avoid novel stimuli, but there is good evidence that children (and experimentally naive monkeys) tend to *approach* novel stimuli (Mendel, 1965; Reese, 1963b; Reese, 1964a; but see Greene, 1964, for an opposing interpretation).

No published theory of transposition predicted any effect of the upward–downward direction, but if Hull's (1949; 1952, p. 7) "stimulus intensity dynamism" were added to an absolute theory of transposition, an effect could be predicted. The addition of the stimulus intensity dynamism to Spence's (1942) absolute theory would generate a predicted interaction between the upward–downward and positive–negative directions. The exact nature of the interaction would depend on the magnitudes of the stimuli used.

Two-stimulus problems can provide data on the effect of the positive–negative direction, and three-stimulus problems can provide data if the correct stimulus is one of the extremes. If the intermediate stimulus were correct, the problem would be irrelevant because the transposition test would necessarily be in the negative direction, since the shift would have to be in the direction of one or the other negative stimulus. The effect of the upward–downward direction can be assessed in all of these problems.

TABLE 4-12
Effects of Direction of Test on Transposition

Study	Dimension	Subjects	Steps	Percentage transposition			
				Negative down	Positive down	Negative up	Positive up
Köhler (1918)	Brightness	Chicks	1	61	67	71	72
Ehrenfreund (1952)	Brightness	Rats	$\frac{1}{3}$	—	90	—	83
			$\frac{2}{3}$	—	80	—	87
			1	—	44	—	26
			$1\frac{1}{3}$	—	58	—	42
Hebb (1938)	Brightness	Rats	1	—	82	—	81
T. S. Kendler (1950)	Brightness	Rats	1	—	67	—	80
			2	—	33	—	70
			3	—	67	—	60
			4	—	50	—	80
S. J. Lachman (1956)	Brightness	Rats	1	92	90	80	88
Maltzman (1949, Exp. 1)	Brightness	Rats	1	—	22	—	42
Kinnaman (1902)	Brightness	Monkeys	?	73	—	—	69
Köhler (1918)	Brightness	Chimpanzee	1	95	—	—	87
H. E. Jones and Dunn (1932)	Brightness	Children	1	50	55	42	38
Köhler (1918)	Brightness	Child	1	100	—	—	100
Klüver (1933)	Weight	Monkeys	1	87[a]	83[a]	98[a]	74[a]
Bingham (1922)	Size	Chicks	1	b	—	—	b
Flory (1938) 2.2 to 1	Size	Rats	1	—	58	—	95
			$2\frac{1}{2}$	—	32	—	60
3.4 to 1			1	—	82	—	86
			$1\frac{1}{3}$	—	70	—	74
Gulliksen (1932a)	Size	Rats	1	65	62	78	83
Maier (1939)	Size	Rats	$\frac{1}{3}$	92	98	—	—
			$\frac{2}{3}$	60	80	—	—

Source	Subjects	Dimension						
Klüver (1933)	Monkeys	Size	1	52	56	—		—	—
Spence (1937b)	Chimpanzees	Size	1½	51	49	—		—	—
Corbascio (1964)	Children	Size	1	95	56	87	96	57
			3	93	54	100	98	91
H. E. Jones and Dunn (1932)	Children	Size	1	63	57	58		48
I. M. L. Hunter (1952a) Exp. 1	Children	Size	1	—	88	—		81
Exp. 2	Children	Size	1	100	70	80		100
Ross et al. (1965)[c]	Children	Size	1	84	66	74		76
Rudel (1958)	Children	Size	1	—	—	76		75
			2	—	—	70		55
			3	—	—	72		53
			4	—	—	85		62
			5	—	—	87		90
			6	—	—	88		90
Stevenson and Iscoe (1954)	Children	Size	1	80	59	86		64
Zeiler (1965b)[d]	Children	Size	1	88	88	91		91
			2	82	82	85		85
			3	86	86	86		86
McKee and Riley (1962)	Children	Loudness	1	72	86	89		95
Riley and McKee (1963)	Children	Loudness	1	91	95	95		92
Shirai (1963) Exp. 1	Children	Size, brightness and shape	1	56	45	62		40

[a] See Table 4–13.
[b] Means not given, but more transposition in positive upward direction than in negative downward direction reported.
[c] These data were omitted from the published report, but were sent to me by Dr. Ross (personal communication, 1965).
[d] Separate data not reported for positive–negative direction, but Zeiler reported that it had "virtually" no effect.

TABLE 4–13
WEIGHT TRANSPOSITION (KLÜVER, 1933)

Subjects	Sample size	Direction	Transposition (%)
Java monkeys	3	Positive up	74.2
Java monkeys	3	Negative down	85.0
Spider monkeys	2	Positive down	87.7
Spider monkey	1	Negative up	96.7
Cebus monkey	1	Negative down	94.4
Lemur	1	Positive down	70.0
Lemur	1	Negative up	100.0

TABLE 4–14
EFFECT OF DIRECTION OF TEST IN INTERMEDIATE-STIMULUS PROBLEMS

				Transposition (%)		
Study	Dimension	Subjects	Steps	Down-ward	Up-ward	Difference (up – down)
Ebel and Werboff (1966)	Size	Dogs	1	31	24	–
W. L. Brown et al. (1959)	Size	Monkeys	$\frac{1}{2}$	31	84	+
Gentry et al. (1959)	Size	Monkeys	$\frac{1}{2}$	74	74	0
Gonzalez et al. (1954)	Size	Chimpanzees	$\frac{1}{2}$	79	62	–
Spence (1942)	Size	Chimpanzees	1	5	31	+
Zeiler (1965b)	Size	Children	1	64	41	–
			2	28	21	–
			3	12	43	+
Zeiler and Gardner (1966b)	Size	Children	$\frac{1}{2}$	12	12	0
			1	31	31	0
			$1\frac{1}{2}$	94	75	–
Wohlwill (1960a) Exp. II	Physical numerosity	Children	1	50	37	–
Price (1960) (control group only)	Weight	Children	1	39	44	+
			3	30	24	–

The available data are presented in Tables 4-12, 4-13, and 4-14.[4] Tables 4-15 and 4-16 summarize the data of Tables 4-12 and 4-13. In general, it appears that in intermediate-stimulus problems (Table 4-14), there is more trans-

[4] Upward and downward tests were used in 12 other studies in which separate data were not reported (Adams, 1937; Balla and Zigler, 1964; Helson, 1927; Kuenne, 1948; Marsh and Sherman, 1966; Martin and Blum, 1961; Riley et al., 1964; Stevenson and Bitterman, 1955; Stevenson and Weiss, 1955; Stevenson et al., 1955a; Taylor, 1932a; Zeiler and Price, 1965). Okano (1957) obtained more transposition in "infants and rats" trained with the larger stimulus correct than with the smaller correct, but the available report does not indicate what the directions of the tests were.

TABLE 4-15

SUMMARY OF TABLES 4–12 AND 4–13: ONE-STEP TESTS ONLY[a]

Difference in transposition	Negative up Negative down	Positive up Positive down	Negative up Positive up	Negative down Positive down	Negative up Positive down	Negative down Positive up
− 22.5 to − 17.6	7.1	4.5	6.7			11.8
− 17.5 to − 12.6		4.5		6.7	7.1	
− 12.5 to − 7.6	14.3	9.1	6.7		7.1	5.9
− 7.5 to − 2.6	21.4	18.2	20.0	26.7		5.9
− 2.5 to 2.4		9.1	26.7	13.3	14.3	23.5
2.5 to 7.4	28.6	18.2	13.3	20.0	21.4	11.8
7.5 to 2.4	14.3	9.1	6.7	6.7	14.3	23.5
12.5 to 17.4	14.3	4.5			21.4	11.8
17.5 to 22.4		9.1	13.3	13.3		
22.5 to 27.4			6.7		7.1	
27.5 to 32.4		4.5		6.7		
32.5 to 37.4		9.1			7.1	
37.5 to 42.4				6.7		5.9
No. of comparisons	14	22	15	15	14	17

[a]Table gives relative frequency in each interval (top direction minus bottom direction). The midpoint of the middle interval is zero.

position downward than upward. In other problems on the Near Test (Table 4-15), there is more transposition upward than downward, especially when both tests are in the positive direction, but also when both are in the negative direction. When the tests are both in the upward direction, there is no consistent difference between negative and positive transposition; but when both are in the downward direction, there is more negative transposition than positive transposition. There is more negative transposition upward than positive transposition downward, and more negative transposition downward than positive transposition upward. On tests at other distances (Table 4-16), the trends are essentially the same as on the Near Test, except when negative and positive transposition are compared with the upward–downward direction controlled. When both tests are upward, there is more negative transposition than positive transposition; but when both tests are downward, the trend is reversed.

Both kinds of directionality affect two-stimulus transposition, but the effect of the positive–negative direction is greater than the effect of the upward–downward direction. Honig (1962) gave pigeons tests in the positive–downward and negative–upward directions, using a free-responding technique. After successive discrimination training, there

TABLE 4–16

Summary of Tables 4–12 and 4–13: Other Tests[a]

Difference in transposition	Negative up Negative down	Positive up Positive down	Negative up Positive up	Negative down Positive down	Negative up Positive down	Negative down Positive up
− 22.5 to − 17.6				20.0		
− 17.5 to − 12.6		8.3				
− 12.5 to − 7.6						
− 7.5 to − 2.6		16.7	14.3	20.0	–	33.3
−2.5 to 2.4	50	8.3	42.8	60.0	50	33.3
2.5 to 7.4	50	25.0			50	33.3
7.5 to 12.4		8.3				
12.5 to 17.4			14.3			
17.5 to 22.4			14.3			
22.5 to 27.4			14.3			
27.5 to 32.4		16.7				
32.5 to 37.4		8.3				
37.5 to 42.4		8.3				
No. of comparisons	2	12	7	5	2	3

[a] See footnote, Table 4–15.

were 80 per cent transposition responses at one step in the positive–downward direction—185 out of 230 responses—and there were 100 per cent transposition responses—out of a total of 5 responses—in the negative–upward direction (see Table 4-5). I find it impossible to decide which test elicited the most transposition, since the percentage measure disagrees with the raw-frequency measure. Transposition responses did not predominate at any of the other distances studied. After simultaneous discrimination training, transposition responses were not predominant at any distance in the positive–downward direction, and not at one step in the negative–upward direction. However, on Far Tests in the negative–upward direction, transposition responses were predominant, indicating that after simultaneous discrimination training there was more negative transposition upward than positive transposition downward on the Far Tests.

According to secondary sources, more negative than positive transposition was also obtained by Bierens De Haan (1928) in bees and monkeys, by Takagi (1935a; 1935b; 1937) in the tomtit, and by Sato (1936) in children, although Motoyoshi (1948) obtained the opposite effect in children. The upward–downward directionality of the tests was not specified in my sources.

Rudel (1958) obtained essentially no difference between positive and negative transposition at one, five, and six steps; but at two, three, and four steps, there was much more transposition in the negative direction than in the positive direction (see Table 4-12). M. S. Scott (1966) obtained a similar result in mentally retarded subjects. There was only very little more negative transposition than positive transposition at one step, but at four steps there was considerably more negative transposition than positive transposition. (Scott did not report separate means, and therefore her study is not included in Table 4-12.) Zeiler (1965b) obtained no difference at one, two, and three steps; but he used a three-stimulus problem with an extreme stimulus correct, and Rudel and Scott used two-stimulus problems.

There is some evidence that distance also influences the effect of the upward–downward direction of the shift, but the data are too contradictory to be conclusive (see Table 4-17). Delay between the end of training and the beginning of testing seems to enhance transposition upward more than transposition downward (Spence, 1942).

Two other studies, both testing children, seem to be relevant (Jackson and Eckhardt, 1940; Rudel, 1959). In both studies, a single stimulus was presented, with reward, during the training phase; several stimuli were presented during a testing phase. In both studies, the predominant response in the testing phase was to the stimulus one or two steps above the absolute stimulus. This finding suggests that the absolute response can occur even without comparison among stimuli during training, but that it is shifted upward from the actual absolute stimulus, presumably by the effect of the stimulus intensity dynamism. If absolute responses did not occur, and only the stimulus intensity dynamism determined responses, as Rudel suggested, then the largest stimuli (three to five steps above the absolute stimulus) should be chosen predominantly. Rudel found that the largest stimuli were chosen no more often than the smallest, contradicting the suggestion; but Jackson and Eckhardt found more responses to the largest stimulus than to the smallest stimulus, although there were not as many responses to the largest stimulus as to the absolute stimulus nor as many as to the stimulus one step above the absolute stimulus. (Spence's [1941] data yielded no evidence for the operation of the stimulus intensity dynamism; the preferred stimulus before training was in the middle of the range of stimuli, and after training with the middle stimulus nonreinforced and the others reinforced, the smallest stimulus was preferred. Only one subject—a chimpanzee—was tested, however, and it was experimentally sophisticated. Previously acquired preferences could have obscured the effect of the stimulus intensity dynamism.)

Other data obtained by Jackson and Eckhardt also conform with expectations based on absolute theory. The design and data are summarized in Table 4-18. Increasing the number of large negative stimuli in the

TABLE 4-17

Effect of Distance on Upward and Downward Transposition

Percentage transposition upward minus percentage transposition downward

Study	Dimension	Subjects	Problem	Difference										
				$\frac{1}{3}$ step	$\frac{1}{2}$ step	$\frac{2}{3}$ step	1 step	$1\frac{1}{3}$ steps	$1\frac{1}{2}$ steps	$1\frac{2}{3}$ steps	2 steps	$2\frac{1}{2}$ steps	3 steps	4 steps
Ehrenfreund (1952)	Brightness	Rats	Two stimulus	−7		+7	−18							
T. S. Kendler (1950)	Brightness	Rats	Two stimulus				+13			−16	+37		−7	+30
Flory (1938)	Size	Rats	Two stimulus				+19	+4				+28		
Spence (1937b)	Size	Chimpanzees	Two stimulus				+23				+38			
Corbascio (1964)	Size	Children	Two stimulus				−4						+10	
M. S. Scott (1966)	Size	Retardates	Two stimulus				+4							+24
Zeiler (1966a)	Size	Children	Intermediate stimulus				−23				−8		+21	
Zeiler and Gardner (1966b)	Size	Children	Intermediate stimulus		0		0							
Price (1960)	Weight	Children	Intermediate stimulus				+5		−19					
Zeiler (1966a)	Size	Children	Other				+4				+4		−6	+2

TABLE 4–18

DESIGN AND DATA OF THE JACKSON AND ECKHARDT (1940) STUDY[a]

| | | Stimulus chosen on test (%) | | |
| | | --- | --- | --- |
Group	Training condition	1–3	4–6	7–9
I	No. 5 alone, rewarded	4	62	34
II	No. 5 rewarded, No. 7 nonrewarded	28	52	20
III	No. 5 rewarded, Nos. 7 and 9 nonrewarded	50	33	17

[a] Stimulus No. 1 was the smallest, and No. 9 was the largest.

training phase should increase the amount of generalization of the inhibitory potentials to the other stimuli; and with the design used, the smallest stimuli in the test phase should therefore have the greatest net response-evocation potentials, and should elicit the greatest number of responses. Concomitantly, the numbers of responses to the largest stimuli should be depressed. This pattern of results was obtained, as Table 4-18 shows. It might also be noted that the difference between Groups II and III in the table is inconsistent with relational theory, since the "small" training stimulus was correct for both groups, but the groups differed in their performance on test trials. The relational response in both groups would be to the smallest stimuli, but these stimuli were preferred only in Group III.

The grouping of the stimuli in Table 4-18 obscures another finding: Stimulus 5, the positive absolute stimulus, was chosen more frequently in Group II than any other stimulus, suggesting that absolute responses predominated in Group II. (In Group III, Stimulus 4 was chosen most frequently.) Rudel included a group like Jackson and Eckhardt's Group II, and obtained the same pattern of results; the absolute response predominated, and there were more responses to the smallest test stimuli than to the largest ones.

The direction of the transposition test was varied in two studies of pitch discrimination in human subjects (McKee and Riley, 1962; Riley and McKee, 1963). There should be more negative transposition of pitch than positive transposition, for the reasons already discussed; but since pitch is not an intensity dimension, there is no stimulus intensity dynamism, and there should be no effect of the upward–downward direction. In line with these expectations, negative transposition averaged 80 per cent and positive transposition averaged only 54 per cent, but transposition upward and downward both averaged about 67 per cent. However, there may have been a weak interaction between the two kinds of direction, since on positive tests there was more transposition upward (58 per cent) than downward (50 per cent), and on negative tests there was more transposition downward (84 per cent) than upward (76 per cent). Razran (1938a) also obtained a weak effect of the upward–downward direction, in a study in which the salivary response of human adults was conditioned to a musical interval. Generalization to an interval one octave higher than the conditioned interval was somewhat greater than generalization to an interval one octave lower (62 per cent generalized responses versus 55 per cent). It may be, therefore, that stimulus intensity is not the variable determining the effect of the upward–downward direction; but alternatively, it may be that pitch is actually some kind of intensity dimension, in human subjects at least.

Multiple Tests

Klüver (1933) gave monkeys a variety of transposition tests, with changes in distance, form, and other stimulus properties, and obtained more transposition in the later tests than in the early ones. The same effect was obtained in chimpanzees in two studies by Spence (1937b; 1942) and in one by Gonzalez et al. (1954). In all four studies, the tests were interspersed among training trials, and all test responses were rewarded. Using a similar procedure with rats, Gayton (1927) obtained evidence suggesting that there may have been some increase in transposition over multiple tests.

Bingham (1922) found more transposition on the second test given to chicks than on the first test, apparently without further training between the two tests. However, the first test was negative and downward and the second was positive and upward, which makes the interpretation of the finding ambiguous. Only two studies investigated the effects of the directions of testing on transposition in chicks; but, as indicated in Table 4-12, these studies suggest that chicks transpose more in the positive direction than in the negative direction, and transpose more upward than downward. Both trends would enhance transposition on the second test in Bingham's study.

Köhler (1918) found less transposition in chicks on the second test than on the first test, contrary to Bingham's finding; but in Köhler's experiment, the first test was positive and the second was negative, reversing the order used by Bingham. The greater frequency of positive transposition in chicks than negative transposition would explain the discrepancy between the order effects obtained by Bingham and Köhler; but unfortunately, these are the only two studies in which chicks were given positive and negative tests, and therefore the validity of this argument remains to be established. (Kroh [1927] also gave multiple tests to chickens, but the available report did not give separate data for the different tests.) D. H. Cohen (1963) found that transposition in pigeons dropped significantly over four tests, even though 90 retraining trials were given before each test.

Gulliksen (1932a) and Heyman (1951) found very little effect of order of testing in rats, with retraining between tests. However, Flory (1938) obtained fairly large order effects in rats, which transposed more on the second test especially when it was a Far Test. Helson (1927) gave rats a one-step transposition test and then a series of tests with "all manner of combinations" of the stimuli. Performance on the latter series was better than on the one-step test, perhaps indicating an effect of multiple testing.

Bagshaw and Pribram (1965) found that normal monkeys transposed about 22 per cent more on the second administration of a one and one-half step test, given after retraining, than on the first administration of the test. (However, amygdalectomized monkeys transposed about 31 per cent *less* on the second test, and monkeys with inferotemporal lesions transposed about 6 per cent less on the second test. The operations were performed between the tests.)

In the study by Perkins and Wheeler (1930) on transposition in goldfish, 81 per cent of the subjects showed an increase in transposition with multiple testing, except that many of the subjects showed a drop after many days of tests.

Kuenne's (1946) data showed little effect of multiple testing in children, but there was slightly more transposition on both the Near Test and the Far Test given first than given second. Caron (1967) obtained this effect on the Near Test, but obtained no difference on Far Tests. M. S. Scott (1966) reported that the order of testing had no statistically significant effect on transposition, but she did not report the means. Stevenson and Iscoe (1954) used a three-stimulus problem with the largest or smallest stimulus correct, and found more transposition on the second test than on the first test. However, the second test was two steps from the first test and one step from the original discriminanda; the first test was in the positive direction and the second was in the negative direction; and the first "test" was learned to a criterion before the second test was given. The confounding of these variables makes the finding ambiguous (see sections entitled "Effect of Direction of Transposition Test" and "Distance" [this Chapter] and "Multiple-Problem Training" [Chapter 3]). I. M. L. Hunter (1952a, Experiment II) obtained somewhat more transposition on the second test than on the first test, but order was confounded with overtraining. Zeiler and Salten (1966, Experiment 1) obtained no effect of repeated tests with interspersed retraining trials.

In two other studies of transposition in children, with all test-trial responses rewarded, there was more transposition on the Near Test given second than given first, but there was slightly less transposition on the Far Test (three steps) given second than given first (Reese, 1964b[5]; Reese and Fiero, 1964[5]). This order effect seemed to be greater when the stimuli

[5]The relevant data were omitted from the reports cited.

used were distinctive (2 to 1 area ratio) than when they were similar (1.3 to 1 ratio) (Reese, 1964b[5]). In line with this conclusion, Zeiler (1965b) and Whitman (1965) found no order effect with similar stimuli (1.4 to 1 ratio), even though they retrained the subjects on the original discrimination between tests; and Reese (1961[5]) found no order effect with moderately similar stimuli (1.6 to 1 ratio).

In two studies in which only transposition responses were rewarded there was less transposition on the test given second than on the test given first, regardless of distance (Reese, 1962a; Stevenson and Bitterman, 1955).

In a study of brightness discrimination thresholds in the dancing mouse, Yerkes (1907, pp. 126–128) found that the difference thresholds became smaller as testing continued, suggesting that the discriminative capacity of the animal improved over the series of tests. This finding, considered with the data on the effect of multiple testing on transposition, suggests that presenting a series of discriminations increases the likelihood that the subject will respond to the relative characteristics of the stimuli. Multiple-problem training apparently has an effect similar to but stronger than this effect of multiple testing.

CHAPTER 5

Subject Variables

"Subject variables" include the variables that are predicated about the organism. The ones included here are grouped together for convenience of presentation, but it might be noted that it has been more convenient to deal with others elsewhere. For example, individual differences are considered in Chapter 2, "comparison" behavior is considered in Chapter 3, and "selective attention" is considered in Chapter 11.

Effect of Noticing Change in Stimuli from Training to Test

Washburn (1926, p. 242) suggested that subjects transpose because they fail to notice the change in stimuli from the training phase to the test phase. Köhler (1918), Perkins and Wheeler (1930, p. 47), and Gulliksen (1932b, pp. 501–502) also believed that calling attention to the change in stimuli would disrupt transposition. In a study by Köhler (1918) a chimpanzee gave absolute responses on the first two trials of a transposition test; and Köhler observed that "From the animal's behavior it appeared that the [test] situation was new and strange" (p. 224). Similarly, Taylor (1932a) reported, in a study of transposition[1] in chicks, that in about one-third of the transposition tests, the subject "approached the boxes, hesitated, apparently observing the stimulus carefully, then ate from the positive gray [the absolute stimulus] .... The responses to the neutral boxes [transposition responses] were practically all made immediately" (p. 25).

Wertheimer (1925), discussing the recognition of a melody played in a new key, remarked that "one is often not even aware that a transposition has been made" (p. 4). Klüver (1933) mentioned that 10 of 13 children he tested in the transposition situation responded relationally, and "The majority of children did not even seem to notice the changes in 'absolute' size" (p. 321). He noted that this observation was "in line with the observations made by Frank" (H. Frank, 1926; H. Frank, 1928; neither paper available in English). Using the intermediate-size problem, Spiker and Terrell (1955) found that children who commented on the change of stimuli

[1]Taylor used a two-stimulus brightness-discrimination problem, not the intermediate-size problem as Rudel (1957) appeared to assert.

from the training to the test phase transposed significantly less (and gave significantly more absolute responses) than subjects who made no comment. The group that made no comment presumably included many subjects who failed to notice any change in the stimuli. Shirai (1963, Experiment I) obtained the same result in college students. Stevenson and Weiss (1955) also obtained this effect in college students, using a four-stimulus problem with an extreme or intermediate stimulus correct (in subgroups), and found that the probability of noticing the change was directly related to distance and inversely related to delay between the training and test phases. More subjects noticed the change on a two-step Far Test than on the Near Test, and more noticed the change when testing was immediate than when it was delayed. However, Zeiler and Salten (1966, Experiment 1) also used the intermediate-size problem, and found no difference between the performance of children who spontaneously referred to the change and those who did not.

As was pointed out in Chapter 3 in the section entitled "Stimulus Similarity," data obtained by McGrade (1958) suggest that tactual cues might be more similar to one another than visual cues produced by the same stimuli. The extremely high level of transposition obtained by McGrade with tactual cues (about 95.5 per cent transposition), in comparison with the normal level obtained with visual cues (79 per cent transposition) can be interpreted to indicate that most of the subjects failed to notice the change in tactual cues in the shift to the transposition test, and that more of the subjects recognized the change in visual cues. Alternatively, it might mean that the relation between the tactual cues was easier to perceive, but the faster initial learning with visual cues than with tactual cues argues against this explanation.

Wohlwill (1957) reported data that could be interpreted to indicate that noticing the change interferes with two-stimulus transposition in college students. Changing the conditions of presenting the stimuli apparently reduced transposition. Similarly, Shirai (1963, Experiment I) found that after two-stimulus discrimination learning, children generally transposed less to a three-stimulus test set than to a two-stimulus test set.

G. R. Thompson (1965) found that transposition occurred in mental retardates when the stimuli varied in only one dimension (size); chance responses occurred when size and brightness were both varied; and absolute responses occurred when size, brightness, and form were varied. This pattern of results is consistent with the hypothesis that noticing the change reduces transposition, on the assumption that the greater the number of dimensions transposed, the greater is the likelihood that the subject will notice the change.

Jackson (1939) also found that the frequency of transposition depended on the number of dimensions changed. After training with four-dimensional stimuli, children gave more transposition responses when two dimensions were transposed and two were eliminated than when one was transposed and three were eliminated, and under both conditions there were more transposition responses than when all four dimensions were transposed. Since it is not reasonable to assume that the changes would go unnoticed, and since transposition occurred, the responses must have been made to specific stimulus elements or to specific stimulus relations rather than to a *Gestalt* composed of all four stimulus elements or relations. Unfortunately, the results of this study must be accepted only tentatively, because (a) the sample size was small (eight children), (b) the subjects had already been given eight days of training and testing with the four-dimensional stimuli (over 200 trials), and (c) the number of dimensions transposed was varied within subjects rather than between groups.

Okamoto and Okuno (1958) obtained a similar effect, using three-dimensional stimuli. On test trials, either size, size and color, size and form, or all three dimensions were transposed. Transposition dropped as the number of dimensions transposed increased.

Stevenson *et al.* (1955b) found that altering the brightnesses of the test stimuli in a size-discrimination problem reduced transposition, presumably by increasing the ease of discriminating between the training and test situations.

Shirai (1954) found that size transposition and memory of absolute size were negatively correlated in human adults. Subjects who were less accurate in remembering absolute sizes transposed more than those who were more accurate. Furthermore, 74 per cent of the incorrect recognitions of the changes in size from training to test were associated with transposition responses. Transposition averaged 50 per cent when standard training and testing procedures were used; but when the brightness as well as the size of the transposition stimulus was altered, transposition averaged only 30 per cent. Of 10 subjects who gave the absolute response on the standard test, all also gave the absolute response on the test with the brightness alteration; and of 10 who transposed on the standard test, 4 shifted to the absolute response when the brightness was altered. These data are not unambiguous, but are consistent with the assumption that noticing the change reduces transposition.

Several investigators, however, obtained transposition in subjects that apparently recognized the change in stimuli (rabbits: Washburn and Abbott, 1912; rats: Hebb, 1937b; Lashley, 1938b, p. 169; monkeys: Klüver, 1933; children: Alberts and Ehrenfreund, 1951; Jackson, 1939; Jackson and Dominguez, 1939; Jackson *et al.*, 1938; human adults: Dees and Grindley, 1947). (See also Blum and Blum, 1949.) The behavior that can be taken as evidence that the subject recognized the change in stimuli includes hesitation (increased latency of response), vacillation, intensified observing responses (or attention), increased emotionality, and the like. In all four of the studies using children as subjects, the response latencies were greater on the first test trial than on training trials, implying that the subjects noticed the change in stimuli, or perhaps noticed only that some unidentified change had occurred. Nevertheless, transposition was obtained in each study. The amount of transposition was not related to the amount of change in response latency (my analysis of data presented by Jackson *et al.*, 1938).

Corbascio (1964) attempted to assess the effects of alerting the subjects to the change in stimuli, but the sample sizes were quite small and the results are ambiguous (see Table 5-1).

CONCLUSION

Transposition usually occurs when the subject does not notice the change in stimuli, but it often occurs even when some change is apparently noticed. Failure to notice the change is therefore not the only basis for transposition.

Ternus (1926) reported that under certain conditions a figure might appear to move and to change in size or brightness. For example, the figure represented by the three broken lines in Fig. 5-1*A* was presented after the subjects had seen the figure represented by the solid lines (in the actual experiment, all of the lines were solid; Fig. 5-1*A* shows the lengths and positions of the lines). The figure appeared to move to the right and to expand in size. Similarly, when light gray, middle gray, and dark gray points occupying the positions indicated by the circles in Fig. 5-1*B* were shown after the presentation of white, light gray, and middle gray points occupying the positions indicated by the dots, the line of points appeared to shift to the right and to grow darker. According to Ternus, "Experiments of the type reported here were first made by J. Pikler" in 1917. (Ternus, 1926, footnote 1, p. 150. No reference was cited, but perhaps the reference was to Pikler's 1917 *Sinnesphysiologische Untersuchungen*.) Koffka said that Schumann was the first to observe this kind of phenomenon. According to Koffka, Schumann found that "in the successive comparison of two circles, or lines of different length, an extension or a shrinking appeared in the field of vision according as the eyes passed from the smaller to the larger or from the larger to the smaller object" (Koffka, 1925, p. 222). The Schumann study was also described by Lindworsky (1931, pp. 238–239), but neither Koffka nor Lindworsky gave a reference to any published report. Werner (1948, pp. 220–221) described the same kind of finding: when shown line *a* and then line *b* in Fig. 5-1*C*, many subjects experienced a lengthening of the line; when shown line *b* and then line *a*, many experienced a shrinkage of the line. (Werner gave

TABLE 5-1

PERCENTAGE TRANSPOSITION OBTAINED BY CORBASCIO (1964)

Stimuli		Instruction	One-step test			Three-step test		
Training[a]	Test[a]		Sample size	Trial 1	(10 trials)	Sample size	Trial 1	(10 trials)
Background	Background	"Now watch"[b]	—	—	—	6	100	—
		None[b]	—	—	—	9	56	—
		"Now be careful . . ."[cd]	5	100	(100)	5	80	(72)
		None[c]	5	100	(100)	20	75	(72)
Background	No background	"Now be careful . . ."[cd]	5	80	(98)	5	80	(88)
		None[c]	5	80	(92)	5	100	(90)
No background	No background	"Now watch"[b]	—	—	—	25	84	—
		None[b]	—	—	—	10	90	—

[a] Background stimuli were mounted on cards to provide a delimited background; No-background stimuli were held up by the experimenter, were not mounted, and had no delimited background.

[b] Preliminary experiment.

[c] Main experiment.

[d] "Now be careful and do the same thing you have done before."

139

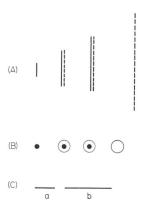

FIG. 5-1. Illusions of movement. See text for explanations. (A) After Ternus, 1926, Fig. 24, p. 159. (B) After Ternus, 1926, Fig. 1, p. 150. (C) After Werner, 1948, p. 221.

as a reference a paper by Jaensch published in 1920.) The effect is also known as the phi-phenomenon (for example, Hartmann, 1942, p. 175; see also Koffka, 1924).

One might speculate that even if the subject notices the change in the stimuli from the training phase to the test phase, he might perceive the test stimuli as the training objects somehow shifted in size or brightness. Such a subject should transpose, even though he noticed the change. Sherman (1966) tested more than 380 preschool children, and reported that about 10 per cent spontaneously remarked about the change in the sizes of the stimuli on the transposition test. According to Sherman, these children "thought that E [the experimenter] changed the original pair of stimuli into a larger pair; or that the original pair spontaneously expanded" (footnote 1, p. 58). Apparently the level of transposition in these children was as high as in the children who did not comment about the change in stimuli.

Speed of Original Learning

It is popularly believed that fast learning is unstable and slow learning is stable, but the experimental evidence from studies of serial learning contradicts this notion.[2] Fast learners actually have better retention than

[2]This "principle" might well be derived from the saw, "plodding wins the race." Croxall (1866, pp. 179–180) interpreted Aesop's fable of the hare and the tortoise consistently with this principle, but L'Estrange (1708, pp. 149–150) did not. Meumann (1913, p. 171), who studied with Wundt (Boring, 1950, p. 429), was one of many psychologists who also accepted the principle.

slow learners (see, for example, reviews by W. S. Hunter, 1929; Lyon, 1916; McGeoch and Irion, 1952; Underwood, 1954[3]). Popular belief also seems to be that slow learners learn more about the total situation than fast learners, but here the experimental evidence is not conclusive. Fast learners retain memorized prose and poetry somewhat better than slow learners (for example, Lyon, 1916), but there has been no test for retention of the theme or plot, which can be considered to be the important aspect of the "total situation." According to Wheeler (1929), the fast learner usually "apprehends more detail which gives him an opportunity to perceive the material in a greater variety of relationships. In case of unfamiliar material, . . . the slow learner who spends more time establishing relationships between details forgets less than the rapid and superficial learner" (pp. 250–251). In the transposition problem, better grasp of the total situation should probably increase transposition; and if slow learners learn more about the total situation, they should transpose more than fast learners. The experimental evidence is summarized in Table 5-2 (where F stands for fast and S stands for slow) and discussed below.

Two-Stimulus Problems

Bingham (1922) suggested that transposition is probably more likely to occur the better the training, generalizing from his results with chicks. However, Taylor (1932a) reported that there seemed to be the opposite relation between learning speed and transposition in chicks; the better learners gave fewer transposition responses. Heyman (1951) reported data that indicate that learning speed is unrelated to transposition in rats. (Heyman reported data for each rat individually; I divided the subjects into fast and slow learners at the median number of trials to criterion. The fast learners averaged 77 per cent transposition, and the slow learners averaged 75 per cent transposition.) Bagshaw and Pribram (1965) found no relation between learning speed and transposition in monkeys.

Ross et al. (1965) obtained significantly more transposition in both mentally normal and mentally retarded children, the fewer the errors in original learning; and Stevenson et al. (1955a) obtained the same effect in normal subjects, but not at a statistically significant level. Okamoto and Okuno (1958) obtained the opposite effect in young children (about three to five years old) when all three dimensions of three-dimensional stimuli were transposed, but obtained no effect when one dimension was transposed and when two dimensions were transposed. No effect was obtained in older children (about six and seven years old). Kuenne (1946),

---

[3] Underwood concluded that when associative strengths are equated, fast and slow learners have equal retention. However, his data supported the conclusion that for ordinary methods of training and testing, there is a difference favoring fast learners.

TABLE 5–2

RELATION OF LEARNING SPEED TO TRANSPOSITION

| | | Percentage transposition | | |
| | | Fast | Slow | Direction of |
Study	Subjects	learners[a]	learners[a]	difference
Bingham (1922)	Chicken	—	—	F > S
Taylor (1932a)	Chicken	—	—	F < S
Heyman (1951) $\frac{1}{2}$ step	Rat	91	89	F ≥ S
1 step	Rat	81	76	F ≥ S
1$\frac{1}{2}$ steps	Rat	58	60	F ≤ S
Bagshaw and Pribram (1965)	Monkey	81[b]	71[b]	F > S
Gonzalez et al. (1954)	Chimpanzee	69	73	F ≤ S
Spence (1939b)	Chimpanzee	—	—	F > S[c]
Alberts and Ehrenfreund (1951)	Human	—	—	F = S[d]
Caron (1966)	Human	—	—	F > S
Kuenne (1946)	Human	—	—	F = S
Okamoto and Okuno (1958) young	Human	—	—	F < S[e]
old	Human	—	—	F = S
Ross et al. (1965)	Human	—	—	F > S
Sherman (1966)	Human	—	—	F = S
Stevenson et al. (1955a)	Human	—	—	F > S
Terrell (1958)	Human	94[f]	97[f]	F ≤ S
Terrell and Kennedy (1957)	Human	98[g]	70[g]	F > S
Zeiler and Salten (1966) Exp. 1	Human	—	—	F > S

[a] Dashes indicate that means were not reported.

[b] Preoperative means of fastest learning group and slowest learning group. Correlation reported to be low.

[c] But F = S when method of learning was partialled out.

[d] In seven groups, r ranged from −.51 to +.40.

[e] Only when all three dimensions changed; when one or two dimensions changed, F = S.

[f] Means of two fastest learning groups and two slowest learning groups.

[g] Means of fastest group and slowest group. Three intermediate groups averaged 70 per cent transposition.

Alberts and Ehrenfreund (1951), and Sherman (1966) found no relation between learning speed and transposition in children.

Terrell and Kennedy (1957) found that there was faster original learning and more transposition when candy was used as a reward than when nonconsumables were used, suggesting a relation between learning speed and transposition; but Terrell's (1958) data did not confirm this apparent relation. The data of Terrell's later studies (Terrell, 1959; Terrell et al., 1959) are indeterminate with respect to this point, since "virtually all subjects transposed on every trial." (The Terrell studies are also discussed in the section entitled "Reward," Chapter 3. See also the discussion of

Zeiler's [1965b] study in the section entitled "Stimulus Similarity," Chapter 3.)

INTERMEDIATE-STIMULUS PROBLEMS

Gonzalez *et al.* (1954) tested chimpanzees in the intermediate-size problem, and even though there were only four subjects, there was clearly little or no relation between learning speed and amount of transposition. Spence (1939b, Problem 1), however, tested 17 chimpanzees, and obtained a close relation between learning speed and transposition. For the 15 subjects which solved the problem, the correlation between trials to criterion and transposition was −.83. (The correlation coefficients given here are Pearson r's which I computed from the data of Spence's Table 3, p. 15, and Table 4, p. 23. All are significant at beyond the .005 level.) The difference between the results of these two studies is attributable to the use of different kinds of stimuli. Gonzalez *et al.* used stimuli varying in size; Spence used stimuli varying only in position, as shown in Table 5-3.

Spence gave four training problems, each with a different stimulus setting. He noted that the subjects that transposed 80 per cent or more tended to learn all four problems simultaneously, and the other subjects tended to learn them at different rates. The error curves for the four problems approached zero (perfect performance) at points that were closer

TABLE 5–3
THE STIMULUS SETTINGS USED BY SPENCE (1939b, PROBLEM 1)

Problem	Available positions[a]										
	1	2	3	4	5	6	7	8	9	10	11
Training	o	o	+	o	o						
		o	o	+	o	o					
			o	o	+	o	o				
				o	o	+	o	o			
Test		o	o	+	o	o					
			o	o	+	o	o				
				o	o	+	o	o			
Training		o	o	+	o	o					
			o	o	+	o	o				
				o	o	+	o	o			
					o	o	+	o	o		
Test	o	o	+	o	o						
		o	o	+	o	o					
			o	o	+	o	o				

[a] The symbol "o" indicates the positions of negative stimuli; "+" indicates the positions of positive stimuli.

together for the "successful" subjects (the ones that transposed at a high level) than for the other subjects. Spence devised two indices of the tendency to learn the four problems simultaneously, in order to assess its apparent relation to transposition. The first index—the average deviation of the points at which the error curves fell below two errors—correlated .93 with trials to criterion and − .89 with transposition, and the second index— the range between the earliest and latest points at which the error curves fell below two errors—correlated .95 with trials to criterion and − .91 with transposition. These correlations indicate that subjects that learned the four training problems simultaneously learned them more rapidly and transposed more than subjects that learned them separately.

When the effect of the method of learning was partialled out, the correlation between trials to criterion and transposition dropped considerably (to −.01 when the first index was partialled out, and to .27 when the second index was partialled out). It therefore appears that the correlation between learning speed and transposition was largely a spurious product of the relations of these two variables to the method of learning. Spence reported that all of the "successful" subjects, which transposed 80 per cent or more, "usually went to the far side of the cage between trials and thus approached the apparatus from a distance. From such a position . . . the visual appearances of the different settings are more alike than from a close position. . . . Moreover, . . . as these subjects approached, they gave the appearance of attempting to place themselves equidistant from the two ends of the setting" (p. 47). This behavior "appeared with much less frequency and constancy" in the other subjects (p. 48). The method used by the successful subjects would make the various stimulus settings virtually indistinguishable from one another, and would therefore yield simultaneous learning of the four training problems and a high level of transposition.

Rudel (1960) suggested that fast learning of the original discrimination is associated with a high level of transposition in the intermediate-size problem. Caron (1966) and Zeiler and Salten (1966, Experiment 1) obtained confirmatory evidence; but Reese (1964b)[4] obtained the opposite trend, although not at a statistically significant level (r between trials to criterion and transposition = .24).

Figure 5-2 presents previously unreported data from four of my studies of transposition (Reese, 1961; Reese, 1962a; Reese, 1946b; Reese and Fiero, 1964). Inspection of these data indicates that if there is a relation between learning speed and transposition, it is probably complex, and it may interact with age of subjects, training criterion, and stimulus similarity.

---

[4]The relevant data were omitted from the previous report.

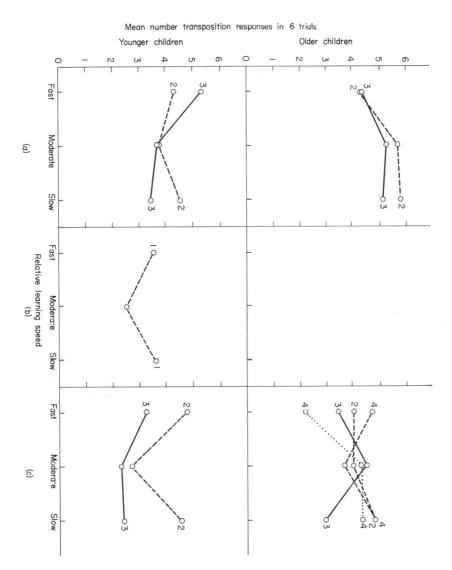

FIG. 5-2. Learning speed and transposition in the Reese studies (previously unreported data): (a) 1.3 to 1 area ratio, (b) 1.6 to 1 area ratio, and (c) 2 to 1 area ratio. Training criterion (---) low (5/5 and 8/10), (——) moderate (9/10), and (···) high (14/15).

Study	Rewarded responses
1. Reese (1961)	All
2. Reese (1962a)	Transposition
3. Reese (1964b)	All
4. Reese and Fiero (1964)	All

145

Ten of the comparisons in Table 5-2 suggest that fast learners transpose somewhat more than slow learners, five comparisons suggest the opposite trend, and four comparisons suggest no trend. These data and the data from my own studies suggest that there is a positive relation between learning speed and transposition, but that the relation can be weakened or even reversed by other variables that have yet to be identified with any degree of confidence.

Concept Knowledge

It is well established that verbalization usually facilitates learning in children (for example, Liublinskaya, 1957; Pyles, 1932; Shepard and Schaeffer, 1956; Weir and Stevenson, 1959), but Luria (1961) and Lovaas (1964) have shown that in young children verbal operant behavior sometimes has only sporadic and weak control over nonverbal operant behavior (see also T. S. Kendler, Kendler, and Learnard, 1962; Reese, 1962b).

One of the perplexing problems in research on the effects of concept knowledge on transposition is to determine whether or not the subject possesses the relevant concepts. The determination is necessarily based on the subject's overt responses, since neurological evidence is impossible to obtain, but the selection of the kinds of responses deemed to be appropriate has seldom been ingenious. One method is to determine whether the subject will verbalize the solution of the discrimination problem in terms of the relational concept, spontaneously or in response to appropriate questions, which may be completely formalized or may include probes. If completely formalized questions are used, some subjects may fail to give appropriate answers because they fail to understand the questions; but if probes are used, it is possible that the examiner may inadvertently lead the subject to an appropriate (or inappropriate) answer. Furthermore, the questions are necessarily asked at the end of the experimental session, and there is no way to determine whether or not the subject's response really indicates what he was doing during the learning session. Some subjects might not remember or might have changed sets. The method is intended to identify the subjects who used the relevant concepts, but it probably does not identify all of them. It certainly identifies none of the subjects who possessed the relevant concepts but did not use them.

A second method, or actually group of methods, is to try to get the subject to emit appropriate labels for the stimuli. In an intermediate-size discrimination, for example, the experimenter might point to the middle-sized stimulus and ask the subject, "What do you call this one?" It is very likely that the subject will misunderstand the question, especially since investigators using this method have often deliberately avoided reference to "size" in the questions asked. Another drawback is that the examiner must often make a subjective evaluation of the subject's response to determine whether or not it is appropriate. Such responses as "middle-sized," "medium," and "medium-sized" are easy to evaluate; but such responses as "mama one," "regular size," "little bit bigger," and "sister" are hard to evaluate. One solution to the problem of misunderstanding the question is for the examiner to say, "This is the big one" (pointing to the largest stimulus), "this is the little one" (pointing to the smallest one), "and this is the ...?" (with a rising inflection and pointing to the middle-sized one). Aside from the problem of obtaining idiosyncratic responses, this variation does not allow a determination of whether the subject knows what "big" and "little" mean if it becomes apparent that he does not know what "middle-sized" means.

Although this kind of test has usually been given at the end of the experimental session, it has sometimes been given before training begins, usually several days beforehand. The advantage of giving the test before the experimental session begins is that the subjects can be classified into "verbal" and "nonverbal" groups, permitting the formation of sub-groups of equal size for the administration of different experimental treatments. However, this advantage is largely lost if the investigator repeats the test at the end of the experiment, since typically a substantial number of subjects is found to have changed from the nonverbal classification to the verbal classification. (For stylistic purposes, I am omitting the quotation marks from these designations. The special meanings should be kept in mind, however.)

A third method, sometimes used in conjunction with the second one and given after it, is to try to get the subject to point correctly when the experimenter supplies the verbal labels. In the intermediate-size problem, for example, the experimenter might tell the subject, "Point to the middle-sized one." (It would be better to tell the subject to put his finger on the one named, since even young preschoolers have sometimes already learned that "it is not polite to point.") In the terminology of Osgood, Suci, and Tannenbaum (1957, p. 8), the second method requires the subject to "decode" the stimuli, by emitting appropriate labels, and the third method requires the subject to "encode," by pointing appropriately in response to the label. (The theoretical implications of separating these two processes are discussed in the section entitled "Mediation Theory," Chapter 8.)

The problem is twofold. First, all of the available techniques are at least partly inadequate. Second, the available techniques were developed to assess *verbal* concepts, but it is quite possible that some subjects

TABLE 5-4

TABLE 5-4

KNOWLEDGE OF RELATIONAL SIZE CONCEPTS AS A FUNCTION OF AGE LEVEL

Age range (years)	Approximate midpoint	Study	Sample size	Possessed concept (%)	Verbalized solution (%)
		Two-Stimulus Problem			
1.2–2.7	2.0	I. M. L. Hunter (1952a) Exp. III	12	0	0
1.7–2.8	2.3	Rudel (1958)	40	— 10[a]	—
2.6–3.6	3.1	Sherman (1966) Exp. 3	45	91	—
2.8–3.8	3.3	Rudel (1958)	37	— 97	—
2.9–3.9	3.4	Sherman (1966) Exp. 2	73	97	—
2.9–3.8	3.4	R. E. Cole et al. (1964)	27	100	4
3.0–3.9	3.5	Alberts and Ehrenfreund (1951)	22	100	38
3.0–3.9	3.5	Sherman (1966) Exp. 4	75	96	—
2.5–4.6	3.6	Corbascio (1964)	147	96	7
3.0–4.2	3.6	Sherman (1966) Exp. 1	60	100	—
3.2–5.0	4.1	R. C. Johnson and Zara (1960)	41	— 27	—
2.8–5.8	4.3	Kuenne (1946)	44	93	70
4.0–4.9	4.5	Stevenson et al. (1955a)	20	—	60
4.6–5.4	5.0	Alberts and Ehrenfreund (1951)	18	100	89
4.9–5.3	5.1	I. M. L. Hunter (1952a) Exp. I	24	—	67
3.7–6.8	5.2	Zeiler and Jasper (1966)	60	93	—
5.0–5.9	5.5	I. M. L. Hunter (1952a) Exp. II	55	—	53
Grades 4–7	—	Stevenson and Iscoe (1954)	140	—	79
Retarded	—	M. S. Scott (1966)	80	30	—
Retarded	—	Stevenson and Iscoe (1955)	44	—	7
		Intermediate-Stimulus Problem			
2.0–2.9	2.5	Thrum (1935)[b]	11	18	—
2.5–3.4	3.0	Marshall (1966) boys	12	25	—
2.5–3.4	3.0	Marshall (1966) girls	10	10	—
3.0–3.9	3.5	Thrum (1935)[b]	16	31	—
3.3–3.7	3.5	Caron (1965) boys	38	18 (24)[c]	—
3.3–3.7	3.5	Caron (1965) girls	38	21 (24)[c]	—
3.5–4.4	4.0	Marshall (1966) boys	38	47	—
3.5–4.4	4.0	Marshall (1966) girls	48	54	—
3.8–4.2	4.0	Caron (1965) boys	75	37 (27)[c]	—
3.8–4.2	4.0	Caron (1965) girls	58	50 (50)[c]	—
3.9–4.6	4.2	Beaty (1966)	63	11	—
3.2–5.5	4.4	Spiker and Terrell (1955)	48	52	—
3.3–5.6	4.5	Spiker et al. (1956)	84	36[d]	—
3.6–5.3	4.5	Reese (1961)	49	— 41	—
3–5	4.5?	Gonzalez and Ross (1958)	25	— 40	—
4.0–4.9	4.5	Thrum (1935)[b]	7	57	—
4.3–4.8	4.6	Caron (1965) boys	76	61 (51)[c]	—
4.3–4.8	4.6	Caron (1965) girls	78	68 (76)[c]	—
3.9–5.9	4.9	Zeiler and Paalberg (1964b)	119	23	—
4.5–5.4	5.0	Marshall (1966) boys	77	73	—

TABLE 5–4 (*continued*)

Age range (years)	Approximate midpoint	Study	Sample size	Possessed concept (%)	Verbalized solution (%)
4.5–5.4	5.0	Marshall (1966) girls	67	63	—
4–5	5.0?	Zeiler (1963a)	348	— 20	—
4–5	5.0?	Zeiler (1963b)	36	— 39	—
4–5	5.0?	Zeiler (1963d)	120	— 14	—
4–5[e]	5.0?	Zeiler (1965b)	118	20	—
4–5	5.0?	Zeiler and Lang (1966b)	64	—	36
3.7–6.8	5.2	Zeiler and Jasper (1966)	112	21	—
4–6	5.5?	Stevenson and Bitterman (1955)	24	17	0
4.8–6.1	5.5	Rudel (1957)	23	39	17
5.5–6.0	5.8	Reese (1962a)	21	— 43	—
5.5–6.5	6.0	Marshall (1966) boys	65	85	—
5.5–6.5	6.0	Marshall (1966) girls	42	98	—
6.1–6.8	6.5	Reese (1962a)	20	— 55	—
5–7	6.5?	Zeiler and Salten (1966)	20	—	40[f]
6.3–7.9	7.1	Reese and Fiero (1964)	76	— 93	—
7–8	8.0?	Zeiler and Gardner (1966b)	176	100	100
7.0–9.8	8.4	V. Graham et al. (1944)	56[g]	91[h]	—
Brain damaged	—	Rudel (1960)	28	36	4
Mongoloid	—	Rudel (1960)	15	7	0
Other Problems					
2.0–2.9	2.5	Thrum (1935)[b] smallest	11	36	—
3.0–3.9	3.5	Thrum (1935)[b] smallest	16	62	—
4.0–4.9	4.5	Thrum (1935)[b] smallest	7	100	—
2.0–2.9	2.5	Thrum (1935)[b] largest	11	54	—
3.0–3.9	3.5	Thrum (1935)[b] largest	16	88	—
4.0–4.9	4.5	Thrum (1935)[b] largest	7	100	
4–5	5.0?	Zeiler (1965b) largest and smallest	118	100	—
4–6	5.0	Elkind (1964) largest and smallest	90	100[i]	—

[a] Met one or other criterion.

[b] Summary of first-test data from Thrum's Table 1 (Subjects 1–25) and Table 4 (Subjects 26–34). Percentage of subjects responding correctly at least 70 per cent of the time.

[c] Number in parentheses is percentage responding at least 56 per cent correctly when told to put finger on middle-sized one (second test, nine trials). Other number is percentage who emitted appropriate label (first test).

[d] At least 36 per cent; 84 children were tested to obtain 30 concept and 30 no-concept subjects.

[e] As reported by Zeiler (1967).

[f] Spontaneous.

[g] Subjects who solved discrimination; no data given for 19 Ss who failed to learn.

[h] Used conventional term; other 9 per cent used terms that are probably acceptable.

[i] Approximate.

149

possess equivalent nonverbal concepts which can function as well as the verbal ones. Since there is no good way to determine whether or not a subject possesses nonverbal concepts, it is necessary to concentrate attention on the effects of verbal concepts; but relatively great variability in the behavior of nonverbal subjects is to be expected, because some of them presumably possess nonverbal concepts that are relevant.

Tables 5-4 and 5-5 and Fig. 5-3 summarize the available evidence on the relation between age level and knowledge of verbal concepts of intensity relations.[5] Whitman's (1965) data, summarized in Table 5-5, show that the training condition influences the percentage of children who are assessed as possessing the concept of middle-sizedness. The lowest percentages were in the groups given the "no pretraining" condition, which was the condition that was most closely similar to the standard methods of training. The pattern of findings suggests that estimates of the percentages of verbal children at three to five years of age in studies using the standard methods of training are fairly gross underestimates.

Two-Stimulus Problems

Jackson *et al.* (1938) said, ". . . our general observations seem to indicate that although the subjects [three to six years of age] may readily understand the concept 'bigger than,' they do not transfer by such verbal analysis on critical trials. Language did not appear to be a factor in making a choice between the transposed stimuli among our subjects" (pp. 581–582). The subjects were tested only on Near Tests. M. S. Scott (1966) also obtained no relation between concept knowledge and Near Test transposition. In neither of these studies were the means of the verbal and nonverbal groups reported. This may be important, because in five other studies in which there was no statistically significant relation between concept knowledge and Near Test transposition, the direction of the obtained relation was consistently in favor of the verbal groups (Kuenne, 1946; McKee and Riley, 1962; Rudel, 1958; Sherman, 1966; Stevenson *et al.*, 1955a). Furthermore, Stevenson and Iscoe (1954), using a three-stimulus problem with the largest or smallest stimulus correct (in subgroups), found significantly more Near Test transposition in subjects who verbalized

[5]Rudel's (1958) interpretation of the H. Thompson (1940) and Welch (1939) developmental studies as evidence that "most children under three do not understand verbal reference to size . . . " was erroneous. Welch deliberately omitted verbal reference to size in the tests, and Thompson asserted that two-and-a-half-year-olds could respond correctly to the size reference if the stimuli were markedly different. Actually, they may be able to do so even with relatively small differences between the stimuli. Binet found that his own two-and-a-half-year-old daughter could correctly indicate the relative sizes of two lines when the difference between the longer and shorter lines was as little as one-twentieth of the length of the shorter line (according to Bühler, 1930b, p. 75; no reference cited).

the problem solution than in subjects who did not. (Their nonverbal group averaged about 9 months younger than the verbal group, but the age difference was probably irrelevant, because the subjects ranged from 9 to 14 years of age.)

Kuenne (1946) obtained significantly more Far Test transposition (five steps) in verbal children than in nonverbal children. Rudel (1958) obtained no statistically significant differences between verbal and nonverbal children; but the trends suggested that the verbal children transposed more than the nonverbal children at two, five, and six steps, and transposed less than the nonverbal children at three and four steps.

TABLE 5–5

WHITMAN'S DATA ON CONCEPT OF MIDDLE-SIZEDNESS AS A
FUNCTION OF AGE LEVEL AND PRETRAINING CONDITION[a]

Age range	Pretraining condition		
	No pretraining (%)	Perceptual (%)	Verbal (%)
3.2–3.9	0	10	50
4.1–4.9	30	40	80
5.0–5.9	40	80	90

[a]There were 10 subjects per cell. The pretraining conditions are discussed in this section.

Alberts and Ehrenfreund (1951) examined the concept variable, but did not report its relation to transposition. (The study is nevertheless widely cited as providing evidence on the relation of transposition to concept knowledge, probably because Alberts and Ehrenfreund reported that the older children verbalized the principle of solution more frequently than the younger children and transposed more than the younger group. However, the relations of concept knowledge and transposition to age level were not strong enough to justify the inference that concept knowledge and transposition were related to each other.)

Kuenne (1946) noted that the effect of concept knowledge seems to be related to age level. Data obtained by Marsh and Sherman (1966) also indicate that transposition can be brought under verbal control in older children but not in younger children. Zeiler (1965b) has questioned the conclusion, since he obtained the high flat gradient of transposition in verbal children when a 2 to 1 ratio of stimulus areas was used, but obtained a decreasing gradient when a 1.4 to 1 ratio was used. Zeiler's findings and interpretation are discussed in detail in the section entitled "Stimulus Similarity" (Chapter 3), where a qualification of his interpretation is suggested.

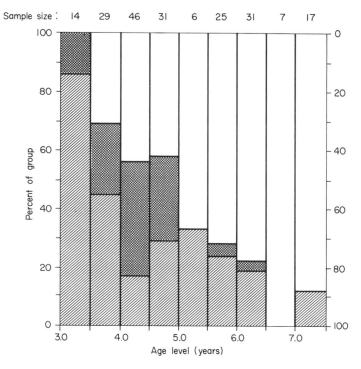

Sample size : 14   29   46   31   6   25   31   7   17

FIG. 5-3. Knowledge of concept of middle-sizedness as a function of age level (previously unreported data from Reese, 1964b): open area indicates concept, crosshatched area indicates questionable, and diagonal lines indicate no concept.

I. M. L. Hunter (1952a, Experiment III) obtained a high level of transposition in preverbal children, using a task designed so that absolute theory would predict absolute responses and relational theory and mediation theory would predict transposition. Since transposition occurred, and since mediation could not occur in the preverbal children, Hunter concluded that the study supported relational theory. However, Grice (1953) showed that Spence's (1942) absolute theory could predict transposition in the task, by using appropriate values of the constants in the generalization equations.

According to Oléron, deaf and hearing children do not differ in two-stimulus transposition of size and weight (Oléron, 1957; Oléron, 1963), but the deaf are inferior in transposition of speed (fast and slow rotating discs, flickering lights, moving trucks) (Oléron, 1963). (Kol'tsova [1961] attempted to study the transposition of speed in normal children, but the data are ambiguous because of the design of the study. In the one condition apparently demonstrating response to relations, the subjects could have been responding and withholding response on a simple alternation. In the other experimental condition, in which a simple alternation was incorrect, there was no apparent relational responding.)

The language deficiency of the deaf apparently may sometimes have a detrimental effect on transposition, and sometimes not. (Language deficiency in otherwise normal children may also be irrelevant. Köhler [1918, p. 225] reported that a "three-year-old child of fairly low vocabulary for its age" transposed on all 20 of the test trials that were given.) Furth (1964) and Youniss (1965) argued that cognition is not necessarily verbal, but the validity of their argument was challenged by Blank (1965). In a reply to Blank, Furth (1965) clarified his position and made the important point that it is necessary to distinguish between *knowledge* of a concept and *use* of the concept, noting that Inhelder and Piaget (1964, p. 293) had also emphasized this distinction. Furth's position is not that the deaf are totally unfamiliar with the English vocabulary, but that they lack linguistic competence. Furth and Youniss (1965) have reported confirmatory evidence for this position.[6]

Rexroad (1926) demonstrated experimentally that the color "green" and the printed word "green" are functionally equivalent to each other in college students, and are at least partially equivalent to the word "green" spoken by the investigator. Ivashchenko (1958) obtained similar results. According to Rexroad: "This is a laboratory example of Weiss' distinction between biosocial equivalence and biophysical equivalence" (p. 458); but it seems to miss the mark slightly as an example, because Weiss (1925, pp. 78–82) was discussing the equivalence of behaviors rather than the equivalence of stimuli. "Biophysical" equivalence was supposed to have an "anatomico-physiological" basis, and "biosocial" equivalence was based on the effects of the behaviors "as stimuli for other individuals" (p. 79). Accepting a dinner invitation (in Weiss's example, pp. 79–80) by writing, telegraphing, sending a messenger, and telephoning are four behaviors whose products may function as equivalent stimuli; but it is surely trivial to classify such *behaviors* as equivalent on the basis of the equivalence of their *products*. (See Hebb, 1949, and Berlyne, 1965, for other views on "response equivalence.") Rexroad's demonstration, however, was not trivial, even if the emphasis was misplaced. The equivalence of the different stimuli presumably resulted from the commonality of meanings, and the mediating link could have been either a visual image of the color or a covert verbalization of the color name (among other possibilities). There is some evidence (Reese, 1965b) that the use of visual images as mnemonics is as effective as using verbal context, suggesting that visual images are as

[6]Furth's reply to Blank is available only in mimeographed form, since it was unfortunately not accepted for publication by the editors of the *Psychological Bulletin*, in which Furth's original paper and Blank's criticism had appeared.

effective in mediation as verbal processes are. There is no reason to doubt that the same might be true in the transposition situation.

Polosina (1934) trained children to respond to cards containing similar figures and not to respond to cards containing dissimilar figures. The children transferred the discrimination to cards containing new figures, and Razran (1939, p. 317) identified the transfer as "transposition of similarity." However, it was probably actually mediated generalization, since the children were eight years old and undoubtedly knew the concepts required for mediation, and since there was more transfer in children with higher school achievement.

Wesman and Eisenberg (1941) trained college students on eight two-stimulus problems, gave a transposition test after each problem had been solved, and asked about the basis of solution after each transposition test. The answers to the questions were used to identify "specific" responses. A response was categorized as specific if the subject reported that it was based on a quality other than the relevant dimensional quality. For example, "it is easier to handle" would indicate a specific response on a size-discrimination problem. When a group-training procedure was used, transposition averaged 69 per cent, absolute responses averaged 20 per cent, and specific responses averaged 11 per cent. When subjects were trained and tested individually, transposition averaged 56 per cent, absolute responses averaged 16 per cent, and specific responses averaged 28 per cent. Although it is neither necessary nor desirable to interpret the introspective reports as factually accurate, since, for example, a subject may be unaware of the reason for his choice but unwilling to admit that he is, these data nevertheless suggest that cognitive factors must be taken into account in any theory dealing with transposition in articulate subjects.

INTERMEDIATE-STIMULUS PROBLEMS

In what might be called a "zero-step" transposition test, V. Graham, Jackson, Long, and Welch (1944) obtained transfer from "middle size" to "middle density," and although the amount of transfer increased with age level, the youngest subjects were seven years old, and all subjects who solved the discrimination problem were found to possess the relevant verbal concepts.

In 14 studies, listed in Table 5-6, verbal children were not significantly different from nonverbal children in intermediate-stimulus transposition. However, in five of these studies, the general trend favored the verbal group; in one study there was no difference between the groups; and in one the trend was reversed and favored the nonverbal group. In the reports of the other seven studies, not enough data were presented to make it clear what the directions of the obtained trends were, although the data presented suggest that reversed trends were probably obtained in three of these studies.

TABLE 5–6

STUDIES OBTAINING NO SIGNIFICANT EFFECT OF CONCEPT
KNOWLEDGE ON INTERMEDIATE-STIMULUS TRANSPOSITION

Study	Age range (years)	Direction of obtained trend			
		V > NV[a]	V = NV[a]	V < NV[a]	Indeterminate
Caron (1966)	3.3–4.8			x	
Gonzalez and Ross (1958)	3–5	x			
Reese (1961)	3.6–5.3	x			
Reese (1962a)	5.0–6.8	x			
Reese (1964b)	2.9–7.6	x			
Rudel (1957)	4.8–6.1			?	
Rudel (1960)	b			?	
Zeiler (1963a)	4–5	x			
Zeiler (1963b)	4–5		x		
Zeiler (1963d)	4–5			?	
Zeiler (1965b)	5–6				x
Zeiler and Lang (1966b)	4–5				x
Zeiler and Paalberg (1964b)	3.9–5.9				x
Zeiler and Salten (1966) Exp. 1	5–7				x

[a]V indicates verbal, NV indicates nonverbal. "?" indicates probable trend.
[b]Brain-damaged and mongoloid children.

The point to be noted is that the nonverbal group was seldom found to be superior to the verbal group, and was never found to be significantly superior to the verbal group.

There are other studies in which statistically significant differences favoring the verbal group were obtained. Whitman (1965), Marshall (1966), and Caron (1967) obtained significantly more transposition of intermediate size in verbal children than in nonverbal children. Price (1960) found, in an intermediate-weight problem, that relevant verbal pretraining (learning relational names for the stimuli) facilitated transposition; and Spiker and Terrell (1955) obtained similar results with an intermediate-size problem.

Spiker, Gerjuoy, and Shepard (1956) found that nonverbal children solved a standard intermediate-size problem as rapidly as verbal children, but were inferior to the verbal children on a task in which the absolute sizes of the stimuli varied from trial to trial. Perhaps the verbal children transposed more from trial to trial than the nonverbal children did, but an alternative explanation of the finding is that acquired distinctiveness of cues facilitated the complex learning in the verbal children (see Reese, 1962b; Reese, 1963a).

Zeiler and Salten (1966, Experiment 2) attempted to control transposition by the use of instructions given after the training criterion had been met and before the test began. The subjects in one group were given instructions intended to emphasize the relation and its invariance with change in absolute

qualities, and the subjects in the other group were given instructions emphasizing the absolute size of the correct training stimulus. Two subjects were
given the intermediate-size problem and four were given the two-stimulus
problem. The "relational" instructions increased transposition in both
kinds of problem, and the "absolute" instructions increased absolute
responses; but in neither kind of problem were the instructions completely
effective. The instructions appeared to be more effective in the two-stimulus
problem than in the intermediate-stimulus problem. In almost all of the
studies of two-stimulus transposition, the absolute response has not been
predominant at any distance. It usually has a maximum frequency no greater
than the chance level. Zeiler and Salten, however, obtained clearly predominant absolute responses on the Far Tests after the absolute instructions
were given.

In a similar study, Riley et al. (1966) gave instructions designed to arouse
relative or absolute responses. A "relative" group was instructed during
training to "find the middle-sized one"; one "absolute" group was told, "See
this one? The star will always be hidden under this one"; and a second
absolute group was told, "Find the one that fits the board" (the board on
which the stimuli were presented contained three strips which were the
same width as the middle-sized stimulus). These special instructions were
given during training, but not during testing. On a one-trial test, at a
distance of one step, about 83 per cent of the subjects in the absolute groups
gave absolute responses, compared with 28 per cent in the relative group.
About 61 per cent of the relative group transposed, and only 17 per cent of
the two absolute groups transposed. (The other subjects gave the nontransposition-nonabsolute response.) No control group was tested, but
comparing these percentages with the percentages obtained in similar
studies using "standard" training methods suggests that the absolute instructions interfered with transposition, but that the relative instructions had
no effect, as Zeiler (1966b) also noted.

Big and little are obviously relevant concepts in a two-stimulus size
discrimination problem, and middle-sized is clearly relevant in the intermediate-size problem; but Spiker et al. (1956) pointed out that the subject
does not need the concept of middle-sizedness to solve the intermediate-
size problem on a verbal basis, since "not big and not little" should serve
equally well. (However, Stevenson and McBee [1958] found that four-year-
old children solved the intermediate-size problem more slowly than a three-
stimulus problem with an extreme stimulus correct, and six-year-olds
exhibited the same effect when the discrimination was especially difficult.)

The suggestion has experimental support, obtained in a study of
preschool children tested at one and three steps (Reese, 1966). A control
group was trained and tested under standard conditions, and two experimental groups were trained under conditions designed to elicit verbal

mediators and to associate the choice response with them. The subjects in one experimental group were told before each response during training that the reward was under the "medium" stimulus, and the subjects in the other experimental group were told that it was "not under the big one or the little one." During the transposition tests, these verbalizations were not given by the experimenter. The data indicated that the two kinds of verbal training were equally effective, and produced better performance during training than the control condition and more transposition on both tests than the control condition. As shown in Fig. 5-4, there were distance effects in all three groups, indicating that even though the performance of the experimental groups was influenced by the verbal training, it was still also influenced by the absolute stimulus qualities. Shepard (1956) obtained a similar effect. Verbal training increased generalization, but there remained a drop in the generalization gradient as the distance between the test stimulus and the conditioned stimulus was increased.

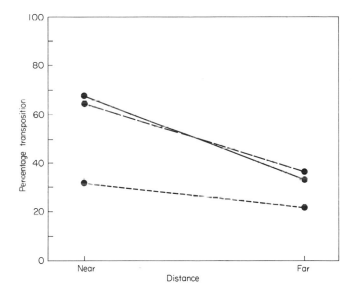

FIG. 5-4. Transposition in the Reese (1966) study: (———) medium, (— —) not-big not-little, and (- - -) standard. (Drawn from Reese, 1966, Table 2, p. 126, younger and older groups combined.)

In an unpublished study, I used the same "standard" and "not-big not-little" conditions as in the study described above, and added a condition in which the child was asked before each response during training, "Is it under the big one, the little one, or the middlesized one?" (The sequence of size names was varied across trials.) The idea was to see if this "perceptual" condition, in which the child's attention was called to the relevant dimension, would have the same effect as the more direct statement given to the child in the not-big not-little condition. The children were four- and five-year-olds. The sample sizes, trials to criterion, and transposition scores are given in Table 5-7. The perceptual group appeared to fall about midway between the other two groups in learning speed, but the difference between the standard condition and the perceptual condition was not reliable, although the other differences were statistically significant. The only reliable effect on transposition was the order effect; there was more transposition on the first test, whether it was a Near Test or Far Test, than on the second test.

TABLE 5–7
UNPUBLISHED STUDY BY REESE[a]

Measure	Group		
	Standard	Not-big not-little	Perceptual
Sample size	13	19	18
Mean trials through criterion	90.4	28.2	63.8
Median trials through criterion	71	10	33
Mean percentage transposition (6 trials):			
one step	47.4	40.4	23.1
three steps	24.3	32.5	27.8
Percentage transposition (trial 1):			
one step	62.5	45.5	11.1
three steps	40.0	62.5	33.3

[a]Training criterion was 9 correct of 10 consecutive responses. All test-trial responses were rewarded. See text for description of study.

The data for the training phase indicate the telling the child which sizes are incorrect facilitates learning more than calling his attention to the relevance of the size dimension, and suggest that calling his attention to the relevant dimension may yield some facilitation. Although the latter effect was not reliable in this study, the difference between the learning scores of the standard and perceptual groups was almost as large as the difference between the perceptual and not-big not-little groups.

Two conclusions can be drawn from the transposition data. First, the previously obtained effect of the not-big not-little instruction was not replicated; and, second, neither experimental condition had any reliable effect on transposition.[7]

[7]I am inclined to doubt the reproducibility of the data of this study, and have summarized them there only because they disagree with my previous findings.

CONCLUSION

It is likely that nonverbal cues can facilitate transposition, but there is no direct evidence for this speculation. The research on the effect of verbal concepts indicates that they facilitate two-stimulus transposition in older children, but sometimes do not in younger children. Young verbal children may be able to use the conceptual labels correctly only if the stimulus differences are large. Verbal concepts generally facilitate inter- mediate-stimulus transposition, but sometimes the effect is weak. Instruc- tions can enhance the verbal control of transposition responses.

Age

Köhler (1918) predicted an increase in the absolute response with increas- ing age of subjects, because of an improvement in the ability to recognize absolute stimuli and to retain the discrimination on the test trials (see also Koffka, 1925, p. 141).

TWO-STIMULUS PROBLEMS

The data on the effect of age level on two-stimulus transposition are summarized in Table 5-8. Riekel (1922) found that transposition decreased with age within the range from two to six years. (Overall transposition of brightness and color averaged 70 per cent, and overall transposition of size averaged 27 per cent, but the percentages at different age levels were not given in my secondary sources.) Shirai (1963, Experiment IV) obtained additional evidence supporting Köhler's suggestion. With increasing age level, there was an increase in the accuracy of recognizing the absolute stimulus in a one-step test set. Data reported by Wohlwill (1960a, Experiment 2) also support the suggestion. Older children (eleven to thirteen years of age) were apparently better able to recognize the absolute stimulus of an intermediate-stimulus problem on a test with the stimuli presented in pairs than were younger children (seven and eight years of age).

Shirai found that transposition increased from four to five years of age, decreased from five through thirteen years of age, and then remained constant through nineteen years of age (at a level of about 30 per cent trans- position) (Shirai, 1939; Shirai, 1941; see also Shirai, 1963, Experiment I). However, in another study, Shirai found that transposition increased from a level of 83 per cent at two years of age to 95 per cent at three years of age, remained constant until eleven years of age, and then dropped to 80 per cent at twelve to thirteen years of age (Shirai, 1951). (Shirai gave the per- centage for two-year-olds as 74.7, but included in the computation one child who failed to learn the initial discrimination. I omitted this subject in computing the percentage given here.)

The age differences in the last study (Shirai, 1951) were not statistically

TABLE 5–8

RELATION BETWEEN AGE LEVEL AND TWO-STIMULUS TRANSPOSITION

Study	Age range (years)	Trend in transposition with increasing age level		
		Decrease[a]	No change[a]	Increase[a]
Near Test				
Alberts and Ehrenfreund (1951)	3.0–5.4		⊗	
Jackson *et al.* (1938)	2.4–5.8		⊗	
H. E. Jones and Dunn (1932)	b			x
Kasianova[c,d]	1.5–7			x
Kuenne (1946)	2.5–5.8		⊗	
Maekawa (1955)[c]	3–6			x
Marsh and Sherman (1966)	2–4			x
Okamoto and Okuno (1958)[c]	3.6–7.5			x
Oléron (1957)[c]	4–7[e]			x
Riekel (1922)[c]	2–6	x		
Riley and McKee (1963)	f	⊗		
Rudel (1958)	1.7–3.8			⊗[g]
Sato and Kitagawa (1947)[c]	4–6			x
Sherman (1966)	2.5–3.9		⊗	
Shirai (1939; 1941)	4–5			x
	5–13	x		
	13–19		⊗	
Shirai (1951)	2–3			⊗
	3–11		⊗	
	11–13	⊗		
Stevenson *et al.* (1955a)	4.0–4.9[h]			⊗
Terrell (1958)	4–9		⊗	
Terrell (1959)	5–9			⊗
Terrell *et al.* (1959)	5–11		⊗	
Terrell and Kennedy (1957)	4–9	⊗		
G. R. Thompson (1965)	Retarded		⊗	
Vatzuro (1959)[c]	9–14			x
Zakher (1963)[c]	Preschool			x
Far Test				
Alberts and Ehrenfreund (1951)	3.0–5.4			x
Kuenne (1946)	2.5–5.8			x
Rudel (1958)	1.7–3.8			x
G. R. Thompson (1965)	Retarded			x

[a]The symbol "x" indicates direction of trend obtained, and "⊗" indicates trend not statistically significant.

[b]Mean 5.7 years (S.D. .3).

[c]Presumably used Near Test; trend presumably significant (cited from secondary sources).

[d]Cited by Zaporozhets (1965).

[e]Deaf children.

[f]Grades 2 and 3, college.

[g]Age level confounded with concept knowledge.

[h]Also Grades 2, 5, 8, and 10, and college.

significant. In 12 other studies, included in Table 5–8, there were no statistically significant age differences in Near Test transposition. In seven of these, the obtained means of different age groups were virtually identical; in three the obtained trends favored the older groups; and in two the obtained trends favored the younger groups.

Marsh and Sherman (1966) found that four-year-old children transposed more than two-year-olds, and Okamoto and Okuno (1958) obtained a positive relation between transposition and age in children 3.6 to 7.5 years old. Sato and Kitagawa (1947) and Maekawa (1955) obtained the same results in the age range from three to six years. H. E. Jones and Dunn (1932) obtained a correlation of .18 ($\pm$ .08) between age and Near Test transposition. The age range in the Jones and Dunn study was more restricted than in most of the other studies, but Jones and Dunn gave much less training on the initial discrimination (six trials) than was given in the other studies (training to various criteria). The small number of training trials perhaps contributed to the effect obtained, since older children generally solve discrimination problems more rapidly than younger children (see Table 5-9). This age difference is also found in infant monkeys (Harlow, Harlow, Rueping, and Mason, 1960; and with less clear-cut results, Mason, Blazek, and Harlow, 1956). Shirai (1951) and Stevenson et al. (1955a) obtained mixed relations between age and learning speed in human subjects. In Shirai's study, there was an increase in learning speed between the ages of two and four years, then a decrease in learning speed from five through thirteen years. Stevenson et al. obtained the increase from the preschool level to the fifth-grade level, then a decrease from the fifth-grade through the college level. It has been suggested that the slower learning speed at the older age levels is attributable to the use of more complex hypotheses by the older subjects (for example, T. S. Kendler, Kendler, and Learnard, 1962, pp. 583–585; Rabinowitz and Cantor, 1966; Shirai, 1951; Stevenson et al. 1955a).

Berman (1963) found that two-year-old children were inferior to four-year-old children in solving a "relative" discrimination problem, which could mean that they transposed less than the four-year-olds; but they were also inferior on an "absolute" discrimination problem (see Chapter 6). Vatzuro (1959) and Zakher (1963) reported that relational responding increased with age level (even though Vatzuro's normal subjects were nine to fourteen years old). Kasianova (cited by Zaporozhets, 1965) found that younger children transposed less than older children in a two-stimulus problem, but the amount of transposition increased considerably at all age levels after special training was given. In the special training, the children were taught to compare objects with respect to size, "putting cups one into another, cardboard blocks, and other things of different size." Zaporozhets implied that the special training teaches the child to perceive the size relation (see also Zaporozhets, 1958, pp. 283–284); but it seems to be at least

TABLE 5–9

STUDIES REPORTING DATA ON RELATION BETWEEN AGE LEVEL AND LEARNING SPEED

Study	Age range (years)	Increase in learning speed with increase in age level
Two-Stimulus Problems		
Alberts and Ehrenfreund (1951)	3.0–5.4	Yes
Berman (1963)	2.0–4.8	Yes
Brackbill and Jack (1958)	5–6	No
G. N. Cantor and Spiker (1954)	3–5	No
Hill (1962)	0.7–8.8	Yes
H. E. Jones and Dunn (1932)	Mean 5.7 (S.D. .3)	Yes[a]
Kuenne (1946)	2.5–5.8	Yes
Marsh and Sherman (1966)	2.5–5.0	Yes[a]
Murphy and Miller (1959)	[b]	Yes
Roberts (1932) (Task I)	2–5	Yes[a]
Rudel (1958)	1.7–3.8	Yes
Sherman (1966)	2.5–3.9	No
Shirai (1951)	2–13	Mixed
Shirai (1963)	4–10	Yes[c]
Stevenson and McBee (1958)[d]	3.4–6.8	No
Stevenson and Iscoe (1954)[d]	9.2–14.2	No
Stevenson and Iscoe (1955)[e]	9–40	No
Stevenson et al. (1955a)	4.0–4.9[f]	Mixed
Terrell (1958)	4–9	No
Terrell (1959)	5–9	No[a]
Terrell et al. (1959)	5–11	No[a]
Terrell and Kennedy (1957)	4–9	Yes
Trabasso, Deutsch, and Gelman (1966) pilot study	2.5–9.5	No
G. Weiss (1954)	3–5	Yes
Wohlwill (1960a)	4.9–12.1	Yes
Zakher (1963)	Preschool	Yes[a]
Intermediate-Stimulus Problems		
Caron (1966)	3.3–4.8	Yes
V. Graham et al. (1944)	7.0–9.8	Yes[a]
Hicks and Stewart (1930)	2–5	Yes
Marshall (1966)	2.5–6.5	No
Martin and Blum (1961)	Mean 6.3 (S.D. 1.6)	No
Reese (1962a) easy problem	5.0–6.8	No
hard problem	5.0–6.8	Yes
Reese (1964b) easy problem	2.9–7.6	Yes
hard problem	4.2–7.6	Yes
Spiker et al. (1956)	3.3–5.6	No
Stevenson and McBee (1958)	3.4–6.8	Yes
Whitman (1965)	3–5	Yes
Wohlwill (1960a)	7.0–12.8	Yes[a]

[a] Nonsignificant trend, or report not entirely clear.
[b] Grades 1 to 4.
[c] Brightness, but not size and shape.
[d] Three-stimulus problem with largest or smallest correct.
[e] Feeble-minded sample.
[f] Also Grades 2, 5, 8, and 10, and college.

equally likely that the special training serves only to focus the child's attention on the size relation, which he can already perceive. Young children
apparently tend to ignore the size relation in the experimental situation, but
they almost certainly can respond to it, since "children of less than a year
can obviously distinguish big from little things, e.g., they will readily select
the larger of two cookies" (Rudel, 1958, p. 386).

The suggestion is that the discrimination is more likely to occur when the
subject is appropriately motivated, with cookies for example, than when he
is not. Ricciuti (1965) tentatively suggested a similar explanation of part
of his data, which showed that about 30 per cent of the infants he tested
(twelve to twenty-four months old) spontaneously grouped objects on the
basis of size (when form and color were constant) but only 14 per cent spontaneously grouped on the basis of form (when size and color were constant).
Size preferences were observed, but no form preferences. Ricciuti suggested,
in effect, that the subjects may have been motivated to group the sizes but
not motivated to group the forms. (He recognized, however, the alternative
that the lack of form preferences could have resulted from the difficulty of
the form discrimination.)

On Far Tests, Kuenne (1946), Alberts and Ehrenfreund (1951), and Oléron
(1957) obtained significantly less transposition in younger children than
in older children; but Rudel (1958) found no significant age effect on Far
Test transposition. Rudel's younger group was not as old as the youngest
groups in the studies by Kuenne and Alberts and Ehrenfreund, and her
older group was about as old as their youngest groups (see Table 5-8). There
was also a narrower age difference between the groups in Rudel's study
than in the latter two studies. These differences might account for the
discrepancy in results, but there were also procedural differences. Furthermore, the obtained trend in Rudel's study favored the older group at two,
five, and six steps and was reversed only at three and four steps. G. R.
Thompson (1965) obtained a positive but nonsignificant correlation between
age of mentally retarded subjects and Far Test transposition.

INTERMEDIATE-STIMULUS PROBLEMS

Spence (1939b, Problem 1) tested seven "more or less" experimentally
naive chimpanzees ranging in age from three to twenty-one years. The
correlation between age and transposition was −.50, and although it was
not a statistically significant correlation, it suggests that there was an
inverse relation between age and transposition. (The correlation for the
whole group, including 10 other chimpanzees that were experimentally
sophisticated, was −.52, which was also nonsignificant.) However, the older
subjects tended to use an inferior learning strategy, which also yielded a
low level of transposition. (See the discussion of this study in the section
entitled "Speed of Original Learning," this chapter; the correlation between

age of naive subjects and the first index of simultaneous learning was .70.) When the effect of the learning strategy was partialled out, the correlation between age and transposition increased to .66, suggesting that with strategy held constant, the older subjects would transpose more than the younger subjects. These suggestions are quite tentative, however, because the correlations were all statistically nonsignificant.

Table 5-10 summarizes the data on the effects of age level on intermediate-stimulus transposition in human subjects. In studies by Hicks and Stewart (1930), Reese (1962a; 1964b), and Caron (1967), Near Test transposition of intermediate size seemed to increase slightly with increasing age in children. Martin and Blum (1961) did not report separate means for age groups, since there was no statistically significant relation between age and Near Test transposition, but the relation was also nonsignificant in the Hicks and Stewart and Reese studies. Marshall (1966) obtained a significant increase in Near Test transposition with increasing age level.

V. Graham *et al.* (1944) gave an intermediate-stimulus problem in which the concept of "middle size" had to be generalized to "middle density." The generalization increased with increasing age, but the subjects were older than in the other studies cited (see Table 5-10), and this kind of transfer is probably verbally mediated (see Blank and Bridger, 1964).

Reese (1962a) found less Far Test transposition in preschool children than in kindergarten children when the stimuli were distinctive (2 to 1 area ratio), but found no effect when the stimuli were similar (1.3 to 1 area ratio). In a later study, however, Reese (1964b) found no significant age differences at either level of stimulus similarity (using comparable age groups and the same area ratios in the two studies). The trends favored the younger groups. Whitman (1965) tested children who were three, four, and five years old, using a stimulus ratio of 1.4 to 1, and found that transposition at three and six steps increased significantly with age. Caron (1966; 1967) also obtained significant increases in Far Test transposition with increasing age level, testing within the age range from three to five years.

CONCLUSION

The evidence is not impressive, because of the frequency of nonsignificant trends, but suggests that older children transpose somewhat more than younger children do. There are contradictory data, but it seems likely that the contradictions are attributable to procedural variables.

Intelligence

Vatzuro (1959) reported that relational responding was greater in normal children than in mentally retarded children. Using two-stimulus problems,

TABLE 5–10
RELATION BETWEEN AGE LEVEL AND INTERMEDIATE-STIMULUS TRANSPOSITION

Study	Age range (years)	Change in transposition with increasing age level		
		Decrease[a]	No change[a]	Increase[a]
	Near Test			
Caron (1967)	3.8–4.8			x
V. Graham et al. (1944)	7.0–9.8			x
Hicks and Stewart (1930)	2–5			x
Marshall (1966)	2.5–6.5			x
Martin and Blum (1961)	b		⊗ [c]	
Reese (1962a)				
2 to 1 series	5.0–6.8			⊗
1.3 to 1 series	5.0–6.8			⊗
Reese (1964b)				
2 to 1 series	2.9–7.6			⊗
1.3 to 1 series	4.2–7.6			⊗
	Far Test			
Caron (1966)	3.3–4.8			x
Caron (1967)	3.8–4.8			x
Reese (1962a)				
2 to 1 series	5.0 6.8			x
1.3 to 1 series	5.0–6.8		⊗	
Reese (1964b)				
2 to 1 series	2.9–7.6	⊗		
1.3 to 1 series	4.2–7.6	⊗		
Whitman (1965)	3–5			x

[a] See footnote a, Table 5–8.
[b] Mean 6.3 (S.D. 1.6).
[c] Trend nonsignificant, no means reported.

H. E. Jones and Dunn (1932) found a low correlation between mental age and Near Test transposition; but only six training trials were given on each problem, which could have yielded a difference in original learning related to mental age. Jackson and Jerome (1943) found that gifted children learned the original discrimination faster than dull children, and transposed somewhat but not significantly more. O'Connor and Hermelin tested imbeciles and mentally normal children, and obtained results exactly paralleling those of Jackson and Jerome (see Table 5-11).[8] Balla and Zigler (1964), however,

[8] The results were summarized briefly by O'Connor (1965, p. 75), and further details (including the material presented in Table 5–11) were kindly sent to me by Dr. O'Connor (personal communication, 1965). The experiment was incidental to a series of studies of reversal learning reported by O'Connor and Hermelin in 1959, and was omitted from their published report.

found no reliable difference between normal and retarded subjects on the training task, and no consistent difference on the transposition test. G. R. Thompson (1965) obtained no consistent relation between the IQ of mentally retarded subjects and transposition.

Kuenne (1946) obtained a weak and nonsignificant positive relation

TABLE 5–11
DATA FROM THE O'CONNOR AND HERMELIN STUDY[a]

Group	Mean CA (years)	Mean MA (years)	Mean IQ	Mean trials to criterion	
				Training	Transfer
Imbeciles	11.4	4.9	42.9	36.0	2.9
Normals	5.1	—	—	28.4	2.1

[a]Training was on Stimuli 1 and 2 of a series; transfer was on Stimuli 2 and 3 (Near Test). The groups were not significantly different in training or transfer, but the difference in training "might be on the border line of significance" (O'Connor, personal communication, 1965).

between mental age and Near Test transposition, but obtained a significant positive relation on a five-step Far Test. However, the subjects in Kuenne's study were approximately normal mentally, and the mental age groups also differed in chronological age. Ross *et al.* (1965) found that mentally normal children gave more transposition responses than mentally retarded children in a delayed-reward condition, but the difference was not statistically significant.

Using the intermediate-size problem, Martin and Blum (1961) found a nonsignificant positive relation between transposition and intelligence, comparing normal subjects and mentally retarded subjects. Baumeister *et al.* (1964) obtained the same effect, using a task requiring choice of the intermediate stimulus or the largest stimulus (in subgroups). Caron (1967) obtained very low and nonsignificant correlations in normal children in the intermediate-size problem, but the obtained correlations were positive.

Rudel (1959) concluded from the results of her generalization study (discussed in section entitled "Effect of Direction of Transposition Test," Chapter 4) that mentally normal children exhibit both absolute and relational responses, but that mongoloid subjects respond, in this kind of task, neither absolutely nor relationally. The mongoloid subjects tended to choose a large box in the middle of the array of test boxes. In another study using a standard intermediate-size transposition test, however, Rudel (1960) obtained relational responses in mongoloid subjects; and in one condition (easy discrimination, immediate test), the mongoloid group gave more relational responses than normal children and more than brain-damaged children.

In general, the data of the studies reviewed in this section indicate that more intelligent subjects tend to transpose somewhat more than less intelligent subjects. However, the effect is not an impressive one.

Sex Differences

Caron (1965) found, in a normative survey he conducted, that preschool girls were more likely to possess the concept of middle-sizedness than preschool boys were. On the basis of this finding, he predicted that girls would transpose intermediate size more than boys would; and in a study of the effects of multiple-problem training on transposition (Caron, 1966, discussed in section entitled "Multiple-Problem Training," Chapter 3), he confirmed the prediction. In a later study, Caron (1967) obtained no significant sex difference in transposition, but a different kind of multiple-problem training was used. The training included a "warm-up" problem with stimuli that were about the same size as the stimuli in the formal training problem. (Marshall [1966] found no consistent sex difference in knowledge of the concept of middle-sizedness within the range from 30 to 78 months of age.)

Sherman (1966) used multiple-problem training procedures with two-stimulus problems, and found no sex difference in transposition. Sato (1936) and Motoyoshi (1948) also obtained no sex difference, apparently using single-problem training with the two-stimulus discrimination situation.

In my six studies of intermediate-size transposition (including the unpublished study described in the section entitled "Concept Knowledge," this chapter), a total of 246 boys and 245 girls were tested. They ranged in age from 2.9 to 7.9 years, and were divided into a total of 28 different experimental groups. The data of the 1961 study, summarized in Table 5-12, agree with Caron's data on the Near Test, but

TABLE 5–12

SEX DIFFERENCE IN TRANSPOSITION

Effects of concept knowledge and distance (Reese, 1961)[a]

Group	Sex	Sample size	Percentage transposition		
			Near	Middle	Far
Verbal	Male	10	36.7	26.7	25.0
	Female	8	60.4	16.7	18.8
	M − F		−23.7	+10.0	+6.2
Nonverbal	Male	9	44.4	20.4	13.0
	Female	10	63.3	3.3	6.7
	M − F		−18.9	+17.1	+6.3

[a] Data previously unpublished. Age range 43 to 64 months.

TABLE 5–13

SEX DIFFERENCE IN TRANSPOSITION

Effects of concept knowledge, stimulus similarity, age level, and distance (Reese, 1964b)[a]

Group	Sex	Sample size	Percentage transposition	
			Near	Far
2 to 1 ratio	Male	61	51.9	19.1
	Female	59	45.5	16.4
	M − F		+6.4	+2.7
1.3 to 1 ratio	Male	45	73.0	25.9
	Female	44	83.0	27.3
	M − F		−10.0	−1.4
Verbal	Male	64	66.7	20.6
	Female	56	68.2	25.0
	M − F		−1.5	−4.4
Nonverbal	Male	32	55.7	24.0
	Female	36	48.6	18.5
	M − F		+7.1	+5.5
Questionable	Male	10	40.0	25.0
	Female	11	69.7	9.1
	M − F		−29.7	+15.9
35–59	Male	64	51.3	22.9
	Female	58	49.1	22.1
	M − F		+2.2	+.8
60–83	Male	34	76.5	24.0
	Female	36	75.5	20.4
	M − F		+1.0	+3.6
84–90	Male	8	70.8	6.2
	Female	9	85.2	16.7
	M − F		−14.4	−10.5

[a] Data previously unreported. Data are for main effects; interactions ignored.

disagree on the Far Tests. On the Far Tests, boys were superior to girls. Concept knowledge seemed to be irrelevant to the sex difference. However, the data of the 1964b study, summarized in Table 5-13, do not agree with the 1961 data. The reversal in the direction of the sex difference with increasing distance of test was obtained only in children whose classification was "questionable" with respect to concept knowledge. Verbal girls were superior to verbal boys at both distances, and nonverbal girls were inferior to nonverbal boys at both distances. Figure 5-5 shows the effect of distance in the 28 groups of all six studies. Girls tended to transpose more than boys on the Near Test, but they tended to transpose less than boys on the Far Tests.

The 1964b data (Table 5-13) suggest that the sex difference is affected by stimulus similarity (ratio of areas). With distinctive stimuli, boys were

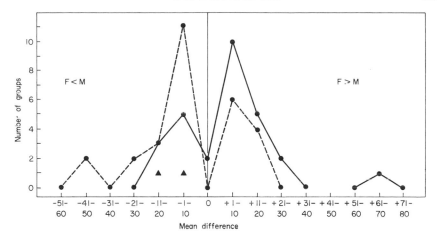

FIG. 5-5. Distance effect on sex differences in the Reese studies: mean percentage transposition by females minus mean percentage transposition by males. (——) One step (28 groups), (- - -) three steps (28 groups), and (▲) two steps (2 groups).

superior to girls; with similar stimuli, girls were superior to boys. The effects seemed to be weakened by increasing the distance of the test. The data of the 1962a study, summarized in Table 5-14, fail to confirm these trends. With distinctive stimuli, girls were superior to boys; with similar stimuli, boys were as good as or superior to girls, depending on the distance of the test.

The 1964b study also suggested that age level may influence the sex difference. Younger boys seemed to be superior to girls, and older boys inferior to girls. Table 5-15 presents the data from all six studies on the effect of age level, and it can be seen that age level had no consistent effect on the sex difference.

TABLE 5–14

SEX DIFFERENCE IN TRANSPOSITION

Effects of stimulus similarity and distance (Reese, 1962a)[a]

Stimulus ratio	Sex	Sample size	Percentage transposition	
			Near	Far
2 to 1	Male	10	66.7	43.3
	Female	10	71.7	46.7
	M − F		−5.0	−3.4
13. to 1	Male	10	78.3	56.7
	Female	11	78.8	51.5
	M − F		−.5	+5.2

[a]Data previously unpublished. Age range 60 to 81 months.

TABLE 5–15

SEX DIFFERENCE IN TRANSPOSITION

Effects of age level and distance (Reese studies)

Age level (months)	Study[a]	Sex	Sample size	Percentage transposition Near	Percentage transposition Far
34–43	E	Male	19	45.6	24.6
		Female	23	49.3	30.4
		M − F		−3.7	−5.8
35–59	C	Male	64	51.3	22.9
		Female	58	49.1	22.1
		M − F		+2.2	+.8
41–71	F	Male	25	32.0	32.7
		Female	20	35.0	23.3
		M − F		−3.0	+9.4
43–64	A	Male	19	42.1	19.3
		Female	18	62.0	12.0
		M − F		−19.9	+7.3
44–63	E	Male	19	59.6	35.1
		Female	22	71.2	32.6
		M − F		−11.6	+2.5
60–81	B	Male	20	72.5	50.0
		Female	21	75.4	49.2
		M − F		−2.9	+.8
60–83	C	Male	34	76.5	24.0
		Female	36	75.5	20.4
		M − F		+1.0	+3.6
76–95	D	Male	38	62.3	16.2
		Female	38	63.4	16.7
		M − F		−1.1	−.5
84–90	C	Male	8	70.8	6.2
		Female	9	85.2	16.7
		M − F		−14.4	−10.5

[a] Studies are indicated by the following: A, Reese, 1961; B, Reese, 1962a; C, Reese, 1964b; D, Reese and Fiero, 1964; E, Reese, 1966; and F, Reese, unpublished study.

Table 5-16 summarizes the data of the study with Fiero. These data suggest that the level of the training criterion can reverse the distance effect on the sex difference.

The data on the effect of distance on the sex difference are not consistent with the data obtained by Caron (1966), because Caron's data are for a Far Test. It may be that the difference in results is attributable to Caron's use of multiple-problem training procedures, since I used single-problem training in all six of my studies. However, in the studies summarized in Tables 5-17 and 5-18, procedures were used that were designed to elicit verbalizations. In the 1966 study (Table 5-17), the subjects in Group I were

TABLE 5–16
SEX DIFFERENCE IN TRANSPOSITION
Effects of training criterion and distance (Reese and Fiero, 1964)[a]

Training criterion	Sex	Sample size	Percentage transposition	
			Near	Far
5/5	Male	14	78.6	6.0
	Female	14	65.5	25.0
	M – F		+13.1	−19.0
9/10	Male	12	44.4	19.4
	Female	12	61.1	8.3
	M – F		−16.7	+11.1
14/15	Male	12	61.1	25.0
	Female	12	63.9	15.3
	M – F		−2.8	+9.7

[a] Data previously unpublished. Age range 76 to 95 months.

told before each response during the training phase that the reward was under the "medium" stimulus object, the subjects in Group II were told that it was "not under the big one or the little one," and the subjects in Group III were given standard instructions omitting size references. In the unpublished study (Table 5-18), the verbal group was given the not-big not-little instruction, the perceptual group was given instructions designed to focus attention on the size dimension, and the control group was given the standard instructions omitting size references. The data show that even when the subjects were encouraged to use available mediators, there was no consistent sex difference favoring girls.

The age range in these two studies was 34 to 71 months, which includes the range of Caron's subjects (40 to 57 months). Therefore, the difference in results is apparently not an age difference.

CONCLUSION

Preschool girls transpose somewhat more than preschool boys on the Near Test, but transpose somewhat less than boys on Far Tests unless multiple-problem training is given. After multiple-problem training, girls transpose more than boys on Far Tests. The effect of multiple-problem training on the sex difference is not attributable to an effect on the probability of using available mediators. (It is also not attributable to a difference in immediate memory, since Van De Moortel [1965] has shown, in a review of the developmental literature, that there is no sex difference in immediate memory.) The cause of the effect is not known.

TABLE 5–17

SEX DIFFERENCE IN TRANSPOSITION

Effects of training condition, age level, and distance (Reese, 1966)[a]

Age level[b]	Group	Sex	Sample size	Percentage transposition	
				Near	Far
Younger	I	Male	5	60.0	23.3
		Female	9	53.7	29.6
	II	Male	7	52.4	23.8
		Female	7	59.5	38.1
	III	Male	7	28.6	26.2
		Female	7	33.3	23.8
Older	I	Male	7	76.2	40.5
		Female	7	83.3	38.1
	II	Male	6	57.1	35.7
		Female	8	79.2	41.7
	III	Male	6	40.0	26.7
		Female	7	50.0	16.7
Both levels	I and II	Male	25	64.0	32.7
		Female	31	68.3	36.6
		M – F		–4.3	–3.9
	III	Male	13	30.8	24.4
		Female	14	41.7	20.2
		M – F		–10.9	+4.2
Younger	All groups	Male	19	45.6	24.6
		Female	23	49.3	30.4
		M – F		–3.7	–5.8
Older	All groups	Male	19	59.6	35.1
		Female	22	71.2	32.6
		M – F		–11.6	+2.5

[a] Data previously unpublished.

[b] Younger indicates 34 to 43 months; older indicates 44 to 63 months. See text for description of groups.

Phylogenetic Comparisons

Species differences in transposition have not been investigated in any one study, and comparisons across studies are of doubtful validity because of procedural differences. A number of studies, however, have demonstrated transposition in a variety of species, and a tentative conclusion about the relation between phylogenetic status and transposition can be suggested. The data are summarized in Table 5-19. (Table 5-20 lists additional studies included in Shirai's [1951] master's thesis.)

TABLE 5–18
SEX DIFFERENCE IN TRANSPOSITION
Effects of training condition and distance (Reese, unpublished study)[a]

Condition	Sex	Sample size	Percentage transposition	
			Near	Far
Verbal	Male	9	27.8	37.0
	Female	7	40.5	23.8
	M – F		–12.7	+13.2
Perceptual	Male	9	24.1	33.3
	Female	8	20.8	22.9
	M – F		+3.3	+10.4
Control	Male	7	47.6	26.2
	Female	5	50.0	23.3
	M – F		–2.4	+2.9

[a]The study is described in the section entitled "Concept Knowledge," this chapter. Other data are given in Table 5-7, but the sample sizes in Table 5-7 and this table are different because sex of subject was not recorded on data sheets and the names of five subjects were ambiguous with respect to sex. Age range about 41 to 71 months.

INSECTS

Using stimuli differing in brightness, Bierens de Haan (1928) found absolute responses in bees, but Hörmann (1934) was able to demonstrate relative choices. Hertz (1929) concluded that bees can discriminate and transpose "degrees of openness," but she tested for transposition in only one direction on the dimension, and spontaneous preferences cannot be ruled out as a basis for the "transposition" obtained.[9] In discussing other studies by Hertz, C. J. Warden et al. (1940, pp. 696–698) pointed out that there was a relation between the attractiveness of the patterns used and the likelihood of effective intermittent stimulation, and that Zerrahn (1933) had shown that the attractiveness of "paddlewheel patterns" is directly proportional to the number of radii. Wolf and Zerrahn-Wolf (1937) also concluded that flicker rather than form determined the response. Warden et al. said; "It is very likely, therefore, that insects, such as the honeybee, *distinguish patterns, not on the basis of form, but primarily through the relative stimulating efficiency of intermittent illumination*" (p. 698, their italics). However, Warden et al. reported that Hertz also showed that bees "could be trained to react to one of two grays regardless of their absolute brightness"

[9] She used as synonyms for "degree of openness," *richness of contrast* (p. 257), *degree* or *richness of articulation* (pp. 257 and 262), and *relative continuity* or *discontinuity of contours* (pp. 261 and 263). There was some evidence, in the first experiment (pp. 254–255), that the bees spontaneously preferred a circle to a star, which weakens the argument that the bees might have spontaneously preferred the more "open" figures on the transposition tests.

TABLE 5-19

UNIDIMENSIONAL TRANSPOSITION IN INFRAHUMAN SPECIES[a]

Subject	Study	Dimension		
		Brightness	Size	Other
Bee	Bierens de Haan (1928)	No		
	Hertz[b]	Yes		
	Hertz (1929)	Yes		Yes (flicker?)
	Hörmann (1934)	Yes		
Wasp	[c]		Yes	
Goldfish	Perkins (1931)	Yes[d]		
	Perkins and Wheeler (1930)	Yes[d]		
Fish	Burkamp (1923)	No		
	Herter (1929)	Yes	Yes	
Turtle	Casteel (1911)		Perhaps	
	Spigel (1963)	No		
Tortoise	Kuroda (1933)	No		
Chicken	Bingham (1913; 1922)		Yes	Yes? (color)
	Breed (1912)			No (speed)
	Cutsforth (1933)	Yes		Yes (color)
	Jaensch (1920)	Yes	Yes	Yes? (color)
	Katz and Révész (1921)	Yes		
	Katz and Toll (1923)	Yes		
	H. Keller and Takemasa (1933)	Yes		
	Köhler (1915; 1917; 1918)	Yes		
	Kroh (1927)		Yes	
	M. H. Lewis (1930)			
	Pattie and Stavsky (1932)	Yes		Yes (speed)

Chicken	Révész (1924)		Yes	
	Riekel (1922)	Yes	Yes	Yes? (color)
	Takei (1927)	No	Yes	
	Takemasa (1934)	Yes		
	Taylor (1932a)	No		
Gamecock	H. M. Johnson (1916)			No (coarseness)
Bird	Borovski (1936)	No		
	Sadovinkova (1923)	Yes		Yes (position)
Tit	Takagi (1935a; 1935b; 1937)	Yes		
Crow	Coburn (1914)		Yes	
Parakeet	Campbell and Kral (1958)	Yes		
Pigeon	D. H. Cohen (1963)	Yes		
	Honig (1962)			Yes (color)
	Rudolph[e]			Yes (color)
	Towe (1954)		Yes	
	Zeiler (1965a)		No[d]	
	Zeiler[f]		No[d]	
	Zeiler and Price (1965)		No[d]	
Rabbit	Washburn and Abbott (1912)	Yes		
Hedgehog	Herter (1932; 1933; 1934)	Yes		
Mouse	Hopkins (1927)	Yes		
	Moody (1929)	Yes (?)		
	Yerkes (1907)	Yes		
Guinea pig	Hadley (1927)	Yes		
	Wissenburgh and Tibout (1921)	Yes		

Table 5–19 (continued)

Subject	Study	Dimension		
		Brightness	Size	Other
Rat	Adams (1933; 1937)			Yes (weight)
	Baker and Lawrence (1951)		Yes	
	Blue and Hegge (1965)			Yes (loudness)
	Chang (1936)		Yes	
	Chisum (1965)	Yes		
	Ehrenfreund (1952)	Yes		
	Flory (1938; 1939)		Yes	
	Gayton (1927)	Yes		
	Grether and Wolfle (1936)	Yes	Yes	
	Gulliksen (1932a)		Yes	
	Gulliksen (1936)		Yes	
	Hebb (1937b)	Yes	Yes	
	Hebb (1938)	Yes		
	Helson (1927)	Yes		
	Heyman (1951)	Yes		
	I. M. L. Hunter (1952b)		Yes (?)	
	I. M. L. Hunter (1953b)		Yes	
	F.N. Jones (1939b)	Yes		
	Kendler (1943; 1950)	Yes		
	S.J. Lachman (1956)	Yes		
	Lashley (1912)		Yes	
	Lashley (1938b)		Yes	
	Lawrence and DeRivera (1954)	Yes		No (numerosity)
	Mackintosh (1965b)		Yes	
	Maier (1939)		Yes	

Animal	Reference			
Rat	Maltzman (1949)	No		
	McCulloch (1935)		Yes	Yes (weight)
	Meyer (1964b)		Yes	
	Nahinsky (1960)			
	Okano (1957)		Yes	Yes (?)
	Riley (1958)	Yes		
	Riley et al. (1960)	Yes		
	Riley et al. (1963)	Yes		
	R. Thompson (1955)	Yes	Yes	
	Wolfle (1937)	Yes		
Cat	Warren (1964)		Yes	
	Warren (1964)		No[d]	
Dog	Beritoff and Topurin (1929)			No (loudness)
	Bregadze (1937)			No (pitch)
	Ebel and Werboff (1966)		No[d]	
	Kleshchov (1933)			Yes (pitch)
	Usnadze (1927)			Yes (loudness)
Monkey	Bagshaw and Pribram (1965)	Yes	Yes	
	Bierens de Haan (1928)		Yes	
	W. L. Brown et al. (1959)		No[d] (?)	
	Gentry et al. (1959)		Yes[d]	
	H.M. Johnson (1916)			Yes (distance)
	Kafka (1931)		Yes	
	Kinnaman (1902)	Yes		Yes (coarseness)
	Klüver (1933)	Yes	Yes	Yes (loudness), (weight)

177

TABLE 5-19 (*continued*)

Subject	Study	Dimension		
		Brightness	Size	Other
Monkey	Ohtsuka (1937; 1942)	Yes	Yes (?)	
	Ohtsuka (1939)			No (position)[d]
	Schwartzbaum and Pribram (1960)	Yes		
	Verlaine (1935)		Yes	
Chimpanzee	Gonzalez et al. (1954)		Yes[d]	
	Harrison and Nissen (1941)	Yes	Yes	Yes (position)
	Köhler (1915; 1917; 1918)		Yes	Yes (color)
	Nissen (1942)		Yes	
	Spence (1936b; 1937b; 1938)			Yes (position)[d]
	Spence (1939b)		Yes	
	Spence (1941)		Yes	
	Spence (1942)		No[d]	

[a] "Yes" means transposition was obtained; "No" means it was not obtained.
[b] Cited in C.J. Warden et al. (1940, p. 695).
[c] See C.J. Warden et al. (1940, p. 694).
[d] Intermediate-stimulus problems.
[e] Cited in Riley (1965b, pp. 308–310).
[f] Personal communication, 1966.

178

TABLE 5–20
ADDITIONAL STUDIES LISTED BY SHIRAI (1951)[a]

Study	Species	Dimension
Verlaine (1927)	Bee	Brightness
Schaller (1926)	Fish	Form
Hertz (1928a)	Jaybird	No information
Hertz (1928c)	Raven	No information
Herter (1933; 1934)	Hedgehog	Brightness, color
Odani (1934)	Rat	Brightness

[a] Shirai did not mention the findings of these studies. She discussed the findings of other studies, which are included in the text. It is possible that not all of these studies dealt directly with transposition.

(p. 695), suggesting that brightness relations can be sensed by the bee (it is not clear which of the Hertz studies was being cited). These writers also said that "Wasps apparently react to a multiplicity of spatial relationships, involving size, brightness, and form" (p. 694). They referred to untranslated studies in French and German, and to a report by G. W. Peckham and Peckham (1898); but if the report by the Peckhams is characteristic of the other references, which I have not examined, then the conclusion of Warden *et al.* was probably based upon demonstration of the ability of the wasp to relocate sites that it has temporarily abandoned, as in relocating the nest and in relocating prey.

FISH

Perkins and Wheeler (1930) obtained brightness transposition in the goldfish (the paper by Wheeler and Perkins, 1929, appears to be a preliminary report of these studies), and Perkins (1931) confirmed this finding. Herter (1929) apparently also obtained brightness transposition in fish, but Burkamp (1923) obtained absolute responses in fish.

TURTLES

Casteel (1911) presented evidence suggesting that transposition of size occurs in turtles. Spigel (1963) obtained little brightness transposition in turtles, but the test may have been inappropriate. Of five turtles given a black–gray discrimination, with gray positive, four solved the problem; but on a gray–white transposition test, with no reinforcement for any response, transposition averaged only 58 per cent over six trials. The fastest two learners were given the gray–white discrimination problem two weeks after the black–gray problem had been solved, and failed to learn within 200 trials. Of four other turtles given only the gray–white discrimination, none solved the problem in 200 trials. It is apparent, then, that the gray–white discrimination was much more difficult than the black–gray discrimination, probably accounting for the failure to obtain transposition. The ratio of brightnesses was 1 to 1.91 millilamberts for the black–gray discrimination and 1 to 1.58 millilamberts for the gray–white discrimination.

Kuroda (1933) also used a black–gray–white series, and seems to have obtained similar results in tortoises.

FOWL

Takei (1927) used a black–gray–white series, testing chicks, and obtained results similar to Spigel's and Kuroda's even though transposition was up-ward and the chicks initially preferred the brighter (positive) training stimulus. Taylor (1932a) used the same kind of stimulus series with chicks, and also obtained no transposition. In fact, this was one of the few studies obtaining a predominance of absolute responses on test trials. (Wesman and Eisenberg [1941] obtained an average of only 56 per cent transposition by college students trained individually on problems like this, with markedly distinctive stimuli, but they obtained 69 per cent transposition in a "group" study [see section entitled "Multiple-Problem Training," Chapter 3, for details of the study]. On the first problem, there was only 45 per cent trans-position in subjects trained individually, and 63 per cent in subjects trained as a group.) Transposition of brightness was obtained in chickens in nine other studies, apparently using stimuli that were more similar to one another than were the stimuli used by Takei and Taylor (see list in Table 5-19). In one of these studies, by M. H. Lewis (1930), chicks clearly transposed bright and dim relations, and apparently also transposed the intermediate bright-ness relation. The description of procedures was very poor, however, and the results are therefore somewhat ambiguous.

Takei (1927) obtained 65 per cent transposition of size at one "step" in chicks. The ratio of stimulus areas was 4 to 1 during the training phase and was 2.25 to 1 on the test (the training-stimulus areas were 7 cm² for S⁻ and 28 cm² for S⁺; the test-stimulus areas were 28 and 63 cm²). Jaensch (1920), Bingham (1922), Riekel (1922), Révész (1924), and Kroh (1927) also seem to have obtained transposition of size in chickens.[10]

---

[10]Referring to a preliminary report of Bingham's size-transposition data (Bingham, 1913), Watson said, "From experiments now in progress at the Nela Physical Laboratory (Johnson), it would seem that this observation cannot be confirmed" (Watson, 1914, footnote 16, p. 367). According to Bingham, Watson's remark was based on "having been informed by Johnson that the latter failed to secure positive evidence in this relative stimulus problem with a single adult game bantam" (Bingham, 1922, p. 18). Johnson himself disclaimed Watson's interpreta-tion, and pointed out that " ... the two problems are so different that there is little basis for comparison" (H. M. Johnson, 1916, footnote 6, p. 182).

In 1915, Köhler demonstrated size constancy in hens (and chimpanzees). The subjects were trained to choose the larger of two rectangles, and continued to do so when the larger rectangle was placed farther from the subject than the smaller one, even when the smaller one gave a larger retinal image. Götz (1926) obtained the same effect in hens, using grains differing in size.

Perkins and Wheeler (1930) seem correctly to have detected "hints of transposability" in Breed's (1912) results with chicks, using form and color. However, Bingham (1922) and Takei (1927) found no evidence of form transposition in chicks. Bingham (1922) also obtained no transposition of flicker in chicks, and Jaensch (1920) and Riekel (1922) seem to have obtained no transposition of length. Pattie and Stavsky (1932) obtained transposition of speed.

H. M. Johnson (1916) obtained no transposition of "coarseness" (width of striae) in the single Indian gamecock which solved the initial discrimination. In fact, there was a predominance of absolute responses (68 per cent absolute responses).

Lashley (1916) obtained transfer of responses to color in the bantam gamecock, but since both the relative value and absolute value of either the positive or negative stimulus remained unchanged on test trials, the transfer cannot properly be classified as transposition.

Sadovinkova (1923) obtained transposition of spatial relations in songbirds, Takagi (1935a; 1935b; 1937) obtained brightness transposition in the tomtit, and Campbell and Kral (1958) obtained responses to brightness relations in the parakeet. Borovski (1936) apparently failed to obtain brightness transposition in birds.

Coburn (1914) concluded that his data indicated that crows can respond to relative size, but Bingham (1922) argued that the nature of the training rendered the conclusion doubtful. Every critical problem in Coburn's study included stimuli that were identical to or highly similar to stimuli of previous problems, and there were changes in the absolute values of the stimuli from problem to problem throughout training. Bingham correctly suggested that the latter procedure may have resulted in the development of a "relative difference preparation" (p. 99), judging from the data on the effects of multiple-problem training reviewed in Chapter 3. However, Bingham overlooked a very suggestive finding on the last six problems (Series 11–16). On these critical problems, transposition ranged from 64 to 80 per cent (the median was 70 per cent), which is relatively low, since these problems were preceded by 10 problems in all of which the same relative stimulus was positive. As already noted, multiple-problem training should tend to increase transposition; furthermore, in each of these critical problems only transposition responses were rewarded, and the scores were therefore inflated by relearning. There was also possibly a preference in the crows for the larger stimulus, which was correct in all problems. (The subjects had already learned to approach the brighter of two lights, and anyway had a spontaneous preference for the larger stimulus. Initially, the larger stimulus was brighter than the smaller, although on later tests with brightness and size varied independently, size controlled responses.) That the obtained percentages of transposition were relatively so low indicates that there must have been considerable interference with transposition.

Spence's (1937b) theory can account for the interference with transposition on the basis of absolute preferences and aversions acquired during training. For example, in Series 12 the stimuli were circles with diameters of 6 and 9 centimeters, and 70 per cent of the responses on 10 trials were to the larger (transposition) stimulus. The frequencies of reward and of nonreward of responses to the 8 stimuli used over the 11 preceding problems are given in Table 5-21; and it is obvious that an approach tendency already conditioned to Stimulus 6 and generalized from Stimulus 5 would compete with the approach tendency already conditioned to Stimulus 9, and would interfere with transposition. In the next problem (Series 13), using circles with diameters of 4 and 6 centimeters, 64 per cent of the responses on 42 trials were to the larger stimulus, clearly exhibiting the effect of extinction of the response to Stimulus 6 on the preceding problem (generalized and conditioned inhibition presumably conflicted with the approach tendency generalized from Stimulus 5 to Stimulus 4).

Honig (1962) and Rudolph (cited by Riley, 1965b, pp. 308–310) obtained transposition of wave length in pigeons, D. H. Cohen (1963) obtained transposition of brightness, and Towe (1954) obtained transposition of size. Zeiler (1965a) and Zeiler and Price (1965) obtained absolute responses in pigeons in intermediate-size problems; and in two further studies, both only partially completed, Zeiler has confirmed this finding (Zeiler, personal communication, 1966). Honig (1965, Study 3) also obtained absolute responses in pigeons after training on "stimulus-difference" discriminations, in which the birds were required to learn to respond to one side when two identical stimuli were presented, and to respond to the other side when two different stimuli were presented. The training stimuli had wave lengths ranging from 500 to 570 millimicrons, and the test stimuli had wave lengths ranging from 590 to 630 millimicrons. The pigeons "demonstrated a consistent preference for the values closer to the original training range."

RABBITS AND HEDGEHOGS

Washburn and Abbott (1912) obtained transposition of brightness in the rabbit, and Herter (1932) demonstrated relative brightness responses in hedgehogs.

TABLE 5-21
DATA FROM THE COBURN STUDY

Training series	Stimuli								Mean number of responses		Correct responses (%)
	2	3	4	5	6	7	8	9	Incorrect	Correct	
1	−			+					0	0	—
2				−				+	1.5	3.5	70
3	−							+	1.0	19.0	95
4	−			+					6.5	53.5	89
5		−		+					4.5	25.5	85
6	−	+							26.0	74.0	74
7		−		+					16.5	73.5	82
8		−			+				0.5	7.5	94
9		−		+					10.0	54.0	84
10	−								1.0	9.0	90
11		+	−		+				2.0	8.0	80
(Total rewarded responses)	(0)	(83.0)	(0)	(206.5)	(15.5)	(0)	(0)	(22.5)			
(Total nonrewarded responses)	(34.5)	(31.5)	(2.0)	(1.5)	(0)	(0)	(0)	(0)			
12					−			+	3.0	7.0	70
13			−		+				15.0	27.0	64

MICE

Rowley and Bolles (1935) found that changing the size and brightness of shapes did not affect the performance of white mice. In a study of brightness discrimination thresholds in mice, Moody (1929) gave six phases of training, varying the positive stimulus brightness within each phase and the negative stimulus brightness only between phases. The negative stimulus of the later phases was as bright as the positive stimulus of early phases, or even brighter. A high level of performance was obtained on the first ten trials of each of these later phases (73 to 83 per cent correct responses), suggesting that transposition occurred. However, preliminary data reported by Moody indicated that the mice were positively phototropic, and therefore the data are ambiguous with respect to transposition. Data presented by Yerkes (1907, Table 24, pp. 163–164; Table 26, pp. 167–168) suggest that brightness transposition occurs in the dancing mouse, because although the stimulus lights used in the study differed in color (red–green) as well as brightness, Yerkes concluded that "the animals depend upon brightness when they can, and . . . their ability to discriminate color differences is extremely poor" (p. 169). Hopkins (1927) obtained brightness transposition in mice.

GUINEA PIGS

Wissenburgh and Tibout (1921) apparently demonstrated perception of brightness relations in guinea pigs. Hadley (1927) trained guinea pigs on a discrimination with size and brightness confounded, and obtained 86 per cent transposition on a 10-trial Near Test with size and brightness still confounded. On a "zero-step" test with the sizes the same as during training but with the brightness difference eliminated, the subjects gave only 74 per cent correct responses on 20 trials, even though differential reinforcement was given throughout the "test." These findings seem to indicate that the subjects initially learned much more about the brightnesses than about the sizes. Alternatively, it is possible that the findings indicate that there was less generalization between the brightnesses than between the sizes, but the high level of transposition obtained with the confounded stimuli seems to be inconsistent with this interpretation.

RATS

It has been demonstrated that rats can transpose brightness (17 studies), size (15 studies), weight (two studies), and loudness (one study). (The studies are listed in Table 5-19.) They cannot transpose physical numerosity (Lashley, 1938b, pp. 171–172). No brightness transposition was obtained in one study (Maltzman, 1949). There was, in fact, a predominance of absolute responses, whether the stimuli were markedly different (.29, 1.5, and 5.2 foot-candles) or were more similar (.55, 1.15, and 2.2 foot-candles).

Meyer (1964b) trained six groups of rats with Stimuli 2 and 4 or 2, 4, and 6 of a series of seven stimuli varying in size. The experimental conditions were the same as were used in a previous study (Meyer, 1964a; see also Table 6-1). In the test trials, each of the 21 possible pairs of the seven stimuli in the series was presented once. Transposition averaged 74 per cent, and Meyer reported that 81 per cent of the responses were consistent with predictions derived from Spence's (1942) theory. Relational theory would presumably predict transposition on all pairs, and therefore only 74 per cent of the responses were consistent with relational theory.

Hebb (1937b) found greater transposition of brightness than size in rats reared in total darkness; but transposition occurred even on the size problem, and Hebb concluded that there is an innate tendency to perceive relative values on these visual dimensions. In another study, Hebb (1938) obtained brightness transposition in rats which were trained and tested after destruction of the striate cortex. He observed in both studies that rats which did not give consistent relational responses gave consistent position responses.

Blue and Hegge (1965) obtained loudness transposition in rats. During training, the most intense of nine loudnesses was positive; and by the end of training, a generalization gradient of response-evocation potential was demonstrated. On test trials, each of the nine loudnesses was increased by 45 decibels. The entire gradient shifted upward, demonstrating transposition.

Nahinsky (1960) trained rats to make one response under a high thirst drive and a different response under a low thirst drive. On test trials with thirst satiated but with high and low hunger drive, the rats performed at better than the chance level. The transfer could have resulted from generalization on the basis of similarity of drive stimuli, as Nahinsky suggested; but it could be classed as transposition, since the subjects could have been responding on the basis of the relative intensities of the drive stimuli.[11]

CATS

Warren (1964) obtained transposition of size in cats when an extreme stimulus in a three-stimulus set was correct, but obtained absolute responses when the intermediate stimulus was correct.

DOGS

Usnadze (1927) "trained a dog to form a CR to the stronger of two sound stimuli, when the stronger followed the weaker stimulus by one second and

---

[11]Babb's (1963) study of transfer between habits based on shock and thirst is not relevant, because the drive stimuli were not the conditioned cues.

was reinforced, two seconds later, by an electric shock. Repeating the first or the second stimulus or making the second stimulus the weaker of the two failed in most cases to produce the conditioned reaction, while some transposition was observed when bells of differing intensities had been substituted for the sounds . . . used in the training" (Razran, 1939, p. 318). However, the "percentage of mistakes remained rather high even after long training" (C. J. Warden et al., 1936, p. 289). Beritoff and Topurin (1929) obtained the same kind of conditioning in the dog, but no transposition. The conditioned response could be elicited only by the specifically trained stimuli.

Bregadze (1937) also obtained no transposition in dogs that had been conditioned to respond to a succession of three musical notes. Kleshchov (1933), however, obtained two-stimulus transposition of tones. The training stimuli differed by a fifth (C^3 vs G^3); and there was more transposition to fifths than to thirds, even when the key was changed, and even when the thirds seemed to be more similar to the training pair than the fifths were (for example, G-B pairs and D#-A# pairs). Furthermore, "this difference between generalizations was the greater the nearer in frequency the tested stimuli were to the trained stimuli" (Razran, 1939, p. 312). (Razran [1938a] obtained essentially the same findings in human adults.)

MONKEYS

In the earliest experimental study providing data on transposition, Kinnaman (1902) demonstrated that monkeys can transpose brightness. Later studies have confirmed this finding (Bierens de Haan, 1928; Klüver, 1933; Ohtsuka, 1937; Schwartzbaum and Pribram, 1960), and it has been shown that monkeys can also transpose other visual qualities (Bierens de Haan, 1928; H. M. Johnson, 1916; Kafka, 1931; Klüver 1933; Ohtsuka, 1942) and can transpose auditory and weight qualities (Klüver, 1933—Klüver's 1929a, 1929b, 1930, and 1931 papers appear to be preliminary reports of these studies). Schwartzbaum and Pribram (1960) and Bagshaw and Pribram (1965) found that normal monkeys transposed more than amygdalectomized monkeys. (The Schwartzbaum and Pribram study was also summarized by Pribram, 1962, pp. 129–131.) The effect of amygdalectomy is not on generalization (Hearst and Pribram, 1964) nor on retention of the discrimination (Bagshaw and Pribram, 1965). Bagshaw and Pribram (1965) suggested that it affects the process underlying transfer of training, but admitted that the nature of this process is not yet specifiable.

Bagshaw and Pribram (1965) also found that inferotemporal cortical lesions interfered with transposition, but not as much as amygdalectomy. The postoperative test was given after retraining, and the retraining scores indicated that there was interference with retention of the original discrimination only in the inferotemporal group. As Bagshaw and Pribram noted, inferotemporal lesions disrupt discrimination and increase stimulus generalization, accounting for the performance of the inferotemporal group.

Gentry *et al.* (1959) obtained intermediate-size transposition in monkeys, but W. L. Brown *et al.* (1959) obtained ambiguous results with this problem (see section entitled "Multiple-Problem Training," Chapter 3). Ohtsuka (1939) obtained no transposition of middle position in monkeys.

CHIMPANZEES

Using two-stimulus problems, Köhler (1915; 1917; 1918) obtained transposition of brightness, size, and color in chimpanzees; and Spence (1937b; 1938) and Nissen (1942) obtained transposition of size. (Spence also reported parts of his data in 1936b and in 1942, footnote 4, p. 262.) Spence (1941) obtained a kind of transposition of size in chimpanzees. The subjects were given training with one negative stimulus and two positive stimuli (either the largest or smallest two of the three), and were given tests with the two positive stimuli. Relational responses were obtained in two experiments (Experiments 1 and 3), but not in a third experiment (Experiment 2). Spence (1942) obtained no transposition of intermediate-size in chimpanzees, but Gonzalez *et al.* (1954) did by using a kind of multiple-problem training procedure.

Spence (1939b) and Harrison and Nissen (1941) obtained transposition of position in chimpanzees.

J. S. Robinson (1955) showed that chimpanzees can learn to respond to the "identity" relation, independently of absolute object qualities, confirming Nissen's (1953) speculation that such learning is possible. In a further study, J. S. Robinson (1960) trained chimpanzees to choose a compound stimulus having two instances of a figure (circle or triangle) and to avoid compounds having one instance of both figures. On equivalence tests, the data indicated that one subject responded on the basis of a "simplicity" relation, choosing the stimulus compound with the fewer different elements; the other two subjects responded on the basis of a "multiplicity" relation, choosing the stimulus compound with more identical elements. The third possible relation, "duplexity" (choosing the compound with two identical elements), was least frequently a basis for responding. Apparently the subjects perceived the relations indicated by their responses, since utilization of the concept of stimulus patterning as an explanation fails to account for the findings.

CONCLUSION

Two-stimulus transposition has been obtained in every species tested, but intermediate-stimulus transposition seems to be rare. (There might be differences among the species in the dimensions that are transposable, but this suggestion is almost idle speculation because of the gaps in the data and the lack of comparability across studies.)

CHAPTER 6

Absolute versus Relative Discrimination Problems

The Standard Absolute and Relative Problems

As the terms are ordinarily used, the "absolute" and "relative" discrimination problems require three stimuli, A, B, and C, ordered on some dimension. The intermediate stimulus B is paired with A on half of the trials, and with C on the other half. In the absolute discrimination problem, the subject must choose B whether it is paired with A or with C. This problem has sometimes been called an intermediate-stimulus problem (McCulloch, 1935; Rudel, 1957; Spence, 1942). In the relative discrimination problem, the subject must choose B when B is paired with A and must choose C when B is paired with C.

Training on a relative discrimination problem is the same as training on one of the kinds of multiple problem considered in Chapter 3 (in the section entitled "Multiple-Problem Training"). However, in Chapter 3 the discussion was centered on the effects of this kind of multiple-problem training on transposition to a new set of stimuli, and here the emphasis is on performance during the training phase.

C. J. Warden and Rowley (1929) and C. J. Warden and Winslow (1931) obtained absolute discrimination learning in doves, and even though the learning was extremely slow—performance was much less than perfect after 1000 trials—their conclusion that discriminations are easier when based on relational factors as opposed to absolute factors was unwarranted. They did not give a relative discrimination problem or a standard discrimination problem, and therefore had no data against which the absolute discrimination learning could be evaluated. Warden and Rowley pointed out that Yerkes and Eisenberg (1915) had obtained standard two-stimulus discrimination learning in the dove in fewer trials; but as Warden and Rowley correctly noted, there were so many other procedural differences that the comparison was not valid.

Campbell and Kral (1958) obtained absolute discrimination in the parakeet; but again no other kinds of problem were included, and the results are ambiguous with respect to the relative difficulty of absolute discrimination learning.

McCulloch (1935) found that rats can solve the relative discrimination problem. He found that on the early trials of a one-step transposition test, the predominant response was absolute, indicating that the response was to absolute components. However, only relational responses were rewarded during the test, and there was a shift to relational responses as the test trials continued. The transposition "problem" was learned much more rapidly by the group that had learned the relative discrimination problem than by a control group that had been given the first task with intermittent reinforcement for responses to all three stimuli. McCulloch concluded that the difference between the groups on the transposition task indicated that relational responses were learned in the relative discrimination problem, but he reported other data that suggest an alternative explanation of the difference between the groups. By the end of the first task, all of the control rats had developed a position habit. A strong position habit would retard the learning of the transposition task; therefore, it is possible that the relative discrimination training did not facilitate transposition, but rather that the control training interfered with it. However, there could have been a combination of facilitation from the one kind of training and interference from the other. This possibility is consistent with the findings of Wolfle (1937), who demonstrated that the absolute discrimination is indeed much harder for rats to learn than the relative discrimination. The median error score on an absolute brightness discrimination problem was more than four times greater than on a relative brightness discrimination problem.

Perkins and Wheeler (1930) suggested, in criticizing the C. J. Warden and Rowley (1929) study, that the absolute discrimination is solved by learning two relational responses (for example, choose "brighter" when A and B are presented; choose "dimmer" when B and C are presented).[1] Wolfle (1937) presented evidence that contradicted this explanation. The group that had learned the absolute discrimination was given a 30-trial "transposition" test on which all three stimuli were presented simultaneously, with all responses rewarded. The subjects gave a median of 93 per cent responses to the absolute stimulus (intermediate stimulus), indicating that an absolute response had actually been learned, and not two relational responses. According to Wolfle, there would have been considerable disturbance of performance on the transposition test if the rats had learned during the absolute discrimination training to respond to the brighter of two lights in a generally "dim" situation and to respond to

[1] Perkins and Wheeler's argument resembles Herbert Spencer's contention that the perception of absolute magnitude depends on the perception of relations (Spencer, 1887, pp. 172–177 and 183). However, Spencer was engaged in the classical task of decomposing mental contents into irreducible elements, and was analyzing the conscious awareness of absolute magnitude. Perkins and Wheeler did not assume any perception or awareness of the absolute magnitudes, only perception of the relative magnitudes. The question of whether or not relation perception involves an awareness of relations is irrelevant here, but is discussed in the section entitled "Gestalt Theory" (Chapter 8).

the dimmer of two lights in a generally "bright" situation. Further tests, given after retraining on the original absolute discrimination, confirmed this conclusion. In these tests, the number of lights varied from two to five, including the originally positive stimulus and one to four other brightnesses. All responses were rewarded. The subjects gave a median of 63 per cent responses to the originally positive stimulus, even though its relative brightness was not constant. In the next stage of the experiment, the combinations of lights used in the tests were presented with reward only for responses to the absolute brightness. Performance began above the chance level, and learning was clearly evident. In the final stage, the absolute brightness and two negative brightnesses were presented one at a time, with reward only for responses to the absolute brightness. Learning was again clearly evident. That learning was possible in the last two stages indicates that the subjects were responding to absolute cues.

Schwartzbaum and Pribram (1960) obtained absolute discrimination in normal and amygdalectomized monkeys, and found that the normal group learned more rapidly than the amygdalectomized group. The absolute discrimination training was given after one of the discriminations had been learned and the other had been used as a transposition test. There was almost perfect transposition in the normal group, and about chance transposition in the operated group; but on the absolute discrimination the normal group quickly reversed the transposition, whereas the amygdalectomized group apparently either continued to respond to the transposition pair at the chance level or began to transpose.

It has been demonstrated that human neonates can make the absolute discrimination spontaneously (Hershenson, 1964; Hershenson, Munsinger, and Kessen, 1965).[2] Studies with children have nevertheless shown that the relative discrimination is easier to learn than the absolute discrimination. Wohlwill obtained this effect in nursery-school children (1957, Experiment 1) and in older children (1960a, Experiment 1). In the latter study, he trained the children on a discrimination between stimuli differing in "physical numerosity," to use Stevens's (1951) term, and then gave a one-step transposition test, on which he obtained virtually perfect transposition. After this phase of the experiment, the subjects were given an absolute or a relative discrimination problem with the same stimuli. Performance on the relative problem was better than on the absolute problem (96 vs 51 per cent correct responses), but many of the subjects verbalized the solution to the relative problem and none verbalized the solution to the absolute problem. In a later

---

[2]Hershenson (1965) pointed out that these studies actually demonstrate only that one stimulus is more attractive than the other stimuli, and emphasized that it is necessary to distinguish between "discrimination" and "attention tropisms." The distinction is akin to Lund's (1914) unwillingness to say that the protozoan *Bursaria* accepted or rejected treated egg yolk on the basis of *taste*.

study (Wohlwill, 1963), it was again shown that the relative discrimination of physical numerosity is easier than the absolute, and it was found that this is especially so when irrelevant cues are present. However, the absolute discrimination was found to be easier than the relative discrimination when numerals were used as stimuli. Wohlwill (1960a, Experiment 2) also found that when the intermediate of three stimuli differing in physical numerosity was correct in training, only 40 per cent of the subjects transposed at one step, and 52 per cent gave the absolute response. In a second phase of training, young children (7.0 to 8.6 years old) performed as well on the absolute problem as on the relative problem, but older children (10.7 to 12.8 years old) were better on the absolute problem than on the relative problem.

Berman (1963) and F. K. Graham, Ernhart, Craft, and Berman (1964) found that children learn a relative size discrimination more rapidly than an absolute size discrimination, and they found more perseveration of relational responses than of absolute responses. They concluded that the results support the assumption that children can respond to relational cues. However, the superior performance on relative discrimination problems could result from the occurrence of transposition between the stimulus pairs, since this would facilitate performance on relative problems and would interfere with performance on absolute problems (see Spiker et al., 1956). Transposition does not necessarily require responses to relational cues, and therefore the superior performance on relative problems does not necessarily indicate responses to relational cues.

Line (1931) reported that children solved the absolute discrimination problem more rapidly than the relative discrimination problem "if the presentations were distinctly separated" (p. 82). Unfortunately, Line only summarized the study, and it is impossible to determine conclusively whether he meant separation in *space* between the stimuli (which he had varied in standard two-stimulus transposition problems), separation in *time* between the stimuli (yielding successive discriminations), or separation in time between the *pairs* of stimuli. The first interpretation seems to be ruled out by the wording of the quoted clause, and the third interpretation seems to be ruled out by other considerations. (There are difficult technical problems inherent in the third procedure; and the enhancing effect of delay on transposition should make the relative discrimination quite easy to learn with this procedure.) On the assumption that the second interpretation of the procedure used is correct, the results support the suggestion of Spiker et al. that transposition between problems makes the relative discrimination easier to learn than the absolute discrimination. Transposition is reduced by successive discrimination training, and Marsh (in press) has shown that even after simultaneous discrimination training the predominant response of pigeons on a transposition test with successive stimulus presentations is absolute. Absolute responses might therefore be expected to transfer between stimulus pairs in both of Line's discrimination problems, but they would be correct in the absolute discrimination problem and incorrect in the relative discrimination problem, accounting for the obtained result.

Other Kinds of Absolute and Relative Problems

A study by Meyer (1964a) provides data for rats on somewhat different kinds of absolute and relative problems. The design is outlined in Table 6–1. The stimuli were presented in pairs, and each pair included one positive stimulus and one negative stimulus. The problems given to Groups 1 and 2 were like the relative discrimination problem in that the same direction of relative difference was always correct, and the problems given to Groups 3 and 4 were standard simultaneous discrimination problems. The fifth group was given an absolute discrimination problem. The sixth group was given a kind of absolute discrimination problem, in which the negative stimulus remained constant instead of the positive stimulus. As can be seen in Table 6–1, the order of problem difficulty, as indexed by trials to criterion, was in line with the data already cited; the absolute problems were harder to learn than the relative problems. That there was little or no difference in the difficulties of the relative and standard problems implies that the results are attributable to interference on the absolute problems more than to facilitation on the relative problems.

As Meyer noted, the results supported and extended Hull's (1952) Theorem 14, which states: "Discrimination learning with three discriminanda in the form $- + -$ is possible, but is more difficult than is comparable discrimination learning with two discriminanda, $+ -$, because in the form $- + -$ the conditioned inhibition ($_sI_R$) generalizes upon the reinforced reaction potential from both sides, summating at S_1, the slope of this summation

TABLE 6–1

THE DESIGN AND RESULTS OF THE MEYER (1964a) STUDY[a]

Discrimination problem	Group	Stimulus pairs	Mean trials to criterion
Relative	1	A^+ vs B^-; A^+ vs C^-	11.4
	2	A^+ vs C^-; B^+ vs C^-	10.3
Standard	3	A^+ vs B^-	12.4
	4	A^- vs B^+	12.3
Absolute	5	A^- vs B^+; B^+ vs C^-	37.1
	6	A^+ vs B^-; B^- vs C^+	28.5

[a] The problem and group designations are not the ones Meyer used.

gradient being much less steep than would be a single $_sI_R$ gradient from the same maximum" (Hull, 1952, p. 77). The relative discrimination problem could be formulated as $^- \pm +$, and would be expected to be more difficult than the simultaneous discrimination problem ($- +$) unless transposition occurred from one pair to the other.

Spiker *et al.* (1956) used a kind of relative task based on the intermediate-size problem. The relative problem required the selection of the middle-sized stimulus on each trial, but this stimulus varied in absolute size from trial to trial. Five three-stimulus sets with one-step separations between adjacent sets were used. A control group was given an "absolute" task, the standard intermediate-size discrimination problem. In 30 training trials (six trials per set in the relative task), there were more correct responses on the absolute task than on the relative task, but the difference was statistically significant only for a subgroup of children who did not possess the concept of middle-sizedness.

W. Brown and Whittell (1923) and Wong and Brown (1923) gave college students problems that were similar to the ones used by Spiker *et al.*, except that the number of stimuli was varied across problems, and the stimuli differed in position rather than size. A fixed position was always correct in the absolute problems, and a relative position was correct in the other problems. There were no marked differences between the rates of solving the two kinds of problem.

Perkins and Wheeler (1930) gave this kind of relative problem to goldfish, using 11 three-stimulus sets with varying brightnesses. A subgroup with the brightest light positive and a subgroup with the dimmest light positive learned more slowly than corresponding subgroups given a standard two-stimulus discrimination, but a subgroup given the relative problem with the intermediate brightness positive performed as well as a subgroup given a standard intermediate-brightness discrimination problem.[3] (The fish seemed to have a spontaneous preference for intermediate brightness.) Perkins (1931) repeated the study, using better controls, and found that the relative task, with 10 different three-light combinations, was learned at the same rate as a standard three-light discrimination, regardless of which brightness was positive. (There was again evident a spontaneous preference for the intermediate brightness, and there was also a preference for the dimmest brightness. Graber [1884] found that some other species of fish are negatively phototropic, and still others are positively phototropic [see C. J. Warden *et al.*, 1936, pp. 33–35 and 38–48].)

Grether and Wolfle (1936) obtained the same effect in rats that Spiker *et al.* (1956) obtained in children and Perkins and Wheeler (1930) obtained

[3]These comparisons are based on an examination of Figs. 33 to 38 (Perkins and Wheeler, 1930, pp. 49–50), which included only 22 of the 42 subjects, and which had no specified baseline unit.

in goldfish; the relative task was learned more slowly than the standard discrimination. Furthermore, as the number of different pairs of stimuli in the relative task was increased, learning speed became slower, except that there was no reduction with only two pairs. Wolfle (1935; 1936) also obtained this relation between the extent of stimulus variation and learning speed, testing college students on paper-and-pencil mazes and finger mazes.

Leeper and Leeper (1932) tested college students with these kinds of problems, and found that variations in the size of pencil mazes did not affect learning speed, nor did variations in the pitch and key of melodies used as stimulus items in a paired-associates task. However, there was better learning of a number maze when the numbers remained constant than when they were varied by the addition or subtraction of a constant. In two other experiments, the stimuli differed in rhythm and varied in sound source. When each constant stimulus was produced by a different sound source, there was better learning with the constant stimuli than with varied stimuli; but when all of the constant stimuli were produced by the same sound source, learning was as good with varied stimuli as with constant stimuli.

M. H. Lewis (1930) found that chicks performed as well on a five-stimulus relative problem of the kind used by Grether and Wolfle as on a standard three-stimulus discrimination when the brightest stimulus was positive, and they were better on the relative problem than on the standard problem when the dimmest light was positive. However, with the intermediate brightness positive the relative problem was not solved. Even in a three-stimulus relative problem with the intermediate brightness positive, performance was not as good as on a standard three-stimulus problem with the intermediate brightness positive.

C. J. Warden and Rowley (1929) found an absolute preference for the brighter stimulus in doves, and noted that the same phenomenon had been observed in other fowl, including the chicken (Breed, 1912; L. W. Cole, 1911), crow (Coburn, 1914), sparrow (Tugman, 1914), and bantam gamecock (Lashley, 1916). Hertz (1928b) obtained this preference in jay birds; and Takei (1927) and M. H. Lewis (1930) obtained it in chicks. (Lewis denied it, but gave no basis for the denial: " . . . but it soon appeared that this was not the case" [p. 65]. His subjects apparently learned the discrimination with the bright light positive considerably more rapidly than the one with the dim light positive.) It seems likely, therefore, that Lewis obtained no difference between the rates of learning the relative and standard problems with the brightest light positive because the learning of the standard problem was facilitated by positive phototropism.

Marsh (in press) used another variation of the relative problem, with the stimulus pairs A versus B and C versus D (in the standard version, the pairs are A vs B and B vs C). In the relative problem, A was positive in the first pair, and C was positive in the second pair. In the absolute problem,

B was positive in the first pair, and *C* was positive in the second. Marsh found that pigeons solved the absolute problem more than twice as rapidly as the relative problem. Transposition from one pair of stimuli to the other pair during the training phase would facilitate performance on the relative problem and interfere with performance on the absolute problem; therefore the finding that the absolute problem was easier indicates that little transposition occurred during this phase. The finding could have been predicted, since there was a two-step separation between the stimulus pairs, and since pigeons normally do not transpose beyond one step (see section entitled "Distance," Chapter 4).

After the initial discrimination problem had been solved, Marsh gave a transfer test with stimuli *B* and *C*. He found that subjects that had learned the absolute problem responded at the chance level on the test. Subjects that had learned the relative problem gave absolute responses (responses to *C*) if the test stimuli were presented successively, but gave relational responses (responses to *B*) if the test stimuli were presented simultaneously. The results for the group that had learned the relative problem indicate that both absolute and relational learning occurred, and that the difference between the excitatory potentials of the absolute stimuli, leading to preference for stimulus *C* when the stimuli were presented successively, was completely obscured by the relational habit when the stimuli were presented simultaneously, leading to choice of *B*.

R. C. Johnson and Zara (1960), Sherman and Strunk (1964), M. S. Scott (1966), and Sherman (1966, Experiments 2, 3, 4) studied children's learning on a relative problem like the one used by Marsh and on a standard two-stimulus discrimination problem. Johnson and Zara found that children solved the relative problem more rapidly than the standard problem, but the opposite result was obtained in the other studies. The discrepancy may be attributable to the effects of extraneous variables in the Johnson and Zara study. To reach the learning criterion, the children in the Johnson and Zara study required many more trials than were required by the children in the other studies (see Table 6-2). The extremely slow learning in both groups in the Johnson and Zara study may have resulted from the effects of fatigue and boredom, since the children started each trial eight feet away from the apparatus and since the required manipulation of the apparatus by the experimenter probably yielded relatively long intertrial intervals. The variations in the stimuli presented to the relative-problem group may, however, have maintained a modicum of interest in the task, producing the somewhat faster learning than in the single-problem group. In the other studies, the children were apparently seated immediately in front of the apparatus, and the required manipulations of the materials by the experimenter were of a kind that requires little time.

Zeiler and Jasper (1966, Experiment 4) gave children the same kind of

TABLE 6-2
TRIALS TO CRITERION IN CHILDREN ON SINGLE-PROBLEM AND TWO-PROBLEM TASKS

		Trials to criterion		
	Learning	Single	Double problem	
Study	criterion	problem	Concurrent	Successive
Two-Stimulus Problems				
R. C. Johnson and Zara (1960)	14/15	193	144	—
M. S. Scott (1966)[a]	18/20	—	—	—
Sherman (1966)				
Experiment 2	7/7	12	16	—
Experiment 3	10/10	19	24	—
Experiment 4	7/7	10	14	—
Sherman and Strunk (1964)	7/7	15	21	—
Intermediate-Stimulus Problems				
Beaty (1966)	5/5	28	27^b	34^b
			52^c	61^c
Zeiler and Paalberg (1964b)	5/5	23	29^d	25^d
			$29^{e,f}$	32^e
Zeiler and Paalberg (1964a)[g]	6/6	19	17^d	20^d
			17^e	21^e

[a] Mean log errors was about 0.45 for the two-problem groups and not reported for the single-problem groups.
[b] Three steps between the two sets of stimuli.
[c] Ten steps between the two sets.
[d] One-half step between the sets.
[e] One step between the sets.
[f] Data for 3 subjects. The other 21 in this group failed to reach criterion.
[g] Adult subjects.

relative problem, and varied the ratio of the stimuli in the series and the number of steps separating the two sets of stimuli used in the problems. The problems were solved more quickly with more distinctive stimuli (2 to 1 ratio of stimulus areas) than with more similar stimuli (1.4 to 1 ratio of areas), and were solved more quickly when the sets were separated by one-half or one step than when they were separated by more than one step.

Zeiler and Jasper also tried the procedure with intermediate-stimulus problems. When the two problems were given concurrently, only one subject out of 64 was able to meet the criterion in the 60 trials allowed (Experiment 1); but when the two problems were given successively, all 48 subjects tested were able to meet the criterion (Experiment 3). Zeiler and Paalberg (1964b) and Beaty (1966) had more success with the method, but found that the single problem was solved somewhat more rapidly than the double problem (see Table 6-2). In a study with adults, however, Zeiler and Paalberg (1964a) found no difference in the speed of solving the single-problem and double-problem tasks. In the last three studies, learning was somewhat faster when the problems were given concurrently than when they were given successively.

Patton (1933) used still another kind of relative problem, requiring choice of the one of two pairs of stimuli having a greater within-pair brightness difference, with absolute brightnesses varied across trials. A four-year-old child refused to continue after Trial 80, but his performance was better than chance when he quit. Older children and adults solved the problem, but the problem was a difficult one, judging from the numbers of trials required. Honig (1965) found that pigeons can solve this kind of problem, although it is very difficult for them also.

Sherman (1966, Experiment 4) devised other kinds of absolute and relative problems, using a series of stimuli varying in size. In the absolute problem, preschool children learned to choose Stimulus 4 whether it was presented with Stimulus 1, 2, or 3. In the relative problem, children learned to choose the larger stimulus in three pairs (1 vs 2, 2 vs 3, and 3 vs 4). The absolute problem was solved more rapidly than the relative problem (10 vs 19 trials to criterion). Actually, both problems could be solved on a relational basis. The second problem could be solved on the basis of a relatively constant relation, or on the basis of a constant direction of relation. The first problem could be solved on the basis of a constant direction of relation.

Conclusion

Table 6-3 summarizes the evidence on the relative ease of learning relative, absolute, and standard discriminations. The absolute discrimination problem is harder to learn than the relative discrimination problem; but it can be solved, and the solution is apparently based on absolute properties and not on combinations of relative properties. Even on the relative discrimination problem, absolute properties have an effect on performance. The difference in difficulty is attributable to the occurrence of transposition, which facilitates performance on the relative discrimination problem and interferes with performance on the absolute discrimination problem. However, the relative discrimination is harder to learn than the standard simultaneous discrimination, presumably because transposition in the relative discrimination problem is less than perfect and interfering absolute responses sometimes transfer between the stimulus sets.

TABLE 6-3

RELATIVE EASE OF SOLVING RELATIVE, ABSOLUTE, AND STANDARD DISCRIMINATIONS

Study	R vs A[a]	R vs S[a]	S vs A[a]
Beaty (1966)		−	
Berman (1963)	+		
W. Brown and Whittell (1923)		=	
F. K. Graham et al. (1964)	+		
Grether and Wolfle (1936)		−	
R. C. Johnson and Zara (1960)		+	
Leeper and Leeper (1932)[b]		=/−	
M. H. Lewis (1930)[b]		=/−/+	
Line (1931)	−		
Marsh (in press)	−		
Meyer (1964a)	+	=	+
Perkins (1931)		=	
Perkins and Wheeler (1930)[b]		=/−	
M. S. Scott (1966)		−	
Sherman (1966) Exp. 2		−	
Exp. 3		−	
Exp. 4	−	−	−
Sherman and Strunk (1964)		−	
Spiker et al. (1956)		−	
Wohlwill (1957) Exp. 1	+		
Wohlwill (1960a) Exp. 1	+		
Exp. 2 young	=		
old	−		
Wohlwill (1963)[b]	+/−		
Wolfle (1935)		−	
Wolfle (1936)		−	
Wolfle (1937)	+		
Wong and Brown (1923)		=	
Zeiler and Paalberg (1964a)		=	
Zeiler and Paalberg (1964b)		−	

[a] R indicates relative discrimination, A indicates absolute discrimination, and S indicates standard simultaneous discrimination, "+" means first easier than second.

[b] Effect depended on experimental conditions. See text.

PART III

Studies of Multidimensional Transposition

CHAPTER 7

Form Transposition

The Meaning of Form

According to *Webster's New Collegiate Dictionary* (1953 Edition, p. 326), *form, figure, shape, conformation,* and *configuration* mean "the disposition or arrangement of content that gives a peculiar aspect or appearance to a thing." *Pattern, Gestalt, complex,* and *whole* have been used as roughly synonymous with these terms. The distinctions among the terms are often subtle, and although they may be important for some purposes, they are too esoteric for my purposes. I use the term "form" in a generic sense, to refer to multidimensional stimuli, and do not imply any particular theoretical orientation.

The Meaning of Form Transposition

Studies of transfer between forms are usually classified as studies of "stimulus equivalence"; but for reasons discussed in Chapter 1 (section entitled "Stimulus Equivalence"), I classify them as studies of "form transposition." The term "equivalence" is ambiguous because it implies identity of stimulus functions.

In studying the "transposition" of forms, two kinds of evidence must be considered. One kind of evidence is obtained in studies of form generalization, in which a response is conditioned to one form, usually with a differential conditioning or discrimination learning procedure; and then other forms are presented to see whether they can arouse the response. The other kind of evidence is more indirect. The same initial procedures are used, but the critical evidence is obtained by comparing the difficulties of learning discriminations between various forms. The relative difficulty of a discrimination is assumed to reflect the relative amount of transposition or "generalization" between the forms. Generalization and discrimination are considered to be closely (but inversely) related, and it is clearly desirable to include difficulty of discrimination as a criterion. However, it then becomes impossible to present a thorough review of the relevant literature in a single chapter; and therefore, I have attempted to summarize only the salient findings.

The Transposition of Visual Forms

Michels and Zusne (1965) and Hershenson (1965) reviewed much of the relevant discrimination literature on human subjects and some of the animal work, and Sutherland (1961b) reviewed the literature on animals. Sutherland listed 12 tentative conclusions (pp. 58–59), which are quoted below with additional material not included in his monograph. (Sutherland's review was quite thorough—there were 203 references listed in the bibliography—and should be consulted for details about the research literature.)

(a) "The rat often discriminates in terms of parts of the figures only (usually the base line)." (b) "Chickens and fishes also tend to discriminate in terms of parts of the figure, but discrimination is based rather on the parts which most clearly differentiate the figures, than upon the base lines." There is some evidence that monkeys with lesions in the inferotemporal cortex also discriminate on the basis of base-line cues (Butter and Gekoski, 1966), and form discrimination in the porcupine is also ordinarily based on responses to elements or parts rather than to whole forms (Sackett, 1913).

Kroh (1927) trained hens to react to equilateral triangles, and found that they transferred to right triangles, scalene triangles, and others. According to C. J. Warden *et al.* (1940, p. 801), Verlaine obtained the same kind of effect in bees. Although it is possible that the subjects were reacting to triangularity, it seems more likely that they were reacting to a single angle, a single dominant element in the forms. Winslow (1933) obtained contradictory evidence in chicks. The chicks were trained to select the narrower of two rectangles, and were tested with rectangles having equal base lines but different heights. The subjects tended to choose the taller rectangles, which under the influence of the illusion of "breadth of rectangles" would appear to be narrower. Apparently the chicks were responding not to the base-line or vertical extents, but to the whole figures.

Kerpelman and Pollack (1964) concluded that the bottom attributes of stimuli are the most salient cues for children (ranging in age, in their study, from 3.5 to 7.5 years), but that top-to-bottom scanning increases in importance with increasing age level. In 1960, Ghent suggested that top-to-bottom scanning is likely to be more important in younger children than in older children, because it is likely to be the only direction of scanning used by younger children. Later, however, she concluded that older children and adults tend to scan figures from top to bottom, and younger children tend to begin at the "focal part" of the figure and scan downward (for example, Braine, 1965; Ghent, 1963; Ghent and Bernstein, 1961). If the distinguishing parts of figures are located *above* the focal part, older children are more accurate than younger children in discriminating among the figures. The discrimination is apparently based on parts rather than wholes. Wohlwill (1960b, pp. 273–274) reviewed the developmental studies of whole-part perception, and concluded that whole-perception is more characteristic of younger children than part-perception is; but most of the studies involved verbal descriptions of Rorschach cards, and Line (1931) reached the opposite conclusion from his own research, using more structured stimulus materials. Vernon (1957, Chapter II) also reached the opposite conclusion, on the basis of a review of the research on visual perception.

It is well established that the young child can discriminate between forms before he can reproduce them accurately (for example, Rice, 1930); and there is evidence that this lag is not entirely attributable to insufficiently developed motor skills. It may be, according to Bee and Brandt (1965), that the child fails to notice the relational cues in the forms, and discriminates on the basic of nonrelational cues or elements that he reproduces with fair accuracy when asked to draw the whole form. Within the frame of reference of the child, the reproduction is accurate, since it includes what are to him the salient elements; but the adult sees the drawing as lacking the most important properties determining form. (See also Österreith, 1945; Piaget and Inhelder, 1956, Chapter 12; Piaget, Inhelder, and Szeminska, 1960, pp. 36–40.)

If stimulus differences are so small that they are imperceptible to the subject, then generalization between the stimuli will occur. But it is known that if a human subject has a psychophysical discrimination set, he can discriminate between stimuli between which generalization occurs under other sets. The problem is to determine why he generalizes between discriminably different stimuli. A study of Bindra, Williams, and Wise (1965) suggests a solution. Under a psychophysical set, college students required more time to decide that two identical stimuli were identical than to decide that two dissimilar stimuli were different, and more often judged identical stimuli to be different than they judged dissimilar stimuli to be the same. Sully believed that the awareness of a difference in a sensation or group of sensations often occurs "before we can assign any definite character to that which differs.... Hence perhaps discrimination may be regarded as the earliest and primordial mode of intellectual activity" (Sully, 1891, p. 142). Maier (1941) also concluded that recognition of likeness and difference are separate processes, but he believed that the reaction to likeness is the more primitive process. His conclusion was based on data for rats, but the data of W. R. McAllister, McAllister, and Franchina (1965) for college students point to the same conclusion. The students compared the lengths of successively presented lines, with a one-half-minute or an eight-minute delay between the presentations of the standard line and the comparison line. The longer delay did not affect correct judgments of equality, but did affect correct judgments of difference. When more complicated stimuli are used, however, subjects require more time to recognize test patterns that match a standard pattern than to recognize ones that differ from the standard (J. D. Gould and Schaffer, 1966).

Under the psychophysical set, the human subject apparently adopts a more stringent criterion of sameness than of difference. If a subject under a nonpsychophysical set adopts a less stringent criterion of sameness than he operates with in the psychophysical situation, he might well react to dissimilar stimuli as though they were the same. He might "ignore" or "fail to attend to" differences that are perceptible, as though he has decided that even though the stimuli are not the same, their differences are not important or significant. The response would be determined by elements in the forms, but elements that are salient because the subject considers them to be more important than other elements and more important than the form as a whole.

If the young child is capable of observing the relational characteristics within forms, but does not ordinarily observe them, prolonged experience with the forms might increase the probability that the relational characteristics will be observed. E. J. Gibson, Walk, Pick, and Tighe (1958) found that exposure of visual patterns on the walls of rats' cages during rearing facilitated later discrimination between the same patterns and between patterns that were similar to but not identical to the exposed ones. When the test patterns were very different from the cage patterns, no significant transfer effects were found.[1] The investigators suggested that either shape constancy is learned or relational characteristics are discovered (see also J. J. Gibson and Gibson, 1955).

E. J. Gibson, Gibson, Pick, and Osser (1962) noted that some kinds of transformations of solid objects do not destroy the identifiability of the objects. Perspective transformations, produced by slant, are in this class; the class also includes mirror reversals, produced by turning over a flat object. However, between the ages of four and eight years, the child normally learns that "transformations of rotation and reversal *are* significant for distinguishing graphic forms (i. e., the difference between M and W, C and U, d and b, p and b)" (p. 905). The implication is that the very young child recognizes the change in the figures, and perhaps responds differently; but

[1]In further work, summarized by E. J. Gibson (1963), it was found that the effect was obtained when the patterns exposed in the cage were cutouts, but not when they were painted on a flat surface.

the somewhat older child has learned to ignore the change, yielding object constancy; and the still older child has learned that the change sometimes should be ignored and other times is important.

Salapatek and Kessen (1966) showed newborn human infants a large solid black triangle on a white field, and observed that the ocular orientations of the infants were directed toward a single angle (which one varying with the infant). Salapatek (1966) obtained similar, but less striking, findings. These findings seem to be consistent with the hypothesis of Bee and Brandt, since "it is generally accepted that nearly all visual perception occurs during fixation of the eyes, while little or no information is obtained between fixations" (J. D. Gould and Schaffer, 1965, p. 522). The newborn infants, in other words, probably observed only one salient part and not the whole form.

J. D. Gould and Schaffer (1965) found that the efficiency of visual scanning did not improve with practice in college students, nor was there any change in eye-movement patterns; but Schaffer and Gould (1964) reported that subjects highly trained in tachistoscopic experiments differed from untrained subjects in that the trained subjects scanned more quickly and made fewer fixations than the untrained subjects. As a result, the trained subjects made more errors on the task than the untrained subjects. It is possible that trained subjects see the whole but miss seeing the parts, or that they miss seeing the whole but also miss seeing all but the most salient parts.

Munsinger and Forsman (1966) found that recognition accuracy increased with practice in children. The task was to identify which of four shapes was exposed in a tachistoscope, and it required perception of whole forms. In the task used by Schaffer and Gould, a six-by-six matrix of numbers was presented, and the subject was to determine the frequency of appearance in the matrix of a designated target digit. Since this task required perception of the parts, and practice interfered with accuracy, and the task used by Munsinger and Forsman required perception of the whole, and practice increased accuracy, the implication is that trained subjects have learned to see the whole at the expense of perception of the parts. A further implication is that the probability of perceiving the whole can be influenced by practice, corroborating the suggestion I derived from the Bee and Brandt material.

(c) "Most lower animals do not readily transfer to rotated figures. Higher mammals and to some extent octopuses seem to rely more upon properties of the whole form and are less upset by changes in rotation." (d) "Animals can readily discriminate different orientations of the same figure even when these are mirror-images. Right-left mirror-images are less readily discriminable than up-down." These two generalizations may seem to be contradictory, but both failure of transfer and ease of discrimination learning reflect a low level of transposition. (As Wohlwill and Wiener [1964] pointed out, it is sometimes important to distinguish between rotations and mirror-image reversals—*b* is a rotated form of *q*, a left–right mirror image of *d*, and an up–down mirror image of *p*—but for present purposes, the distinctions can generally be ignored.)

Kroh (1927) obtained evidence contradicting the trend. He trained hens to react to equilateral triangles, and reported that "Some hens even 'identified' an equilateral triangle placed upside down without any difficulty" (p. 25), indicating transposition to an up–down reversal. Similarly, K. U. Smith (1934) found that after cats had learned to discriminate between a triangle and a circle, inverting the triangle, which was the positive figure, had no effect on performance. Karn and Munn (1932) also obtained contradictory data; dogs learned black–white and horizontal–vertical discriminations considerably more rapidly than they learned a discrimination between an upright triangle and an inverted triangle. However, Takei (1927, Experiment III) found that rotation of a rectangle disrupted performance in chicks; Sutherland and Carr (1964) reported confirmatory results for rats; and Schmerler (1965) found that pigeons readily discriminated rectangles differing in orientation, indicating a lack of transposition. P. D. Wilson and Riesen (1966) found that monkeys reared without patterned light readily discriminated between a triangle and its inversion, and Butter and Gekoski (1966) found that simultaneous rotation of both the positive and negative figures in a discrimination problem disrupted performance in monkeys, especially in monkeys with inferotemporal lesions.

Riopelle, Rahm, Itoigawa, and Draper (1964) confirmed the finding of greater generalization to left–right reversals than to up–down reversals, testing rhesus monkeys.

Ernst Mach (1886; pp. 106–114 in the 1914 translation) asserted that 90-degree rotation and up–down mirror-image reversal interfere with transposition, and that 180-degree rotation and left–right mirror reversal do not. (He did not, however, use these terms.) He believed that the same phenomena occur in children: "Children constantly confound the letters *b* and *d*, *p* and *q*" (p. 110); but "The letters *b* and *p*, and *d* and *q* are not confused even by children" (p. 114). Dearborn (1899) obtained corroborative evidence, but much of the evidence from other studies is at least partially contradictory (see Vernon, 1957, pp. 8–30 and 51–56). E. J. Gibson *et al.* (1962) obtained no difference between up–down reversal errors and left–right reversal errors in children from four to eight years of age, using letters and letter–like forms. Munn and Stiening (1931) found that rotating a cross (the positive figure in a discrimination problem) had no effect on the performance of the one subject they tested, a child fifteen months old. Gellermann (1933a; 1933b) found that rotation had little effect on the performance of children and chimpanzees. Newhall (1937) found that form perception in three- to five-year-old children was independent of spatial orientation, even when the orientation was reversed. Davidson (1934) found a similar, but weaker, effect in kindergarten and first-grade children, who were shown a standard form and were to find a matching form among five comparison figures including the standard form, a reversal of the standard form, and three other forms. Most of the errors (71 per cent) were choices of the reversed form. The errors probably did not arise because of confusion about the nature of the response required, since R. H. Peckham (1933) found that children as young as twenty-eight months of age generally got perfect scores on a visual acuity test requiring matching from sample (although with no reversed or rotated figures among the alternatives).

Rice (1930) studied the effect of 90-degree rotation of drawings of a diamond and a spoon on their perception by children ranging from about two and one-half years to about nine years of age. The rotated figures were fairly obviously equivalent to the normal figures until about the end of the fourth year of age. The rotated diamond was clearly discriminated from the normal diamond beginning at seven years of age, and the rotated spoon and normal spoon were discriminated beginning at six years of age. (Hanfmann [1933] demonstrated that children have difficulty in discriminating mirror-image reversals, but my secondary sources did not indicate whether they were left–right reversals, which according to Mach should have been hard to discriminate, or were up–down reversals, which should have been easy to discriminate.)

Davidson (1935) presented evidence partially supporting Mach. There was more confusion (more transposition) between letters that are left–right reversals than between letters that are up–down reversals, but there was some confusion between even the latter ones (see Table 7-1). Furthermore,

TABLE 7–1

PERCENTAGE OF CHILDREN MAKING LETTER-REVERSAL ERRORS (AFTER DAVIDSON, 1935)

		Percentage errors	
Kind of reversal	Letter pair	Kindergarten	First grade
Left–right	d–b	93.8	64.9
	b–d	87.5	60.4
	q–p	95.8	62.1
Up–down	d–q	35.4	27.7
	q–d	13.5	13.5
Rotation	d–p	50.0	18.9
(180°)	q–b	43.8	10.8
	b–q	41.7	15.3
	n–u	25.0	9.9
Other	n–h	35.4	13.5

Wohlwill and Wiener (1964) found that although four-year-old children made relatively few errors on a matching-from-sample task, significantly more of the errors that did occur were choices of left–right reversals than of up–down reversals; Rudel and Teuber (1963b, Experiment I) found that discrimination between left–right reversals was much harder than between up–down reversals. Ghent (1960) obtained a similar effect, but the differences were quite small (by inspection of her Fig. 2, p. 252).

Newson (1955) found that 90-degree and 180-degree rotations of figures were much more readily discriminated from the normal figures by five-year-old children than were mirror-image reversals. The discussion of this study in the available secondary source implies that the mirror-image reversals were left–right reversals, which according to Mach should have been harder to discriminate than the 90-degree rotations but no harder than the 180-degree rotations.

Using a paired-comparisons procedure in which the standard figure was presented in turn with each comparison figure (until the subject judged that the figures were the same), Rosenblith (1965) found that with triangles differing in orientation and with circles missing 20 degrees of arc in different locations, children made almost no up–down reversal errors, but made relatively many left–right reversal errors, indicating greater transposition between left–right reversals than between up–down reversals.[2]

Davidson (1935) found that transposition between reversals was greater in kindergarten children than in first-grade children (see Table 7-1). Brooks and Goldstein (1963) found that young children were highly accurate in identifying up–down reversals of photographs, but the percentage correct identifications increased with age level from 80 per cent at three through six years to 99 per cent at eleven through fourteen years. Ghent and Bernstein (1961) obtained a similar effect, but it was not statistically reliable. Rudel and Teuber (1963b) found that the difference between the difficulty levels of up–down and left–right discriminations became smaller with increasing age level from three and one-half to eight and one-half years. Rosenblith (1965) obtained a decline in left–right reversal errors from kindergarten through fourth grade. Hunton (1955) tested children as young as two years of age, using pictures of real objects, and found that although the youngest children appeared to recognize the inversions, they identified the pictures correctly. (See also Wohlwill's [1960b, p. 270] brief review of the developmental studies of the effects of figural orientation on perception.)

In summary, the data for children indicate that some kinds of rotation and reversal have more effect on transposition than others, and suggest that these changes are less likely to interfere with transposition in younger

[2]Preliminary reports were given by Rosenblith (1961; 1963) and Sekuler and Rosenblith (1964).

children than in older children. It is consistent with the material presented thus far in this chapter to suggest that the younger children actually can discriminate between the standard and reversed figures, but do not realize the significance of the differences, and therefore ignore them and behave as though the changes were not discriminated. In line with this suggestion, Hunton (1955) concluded that the recognition of a figure in normal and inverted positions as the same figure is a result of learned generalization rather than perceptual identity. (Her data showed that children as young as two years of age recognized the pictures as disoriented, and accurate recognition of "identity" increased with age.) Vernon (1957, p. 16) reached the same conclusion. According to Vernon (1957, p. 17), Newson (1955) commented that five-year-old children may be unable to see the difference between a shape and its mirror image even when the difference is pointed out to them, but Vernon interpreted this to mean that the children have an inability "to attach any importance to orientation" (p. 17). These conclusions suggest that the response of the young child is to the salient parts of figures and not to the relations among the parts. (See also Suppes, 1966, p. 148; Wohlwill and Wiener, 1964, p. 1121.)

Testing human adults, Dees and Grindley (1947) obtained virtually perfect transposition after 90-degree rotations of the figures, changes in the retinal position of stimulation, and changes in size. The changes increased the reaction times but did not affect the error rates. The stimuli used in training are shown in Fig. 7-1, and obviously could easily be identified as a diamond, square, line, and T (or inverted T). It seems very likely,

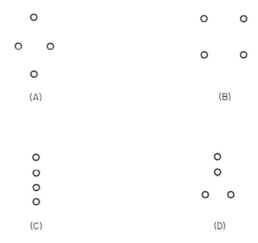

Fig. 7-1. The figures used by Dees and Grindley (1947) in training. (After Dees and Grindley, 1947, Fig. 2, p. 155.)

therefore, that the responses were verbally mediated. Becher (1911) and von Kries (1898) also obtained transposition with changes in the part of the retina stimulated.

(e) "Fishes, rats and octopuses may be able to discriminate in terms of degree of openness of figures, i.e., in terms of differences in some such ratio as amount of contour to area. . . ." Hertz (1929) concluded that bees can discriminate degrees of openness, and that they transpose along this dimension. (See, however, the discussion of the Hertz studies in the section entitled "Phylogenetic Comparisons," Chapter 5.)

Sutherland (1962) has suggested that the analysis of horizontal and vertical extents by the animal underlies this "openness" dimension.

(f) "Animals often have difficulty in discriminating figures whose vertical and horizontal extents at different points on the horizontal and vertical axis are the same. . . ." (g) "Studies which compare the discriminability of figures differing either in horizontal extent only or in vertical extent only yield conflicting results." Sutherland (1963) summarized other data relevant to these generalizations, and outlined a theoretical explanation of the data. Rudel and Teuber (1963b) confirmed the difficulty of these discriminations in children. (See also Sutherland, 1961a.)

(h) "The rat tends to confuse normal squares and circles but this does not apply to other species tested." Lashley (1912) obtained positive transfer in rats between a large circle and a large square, each paired with a small circle (the negative stimulus), in agreement with the generalization. Révész (1924) obtained transfer in a hen from large versus small circles to large versus small rectangles, squares, and triangles, but it is possible that during this phase of the training the positions of the stimuli were not randomly changed from trial to trial.[3] Williams (1926) obtained no evidence of learning in six dogs given 520 to 620 training trials on a circle–square discrimination, contradicting Sutherland's generalization that this discrimination is difficult only for the rat.

Long (1941) found that children can learn to choose the larger of two stimuli regardless of shape, but the subjects were 4.2 to 7.2 years old, and presumably possessed the verbal concepts required for mediated responding (see section entitled "Concept Knowledge," Chapter 5).

(i) "Only higher animals transfer readily when the brightness relationship between figure and background is changed." Gellermann's (1933b) data are in agreement with the generalization, since background changes had little effect on the performance of chimpanzees and children. (Gellermann

---

[3]This possibility is suggested because the second footnote to Révész's Table 1 (p. 403) apparently referred to only one of the series of trials. The footnote read: "The position of the two figures was reversed." C. J. Warden and Baar (1929) sharply criticized Révész for failing to eliminate the possibility of the "Klüge Hans" error, but did not mention this possible failure to control position.

concluded that the transfer was mediated in the children and possibly also in the chimpanzees [see also Gellermann, 1933a], but Lashley [1929b] rejected mediational interpretations of "stimulus equivalence"—"explanations based upon 'symbolism'"—since he believed that "there is clear evidence that the use of symbols depends upon the recognition of similarity, and not the reverse" [p. 545].)

Data reported by Hebb (1937a), Riley (1958), and Zimmermann (1962) are in agreement with the conclusion. Hebb found that transfer by rats reared in darkness was far from perfect when figure–ground relations were changed. Riley found that when the background was changed in such a way that the brightness relation of the stimuli to the ground was constant with changes in the stimulus brightnesses, the performance of rats was unaffected. When the background remained constant and the absolute brightnesses of the stimuli were changed, performance deteriorated, and dropped more the greater the change in absolute brightnesses (and hence the greater the change in the relation between the figure and background brightnesses). Zimmermann found that the performance level of infant monkeys dropped from about 100 to 79 per cent correct when the figure ground brightness relation was reversed.

However, there are data showing that not all figure–ground relations affect form transposition in lower animals. Kroh (1927) found that a hen trained to eat the larger of two grains of corn continued to choose the larger when the same stimuli were presented outdoors instead of indoors, or on a ground of a different size, or on the floor; but when grains of wheat or pieces of bread or meat were presented, the smaller was also taken, regardless of color or form. Wapner (1944) found that different kinds of brightness-relation changes had different effects on form transposition in rats, which is not entirely consistent with Sutherland's generalization. Lashley (1938a) found that changing the background from black to striated brought about only a small drop in the performance level of rats (from 100 to 90 per cent correct responses). Lashley (1929b) also found that reversing the figure–ground brightnesses had no effect on performance. Munn and Stiening (1931) found that changing the figure-ground relations had no effect on the performance of a fifteen-month-old child, who might properly be considered to be a "lower animal."

There is also evidence that changing the brightness relation sometimes affects the performance of "higher animals." Line (1931) found that changing the backgrounds in a brightness transposition test increased absolute responding in children two and one-half to three years old. Gollin (1964), studying conditional discrimination, trained children with the background constant, then changed the background to signal the reversal phase of the conditional discrimination. Virtually all children made an error on the first reversal trial, responding to the originally positive (and now negative) stimulus even though the background had been changed. C. B. Smith (1956) found that changing the background brightness affected the performance of second graders and college students, although a small change had less effect than larger changes. Combining the age groups and treatment conditions in Smith's study, transfer averaged about 80 per cent with a small change, 62 per cent with a moderate change, and 69 per cent with a large change.

Finally, changing the ratio between the stimuli has little, if any, effect on the performance of lower animals and higher animals, until the stimuli become so similar that discrimination is impossible (chicks: Bingham, 1922; crows: Coburn, 1914; rats: Helson, 1927; monkeys: Klüver, 1933; children: Welch, 1939).

(j) "All animals hitherto tested readily transfer to figures of different size: transfer tends to be better to larger figures than to smaller." Sutherland and Carr (1963) trained octopuses to discriminate between horizontal and vertical rectangles of equal size, then gave tests with the sizes increased or reduced. The amount of transfer declined as the amount of change in size increased. K. U. Smith (1934) obtained a similar effect in cats that had learned a triangle–circle discrimination. Reducing the sizes of both figures had little effect on performance except when the reduction was extreme. Other evidence relevant to this generalization is reviewed in Chapter 4 (section entitled "Effect of Direction of Transposition Test").

(k) "Internal distortions of figures have less effect on discrimination than changes in the immediate surround of the figures." (l) "Transfer from filled-in to outline figures and *vice versa* is good. In addition, animals often transfer to figures with broken outlines: the tendency to do so does not appear to correlate with position on the phylogenetic scale." I have found no new evidence relevant to these generalizations. It might be noted, however, that these generalizations are consistent with the assumption that animals tend to respond to the salient parts of figures rather than to whole forms.

OTHER FINDINGS

Several investigators have reported data on the effects of changing the number of stimuli presented. Kroh (1927) trained a hen to eat the larger of two grains of corn, and found that "When offered three grains of different size it ate the larger two, leaving only the smallest. One can say it had not learned the lesson, 'eat the largest grain' but the lesson, 'leave the smallest grain.' A simpler explanation might be that having eaten one of the larger grains the hen was then faced with the situation in which she had originally been trained and responded accordingly" (C. J. Warden *et al.*, 1936, p. 193).

Perkins and Wheeler (1930), testing goldfish, used two lights differing in brightness in the training phase, and tested with three lights including the training pair and one new light. One of the two fish trained with the darkest light positive showed an increase in the performance level from the training to the test phase, and the other showed a decrease. For two other subjects the previously positive light became intermediate in brightness, and both subjects showed a drop in performance. M. H. Lewis (1930) found that changing the number of stimuli temporarily disrupted the performance of chicks, in line with the Perkins and Wheeler data. However, Klüver (1933) found that changing the number of boxes (containing weight discriminanda) did not disrupt the performance of monkeys.

There may be a phylogenetic trend toward less disruption with increasing phylogenetic level, but the evidence for it is obviously extremely tenuous.

Orbeli (1908) seems to have obtained form transposition in dogs, but the available secondary sources gave only examples of figures that were successfully differentiated from the conditioned stimulus figure (through differential conditioning) and gave no examples of figures that could not be differentiated.

Hara and Warren (1961) studied the responses of cats to the Lashley (1938b) figures. The level of transposition was high on virtually all of the test pairs, and there was no difference between normal and brain-injured groups, suggesting that "... the perceptual generalization manifested on equivalence tests is quite a primitive form of behavior" (pp. 92–93). Klüver and Bucy (1939) reported that they obtained form transposition in monkeys lacking both temporal lobes, but did not present detailed results.

Herrnstein and Loveland (1964) demonstrated that pigeons can apparently acquire the concept "person," since the pigeons learned to respond to the presence or absence of human figures in photographs, and generalized to entirely new photographs. If the remarkable transfer obtained did not result from mediation by a concept, then the basis for the transfer is unknown.

Zimmermann (1962) obtained form transposition in infant rhesus monkeys, and found that the presence of some aspect of the negative stimulus (a circle) produced more transfer than the presence of the positive stimulus (a triangle). It would be worth while to test the generality of this finding with a wide variety of stimulus forms.

Carter (1937) found that in human adults, fairly small changes in relevant and irrelevant characteristics of the positive stimulus reduced response frequency, but no presentations of the negative stimulus or variations of it were given during the tests, reducing the opportunity for comparisons.

P. D. Wilson and Riesen (1966) obtained form transposition in young rhesus monkeys reared without patterned light, and although separate data were not reported for the different test pairs, it was implied that there was more generalization of a triangle–circle discrimination than of a horizontal–vertical discrimination.

It has been suggested that the process for "coding" forms may be different from the processes for coding colors and intensities (Aarons, Halasz, and Riesen, 1963; Ingle, 1965), since research evidence indicates that there is more interocular transfer of color and intensity discriminations than of form or pattern discriminations (for example, in goldfish, Ingle, 1965; in rats, Sheridan, 1965; and in cats, comparing studies by Aarons *et al.*, 1963; Meyers and McCleary, 1964; and Riesen, Kurke, and Mellinger, 1953). It is apparent that a combination of the method of studying interocular transfer and the method of studying form transposition should become one of the basic research designs used by investigators interested in identifying the processes underlying form perception. Menkhaus (1957) used this technique with hens, and Mello (1965a; 1965b) used it with pigeons.

Mello found that pigeons trained with one eye open and the other eye occluded transferred maximally to a mirror-image reversal of the positive stimulus when the trained eye was occluded and the other eye was open. Cumming, Siegel, and Johnson (1965) pointed out that the interorbital septum in the pigeon is "paper thin," and an image projected trans-septally would be a mirror-image reversal. If projection occurred during the training with one eye, then simultaneously the other eye would be trained with a mirror image. Mello (1965b) argued that interretinal projection is anatomically possible only between the anteromedial portions of the orbits, which in her study could not have been stimulated by the discriminanda because of the construction of the occluding goggles used. Stimulation could fall only on the temporal retina, which comprises the posterolateral portion of the orbit, where interretinal image projection cannot occur.

Mello's findings have been replicated in the chick, and her argument that the transfer is interhemispheric rather than interorbital has received experimental support (Schabtach, 1966). As in the pigeon, interorbital projection in the chick is possible only if the stimuli are located in the lateral visual field, and it can therefore be excluded by restricting vision to the anterior field. Schabtach demonstrated that interocular mirror-image transfer occurs in the chick, and is as great when vision during monocular training is restricted to the anterior field as when it is unrestricted.

Other Kinds of Form Transposition

Woodworth (1908) described a kind of transfer that could be classed as form transposition. The subject is shown two standard stimulus cards exemplifying a particular relation, and must select from an array of other cards the stimulus that forms the same relation when paired with a third standard card. A boy three and one-half years old was tested, and Woodworth reported that "It was clear that he was able to detach a relation from one pair of terms and transfer it to another, and that the transfer was not always accomplished by aid of the name of the relation" (pp. 490–491). This kind of "transposition" seems to be an instance of Stout's third class of "relative suggestions," in which "the mental production consists in supplying terms in one series corresponding to terms in a parallel series" (Stout, 1918b, p. 57). Stout included what might be called color transposition in this class. "In passing from actual scenery to the coloured picture, and from the coloured picture to its reproduction in black and white, there is a 'transposition of values' delicately adjusted, so that the values may as far as possible preserve their relation to each other" (p. 57). (C. S. Lewis [1949], the British author, used the term "transpositon" in this sense.) Stout also included melodic transposition in this class: "A very clear instance of this third class of relative suggestions is supplied by the singing or mental repetition of a tune in a different key from that in which it has been previously heard" (p. 57). Transposition of this kind is also found with changes in timbre and other musical characteristics, no doubt including changes in tempo within broad limits (Mach, 1914, p. 259), although the anecdotal evidence for this last has probably never been verified experimentally.

Willmann (1944) investigated another kind of musical transposition, between visual designs and melodic themes. Professional composers wrote melodic themes for four visual designs, and listeners attempted to identify the appropriate design, in a multiple-choice test, by listening to each theme. The listeners were significantly better than chance in accuracy, indicating transposition of melodic themes to visual designs in the listeners, and indicating transposition of visual designs to melodic themes in the composers. Osgood et al. (1957, pp. 20–24) summarized similar findings indicating transposition in listeners who were allowed to draw their own designs after listening to musical passages, and Köhler (1929, p. 242) referred to a similar phenomenon, illustrated in Fig. 7-2.[4] Hartmann (1942, pp. 198–199) illustrated the same phenomenon with different figures and different nonsense names.

Transfer from one sensory modality to another has been classified as synesthesia (Osgood et al., 1957, p. 20; Willmann, 1944), as a "simple structure-function in Köhler's sense" (von Schiller, 1933, as quoted in Katz, 1937, p. 73), and as a transposition phenomenon (von Hornbostel, 1925,

---

[4]In an unpublished study with 37 children ranging from about 34 to 47 months of age, I found that only 65 per cent of the group identified Köhler's figures "correctly." (Positions of the figures were counterbalanced, and the order of the names in the question was counterbalanced.) In a study with adults, Holland and Wertheimer (1964) found that the "fittingness" of the names for these figures apparently depends on the fittingness of individual letters rather than on any possible emergent Gestalt quality of the words.

Fig. 7-2. Transposition between words and visual designs. According to Köhler, it is easy to decide which figure to call "maluma" and which to call "takete." (After Köhler, 1929, Figs. 18 and 19, p. 243.)

p. 215; von Schiller, 1933). (See review by Ryan, 1940.) The argument of von Hornbostel was that brightness, for example, is an attribute of sounds and smells as well as colors, and transposition along this dimension should occur whichever modality is affected.

Blank and Bridger (1964) distinguished between two kinds of cross-modal transfer, which they called "cross-modal equivalence" and "cross-modal concepts." In studies of cross-modal equivalence, the subject is required to select from stimuli presented in one modality a stimulus that has previously been presented in another modality. The essential characteristic is that the stimuli presented in the one modality are physically identical to the stimuli presented in the other modality. In studies of cross-modal concepts, the subject learns a response with stimuli presented in one modality, and must transfer the response to stimuli presented in another modality. The essential characteristic is that the stimuli in the one modality are physically different from the stimuli in the other modality. It is probably unfortunate that "concepts" was used to label this second kind of cross-modal transfer, because concepts implies a verbal mediating process. If this implication is ignored, then the distinction between cross-modal equivalence and cross-modal concepts is obviously based on a difference in experimental procedures, and there is no necessary implication that the underlying processes are different.

Cross-Modal Equivalence

Blank and Bridger (1964) concluded from their own research that cross-modal equivalence does not depend upon verbal processes. The conclusion was based on the observation that subjects who performed successfully nevertheless failed to verbalize the basis of their correct responses. The subjects were children ranging from three to six years of age, and Bugelski and Scharlock (1952) have shown that even college students often fail to report implicit verbalizations when questioned. Therefore, the evidence for the conclusion is not convincing. Furthermore, even if the responses were not verbally mediated, they may have been mediated by some other process. There is some evidence that a relation can be *thought* before it can be put into the accepted verbal form (Hazlitt, 1930; see also section entitled "Concept Knowledge," Chapter 5), and therefore a failure to verbalize does not necessarily indicate that mediation did not occur. Farber (1963) concluded that there is a reciprocal interaction between overt behavior and cognitive processes, such that the cognition may sometimes be a result of the behavior, may sometimes mediate the behavior, and may sometimes be independent of the behavior but correlated with it to the extent that both are affected by the same environmental events. The problem is obviously capable of no easy solution.

Hartmann (1942, pp. 184–185) referred to the recognition of the numeral *8* "traced fairly large by someone else's finger across the middle of our bare backs" as a product of "some kind of transposition from the cutaneous domain to the visual." This kind of transposition can be classed as cross-modal equivalence.

Rudel and Teuber (1964; also reported by Rudel, 1963) found that tactual-to-visual transfer and visual-to-tactual transfer in three- to five-year-old children were greater than tactual–tactual transfer, but less than visual–visual transfer. They concluded that the supramodal linkage need not be verbal, but their evidence suggests that whatever it is, it is learned, since transfer increased with increasing age level. Birch and Lefford (1963) and Zaporozhets (cited by H. L. Pick, 1963, p. 187) also studied cross-modal equivalence, and found that transfer improved with increasing age level during childhood.[5]

Rudel and Teuber (1963a) obtained cross-modal transfer of practice effects on the Müller-Lyer illusion in human adults. The illusion was obtained with both tactual and visual presentation of the patterns, but decreased in magnitude across trials. After 80 trials with one mode of presentation, six test trials were given with the other mode of presentation, and it was found that although there was some recovery of the strength of the illusion, it was still significantly weaker than it would have been without the previous training in the other modality.

Jastrow (1886) required adult subjects to reproduce in one modality a stimulus length received in another modality, using vision, touch, and proprioception (arm movement). He concluded that the connection between the senses "seems to be a loose one" (p. 550). Using a psychophysical technique, Kelvin (1954) appeared to demonstrate virtually perfect transfer between the visual and tactual senses in human adults; but Kelvin and Mulik (1958) showed that the result was an artifact of the experimental procedure, and that transfer was actually far from perfect.

[5]M. Cole, Chorover, and Ettlinger (1961) concluded that their study yielded no evidence of transfer from the auditory to the visual modality in children. However, their experimental design, which was only outlined in the brief published report, does not seem to have been appropriate.

In some studies more transfer from tactual to visual modalities has been obtained than from visual to tactual (Gaydos, 1956; Krauthamer, 1959; O'Connor, 1965, p. 77; A. D. Pick, Pick, and Thomas, 1966; Rudel and Teuber, 1963a), but in other studies about equal transfer has been obtained in both directions (Rudel and Teuber, 1964). A significant opposite trend has not been reported.[6] It is apparently easier to identify the salient tactual features of the standard object when it is presented visually than to identify its salient visual features when it is presented tactually.

Ettlinger (1960a) obtained no evidence of transfer between the visual and tactual modalities in monkeys. Moffett and Ettlinger (1966a) showed that monkeys can easily learn to make opposite responses in these different sense modalities. The animals learned to choose one object when the discrimination was tactual and the other object when the discrimination was visual. The investigators concluded that "transfer of training did not take place between sense modalities" (p. 206), and that "tactile and visual learning take place in independent functional systems" (p. 206). (Biederman [1966] pointed out that the study lacked an appropriate control condition, but Moffett and Ettlinger [1966b] challenged his argument.) The results of another study by Ettlinger (1961) are difficult to interpret, because the subjects had an opportunity during the first task to learn on the basis of the cues in the modality to which they might have transferred. W. A. Wilson and Shaffer (1963) obtained no transfer between the visual and tactual modalities in monkeys, but suggested that the reason there is no transfer may be that monkeys do not respond to the same components of the stimuli in the different modalities. Using stimuli designed to increase the likelihood that the same elements would be effective in both modalities, these investigators obtained significant transfer from the tactual to the visual modality, but they did not test for transfer in the opposite direction.

In monkeys there is generally more "nonspecific" transfer from tactual to visual modalities than from visual to tactual, as demonstrated in studies of learning sets with the two modes of stimulus presentations (M. Wilson, 1964; M. Wilson and Wilson, 1962), but equal transfer has been obtained (M. Wilson, 1965) and a significant opposite trend has been reported (M. Wilson, 1966). M. Wilson's (1966) analysis suggests that the amount of cross-modal transfer might depend upon the relative saliency of position and stimulus cues in the two modalities. If position cues are salient, position habits may transfer and interfere with learning-set performance.

CROSS-MODAL CONCEPTS

The transfer from melodic themes to visual designs (Osgood et al., 1957;

[6]Blakeslee and Gunter (1966, Experiment II) obtained trends in the opposite direction in monkeys, but the best transfer was far from perfect, and the difference was not statistically significant.

Willmann, 1944) and from visual designs to nonsense syllables (Hartmann, 1942; Köhler, 1929) are examples of cross-modal concepts. The transfer of cross-modal concepts has also been demonstrated in monkeys (Stepien and Cordeau, 1960) and in preschool children (Blank and Bridger, 1964; Blank and Bridger, 1965; Blank and Bridger, 1966; D. B. Gardner and Judisch, 1963—their 1965 paper is a brief report of the same study—Houck, Gardner, and Ruhl, 1965). The available evidence suggests that the basis for this kind of cross-modal transfer is mediation by verbal symbols (or other kinds of symbols), or is attributable to the perception of supramodal relations.

In a study by von Hornbostel (1931), human observers matched the "brightness" of a standard concentration of benzol with a variable gray, then matched the brightness of the benzol with a variable tone, and finally matched the appropriate tone with a variable gray. There was almost perfect correspondence between the gray selected as matching the benzol and the gray selected as matching the tone; and there was "almost no variation of brightness relationship in different individuals" (von Schiller, 1935, p. 466). "However, some persons are more, others less, sensitive to this kind of experiment" (p. 466). N. E. Cohen (1934) could not replicate these findings; in his study the tone matched to benzol and the tone matched to gray differed by about an octave. Boring (1933, p. 182) also concluded that human adults cannot equate brightnesses of tones, odors, and colors with any great consistency of results, suggesting that the perception of supramodal relations is at best a difficult feat for human observers.

Ohtsuka (1937) obtained evidence suggesting that monkeys can transpose from brightness to size; but the stimuli differing in size also differed in brightness, and the results are therefore ambiguous. Wegener (1965) found no transfer from a brightness discrimination to a loudness discrimination in monkeys. (The means of the experimental and control groups were not significantly different from each other, but the direction of the obtained difference indicated negative transfer.) Since the basis of transfer would apparently have to be the perception of a supramodal relation, Wegener's data could be interpreted as indicating that no supramodal relation was perceived. However, the within-pair brightness and loudness differences in Wegener's study were quite large (.62 and 15.2 foot-candles; 79.8 and 100.7 decibels above .0002 dyne/cm^2), and the successive discrimination procedure was used. Both of these conditions oppose relation perception, as emphasized by the Gestalt psychologists. Therefore, the failure to perceive a supramodal relation may have resulted from the use of suboptimal conditions and not from a general inability to perceive such relations.

Burton and Ettlinger (1960) concluded that their study yielded "no evidence of positive cross-modal transfer between visual and auditory frequency discriminations in the monkey" (p. 1072).

Von Schiller (1933; 1935) trained fish on a brightness discrimination, teaching some to choose the darker of two compartments, and others to choose the brighter. On test trials, the compartments were unilluminated, but one was infused with musk and the other with indol. According to von Schiller, musk has a "bright" smell and indol has a "dark" smell to human observers. (The smell of indol has also been described as "like an outdoor toilet.") Apparently the smells differed in the same way to the fish, because the bright-trained group chose the musk, and the dark-trained group chose the indol. Before training, according to von Schiller, there were no obvious preferences for either smell.

Evidence of cross-modal concepts has also been obtained in rats. In 1918, W. S. Hunter reported that after successive discrimination training with auditory stimuli, rats could transfer the responses to visual and tactile stimuli. Wylie (1916) reported a similar kind of transfer in rats.

SYNESTHESIA

In synesthesia, a stimulus exciting a sensation in one modality simultaneously arouses a sensation in another modality (Werner, 1948, p. 86). "Colored hearing" is an example (see, for example, W. James, 1890, Vol. II, pp. 29–30; Pillsbury, 1934, pp. 355–356; Sully, 1891, p. 269), but other kinds such as color–odor and color–word imagery have also been noted (Gamble, 1909, pp. 5, 106). In addition, it has long been known that certain "tastes" disappear when the nose is closed (see Pillsbury, 1934, pp. 180–182), indicating that the stimulation of the olfactory receptors produces taste sensations. (See Calkins [1916, p. 501] for a list of some of the older references on synesthesia.) According to Boring (1933, pp. 80–81 and 107–108), tonal "volume" and auditory localization are likely to be mediated by visual imagery, but the "visual surrogates" are not essential. Whether or not synesthesia is involved is debatable.

The evidence of synesthesia in young children seems to be largely anecdotal (see Werner, 1948, *passim* in pp. 86–103), and much of it is based on spontaneous verbal reports by the children. Even the *experimental* evidence of synesthesia has come mostly from introspective reports. In spite of the drawbacks of this kind of data, it seems highly reasonable to accept synesthesia as a genuine phenomenon. (See Wells [1919]. There are also numerous examples in creative writing, for example, in the works of Baudelaire [see Bertocci, 1964] and Huysmans [1889, pp. 71–73].) However, whenever verbal reports are used as evidence for the existence of a phenomenon, there is a likely possibility that the phenomenon is a product of verbal or other symbolic processes.

Synesthesia has been assumed to reflect a "primitive organic unity" of the senses (Werner, 1948, pp. 88 and 93; see also Hartmann, 1942, pp. 179–180; von Hornbostel, 1925; Köhler, 1929, Chapter 7, especially pp. 241–245), but it has also been assumed to be a product of meaningful association or mediated generalization (for example, Osgood, 1953, pp. 124, 642–646; Osgood *et al.*, 1957, p. 24). According to Lindworsky (1931), who was an exponent of Act Psychology and Associationism, synesthesia results from association between sensations and images. For example, in colored hearing, the *image* of a color is associated with the *sensation* of a tone. "If colors and tones are tuned to each other in an individual, and, furthermore, if this individual is capable of producing colored images easily, then by reason of the laws of association . . . , tones will often become 'seeing color.' Synesthesia results much less often from the association of accidentally simultaneous impressions. It is a matter of psychological significance here, that the image becomes very vivid, and reaches the intensity of a sensation . . . " (p. 138).

The "doctrine of specific energies of nerves" states in part that "a nerve end when stimulated at all always gives rise to its own peculiar sensation" (Pillsbury, 1934, p. 201; see also Boring, 1950, Chapter 5). This part of the doctrine has generally been accepted (for example, Best and Taylor, 1955, p. 946; Bugelski, 1960, pp. 142–143; Lotze, 1886, pp. 21–23; Pillsbury, 1934, p. 202), but has sometimes been challenged (for example, Ladd and Woodworth, 1911, pp. 350–352). The doctrine is at variance with the "primitive organic unity" notion. (The ability to "see" with the fingers, which has not always been studied with sufficiently tight controls to make the evidence acceptable [see M. Gardner, 1966; Sidgwick and Hodgson, 1884], would not necessarily be contradictory to the doctrine of specific energies, if it were shown that the phenomenon is mediated by temperature receptors or, as has been conjectured, by light-sensitive skin receptors [see Buckhout, 1966; Makous, 1966a, Makous, 1966b, Weintraub, 1966; Youtz, 1966].)

The explanation of synesthesia in terms of primitive organic unity of the senses and the explanation in terms of association can be shown to be closely related. The first explanation requires the assumption that it is possible to perceive supramodal qualities, which might be experienced as discriminably different feeling tones or moods, for example. There is some evidence that such qualities exist in human subjects. Börnstein (1936) showed that the presentation of bright and dark nonoptical stimuli (sounds, smells, tastes, and tactile stimuli) modified the perception of the brightnesses of visual stimuli; Menaker (1966) showed that development in the tactile-kinesthetic modality is delayed in congenitally blind children, compared with normally sighted children of equal age; and according to Hartmann (1942, p. 179), "the Dane, Bartholinus, had reported as far back as 1669 that partially deaf persons could hear better in the light than in the dark. . . ." Aristotle believed that there are supramodal qualities, and that they are perceived by a "deeper-lying faculty," the *sensus communis* (Strong, 1891, pp. 195–196).

If supramodal qualities are the basis of synesthesia, as Werner (1948) suggested, then cross-modal transfer is not necessarily cross-modal and not necessarily transfer. To use von Schiller's experiment as an example, the discriminanda are not the lights and smells existing in the environment, but are produced in the organism by the lights and smells, and are the same whether produced by lights or by smells. It should be immediately obvious that in this case the transfer from the lights to the smells results from mediation by the internal cues, and that the real disagreement between the two explanations of synesthesia is in whether the mediating link is innate or learned. There is no good *a priori* reason to suppose that there are no such innate mediating links (and von Schiller's data suggest that such links exist), and there is good experimental evidence that the required kinds of links can be acquired by learning, as in the studies of the acquired equivalence of cues (see, for example, Reese, 1962b; Spiker, 1956a).

The evidence is spotty, but suggests that cross-modal transfer occurs more readily in lower animals than in subhuman primates, and may therefore be inversely related to phylogenetic level, although Lund (1914) has shown that even the *Bursaria truncatella* can probably discriminate between contact and chemical stimuli. At the human level, cross-modal transfer seems to be a result of mediation by verbal or other symbolic processes.

ACTION FORMS

Katz investigated another kind of form transposition, the transposition of "action forms" (D. Katz, 1950, pp. 128–141). According to Katz, transposition of action forms is exhibited in sports, as by the distance runner who uses a constant pattern of movements but varies his speed by varying the times for each of the movements. Katz demonstrated similar transposition experimentally. Subjects were instructed to write a word ("elev"), then to write it larger. The time required to write each letter was measured and found to be constant. The speed of writing increased directly with increase in the size of the letters. In another phase of the study, in which the subjects were instructed to write more rapidly, then more slowly, relatively the same amount of time was taken for a letter regardless of the speed of writing; the time for a given letter, expressed as a percentage of the total time for the word, was constant with changes in the total time.

In another task, the experimenter tapped a rhythm on a telegraph key (dash dot dot), and instructed the subject to repeat the rhythm at the same rate, and at faster and slower rates. The ratio of the time between the first and second taps to the time between the second and third taps remained approximately constant with changes in the speed of the rhythm, until the rhythm became extremely fast or extremely slow.

Katz also found that transposition of a simple rhythm was more accurate when the simple rhythm was part of a more complex rhythm than when it was presented by itself. He concluded: "The whole fixes its parts more securely and adds to their distinguishing characteristics, producing greater pregnance and making transposition easier" (p. 132). This appears to contradict two of the "essential attributes" of forms: "Form perception prevents the observer from separating the parts," and " . . . the total form quality dominates the qualities of the parts. The more compact the form is [i.e., the greater the pregnance is], the more this holds true . . . " (D. Katz, 1950, p. 45). However, there is reason to believe that Katz's conclusion is valid. According to Mach (1914, citing a communication from Külke), Cornelius taught that it is a great help in the recognition of musical intervals to make note of particular pieces of music that begin with these intervals. Mach wrote: "This excellent device, which I have put to the test in my lectures on acoustics, and have found very effective, apparently complicates matters. One would naturally suppose that it would be easier to make note of an interval than of a melody. Nevertheless, a melody offers a greater hold to memory than does an interval" (Mach, 1914, p. 286).

The transposition of action forms, or the "equivalence of responses" (Lashley, 1929a), is also illustrated by bilateral transfer (for example, Lashley, 1924; Pavlov, 1927, p. 164), and by transfer between fingers. In two experiments by Campbell et al. (1960), college students were trained to avoid a painful noise by depressing a finger, "Finger A," when it was stimulated tactually, and were then given a "transposition" test on which another finger was stimulated for the first time. For example, if the second finger on the left hand were stimulated during training, the third finger on the right hand would be stimulated on the transposition trial. In the first experiment, 16 of 17 subjects transposed, in the sense that they depressed the finger stimulated on the test trial. The other subject depressed Finger A. Even in a group that was specifically instructed during training to depress Finger A regardless of the stimulus, 6 of 17 subjects transposed (the other 11 subjects depressed Finger A). In the second experiment, 19 of 24 subjects given general instructions transposed, and 10 of 24 subjects given the specific-response instructions transposed. The data suggest that most of the subjects given the general instructions and some given the specific-response instructions were set to depress the stimulated finger rather than to depress Finger A. The specific-response instructions were designed to prevent the learning of the more general set, but they were not necessarily completely successful.

Lashley (1929a) also gave the following anecdotal example: "The most striking instance of the sort that has come to my attention is that of a student of piano who, in the stress of a public recital, unknowingly transposed one-half tone upward an entire movement of a Beethoven sonata, a feat which she had never attempted before and could not duplicate afterward even with some practice" (p. 159). Lashley concluded: "We know nothing of the mechanism by which the equivalence is initially established" (p. 159). There is presently no good reason to modify that conclusion.

PART IV

Theories of Transposition

CHAPTER 8

Relational Theories

Background

There has been sharp controversy over the relative merits of the various theories of transposition, but much of it has been fruitless because close examination shows that all of the theories contained deficiencies. As early as 1933, Klüver (p. 325) remarked that the interpretations of transposition phenomena conflicted partly because the theorists had failed to take into account all of the available evidence on transposition, and the remark would still have been apt more than thirty years later. Klüver also suggested that the conflict among the theories resulted partly from a failure of investigators to study many of the factors that might be relevant to the problem. Hebert and Krantz (1965) have pointed out that this is still a problem

It is convenient to classify the theories of transposition as either "relational" or "absolute," but these classifications are somewhat arbitrary. It has long been believed that the subject learns about both the relative and the absolute properties of stimuli[1]; and although the relational theories emphasize relational learning and the absolute theories emphasize absolute learning, neither kind of theory necessarily denies the possibility of the other kind of learning (see section entitled "Historical Background," Chapter 1).

As Spence (1937b, footnote 2, p. 430) noted, there are two major groups of relational theories. In one, represented by the Gestalt school, relation perception is assumed to be fundamental and primitive. In the other, represented by the American configurationists, such as Karl Lashley, the response to relations is assumed to reflect a fairly high order of mental activity involving a relational judgment or a definite experiencing of the relationship as an abstract principle. (Kuenne [1946] also discussed this distinction.) The distinction is not important for present purposes, however,

[1]Early investigators who reached this conclusion include Kinnaman (1902), Köhler (1929), Hicks and Stewart (1930), Rüssel (1931), Klüver (1933), and F. N. Jones (1939a). More recent ones include I. M. L. Hunter (1952a; 1954), Vernon (1952), Nissen, Levinson, and Nichols (1953), Gonzalez et al. (1954), Stevenson and Bitterman (1955), R. Thompson (1955), Hilgard (1956), Wohlwill (1957), Rudel (1957; 1958; 1960), Miller (1959), Wertheimer (1959), Berman (1963), D. H. Cohen (1963), and Baumeister et al. (1964).

because the theories generate similar predictions by adding qualifying assumptions.

Almost all of the proponents of relational theories have ignored an implication of the fact that a relation is necessarily a property of two (or more) objects and not a property of a single object. Stout (1918a, pp. 70–71) said: "According to Stumpf, we may be aware of two notes differing in pitch, and we may be aware that they do so differ, without observing which is higher than the other." My argument here is that there are four cues, two absolute and two relative, but the relative cues are not associated with either single object. As illustrated in Fig. 8-1, which depicts

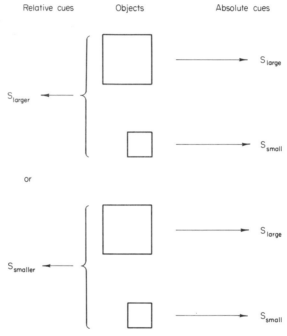

FIG. 8-1. Absolute and relative cues in a two-stimulus size discrimination. (Irrelevant cues have been omitted.)

the absolute cues and the relative cues in a two-stimulus size discrimination, the subject cannot approach the relation "larger" without approaching both objects at once. The problem is to explain how the perception of the relation, which is a property of two objects, gets the subject to approach one of the absolute cues. The solution is simple enough, and deserves to be explicated only because it has heretofore been almost completely ignored. It is clear that the perception of "smaller" requires orientation toward the larger object first and the smaller object second, and that the perception of "larger" requires orientation toward the smaller object first and the larger second. What the subject must learn is to locomote forward when the appropriate relative cue is received, and to move before changing the direction of orientation. The relative cue arouses a response of locomoting forward, and the animal approaches the stimulus toward which it is oriented. Lindworsky seems to have proposed the same explanation in 1919, but his paper has not been translated from the German (see Koffka, 1925, pp. 228–229). Koffka has said of this kind of explanation: "Certainly it does not agree with the description Köhler gives of learning in hens" (Koffka, 1925, Note 208, p. 369, referring to Köhler, 1915, pp. 59–60).

Gestalt Theory

The notion of form perception is basic in Gestalt theory, but it has been pointed out that the Gestalters were not the only psychologists to recognize its existence (see Boring, 1927; Boring, 1930; Spearman, 1937a, Chapter XXIV; Spearman, 1937b; Squires, 1930), and it has been argued that they overestimated and overgeneralized its importance (Helson and Fehrer, 1932). The British Associationists, especially James Mill (1829), argued that the perception, or "idea," of a whole is a synthesis of sensations of its parts, but Sir William Hamilton (1859, pp. 368–372) argued that this doctrine is false. According to Hamilton, "we first obtain a general knowledge of the complex wholes presented to us by sense, and then, by analysis and limited attention, obtain a special knowledge of their several parts" (p. 368). Similar views were expressed by William James (1890, Vol. I, pp. 276–283, 487–488, and 546–547), Woodworth (1918, pp. 96–97), Alverdes (1932, pp. 77–78), Pillsbury (1934, pp. 388 and 390), Bijou and Baer (1965, pp. 151–152), and J. D. Gould and Schaffer (1966); but none of them implied that the wholes have any qualities that are incapable of being analyzed into the several parts. The belief that wholes cannot be analyzed into parts is one of the main tenets of Gestalt theory, and the priority of this belief is properly claimed by the Gestalters. Von Ehrenfels (1890; 1937) had theorized that the "form-quality" is an emergent quality of wholes, but he believed that the whole is analyzable into this quality and the elemental sensations of the parts. Ernst Meumann, who was essentially a Wundtian psychologist (Boring, 1950, p. 429), also accepted the principle of an emergent form-quality (Meumann, 1913, pp. 49–50). (See Line, 1931, pp. 1–24, for a review of these and other relevant theories.)

According to Parsons (1927, p. 244), "the recognition of the form depends upon the unconscious recognition of individual characteristics, and this depends upon physiological processes." Although probably no one would deny the part about physiological processes, virtually all of the Gestalt psychologists denied the part about the dependence of form perception on perception of the elements. In fact, the Gestalt psychologists have emphasized that the perception of the parts is influenced by the nature of the whole. On this point, the British Act Psychologist, G. F. Stout, was in agreement with the Gestalt psychologists. Stout pointed out as an illustration that "The whist-player needs not be told that in every fresh deal the several cards become qualified by their relations within the new whole" (Stout, 1918b, p. 48). Actually, Parsons admitted that the whole is emergent, but he expressed the faith of the elementarist that it will ultimately become explicable in physiological terms (p. 245).

TWO-STIMULUS PROBLEMS

According to Köhler (1918), the perception of a relation and the perception of a form or Gestalt have two characteristics in common: (a) "The individual [elements] appearing in a pair attain an inner union. Their role in this union . . . depends not upon their absolute qualities, but upon their places in the system they compose."[2] (b)"If their places with respect to each other are held constant, but a variation is made in their absolute quality, the Gestalt and the perceived relationship will be transposed" (p. 221). (Elsewhere, however, Köhler [1920, p. 25] said that not all Gestalten are transposable.) No relation need be perceived in order for a Gestalt to be perceived (see Köhler, 1918, pp. 220–221), although a relation among the parts must *exist* in order for the Gestalt to be perceived (Köhler, 1929, pp. 215 and 311). (According to Werner [1948, pp. 220–222], "the establishment of a relation of size between two lengths proceeds initially out of the perceptual togetherness, out of a preliminary figuration . . . " that implicitly contains the abstract relationship. The relation as such is not experienced, but is abstracted from an experienced togetherness or Gestalt; and the abstracted relation and experienced whole are indistinguishable in their effects upon performance. Stout [1918a, p. 73] also believed that form perception is more primitive than relation perception.)

The "inner union" or togetherness depends on the "segregation of a definite whole," and breaks down when the absolute qualities are changed in such a way that the relations among the parts are no longer perceived, or are no longer perceived in the previous way (Köhler, 1929, p. 215). Maier and Schneirla (1935, pp. 357–358) and Stevenson and Bitterman (1955) also postulated that the transposition of a relation may be impaired if absolute properties are changed too much. Changes in the stimuli that eliminate the aspects that characterize the situation for the subject disrupt the behavior. Köhler (1929, p. 214) noted that "when shifted too far toward the periphery of the field, a form will change its character more or less, but

---

[2]Pavlov (1927) also spoke of the "union" of two stimuli into a "single compound" (p. 71), and asserted that " . . . the animal may be affected by the sum total of numerous elementary stimuli acting together as a whole" (p. 38); but he showed that it is possible for single elements within the compound to become effective (pp. 76–77 and 141–144).

excepting this case, the possibilities of transposing a form are very numerous." Furthermore, form can be altered by changing too much "that special set of relations of stimulation which seem to be decisive for the segregation of a definite whole and for the specific dynamical structure underlying form" (Köhler, 1929, p. 215). (Relevant to this point, Hartmann [1942, p. 175] was probably incorrect when he said that a square retains its squareness "whether the length of its sides is two millimeters or two miles," because except when it is seen from a considerable distance, the two-mile square is probably not perceptible as a square, and when it is seen from a considerable distance, it is no longer a two-mile square.) Köhler noted: "Wertheimer has laid great stress upon the point that, for a given form, not all relations of stimulation are equally important. Some of them may be changed considerably without any remarkable effect upon the actual form" (Köhler, 1929, footnote 1, p. 215). Stout (1918a, p. 77) also noted that some relations in a whole are more important than others.

Köhler once identified insight as a "grasp of a *material, inner* relation of two things to each other" (1925, p. 229, his italics). (Romanes [1883, p. 17] used the term "reason" to refer to this kind of process [see also Romanes, 1884, p. 318].) Wheeler (1940) and Helson (1927) considered the occurrence of relational responses to be a criterion of insight but, according to Wapner, Köhler "... does not regard transposition alone, as evidence that insight has occurred. As Köhler defines insight, it is necessarily concerned with an awareness of relations, and he doubts whether an animal who chooses relationally and therefore tends to transpose, need be aware of the fact that his choice is relative" (Wapner, 1944, p. 51, citing personal communication from Köhler).[3]

Gonzalez *et al.* (1954) assumed that spontaneous relational organization is more likely to appear when the differences among the stimuli are small, which would explain the effect of stimulus similarity on transposition. The assumption is in line with Lashley's (1938b) "pinheads and cartwheels" and Koffka's (1922) "crickets and sixteen-inch guns," which were asserted to be too disparate to yield perceptions of size or loudness relations.[4] However, Zeiler (1966a) has reported data that suggest that young children may recognize relations more easily when the stimulus differences are fairly large (2 to 1 area ratio) than when they are smaller (1.4 to 1 area ratio) (see section entitled "Stimulus Similarity," Chapter 3).

[3] Relevant to the problem of awareness, Katz (1937, p. 253) observed: "Man not only *has* consciousness, but he knows that he has it." Lower animals lack this kind of awareness, according to Katz. He cited Betz: "The dog is happy, but he presumably does not know that he is; he has a guilty conscience, but does not know that he has."

[4] With reference to Lashley's "pinheads and cartwheels," Spence (1942) said that it "... describes the experimental finding in a very picturesque manner. However, it explains nothing" (p. 258).

Stevenson and Bitterman (1955) asserted that the distance effect "contradicts a strict relational interpretation of learning which suggests that transposition should not be affected by a change in the absolute properties of the training stimuli as long as their relational properties are unaltered" (p. 274). However, it is doubtful that such a strict interpretation was ever intended, as indicated in the preceding paragraphs, unless the "relational properties" referred to are interpreted as being phenomenological, in which case the statement would be tautological. Spence (1942) pointed out that relational theory does not explicitly predict a distance effect, but he deliberately avoided the question of whether it could or ever would make this prediction.

According to Köhler, the subject learns two habits, one a response to the Gestalt and the other a response to a "more or less definite" absolute stimulus. The trace of the Gestalt ("organization") is much more stable than the trace of a more or less definite absolute stimulus, and therefore the "relative" habit is more likely to control the response after a delay than is the "absolute" habit.[5] Data reported by Gundlach and Herington (1933, Experiment II) support the assumption that the perceived absolute value is only "more or less definite"; adult human subjects had little success in identifying an absolute gray when it was paired with another similar gray (three to five steps from the absolute gray in the Hering series).

A posthumous article by Wertheimer (1959), prepared from notes and said by the editor to be an incomplete exposition of Wertheimer's views, contained many of the same ideas that can be found in Köhler's writings, but is valuable because it was at least an outline of a deliberate attempt to deal with some of the variables that influence the probability of transposition, variables which Köhler dealt with only incidentally and sporadically. In its extant form, Wertheimer's paper reveals typical deficiencies of the Gestalt type of approach, proposing as theoretical assumptions, for example, what are actually restatements of empirical facts, and then using the "assumptions" to explain the facts. However, Wertheimer's discussion makes explicit certain assumptions that remained implicit in Köhler's presentations. One of the most important ones was concerned with the nature of the stimulus in discrimination learning. According to Wertheimer, the subject might learn to respond to a precise absolute value of a stimulus (as assumed in Spence's theory), or to an exact relation (as in the theories based on Helson's concept of adaptation level, discussed later), or to the direction of a relation (as must have been assumed by the Gestalt psychologists).

Wertheimer argued that it would be much harder for a subject to

---

[5] See Köhler (1929, pp. 303–304). Rudel (1957; 1958; 1960) has also expressed this notion. Köhler had earlier, however, denied the possibility of learning the absolute habit (Köhler, 1918, pp. 221–222).

remember a precise absolute value of a stimulus, or an exact relation between two stimuli, than to remember only the direction of a relation, disregarding the absolute value of the relative difference between the stimuli. Therefore, the finding that there is more transposition when the beginning of the transposition test is delayed than when it is immediate implies that the subject can respond to the direction of the relation. However, neither Spence nor the theorists using the adaptation level concept dealt with the consequences of delay, and since appropriate assumptions could be added to their theories to account for the effect of delay on transposition, the finding is not crucial, as Wertheimer apparently believed, except that it demonstrates one way in which these latter theories are presently inadequate. Granting the truth of the premise about the difference in forgetting rate for the different kinds of stimulus properties, Wertheimer's argument can lead to the conclusion that the "absolute-stimulus" and "absolute-relation" theories need revision, but does not require the conclusion that direction of relation can be perceived, unless the needed revisions turn out to be impossible. (D. H. Cohen [1963, pp. 14–15] has suggested that the absolute stimulus is forgotten sooner because it carries a greater "information load" than the relation, but there seems to be no *a priori* reason to expect that increasing the information load would reduce retention, and there is some evidence that increasing the information load aids retention [see, for example, I. M. L. Hunter, 1964, especially Chapter VII; Mach, 1914, p. 206, Reese, 1965b].)

One might speculate that the effect of delay results from "sharpening." "Sharpening" is an increase in the differentiation between figures; "leveling" is a reduction of the differentiation (see Wulf, 1922). Studies of the influence of verbal labels on memory for form imply that the leveling and sharpening tendencies can be brought under verbal control, although they do not directly test this proposition. For example, in a study by DeBold and Mayland (1965), subjects who had learned to associate a diamond-shaped trapezium with the word "sharp" remembered the figure as being "pointier" than it actually was, and subjects who had learned to associate it with the word "even" remembered it as less "pointy" than it actually was. If sharpening in transposition tasks increased the differentiation between the stimuli by distorting the remembered absolute values, then it would be reasonable to suppose that the actual change in absolute values that occurs between the training phase and the test phase would be less likely to disturb the perception of the relation, and that there would therefore be more transposition when the test is delayed than when it is given immediately after the end of the training phase. Although theoretically leveling might occur during the delay instead of sharpening, it seems unlikely that leveling would occur in practice, because leveling would destroy the basis of the discrimination.

Whether or not the Gestalt explanation is correct, there seems to be little doubt that relations are remembered better than absolute qualities, although there is contradictory evidence. Using light reflected from cards, Yerkes (1907, Chapter 8) found that a dancing mouse failed to transfer response from a white-black discrimination to a light-gray—dark-gray discrimination. (P. D. Wilson and Riesen [1966, pp. 92 and 94] referred to transfer in this kind of test as "transposition.") The animal gave only 54 correct responses in the first 100 transfer trials, with differential reinforcement, and required 200 trials to obtain a perfect score on 10 consecutive trials. If the animal had solved the initial discrimination on the basis of the *direction* of the relative difference, there should have been more transfer than was obtained; it can therefore be concluded that the absolute stimulus qualities or the absolute ratio of these qualities exerted some influence on performance. Using transmitted light, there was more transfer, but since the amount of transfer dropped as the ratio between the test lights was reduced, the results for the two kinds of light are not necessarily contradictory. However, the results are definitely only suggestive, since Yerkes tested only one subject with each kind of light.

Spiker (1959, Experiment I), testing nursery-school children, obtained essentially perfect transfer when the ratio was reduced; but the ratio was changed by varying the brightness of the negative stimulus. The brightness of the positive stimulus remained constant, and the response could have been to the absolute value of the positive stimulus or to the direction of the relative difference between the stimuli.

There is fairly good evidence that perceiving a relation between the stimulus and response items in a paired-associates task facilitates learning and retention (for example, Key, 1926; Cree Warden, 1933). The relation can be "natural" or imaginary and bizarre (see Köhler, 1929, pp. 287–288; Reese 1965b), and it apparently can be envisaged as a concrete visual image or described verbally with equal effectiveness (Reese, 1965b). The finding of Salzinger and Eckerman (1965, pretraining task) that a 10-digit number is easier to learn than 10 one-digit numbers presented serially agrees with the general principle; material that is organized or related is easier to learn than unrelated material.

Zeiler (1963b; 1963d) asserted that relational theory cannot predict the occurrence of absolute responses, but the prediction is clearly implicit in the preceding discussion. The prediction of random responses is also possible. (However, it was emphasized that these responses are *random* only with respect to the discriminative cue manipulated by the experimenter [for example, Krechevsky, 1932a; Lashley, 1929a].)

Gestalt theory could have specifically predicted a distance effect, as noted above, and the occurrence of other responses when transposition does not occur; but as Gonzalez and Ross (1958) pointed out: "Relational theorists have not often been concerned with the factors which may be expected to limit transposition" (p. 742). In one exception, Köhler (1918) conducted a series of tests aimed at identifying such factors (according to Koffka, 1925, p. 141; unfortunately, the relevant parts of Köhler's paper were only summarized in the 1938 English translation).

The relational theorists have tended to advance a new *ad hoc* assumption to "explain" each new experimental finding, usually without specifying the details of operation of the newly assumed mechanism (see Hebert and Krantz, 1965; Spearman, 1937a, Chapter XXIV; Spearman 1937b; Taylor, 1932b); for example:

(a) To account for the effect of delay, it was assumed that the subject learns both absolute and relative habits and that the relative habit is retained longer (Köhler, 1929, p. 303; Stevenson and Bitterman, 1955; see also Lashley and Wade, 1946).

(b) To account for the distance effect, it was assumed that changing the absolute properties too much disrupts the perception of the relation. (Köhler implied this in 1918; Stevenson and Bitterman made it explicit in 1955. Klüver's [1933] discussion of the range of stimulus equivalence contains the same idea.)

(c) To account for the correlation between language and transposition, Lawrence and DeRivera (1954) suggested that although children can respond relationally prior to the development of language, they do not necessarily do so in all situations, but the very factors that lead to language development also lead to an emphasis on relational responding as the dominant mode of behavior.

The assumptions in these examples seem to be entirely gratuitous, and as Zeiler (1963c) has pointed out, the relational theorists have not been concerned with specifying the points at which transitions may be expected.

In a criticism of Spence's (1937b) absolute theory of transposition, Razran (1938b) argued that a "*sui generis* conception of relational responses" can generate testable predictions (pp. 535–536), but Spence (1939a) replied that such a conception had so far failed to do so. Spearman (1937b) was even more emphatic in his indictment of Gestalt psychology: the "dynamic theorems . . . are so vague that—like the ancient oracles—anything can be read into them; nothing read out of them" (pp. 382–383). Such laws cannot predict anything, according to Spearman, because of their vagueness, while their vagueness enables them "by far-fetched analogies to be twisted into more or less accord with what we know already" (p. 375). (See, however, Knox's [1939] reply to Spearman. Knox was referring to Chapter XXIV in Spearman's [1937a] book, but this chapter presented essentially the same arguments as the 1937b paper.)

As Kreezer and Dallenbach (1929) noted in another connection, Köhler

(1929) said, in reply to criticism that he should have applied statistical methods to his data: "To my mind this means an inability to see the problems which I had tried to treat in a preliminary way" (pp. 52–53). Kreezer and Dallenbach (1929, footnote 2, p. 432) answered: "We agree with Köhler; qualitative work must precede the quantitative; but after the 'preliminary' work has been done quantitative work should follow."

INTERMEDIATE-STIMULUS PROBLEMS

The classical Gestalt theorists never dealt with the intermediate-stimulus problem, but presumably they would have made the same predictions as for the two-stimulus problem. According to Rudel (1957), Köhler's theory can predict the greater difficulty of learning the intermediate-stimulus problem than of learning the two-stimulus problem. (This is a well-established finding but is not documented in this monograph.) I cannot deduce this prediction from Köhler's 1918 paper as translated in 1938, but Rudel referred to the original 1918 version, parts of which were omitted from the 1938 translation. Presumably, the argument would be that largeness and smallness are obvious relations between two stimuli differing in size; but middle-sizedness is more obvious when the stimuli are spatially ordered in size than when the middle-sized stimulus is not in the middle spatial position. Therefore, the middle-sizedness relation is not as likely to be perceived as the two-stimulus relations. Furthermore, as Lashley and Wade's (1946) discussion implies, the perception of middle-sizedness requires that two two-stimulus comparisons be made successively, increasing the difficulty of the perception of this relation.

SUMMARY

According to Gestalt theory, transposition can occur if the subject has learned to respond to a "configuration" or to a "relation." "Configuration" is synonymous with Gestalt; "relation" means "direction of relation," as brightening or lengthening. The configuration is immediately given in perception, in the sense that no intermediate process is required between the proximal stimulation and the central process corresponding to the percept. The perception of the relation requires an intermediate process, an act of comparison, but apparently no conscious intention to compare nor awareness of the relation is meant to be implied.

Since the laws of transposition are the same for configurations and relations, I will simplify the terminology in the rest of this section by discussing only relations, but it should be kept in mind that configurations are being considered implicitly.

If the stimulus elements are too disparate, no relation is perceptible. (The exact limits must be determined empirically.) If the elements are similar enough to permit relation perception, then the absolute qualities of the elements can be changed within wide limits without affecting the perception of the relation, and transposition occurs. (Again the limits must be determined empirically.) Beyond these limits, the percept changes, and transposition breaks down.

Whether or not the relation is perceived, it is possible to perceive "absolute" values of the stimulus elements. However, if the relation is perceived, the perceived absolute values are not the same as they would be if no relation were perceived. It is difficult for the subject to remember absolute values, and therefore the subject tends to respond to relations whenever possible, although absolute habits interfere with relational habits under some conditions.

Two-stimulus relations are easier to see than multiple-stimulus relations such as middle-sizedness. It has been suggested that the perception of a multiple-stimulus relation requires a series of two-stimulus comparisons, which would account for the difference in ease of perception. However, this does not seem to be a firmly accepted principle in Gestalt theory.

When an extreme change in the absolute properties of the stimulus elements disrupts relation perception, there remains no experimentally established basis for responding to any particular stimulus characteristic. Transposition cannot occur, because its basis has been destroyed; but neither can absolute responses occur, in the usual sense, except on one-step tests. Beyond one step, the stimulus element that might have acquired "absolute habit" is no longer present, and therefore there can be no absolute responses beyond one step. Subjects must, then, respond at the chance level (although it would be incorrect to conclude that the responses are truly *random*).

The occurrence of transposition does not necessarily indicate the presence of reasoning or insight. The latter processes involve not only the perception of relations, but also *awareness* of the relations, particularly cause–effect relations. From this point of view, transposition need not result from any cognitive process, but can be "mechanistic."

Configuration Theory

In Gulliksen and Wolfle's (1938; 1939) "configuration" theory, the subject is assumed to have directional response capabilities (left-turning response and right-turning response, for example), and is assumed to make the responses to stimulus configurations. A configuration is "a pair of stimuli in a given spatial order" (1938, p. 129). Although the configuration was conceived of as neither an absolute stimulus, in Spence's (1937b) sense, nor a relation in the Gestaltist sense (see Gulliksen and Wolfle, 1938,

p. 129), Spence (1942) correctly classified the theory as a Gestalt theory. The perception of a Gestalt, as noted in the preceding section, does not require the perception of a relation. The essential characteristic is that the subject responds to the compound rather than to the elements (see von Ehrenfels, 1937). (It might be noted that in the same sense, Spence's [1952] theory of patterning is also a kind of Gestalt theory, as Hilgard [1956] observed.)

The exposition of Gulliksen and Wolfle's theory is facilitated by reference to an hypothetical problem with two stimulus squares differing in size. One stimulus has an area of four square inches, and the other has an area of sixteen square inches. There are two possible configurations of these two stimuli, one with the larger stimulus on the left and the smaller on the right, and one with the positions reversed. These configurations are represented graphically in Fig. 8-2 by points A and B. Assume that the subject learns to respond left to configuration A and right to configuration B. (In Gestalt theory the subject would be said to have learned to choose the larger of the two sizes.) If the subject is tested with configurations A_1 and B_1 (one step from A and B) and with configurations A_2 and B_2 (two steps from A and B), he will be said to have transposed if he responds left to A_1 and A_2 and right to B_1 and B_2. According to Gulliksen and Wolfle's theory of two-stimulus transposition, transfer to configuration A_i is a function of T, and

$$T = \frac{a_i + k_{ia} w_a - c_{ib} u_b}{b_i - c_{ia} u_a + k_{ib} w_b} \qquad \text{[Gulliksen and Wolfle's Equation T-1, 1938, p. 234]} \qquad (1)$$

where a_i is the pre-experimentally acquired tendency to give the transposition response to A_i; b_i is the pre-experimentally acquired tendency to give the other response to A_i; $k_{ia} w_a$ is the generalized strength of the tendency to give the transposition response to A_i, resulting from correct responses to A during training; $k_{ib} w_b$ is the generalized strength of the tendency to give the other response to A_i, resulting from correct responses to B during training; $c_{ib} u_b$ is the generalized tendency to inhibit the transposition response to A_i, resulting from incorrect responses to B during training (the incorrect response to B is the same as the transposition response to A_i); and $c_{ia} u_a$ is the generalized tendency to inhibit the other response to A_i, resulting from incorrect responses to A during training.

The values of k_{ia} and c_{ia} are assumed to increase in magnitude as the "psychological distance" between A and A_i becomes smaller, and the values of k_{ib} and c_{ib} are assumed to increase as the psychological distance between B and A_i becomes smaller. The terms w_a and w_b symbolize the numbers of correct responses to A and B, respectively, and u_a and u_b denote the numbers of incorrect responses to A and B. Note that these numbers must be positive integers. If it is assumed that the initial response tendencies are equal (that is, $a_i = b_i$), that the numbers of correct responses are equal ($w_a = w_b$),

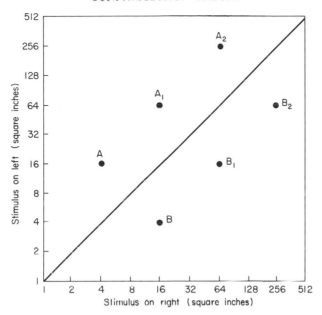

FIG. 8-2. Two-configuration transposition problem, as conceptualized in Gulliksen and Wolfle's theory. See text for explanation.

and that the numbers of incorrect responses are equal $(u_a = u_b)$, then Eq. (1) simplifies to

$$T = \frac{a_i + k_{ia} w - c_{ib} u}{a_i - c_{ia} u + k_{ib} w} \tag{2}$$

(I would be unwilling to assume that $c = k$, as Gulliksen and Wolfle did in further simplifying the equation.)

It is necessary to determine whether, in the general case, T is greater or less than unity. Subtracting the denominator in Eq. (2) from the numerator (to determine which is greater), and rearranging terms:

$$\text{Difference} = (a_i + k_{ia} w - c_{ib} u) - (a_i - c_{ia} u + k_{ib} w)$$

$$= a_i + k_{ia} w - c_{ib} u - a_i + c_{ia} u - k_{ib} w$$

$$= (k_{ia} w - k_{ib} w) + (c_{ia} u - c_{ib} u)$$

$$= w(k_{ia} - k_{ib}) + u(c_{ia} - c_{ib}). \tag{3}$$

Gulliksen and Wolfle assumed that the physical distance between two configurations plotted as in Fig. 8-2 is roughly equivalent to the psychological distance between them. It is apparent from examination of the figure that A_i is nearer to A than it is to B, and since the values of k and c increase as distance decreases

$$k_{ia} > k_{ib} \quad \text{and} \quad c_{ia} > c_{ib}$$

Hence,

$$w(k_{ia} - k_{ib}) > 0 \quad \text{and} \quad u(c_{ia} - c_{ib}) > 0$$

and the difference in Eq. (3) must be positive. This means that the numerator in Eq. (2) must be greater than the denominator, and that T must be greater than unity.

Since T is greater than 1.00, and T is an index of "the amount and direction of transfer to be expected" (Gulliksen and Wolfle, 1938, p. 235), subjects should tend to give the same response to A_i as they learned to give to A, or in other words, they should transpose. (Similarly, subjects should transpose from B to B_i.) Exactly how much transposition is to be expected cannot be specified, because the theorists failed to indicate what function relates T to any response measure.

The theory predicts transposition, but several investigators (for example, T. S. Kendler, 1950; Kuenne, 1946; Price, 1960) have implied that it does not predict the distance effect. If the theory does predict a distance effect, as Gulliksen and Wolfle asserted (1938, p. 245), then T_1 must be greater than T_2 (where T_1 is the T calculated for A_1 and T_2 is the T calculated for A_2). If it is assumed that $a_1 = a_2 = a$, and if the assumptions for Eq. (2) are retained, then

$$T_1 - T_2 = \frac{a + k_{1a}w - c_{1b}u}{a - c_{1a}u + k_{1b}w} - \frac{a + k_{2a}w - c_{2b}u}{a - c_{2a}u + k_{2b}w}. \tag{4}$$

The value of T_1 will be greater than the value of T_2 if the difference between the numerator and denominator of T_1 is greater than the difference between the numerator and denominator of T_2, since both differences are necessarily positive (as already shown in the general case). The difference D between these two differences is

$$\begin{aligned} D &= [(a + k_{1a}w - c_{1b}u) - (a - c_{1a}u + k_{1b}w)] - [(a + k_{2a}w \\ &\quad - c_{2b}u) - (a - c_{2a}u + k_{2b}w)] \\ &= a + k_{1a}w - c_{1b}u - a + c_{1a}u - k_{1b}w - a - k_{2a}w + c_{2b}u \\ &\quad + a - c_{2a}u + k_{2b}w \\ &= k_{1a}w - k_{2a}w - k_{1b}w + k_{2b}w + c_{1a}u - c_{2a}u - c_{1b}u + c_{2b}u \\ &= w[(k_{1a} - k_{2a}) - (k_{1b} - k_{2b})] + u[(c_{1a} - c_{2a}) - (c_{1b} - c_{2b})]. \end{aligned}$$

But from examination of Fig. 8-2, it can be seen that if the constants are linearly (and inversely) related to the distances, then

$$(k_{1a} - k_{2a}) > (k_{1b} - k_{2b}) > 0 \tag{5}$$

and

$$(c_{1a} - c_{2a}) > (c_{1b} - c_{2b}) > 0 . \tag{6}$$

Therefore,

$$(k_{1a} - k_{2a}) - (k_{1b} - k_{2b}) > 0 \qquad \text{[from (5)]}$$

and

$$(c_{1a} - c_{2a}) - (c_{1b} - c_{2b}) > 0. \qquad \text{[from (6)]}$$

Hence, the difference D must be positive, and T_1 must be greater than T_2. A distance effect is therefore predicted.

In Fig. 8-2, the configurations are plotted against logarithmic scales. If untransformed axes were used, the changes in distance from A to the test configurations would be equal to the changes from B, and Eqs. (5) and (6) would become

$$(k_{1a} - k_{2a}) - (k_{1b} - k_{2b}) \tag{5a}$$

and

$$(c_{1a} - c_{2a}) = (c_{1b} - c_{2b}) . \tag{6a}$$

Then T_1 would be equal to T_2, and no distance effect would be predicted. However, using logarithmic axes means that it is being assumed that logarithmic distances are roughly equivalent to the psychological distances with which the theory deals, and using untransformed axes would mean that the assumption is that linear distances are roughly equivalent to the psychological distances. Gulliksen and Wolfle assumed tentatively that the logarithmic relation is a better approximation, because of Weber's law. It might be noted, however, that even if the untransformed axes were used, the distance effect could still be predicted by assuming a nonlinear relation between distance and the k and c terms, since the distance of A_i from B would always be greater, by a constant amount, than the distance from A.

In either case, the "distance effect" that is predicted would be equivalent to the conventional distance effect only if the psychological distance between configurations were directly related to the distance between the absolute stimuli they contain. Although this relation is not explicitly assumed in the theory, it is reasonable to suppose that it was intended. (In Gestalt theory, the Gestalt or perceived relation is either the same for both sets of stimuli or is different, depending upon the differences in the absolute qualities of the stimuli, and this problem therefore does not arise.)

As can be seen in Fig. 8-2, A_i must always be closer to A than it is to B, but at some distance the difference between A_i and A will be for all practical purposes equal to the difference between A_i and B. At that distance T will be approximately equal to zero, and A_i will tend to elicit both responses. This means that the minimum expected frequency of transposition responses is at the chance level, and absolute responses are not expected to predominate at any distance.

Although Gulliksen and Wolfle did not deal with the intermediate-stimulus problem, they gave an extension of the theory to four-configuration problems, and the equations could be extended to the intermediate-stimulus problem. The intermediate-stimulus problem involves six configurations and three directional responses (left, middle, right).

Data obtained by Nissen (1950), R. Thompson (1953), and D'Amato (1961) are inconsistent with the assumption of directional responses. In Nissen's study, chimpanzees solved a two-stimulus simultaneous discrimination problem with the stimuli arranged to require left and right responses in one group of subjects and upward and downward responses in another group. The subjects were then tested with the same stimuli but with the spatial orientation switched between groups. Thompson applied the same design to a transverse patterning problem (see Fig. 3–1), also using chimpanzees as subjects. In both studies there was little decrement in performance when directionality was changed, indicating that the subjects learned approach and avoidance responses (or approach and nonapproach responses), rather than directional responses (unless an unlikely generalization of responses occurred). Bitterman objected to this interpretation of the Nissen data, leading to a brief but rather heated controversy in the *Psychological Review* (Bitterman, 1952; Nissen, 1952a; Nissen, 1952b; Spence, 1952; Weise and Bitterman, 1951).

D'Amato trained rats on a successive brightness discrimination in a Skinner box, with one response lever, and later tested for transfer to a simultaneous discrimination in a Y maze with similar brightnesses. The brighter light was positive in the transfer task, and it was found that rats trained with the brighter light positive in the early problem were superior on the transfer task to rats trained with the dimmer light positive in the early problem. Transfer of specific response tendencies was therefore more important than transfer of any general perceptual factors, and the response tendencies must have been approach and avoidance (or approach and nonapproach) rather than directional.

Weise and Bitterman (1951) considered Lashley's (1938b; 1942) failure to obtain intermediate-stimulus discrimination in rats to be crucial in limiting the applicability of Gulliksen and Wolfle's theory, but several studies obtaining intermediate-stimulus discrimination in infrahuman subjects could have been cited as opposing Lashley's finding (for example, goldfish, Perkins, 1931; Perkins and Wheeler, 1930; chicks, M. H. Lewis, 1930; rats, Wolfle, 1937; infrahuman primates, Spence, 1942).

Ratio Theory

Riley (1958) proposed that the effective stimulus be redefined either as the ratio of the absolute stimulus value to the background ("surround") or as a combination of this ratio and the ratio of the one stimulus value to the other stimulus value. He noted that the first redefinition could be incorporated into Spence's absolute theory, and that the second could be incorporated into relational theory. Assuming that transposition is reduced when either ratio is changed would explain the distance effect and the drop in performance level from training to test, because in typical experiments the ground remains constant, and the change in ratio is therefore greater for Far Tests than for the Near Test (as S. J. Lachman [1956] also noted).

The idea of defining the effective stimulus as a ratio between figure and ground values is not new. According to Riley, Köhler expressed the idea in 1929.[6] Kohlrausch used this kind of definition of the stimulus as early as 1931; and Ernst Mach (1886; footnote 3, p. 80 in the 1914 edition) still earlier suggested that the figure-ground ratio can excite a sensation. Similarly, William James said: "What appeals to our attention far more than the absolute quality or quantity of a given sensation in its *ratio* to whatever other sensations we may have at the same time" (W. James, 1890, Vol. I, pp. 231–232, his italics). Wundt said that "... wherever there occurs a quantitative apprehension of sensations, whether as regards intensity or degree of quality, the individual sensation is estimated by the relation in which it stands to other sensations of the same sense modality" (Wundt, 1896, p. 119).

Bugelski (1956, p. 413) also suggested this kind of definition of the stimulus, and noted that Woodworth (1938, Chapter 24) used the same notion to account for perceptual constancy. (Osgood [1953, pp. 280–285, 295–297] rejected this kind of explanation of constancy, however.) It is interesting to note that Woodworth (p. 601) expressed the notion this way: "According to Weber's law equal brightness ratios should be perceived as equal and the two objects in question should appear equally bright in relation to the [differing background illumination]." The misinterpretation of Weber's law is curious (compare W. James, 1890, Vol. I, pp. 533–549).

---

[6]See Riley (1958, footnote 3, p. 6). The reference was to Köhler (1929, pp. 218–219). The idea was not explicitly stated there, but seems to have been implied. Köhler more clearly expressed the idea in a later paper (1951, pp. 209–210).

Johnsgard (1957) seems to have assumed that both kinds of stimulus can be sensed. He suggested that the "stimulus intensity dynamism," which Hull (1949) believed is related to absolute intensity, is actually related to relative intensity.

Riley (1958) obtained experimental support for his proposal that the stimulus should be redefined. On transposition tests at one and five steps of absolute distance, the background intensity was kept constant in one experimental condition; and in a second condition, the background intensity was changed in such a way that the ratio of stimulus to ground was the same on the tests as during training. The distance effect was obtained when the ground was constant, but there was no decrease in transposition with distance when the ratios were constant.

According to Shirai (1951, pp. 20–21), the importance of the background in brightness discrimination learning was emphasized by Herter (1929), Hörmann (1934), Keller and Takemasa (1933), Takemasa (1934), and Takagi (1935a; 1935b; 1937), among others. The only experimental findings mentioned by Shirai were those of Takagi, who observed that "the more the brightness of the background was separated from the original, the more relative choice decreases. The choice habit of the animals was found disturbed even when only the background was altered, the figures on it being unchanged" (Shirai, p. 21). Line (1931) appears to have obtained a similar effect in children. Line only summarized the relevant study, but reported that absolute responses to brightness were increased by changes in the backgrounds. These findings appear to support Riley's proposal.

Data reported by Campbell and Kral (1958) are also consistent with Riley's proposal. Parakeets were given an absolute discrimination problem, in which a stimulus of intermediate brightness was correct whether paired with a brighter stimulus or with a dimmer one (see Chapter 6). On test trials, the dimmest brightness and the intermediate brightness were presented, with the intensity of the illumination of the surround reduced. On the first test trial, 83 per cent of the subjects responded to the dimmer brightness, rather than responding to the previously positive intermediate brightness; and on 20 test trials, the subjects averaged about 76 per cent responses to the dimmer brightness. As shown in Table 8-1, the positive training ratio (the ratio of the intermediate stimulus to the background on the training trials) was more similar to the ratio of the dimmest stimulus to the background on the test trials than it was to the ratio of the intermediate stimulus to the background on the test trials. Therefore, Riley's theory predicts the obtained results. Kaplan and Helson (1950) obtained similar results in human subjects.

Burkamp (1923) found that when the brightness and color of illumination were changed, aquarium fish continued to respond to the positive absolute

TABLE 8–1
RATIO OF LUMINOSITY OF OBJECT TO LUMINOSITY OF BACKGROUND[a]
(Campbell and Kral, 1958)

	Dim	Intermediate	Bright
Training	.44	.84	1.14
Test	.61	1.41	

[a]Luminosity in log foot-candles.

stimulus. "Increasing the light did not make the fish go to the darker shades, decreasing it did not send them to the lighter shades, nor did colored illumination send them to the grays or to non-training colors" (Woodworth, 1938, p. 606). Katz and Révész (1921) obtained the same kind of result in hens, with colored lights; Köhler (1915; 1917) obtained a similar effect in hens and chimpanzees, using brightness.

Campbell and Kral suggested that the difference between their results and Burkamp's is related to the ecological probability of the change in illumination that occurred. According to Campbell and Kral, brightness constancy tends to occur when changes in the luminosity of an object (the total energy reflected by the object) are ecologically typical or natural, as in Burkamp's experiment. When the changes in luminosity are unnatural, the subject responds as though the changes were natural, and brightness constancy is disrupted. Unnatural changes in luminosity occur when there is an "overnight uniform general change" in the albedo. (The albedo is the ratio of reflected light to incident light. It is invariant with changes in the level of illumination.) Campbell and Kral changed the albedo of the background, and in studies of brightness transposition using standard methods the albedoes of the stimulus objects are changed. The argument suggests that transposition and brightness constancy are mediated by the same processes, but the processes involved were identified by Campbell and Kral only as "inferential cue processes."

A complete evaluation of Campbell and Kral's interpretation would require a review of the literature on brightness constancy that is beyond the scope of this treatise; but it should be noted that without further elaboration the hypothesis fails to account for the distance effect in brightness transposition.

Transposition data, and the data of Campbell and Kral and of Burkamp, can be explained by Riley's (1958) theory. According to the theory, the subject responds to the ratio of the luminosity of the object to the luminosity of the background. The ratio for a given object is constant with changes in illumination, provided the albedoes are unchanged, as in the "constancy" studies (Burkamp, 1923; Katz and Révész, 1921; Köhler, 1915; Köhler, 1917);

but the ratio changes when either albedo is changed, as in the usual transposition experiment and in the Campbell and Kral study and the Line study.

Riley considered only the brightness dimension; and Zeiler (1963c) maintained that Riley's proposals cannot handle transposition of size, because it is "well demonstrated" that size perception is independent of background. Zeiler referred to the Rock and Ebenholtz (1959) studies for support, since they showed that "the effect was not overly impressive" (Zeiler, 1963c, p. 517). However, the effect seems to have been strong enough to support Riley's point. The estimated height of a triangle was 58 per cent greater with a frame than without one, and for a circle it was 82 per cent greater with than without. The effect of the frame on estimated line length was even greater. However, Künnapas (1955) obtained a much weaker effect of frame on estimated line length than Rock and Ebenholtz obtained. Künnapas apparently tested under normal illumination, and Rock and Ebenholtz tested in a dark room and took care to eliminate extraneous cues. Since extraneous cues are usually present in the transposition experiment, it can be argued that the Künnapas study was more relevant than the Rock and Ebenholtz studies, and that Zeiler's conclusion was correct even though he marshalled the wrong evidence to support it. Other evidence is also suggestive; Wohlwill (1962) found that size judgments were not consistently related to variations in the background; and E. J. Robinson (1954) found that although brightness affected size judgments, the effect was weak. Furthermore, Corbascio (1964) used stimuli differing in size, and obtained evidence that is inconsistent with Riley's proposal. Preschool children were trained on a two-stimulus size discrimination, and were then given transposition tests at one, three, and five steps. The stimuli were black paper squares. In one condition they were mounted on white cards to provide clearly delimited backgrounds, and in another condition they were not mounted but were held up by the experimenter to provide no clearly circumscribed background. Children who were trained and tested with the "background" stimuli exhibited the usual distance effect, but those trained and tested with the "no-background" stimuli exhibited a high flat gradient of transposition (see Table 8-2). However, a group trained with background stimuli and tested with no-background stimuli also showed a high flat transposition gradient, and a group trained with no-background stimuli and tested with background stimuli showed the distance effect (see Table 8-2). The data indicate that Near Test transposition was not influenced by the method of presenting the stimuli during either the training phase or the test phase, and Far Test transposition was not influenced by the method of presenting the stimuli during training. However, Far Test transposition was affected by the method of presenting the stimuli on the Far Test, on which elimination of backgrounds increased transposition. It would be difficult to reconcile this finding with Riley's proposal.

TABLE 8–2
PERCENTAGE TRANSPOSITION OBTAINED BY CORBASCIO[a]

Training stimuli	Test stimuli	Distance (steps)		
		One[b]	Three[b]	Five[c]
Background	Background	100	72	61
No background	No background	96	98	93
Background	No background	92	90	—
No background	Background	100	86	—

[a] All tests positive upward.
[b] Trained on Stimuli 3 and 4.
[c] Trained on Stimuli 1 and 2.

Adaptation Level Theories

TWO-STIMULUS PROBLEMS

H. James (1953) extended Helson's adaptation level theory (see Helson, 1964) to the two-stimulus transposition problem by assuming that (a) a neutral point or adaptation level is established in training, (b) the subject learns to avoid stimuli on one side of the adaptation level and to approach those on the other side (for example, approach stimuli more intense than the adaptation level, if the brighter of two stimuli is correct), (c) the location of the adaptation level is independent of reward and punishment, and (d) new stimuli presented after the adaptation level is established will gradually change the adaptation level. If both test stimuli fall on the same side of the adaptation level established during training, random responses are predicted; but if one falls on one side of the adaptation level and the other falls on the other side, perfect transposition is predicted.

C. B. Smith (1956) demonstrated the influence of the adaptation level on brightness perception in second-grade children and high-school students. The same absolute brightnesses were used in the training and test phases, but the background brightnesses were different. Smith used adaptation level theory to predict the amounts of transfer and the difficulty levels of the initial discriminations, and obtained generally supporting results. (For a detailed summary of the rationale, procedure, and findings of the study, see Helson [1964, pp. 414–421].)

James's theory predicts a distance effect, since both distant stimuli fall on the same side of the adaptation level, and near stimuli fall on opposite sides; and it predicts random responses when transposition does not occur. The theory predicts an increase in transposition over test trials even when all test responses are rewarded, since the test stimuli will gradually change the adaptation level until one test stimulus lies below it and the other lies above it. At that point in testing, transposition will begin, since the subject has learned to approach or avoid stimuli relative to the adaptation level, not to approach or avoid specific absolute stimuli. Thomas and Jones (1962) obtained evidence that supports the underlying assumption; the peak of generalization gradients was shifted toward the center of the range of test stimuli presented singly after the presentation of a standard stimulus, even when the stimulus at one end of the range was identical to the standard stimulus. (The standard was presented for only 60 seconds, followed by 12 test series in each of which 5 test stimuli were presented in random order; this procedure could enhance the shift in the adaptation level by maximizing the degeneration of the memory trace of the standard stimulus.)

There is some experimental support for the prediction, but there is also evidence contradicting the prediction since a decrease in transposition over test trials has sometimes been obtained instead of an increase (see Chapter 2). Furthermore, the theory seems to generate as incorrect prediction about the relative amounts of transposition in the positive and negative directions. On a Far Test in the positive direction, both test stimuli lie on the same side of the adaptation level as the positive training stimulus; therefore, subjects should respond at random, because they have equal tendencies to approach both stimuli. If all responses are rewarded, there should be no weakening of the tendency to approach stimuli on that side of the adaptation level; therefore, when the adaptation level shifts, with repeated test trials, the subjects should begin to transpose. On a Far Test in the negative direction, both test stimuli lie on the same side of the adaptation level as the negative training stimulus, and subjects should respond at random because they have equal tendencies to avoid both test stimuli. If all responses are rewarded, the transposition "test" is a reversal problem, and there should be a strengthening of the tendency to approach stimuli on the same side of the adaptation level as the negative training stimulus, and a relative weakening of the tendency to approach stimuli on the same side of the adaptation level as the positive training stimulus. After the adaptation level shifts enough to be between the test stimuli, transposition will occur unless the latter tendency has become weaker than the former. At best, there should be less transposition in the negative direction than in the positive direction. As shown in Chapter 4, the evidence indicates that there is usually more transposition in the negative direction than in the positive direction, contradicting the prediction.

The theory does not handle the intermediate-stimulus problem with symmetrical sets of stimuli, as Zeiler (1963c) noted, because the positive training stimulus is *at* the adaptation level in this kind of stimulus set instead of being above or below it.

INTERMEDIATE-SIZE PROBLEM

Zeiler (1963c) used Helson's adaptation level formulation to construct a theory specifically dealing with the intermediate-size transposition problem. (Zeiler referred to his theory as a "ratio" theory, but the use of the label could lead to confusion with Riley's [1958] ratio theory.) The theory has three basic assumptions. The first is that the subject learns during training to respond to the ratio of the positive stimulus to the adaptation level. This ratio is the "positive training ratio." The second assumption is that the subject responds on the first test trial to the test stimulus ratio that is most similar to the positive training ratio, unless the ratios of all test stimuli are either larger than or smaller than the positive training ratio. In the latter cases, responses are random. (A "test stimulus ratio" is the ratio of a test stimulus to the test adaptation level.) The third assumption is that the adaptation level on test trials is determined by the test-stimulus magnitudes and the training adaptation level:

$$\log(\text{test adaptation level}) = y\left(\frac{\sum \log X_i}{3}\right) + x \log R$$

where $y + x = 1.00$, X_i represents the area of test stimulus i, and R represents the training adaptation level (Zeiler, 1963c, p. 518).

It has been determined empirically that in general, (a) y increases with increasing distance (Reese, 1965c), and (b) at one step it increases with decreasing area ratio of stimuli (Reese, 1965c; Zeiler, 1963c). This means that the influence of the set of test stimuli on the adaptation level, relative to the influence of the set of training stimuli, increases (a) as the amount of overlap between the training and test sets is reduced, and (b) as the discriminability of the stimuli within a set is reduced.

The effect of distance on y can be explained by assuming that as the hypothetical adaptation level determined solely by the test stimuli becomes more discrepant from the hypothetical adaptation level determined solely by the training stimuli, the test stimuli exert relatively more influence on the real adaptation level. That is, with increasing discrepancy between the adaptation level that would be obtained if x equalled zero and the adaptation level that would be obtained if y equalled zero, the *actual* value of y increases. With increasing distance, the two hypothetical adaptation levels necessarily become more discrepant, explaining the effect of distance on y.

The assumption seems to generate an incorrect prediction about the effect of stimulus discriminability. At any given number of steps, the discrepancy between the two hypothetical adaptation levels increases as the within-set differences among the stimuli increase. For example, with a 1.3 to 1 ratio of stimulus areas, the discrepancy is much smaller than with a 2 to 1 ratio of

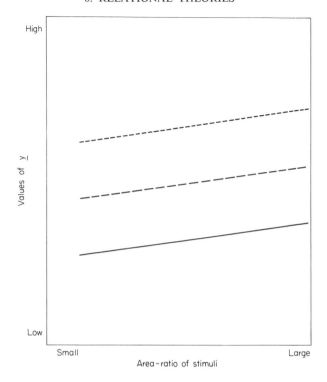

FIG. 8-3. Hypothetical gradients relating y to distance and area ratio of stimuli: (——) one step, (— —) two steps, and (- - -) three steps.

areas. Therefore, the assumption generates the prediction that y increases as the area ratio of the stimuli increases. Figure 8-3 illustrates the predicted relations of y to distance and to area ratio of stimuli; Fig. 8-4 shows the obtained relations. Comparison of these sets of curves indicates that the agreement is actually quite close except on the one-step tests with very small ratios of stimulus areas.

It could be that the curves in Fig. 8-3 are theoretically correct, and that the obtained high values of y at one step are mathematical artifacts. It would not be difficult to construct stimuli which would be easily discriminated from one another in an appropriate psychophysical task, such as the determination of difference limens, but which would be unlikely to be discriminated from one another in a discrimination-learning task. When the area ratio within a set of stimuli is small, the one-step change might well be unnoticed. However, when the difference between two stimuli (or between two sets of stimuli) is unnoticed, the stimuli function as though they were identical; and in order to predict a subject's responses to the stimuli, it would be necessary to treat the stimuli as though they were identical. In

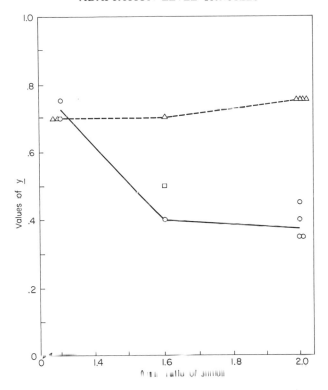

FIG. 8-4. Obtained values of y as a function of distance and area ratio of stimuli. Each symbol represents a different group: (○) one step, (□) two steps, and (△) three steps. (Drawn from data reported by Reese, 1965c, Table 1, p. 414.)

Zeiler's equations, this would require reversing the values of x and y, so that if the theoretically correct value of y for, say, a 1.3 to 1 ratio were .30, it would be necessary to substitute for this value the value of x, .70, in order to predict the observed behavior. A parametric study would be needed to determine the exact point at which the introduction of this mathematical adjustment is required, but it seems unlikely that it would be necessary to use tests beyond one step. If the transition is around a ratio of 1.3 to 1, then to obtain a discrepancy between adaptation levels small enough at two steps to generate a prediction of no discrimination between sets, it would be necessary to use stimuli with a within-set ratio of 1.15 to 1. Even if the transition were around 1.5 to 1, it would be necessary to use stimuli with a ratio of 1.27 to 1 to predict no discrimination at two steps. In order, then, to obtain a high probability that the subjects would fail to discriminate between the training set and the two-step test set, it would probably be necessary to use stimuli that were so similar within a set that discrimination learning would be almost impossible.

Unlike H. James's (1953) adaptation level theory, Zeiler's theory can predict absolute responses, as well as transposition responses. Zeiler's theory also predicts a distance effect. The test adaptation level changes with changes in the amount of separation between the training and test sets of stimuli. However, since x is assumed to be greater than zero, the residual effect of the training stimuli on the adaptation level "damps" the effect of distance on the adaptation level; therefore, distance affects the absolute magnitudes of the stimuli relatively more than it affects the adaptation level. Consequently, distance determines which test stimulus will have a ratio most similar to the positive training ratio. If at a given distance the middle-sized test stimulus has a ratio most similar to the positive training ratio, transposition occurs. As distance is increased, a point is eventually reached at which the ratio of the "absolute" stimulus is the most similar to the positive training ratio, and absolute responses occur. As distance is increased still farther, a point is reached at which the range of test stimulus ratios does not include the positive training ratio. At and beyond that point, random responses occur. (The theory can also predict nontransposition-nonabsolute responses, but only when asymmetrical sets of stimuli are used. In the present context, it is assumed that symmetrical sets are used.)

Zeiler has specified as a boundary condition that his theory deals only with responses on the first test trial, since repeated test trials introduce a number of complicating variables whose effects have not yet been evaluated. He has also discussed some other problems confronting his theory (Zeiler, 1963c, pp. 529–531; Zeiler, 1966b). (See also Riley et al., 1966.)

The theory can be interpreted as a strictly mathematical description of the choice behavior, but Zeiler (1966b) has pointed out that a psychological interpretation is also possible. According to this interpretation, the stimulus is absolute but it is a percept and, paradoxically, the "absolute" percept depends upon the ratio of the physical stimulus to the surround. If two physical stimuli have similar ratios, the stimuli are perceived to be identical; and when the percepts are identical, the responses to them must be identical. As Zeiler (1966b) noted, the theory interpreted in this way is an attempt to quantify the hypothesis that transposition results from a failure to discriminate between the training and test situations. (This hypothesis is discussed in the section entitled "Generalization Theory," Chapter 9, but as already indicated, I have found it necessary to invoke this hypothesis to explain some of the empirical effects on the constants of Zeiler's equations.)

Mediation Theory

Spence (1937a) suggested that "It is possibly only with the advent of verbal processes that the simple mechanism of learning discrimination problems we have proposed [in Spence, 1936a] is transcended" (p. 99). Kuenne (1946) extended the suggestion, and formally hypothesized that Spence's (1937b) theory accounts for transposition in inarticulate organisms, including preverbal children, but that in older children and human adults the behavior is under verbal control. The subject who possesses the relevant concept can respond to the verbal cue and transpose more broadly than the subject lacking the concept.

Theoretically, if the stimuli arouse the verbal responses or labels in the subject, the approach and inhibitory tendencies become conditioned to these labels. On the test trials, different stimuli arouse the same labels, and the labels arouse the same instrumental responses, yielding transposition (see Fig. 8-5).

Lashley (1929b, p. 545) rejected this kind of theory as an explanation of

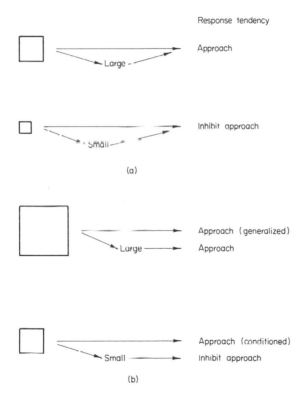

FIG. 8-5. Hypothetical behavior of a "verbal" subject: mediation of the transposition response. (a) Training stimuli and (b) test stimuli. "Large" and "small" represent verbal responses labeling the relative sizes. In the diagram, the approach and inhibitory tendencies are aroused by the verbal cues and the stimulus objects. (However, it is not necessary to assume that they are aroused by the stimulus objects.)

stimulus equivalence, on the argument that "there is clear evidence that the use of symbols depends upon the recognition of similarity, and not the reverse." In the present context, this would mean that the occurrence of the relational concept that mediates the transposition response depends on the recognition of the similarity of the test-stimulus relation to the training-stimulus relation.

The size concepts referred to in the theory are labels for relative stimulus properties. Gayton (1927) implied that verbal ability has been shown to increase absolute responses, apparently referring to data reported by Riekel (1922). Riekel obtained an increase in absolute responses with increasing age level from two to six years, and attributed the increase to the appearance of adequate verbalizations. This effect would come about only if labels for absolute properties were emitted, but the weight of evidence suggests that subjects do not usually emit labels for absolute properties. It appears that relative labels are much more likely to be used.

Even if under appropriate instructions a subject demonstrates that he possesses certain verbal size concepts, he may or may not use the concepts during the training and testing phases of a transposition experiment. In order that a word become an effective mediator in a learning task, the word must not only be emitted at the appropriate times, but it must also become conditioned to some further response such as the approach response in discrimination problems. (See Goss [1961a] for an historical survey of the concept of mediation.) Mediation requires two conditioning processes: one the conditioning of the potential mediator to the external stimulus, and the other the conditioning of the terminal instrumental response to the mediating cue. Osgood et al. (1957, p. 8) used the terms "decoding" and "encoding" to refer to these two processes, and it is important to emphasize that both decoding and encoding must occur in order that mediation occur. Once stated, the proposition seems obvious, but it might not be obvious unless it is stated.

According to Lashley (1926, p. 43), Head's (1920) patients with the "semantic type" of aphasia "lose the ability to distinguish or think certain relationships, although the words which express these relationships are still retained." The loss seems to be associated with a reduced grasp of wholes or of the "full significance" of words and phrases (Head, pp. 142–148, 156–157, and 165). In another kind of aphasia identified by Head, "nominal aphasia," a relation may be recognized, but the patient has difficulty in naming it or in responding to its name (Head, pp. 155 and 161). (According to Fernberger [1919], the type of aphasic disturbance exhibited by a patient may depend upon what imaginal type the patient was before the brain damage occurred.) Both kinds of aphasia should reduce transposition. The patient with semantic aphasia seems to suffer a deficiency in the encoding process, and the patient with nominal aphasia seems to be deficient in the decoding process. No data on transposition by aphasic patients have been published.

There is evidence that the preschool-aged child often does not spontaneously emit the required verbal responses even when they are in his repertory, and that even if the responses are emitted, the young child may be deficient in the encoding process (see, for example, Reese, 1962b; Reese, 1966). Such a child would not be expected to transpose any more than a child who lacked the required concepts entirely.

I have previously used the phrase "mediational deficiency hypothesis" to refer to the inference that certain kinds of age differences reflect a failure of young children to mediate (Reese, 1962b). Flavell (1965) has suggested a more precise terminology, restricting "mediational deficiency" to a deficiency in encoding and introducing the term "production deficiency" to refer to a deficiency in decoding. Production deficiency, then, means that the child does not spontaneously emit the potential mediators; and mediational deficiency means that although the potential mediator is emitted, it exerts no influence on further behavior (see also Flavell, Beach, and Chinsky, 1966). In this restricted sense, the mediational deficiency might result from a complete failure of encoding—the potential mediator elicits no further response—or from encoding of the wrong response. Analogously, there is logically possible a "production error," which would be emitting the appropriate label but not to the appropriate stimulus. According to Zeiler (1967), this kind of "error" does occur. Zeiler reported that "if the subject was given the training set, and was asked to verbally identify and point to one of these stimuli, and then was given a test set larger than the training set, he was frequently confused when asked to indicate the middle-sized stimulus. Under these conditions, the subject sometimes identified the stimulus that had been the middle-sized stimulus of the training set and was the small stimulus of the test set. Similar 'errors' occurred when the child was asked to point to the large training stimulus and then the large test stimulus" (p. 50 in prepublication copy). This failure to transpose the relational label could account for the apparent failure of young children who possess the relevant concept to utilize it on transposition tests.

Marsh and Sherman (1966) trained children on a two-stimulus discrimination with size and brightness confounded, then gave test trials with the sizes transposed one step and the brightnesses not transposed (see Fig. 8-6). On the test trials, a child who was responding to size might transpose, but a child who was responding to brightness would necessarily respond absolutely with respect to size, since the test stimulus that had the same brightness value as the positive training stimulus was also the same size as the positive training stimulus. (All tests were in the positive direction.) During training, one group was required to name the *size* of the stimulus they were choosing, using the words "big" and "little." Another group was

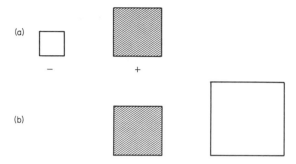

FIG. 8-6. Example of the stimulus sets used by Marsh and Sherman: (a) training stimuli and (b) test stimuli. In the actual experiment, additional sets were used in counterbalancing. (After Marsh and Sherman, 1966, Fig. 1, p. 92.)

required to name the *brightness* of the chosen stimulus, using the words "black" and "white." Transposition on 10 test trials averaged about 74 per cent in the size-verbalization group and about 34 per cent in the brightness-verbalization group. Verbalization was not required on the test trials, but about three fourths of the group verbalized spontaneously. Of the subjects who verbalized spontaneously, about 88 per cent gave overt choices that were consistent with the verbalization.

Marsh and Sherman observed that the very youngest children (2.5 to 3.2 years old) in both verbalization groups failed to transpose above the chance level. To assess the reliability of this finding, they repeated the experiment with a new sample of children from this age range, and with an additional group given no verbalization instructions. Absolute responses predominated (see Table 8-3), and there were no significant differences among the groups. This finding is consistent with the mediational deficiency hypothesis, since it indicates a deficiency in verbal control of overt choices in the very young children. Marsh and Sherman also reported that only one third of the very young children in the size-verbalization group spontaneously verbalized during the test, and none of the spontaneously verbalizing children gave choice reponses that were consistent with the verbalization, lending further support to the mediational deficiency hypothesis. (All of the spontaneous verbalizers in the other two groups of very young children gave responses that were consistent with the verbalization, but these were "absolute" responses and would probably have occurred without the verbalization since absolute responses must have also predominated in the nonverbalizers.)

Gerben and Wischner (1965) found that establishing acquired distinctiveness of conditional cues (background colors) increased the speed of conditional discrimination learning. Verbal pretraining was more effective than motor pretraining, especially in mentally retarded children. The two kinds

TABLE 8-3
PERCENTAGE TRANSPOSITION IN THE MARSH AND SHERMAN STUDY

Measure of transposition	Age range (years)	Experimental condition		
		Verbalization of size	Verbalization of brightness	No verbalization
Trial 1	2.5–3.2[a]	10.0	0.0	30.0
	2.5–3.4[b]	62.5	6.2	—
	4.0–5.0[b]	62.5	25.0	—
10 trials	2.5–3.2[a]	25.0	16.0	34.0
	2.5–3.2[b]	52.9	20.0	—
	3.3–3.4[b,c]	84.4	45.6	—
	4.0–5.0[b]	78.1	33.8	—

[a] Experiment II.

[b] Experiment I.

[c] Estimated by taking weighted means of 2.5–3.2 groups of Exp. I (p. 95) from means of 2.5–3.4 groups of Exp. I (Table 1, p. 93). Not computable from Trial-1 data reported.

of pretraining would presumably have the same effect on attentional processes, and therefore the effect of the pretraining was apparently not a result only of training the children to attend to the conditional cues. Since the motor-response unit was not available to the subject during the conditional discrimination task, the subject would presumably have had to use symbolic representations of the different motor acts, and the most effective symbols would probably be verbal. This would account for the greater effectiveness of the verbal pretraining, since some subjects might have lacked appropriate symbols for the motor responses.

I previously suggested the same kind of explanation of the difference between the findings reported by Jeffrey (1958a; 1958b), who obtained facilitation in preschool children with motor pretraining, and the findings of Murdock (1958) and Reese (1958), who obtained no facilitation in college students and fourth graders with motor pretraining. In Jeffrey's studies the response units were available during the transfer task, but in the Murdock and Reese studies the response units were not available during the transfer task (see Reese, 1962b). Assuming that the retarded subjects in the Gerben and Wischner study were less facile at spontaneously producing the required symbols would explain the lesser effectiveness of the motor pretraining in the retarded children than was obtained in the normal children, but then one might ask why the subjects in the Murdock and Reese studies did not verbalize labels for the motor responses. Murdock used the "star discrimeter" (an apparatus with a lever that can be moved into any of six channels radiating from a central neutral point), and there is evidence that providing college students with labels for the channels facilitates learning with the apparatus (D. E. McAllister, 1953). This finding suggests that college students might not spontaneously label the channels. However, Reese used a double-throw switch with a lever about one and one-half inches long, and the subjects could easily have labeled the responses "up" and "down," although there was no evidence that they did so. Therefore, the conclusion that the facilitation obtained by Gerben and Wischner resulted primarily from verbal processes can be offered only tentatively.

G. R. Thompson (1965) found that groups given "relevant" or "irrelevant" pretraining did not differ in the transposition of size. In the relevant pretraining condition, the subjects were required to name the sizes of toys (for example, "large" or "small"); and in the irrelevant pretraining condition, the subjects were required to name the toys (for example, "car"). Both groups transposed at about the chance level. It could be that the tendency to name the sizes did not transfer at all to the transposition task, or that it did transfer but the subjects, who were mentally retarded, could not use the labels as mediators.

Jeffrey (1965) has argued that "in studying the behavior of children of 4 yr. or older, it probably is more important to ask what role mediators play than whether they are used" (p. 595). According to Jeffrey's argument, the behavior that is usually taken to reflect a deficiency in the use of mediators actually results from the use of inefficient or inappropriate mediators. The argument is consistent with my suggestion that the deficiency in mediation is characteristic of an early stage of concept formation rather than of an early stage of human development (Reese, 1962b), and efforts to determine the conditions under which appropriate mediators are used (such as Reese, 1965a; Reese, 1966; Silverman, 1966) would be importantly supplemented by efforts to determine the conditions under which inefficient or inappropriate mediators are used.

A child who decoded but did not encode might still learn the initial discrimination more rapidly than one who could not (or did not) decode, but the expectation depends on the interpretation of the acquired distinctiveness of cues. If I have interpreted Dollard and Miller's (1950) position on acquired distinctiveness correctly (Reese, 1962b; Reese, 1963a), decoding is required but encoding is not. The response-produced cue combines with the external stimulus to form a compound to which the terminal response is conditioned, as shown in Fig. 8-7a, rather than remaining a separate element separately conditioned to the terminal response, as shown in Fig. 8-7b. The latter case involves both decoding and encoding, as can be seen by comparing Fig. 8-7b with Fig. 8-7c, which illustrates the mediation paradigm. Most psychologists who have discussed Dollard and Miller's theory have used the term "mediating responses" to identify the verbal labels attached to the stimuli (for example, Goss, 1961b; Spiker, 1963b;

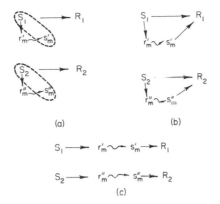

FIG. 8-7. Diagrammatic representation of the controversy about the acquired distinctiveness of cues. (a) Decoding without encoding: acquired distinctiveness of cues (Reese, 1962b; Reese, 1963a); (b) decoding and encoding: acquired distinctiveness of cues (Goss, 1961b; Youniss and Furth, 1963); and (c) decoding and encoding: mediation.

Youniss and Furth, 1963). However, part of the definition of mediating responses is that they intervene between the initial stimulus and the terminal response (Goss, 1961b, footnote 3, pp. 249–250); and my interpretation of Dollard and Miller's theory is that the labels are not assumed to intervene between the initial stimulus and the terminal response, but rather are assumed to become part of the initial stimulus. If this interpretation is correct, acquired distinctiveness could occur even if there were a deficiency in the encoding process, and would facilitate performance in the training phase. If the alternative interpretation is correct, this facilitation would occur only if encoding occurred. There is some evidence that Dollard and Miller's position, as I interpreted it, is incorrect (see Reese, 1963a); but according to J. Cantor (1965, footnote 4, p. 25), this interpretation is required to account for the data of some of the studies of acquired distinctiveness. Marsh and Sherman (1966) also obtained evidence consistent with my interpretation.

White (1965) has shown, from a review of research literature, that the range from five to seven years of age in children is generally a transitional period for a variety of behaviors, which are summarized in Table 8-4. As a possible synthesis of these data, he suggested the hypothesis that before the transitional age, a short-latency "associative level" of functioning and learning is characteristic of children, and that after the transitional age, this level is inhibited and a longer-latency "cognitive level" of operation becomes characteristic.[7] With respect to "mediational deficiency," White's

[7] White (personal communication, 1965) has further suggested that the transitions are "phenotypes which must be associated with change in some genotype which has multifarious effects," implying the possibility of an even broader synthesis than was proposed in his 1965 paper.

TABLE 8–4

WHITE'S SUMMARY OF BEHAVIOR CHANGES FROM AGE FIVE TO AGE SEVEN[a]

Younger pattern	Older pattern
Near but not far transposition	Near and far transposition
Nonreversal shift easier	Reversal shift easier
Classical conditioning increasing	Classical conditioning decreasing
Varying position hinders discrimination	Varying position helps discrimination
Varying positive cue hinders discrimination	Varying positive cue neutral
Little direct inference	Frequent direct inference
Simple discrimination improves	Simple discrimination declines
Prefer tactual exploring	Prefer visual exploring
Color or mixed dominance	Form dominance
No left–right sense	Personal left–right
Form, word, and letter reversals	Decline in reversals
Easily disoriented	Resists disorienting
Fails face–hand test	Passes face–hand test
Increasing prediction of adult IQ	Maximal prediction of adult IQ
Factors I and II account for IQ[b]	Factor III principal factor[b]
Speech expressive and instrumental	Speech internalized
Word associations syntagmatic	Word associations paradigmatic
Lesser effect of DAF[c]	Greater effect of DAF[c]
Little planning before drawing	Planning before drawing
Difficulty drawing "largest" and "smallest" squares	Can perform task
Reinforced by praise	Reinforced by correctness

[a]See White (1965, Table III, p. 209).

[b]Factors I and II are "Sensory-Motor Alertness" and "Persistence"; Factor III is "Manipulation of Symbols" (Hofstaetter, 1954).

[c]DAF stands for delayed auditory feedback.

hypothesis implies that when mediation does not occur in the pretransition stage, it is because it fails to occur in time. The mediated response has a relatively long latency, since it must follow the mediating response; and before it can occur, some short-latency associatively determined response may occur and terminate the trial. In the posttransition stage, the short-latency response is inhibited, allowing time for the occurrence of the mediated response. Data reported by Beiswenger (1966) are consistent with this interpretation.

White suggested that the cognitive styles of "analyzers and nonanalyzers, more or less impulsive types, . . . might be linked to predominantly associative and cognitive function" (p. 215). "Impulsiveness" is defined by a tendency to give responses that have short latencies and are relatively inaccurate, and "reflectiveness" is defined by a tendency to give responses that have longer latencies and are generally accurate. According to White, impulsives fail to inhibit first-available responses, which are determined by associative functions, but reflectives inhibit these responses.

These cognitive styles were identified by Kagan and his associates (for example, Kagan, 1965; Kagan, Moss, and Sigel, 1963), who also suggested: "One of the possible antecedents of an analytic attitude is the ability to inhibit motor discharge . . . " (Kagan *et al.*, 1963, p. 110). Their data indicate that the tendency to exhibit a particular cognitive style has early antecedents and suggest that it may be related to individual differences that develop in the first year of life. Nevertheless, the cognitive style exhibited is not entirely independent of situational and motivational variables, and the relation between the associative-cognitive dichotomy and the impulsive-reflective dichotomy is apparently not close.

It has generally been assumed that the stage of mediational deficiency is a stage of ontogenetic development (T. S. Kendler, Kendler, and Wells, 1960; Kuenne, 1946; Luria, 1957; White, 1965). However, it seems actually to be a stage of cognitive development that is generally but not always characteristic of early childhood. The transitional age is not the same in all experimental situations (see Reese, 1962b), and is not even always the same in a single experimental situation. For example, Boat (1966) obtained mediation in four-year-old children, in the mediated-chaining task; but Leonard (1966) found a deficiency in mediation in this task in seven-year-old children, relative to nine-year-olds and eleven-year-olds. Furthermore, even though Kagan (1965) had little success in inducing a change in the cognitive style of young impulsives to reflectiveness, there has been greater success in inducing a change from the "associative function" to the "cognitive function" (for example, Kasianova, discussed by Zaporozhets, 1965; Lovaas, 1964, Experiments IV and V; Luria, 1961; Reese, 1966; Silverman, 1966).

The research evidence on the effects of verbalization and concept knowledge has shown that verbal groups generally learn the original discrimination more rapidly than nonverbal groups, and sometimes transpose more than nonverbal groups. Often, however, it has been found that the verbal groups transpose no more than the nonverbal groups. This pattern of results could be explained by assuming that the stimulus labels yield acquired distinctiveness of the cues in the training problem, and that whether or not the labels mediate choice responses in the transposition test depends on the stage of cognitive development of the subjects. It must be assumed that acquired distinctiveness occurs even in the younger subjects who are assumed not to mediate. As already pointed out, the assumption that acquired distinctiveness does not involve mediation is debatable. It must also be assumed that the verbal children who transpose at a low level are in the precognitive stage of development and that the verbal children who transpose at a high level are in the cognitive stage. This assumption is also debatable, since the latter group includes children whose age level is below the general transitional age.

An alternative explanation can be based on Spiker's (1956b) suggestion that verbal children are superior to nonverbal children in the delayed-response situation because the verbal children use labels to rehearse the stimulus–response associations during the intertrial interval (see also J. H. Cantor, 1965; Spiker, 1963b). In the transposition situation, rehearsal would facilitate the performance of verbal children on the initial discrimination; but after the discrimination has been learned, some subjects might no longer rehearse. These subjects would not emit the labels on the transposition test, and their verbal ability could not affect their performance. Other subjects might continue to rehearse, and might emit the labels on the test trials, yielding a high level of transposition. It might be noted that the "rehearsal" hypothesis requires that mediation occur. The stimulus must elicit the stimulus label, the stimulus label must elicit the response label, and the response label must elicit the overt choice response.

As pointed out in the section entitled "Concept Knowledge" (Chapter 5), there are alternative ways to decode the intermediate stimulus in a three-stimulus problem. For example, instead of using the word "middle-sized," the subject can use the phrase "not big and not little." Similarly, there may be alternative ways to encode, in both the two-stimulus problem and the three-stimulus problem. The verbal response might mediate not the terminal instrumental response but a perceptual response. (See, for example, T. S. Kendler, 1964; Marsh, 1964; K. G. Scott, 1964; Shepp and Turrisi, in press.[8]) The spontaneous verbalization of a relative-size concept, which requires perception of relative stimulus properties, might bring about increased attention to the relative properties and distract attention from the absolute properties, resulting in a higher level of transposition than would occur without the verbalization. The experimenter could also call attention to the relative properties by making the appropriate verbalizations himself. This would increase the probability of relation perception in the subject, provided that he knows the meanings of the size concepts verbalized by the experimenter. Zaporozhets (1958) has suggested this kind of explanation of the effect of verbalization, and data reported by Whitman (1965) provide experimental support. (The Whitman data are discussed in the section entitled "Multiple-Problem Training," Chapter 5. See also Tighe, 1965.) Jeffrey (1965) obtained evidence suggesting that labeling serves to inhibit responses to irrelevant dimensions, which is consistent with the assumption that in the transposition problem labeling the relative properties of the stimuli distracts attention from the absolute properties.

The basic assumption of this interpretation is that the stimulus labels can mediate a perceptual response: identification of or attention to a particular kind of stimulus dimension. Certain data from studies of reversal

[8]As Marsh (1964) pointed out, it is possible that such a perceptual response develops earlier than true verbal mediation.

learning support the assumption. To show how these data support the assumption, it is necessary to show first how "one-stage" and "two-stage" learning affect reversal. Jakobovits (1966) has argued that there is no useful distinction between "two-stage mediation theory" and "single-stage theory," partly because "the single-stage paradigm could easily be rewritten to include mediating events" (p. 377) and partly because no real single-stage theory exists. (The argument is not as trivial as it may sound here, because as Jakobovits pointed out, attempts have been made to force certain modern theories into the "single-stage" category.) Unfortunately, however, Jakobovits failed to distinguish between *models* and *theories*. (See the paper by R. Lachman [1960] for an analysis of this distinction.) The point is that although no modern theory with any reasonable scope deals *only* with the single-stage model, many modern theories deal with both the single-stage model and the mediation model; and there is obviously a difference between these models.

Figure 8-8a depicts the original learning in a one-stage model of reversal learning. In order to learn the reversal, the nonverbalizing subject must first inhibit the response to the originally positive stimulus (S^+) and then learn to approach the originally negative stimulus (S^-). Figure 8-8b shows the original learning in an "instrumental" two-stage model, in which the verbal labels mediate the terminal instrumental response. In order to learn the reversal, the verbalizing subject must inhibit the response to the old positive stimulus *and* the response to its label, and then must disinhibit the response to the old negative stimulus and its label. The processes required for reversal in the instrumental two-stage model (Fig. 8-8b) should be more difficult than

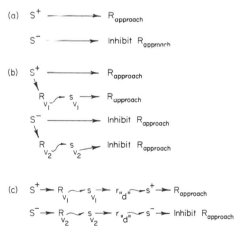

FIG. 8-8. The one-stage and two-stage models of original learning: (a) one-stage model, (b) instrumental two-stage model, and (c) perceptual two-stage model. R_{v_i} labels a value on the relevant dimension, $r_{"d"}$ is an attentional response to the dimension, and s^+ and s^- are the perceived values on the dimension.

the ones in the one-stage model, and therefore the verbalizing subject should reverse more slowly than the nonverbalizing subject (see O'Connor and Hermelin, 1959).

Figure 8-8c shows the original learning in a "perceptual" two-stage model, in which the verbal labels mediate a perceptual response instead of the terminal instrumental response. In order to learn the reversal, the subject must inhibit the response to s^+ and disinhibit the response to s^-. This should be easier than after either of the other two kinds of learning, because in the one-stage model and in the instrumental two-stage model, S^+ and S^- are stimulus compounds that include positions and other irrelevant cues to which the subject will probably respond when the approach to S^+ has been sufficiently weakened, while in the perceptual two-stage model, s^+ and s^- are stimulus elements from which irrelevant cues have been excluded by selective attention.

On the initial task, two-stage learning—whether instrumental or perceptual—should be faster than one-stage learning. However, instrumental two-stage learning in the initial task should interfere with performance on the reversal task, and perceptual two-stage learning in the initial task should facilitate performance on the reversal task.

The usefulness of distinguishing between the two kinds of two-stage learning is illustrated by comparing the effects of verbalization in mentally normal children and mentally retarded children. There is an age difference in the reversal-learning performance of normal children. Younger children perform consistently with the one-stage model or with the instrumental two-stage model, and older children and human adults perform consistently with the perceptual two-stage model (Bedrosian, 1966; T. S. Kendler, 1963; T. S. Kendler et al., 1960; Reese, 1962b). The transitional age is between five and seven years.

It has been shown in studies of reversal learning in retarded subjects that imbeciles instructed to verbalize labels for the stimuli learn the initial discrimination more rapidly than imbeciles not instructed to verbalize stimulus labels, but learn the reversal more slowly than imbeciles not instructed to verbalize labels (O'Connor, 1965; O'Connor and Hermelin, 1959). The difference in initial learning can be explained by assuming that one-stage learning occurred in the non-instructed group, and that two-stage learning occurred in the instructed group. The two-stage learning could have been instrumental or perceptual. If the learning were instrumental, the labels would have either increased the distinctiveness of the cues (without mediation of the choice responses) or mediated the choice responses. If the learning were perceptual, the labels would have mediated the perceptual response. The difference in reversal learning can be explained only by assuming that one-stage learning occurred in the non-instructed group, and that instrumental two-stage learning occurred in the instructed group.

Instrumental two-stage learning would interfere with reversal more than one-stage learning. The obtained pattern of results, then, suggests that perceptual two-stage learning did not occur.

I have suggested elsewhere (Reese, 1962b) that for the imbecile the labels of specific stimulus values are functionally equivalent to nonsense syllables, in that they do not direct attention to any dimension. In effect, "gray" and "white," for example, differ in some unidentified way for the imbecile, and not specifically in "brightness." Stephens (1964; 1966) has reported data that support this contention. Mentally retarded boys were inferior to mentally normal boys in both utilizing and naming conceptual categories. This deficiency in conceptual categorization would lead to the expectation that perceptual two-stage learning seldom occurs in imbeciles.

Campione, Hyman, and Zeaman (1965) have reported findings that can be explained only by assuming that mentally retarded children eventually identify the relevant dimension as such. The children, who had a mean IQ of 35, learned an intradimensional shift more rapidly than an extradimensional shift, even though all of the dimensional values introduced with the shift were different from the values used in the original learning problem. For example, in original learning the stimulus compounds might be a black square, a red square, a black triangle, and a red triangle; and after the shift the compounds might be a yellow T, a white T, a yellow cross, and a white cross. In the intradimensional-shift condition, the same dimension (color or form) was relevant in original learning and after the shift; in the extradimensional-shift condition, the relevant dimension was different in the two tasks. If the various colors were not recognized as falling on one dimension, and the forms on another, then there would have been no basis for the faster learning of the intradimensional shift than of the extra-dimensional shift.

These data can be reconciled with the conclusion that mentally retarded subjects are deficient in conceptualizing dimensions by assuming that the "identification" of the relevant dimension was nonverbal. However, "form" is not a physical dimension, and therefore the identification of form as a dimension probably requires verbalization. The previous conclusion can still be retained, but with emphasis that there is a *deficiency* in conceptualization rather than a complete *lack*.

In the studies of reversal in imbeciles (O'Connor, 1965; O'Connor and Hermelin, 1959), groups of normal children were also tested; and it was found that the normal children performed like the imbeciles instructed to verbalize stimulus labels. Therefore, on the assumption that the normal children spontaneously verbalized to the same extent that the instructed imbeciles verbalized, neither the imbeciles nor the normal children identified the relevant dimension. The normal children in these studies had an average age of 5.1 years, which would place them at the end of the pretransitional stage or at the beginning of the transitional stage. As already indicated, the performance of children at this level is more consistent with the one-stage and instrumental two-stage models than with the perceptual two-stage model.

Bryant (1964) obtained data consistent with the analysis outlined above. The initial task and the transfer task required discrimination among stimuli differing in one or two relevant dimensions and one irrelevant dimension. In one experimental condition, the experimenter named the correct stimulus values after each correct response; in another condition, no labels were supplied. Learning speed was greater in the first condition than in the second in both mentally normal children and severely subnormal children. On the transfer task, with no labeling by the experimenter in either condition, the performance of the normal children was improved by having had the labels supplied in the first task; and the performance of the subnormal children was *worsened* by having had the labels supplied in the first task. If, as I have assumed, the labels of the absolute stimulus values did not direct the attention of the subnormal children to the relevant dimensions, then the persistence of the labels from the first task to the second could have led to confusion, since the precise absolute values of the first-task stimuli were not represented at all in the second task. In the normal subjects, however, if the labels directed attention to the relevant dimensions, then facilitation of transfer-task performance would be expected, since the same dimensions were relevant in both tasks.

Bryant suggested a different interpretation of the results. He hypothesized that subnormal children transfer "negative learning" (learning what to ignore) rather than "positive learning" (learning what to approach), and that normal children transfer positive learning. This hypothesis does not account for the different effects of labeling the previously correct values, because it implies not only that labeling would enhance transfer in the normal group, but also that labeling would have no effect on transfer in the subnormal group. The first implication was supported by the data; but contrary to the second implication, labeling interfered with transfer in the subnormal group. However, Bryant (1965a) obtained evidence supporting his hypothesis, using the design shown in Table 8-5. Severely retarded subjects were better on the "negative" transfer task than on the "positive" transfer task, and normal children were better on the positive transfer task than on the negative transfer task. Bryant suggested, though, that what he had shown might be that normal subjects can transfer on the basis of learning that is "specific," and subnormal children "are less able to do this and . . . have to fall back on learning which is already relatively general" (p. 85). By "specific" learning, Bryant meant that the subjects learn to respond to only one value on the relevant dimension; and by "general" learning, he meant that the subjects learn to ignore all values on the irrelevant dimension.

TABLE 8–5
POSITIVE AND NEGATIVE TRANSFER TASKS IN THE BRYANT (1965a) STUDY[a]

Task	Relevant dimension	Irrelevant dimension	Dimensional value held constant
Initial	Color	Size	Letter
Positive	Color	Letter	Size
Negative	Letter	Size	Color

[a]The colors, sizes, and letters used in the transfer tasks were not the same as those used in the initial task.

(In the 1964 and 1965a studies, the correct stimulus was associated with all values on the irrelevant dimension.)

My analysis implies, on the other hand, that the normal subjects not only learned to respond to the correct value but also learned which dimension was relevant and which was irrelevant, while the specific and general learning suggested by Bryant, which do not require that the subject identify the dimensions, occurred only in the subnormal children. The average age of the normal children was 5.8 years, which is old enough to justify the assumption that mediation occurred. The normal children, then, should have performed equally well on both transfer tasks. They actually showed more positive transfer than negative transfer, as already indicated; but the difference was not statistically significant.[9] The subnormal children were better on the negative transfer task than on the positive one, as my interpretation predicts. On the positive transfer task the previously positive stimulus value did not appear at all, and there was a new irrelevant dimension, providing no basis for transfer in the subnormal children. On the negative transfer task, a new relevant dimension was introduced but the previously irrelevant dimension remained present and irrelevant. Although the specific values on the irrelevant dimension were not the same on the negative transfer task as on the initial task, they seem to have been sufficiently similar that considerable stimulus generalization could be expected, and therefore sufficiently similar that the response (literally nonresponse) to the new elements on that dimension would transfer.

Contrary to the prediction of my analysis, there was transfer on the positive transfer task, since learning speed on both transfer tasks was greater than on the initial task in subnormals as well as normals. However, there was no control for sources of nonspecific transfer, such as warm-up and learning-to-learn, and the objection is therefore not crucial, at least unless further research shows that these sources fail to provide as much transfer as was actually obtained by Bryant.

[9] Bryant did not report the t for this comparison. Using an error term based on the overall analysis of variance, I found that $t = 1.23$. With 36 df, $p > .05$.

In a further study in the series, Bryant (1965b, Experiment I) used a sorting task in order to insure that there was equal experience with all values on the relevant dimension as well as on the irrelevant dimensions. The subjects were moderately retarded children. Bryant found that when the experimenter named the stimuli in the initial sorting task, there was slightly but not significantly better performance on the transfer task than when no names were given in the initial task. It might be that the effect of the labeling in moderately retarded subjects falls midway between the effects in normal subjects and in severely retarded subjects; but the demonstrated effects in the latter two groups were in a different kind of task, and there is no assurance that these effects would be obtained in the sorting tasks used with the moderately retarded group.

In the final study, Bryant (1965b, Experiment II) again used the sorting task, with positive and negative transfer tasks analogous to those of the discrimination learning problems of the previous experiments. The subjects were moderately retarded children. There was essentially equal transfer to both tasks (mean trials to criterion 10.5 on positive and 11.6 on negative). As in the other study using the sorting tasks, it might be that moderately retarded children exhibit transfer effects midway between those of normal subjects and severely retarded subjects, but no firm conclusion will be possible until the latter groups are given the sorting tasks (or the moderately retarded group is given the discrimination learning tasks). It is possible that the only transfer that occurs in the sorting task is nonspecific, and is independent of which dimension is carried over from the initial task to the transfer task.

It can be shown that the two kinds of two-stage model have different implications for the transposition situation, if it is assumed that in the one-stage model subjects tend to respond to absolute cues. Verbal subjects, in order to label the stimuli correctly, must attend to the relative cues. In the perceptual two-stage model, it is assumed that all other cues are ignored; therefore, unless the stimuli are changed so radically that the relative cue changes, perfect transposition is predicted at all distances. The transposed stimuli would be perceptually identical to the training stimuli, because the relative cue is identical.

In the instrumental two-stage model, the verbal label is assumed to mediate the choice response, but the absolute cues are also assumed to have an effect on the choice response. Therefore, as long as the subject continues to label the relative sizes appropriately, and as long as the absolute cues are within the range of generalization, there will be two sources of response-evocation potential, one mediated and one generalized. These will usually not conflict on the Near Test in two-stimulus problems, but will conflict on Far Tests. Therefore, verbalization should enhance transposition on the Near Test and also on Far Tests, but there should be a distance effect. At extreme distances, beyond the range of stimulus generalization, there should be an increase in transposition, provided that the subject continues to label the relative sizes appropriately, because there will remain only the mediated response-evocation potential of the relative cue.

In Spence's 1942 theory of intermediate-stimulus transposition, absolute responses are predicted even on the Near Test. Therefore, if this theory is used to generate predictions from the instrumental two-stage model, the mediated and generalized responses will be predicted to conflict on the Near Test, and less facilitation of transposition will be predicted than from the perceptual two-stage model. However, Spence's theory also predicts that the strength of the absolute response tendency decreases as distance increases. There would be less conflict between the absolute response and the mediated transposition response with increasing distance, and therefore there would be an increase in transposition with increasing distance. This trend is not obtained in verbal subjects, but the obtained trend of decreasing transposition with increasing distance could be predicted by assuming that the probability of occurrence of the appropriate mediator decreases with increasing distance. This assumption seems to be reasonable, since "production errors" should increase with increasing distance.

The data for verbal subjects in both the two-stimulus problem and the intermediate-stimulus problem appear to be more consistent with the instrumental two-stage model than with the perceptual two-stage model. However, verbalization is not the only way to direct the attention of a subject toward the relative cues. One other way seems to be to train the subject with more than one set of stimuli. Multiple-problem training seems to affect transposition in about the way predicted by the perceptual two-stage model. (See section entitled "Multiple-Problem Training," Chapter 11, where it is shown that it is necessary to assume that at extreme distances, the nature of the relative cue changes.)

Hunter's Configuration Theory

I. M. L. Hunter (1954) has hypothesized that transposition is a special case of discrimination between bivariant stimuli, or more accurately, discrimination between bivariant stimulus situations or configurations. Two objects form a single configuration, and changing the positions of the objects does not change the configuration. (Bitterman and McConnell [1954] and Zeiler [1964a] also used the term "configuration" in this sense. In Gulliksen and Wolfle's [1938] theory, however, a configuration is not independent of the positions of the stimulus objects.) A given configuration has both relational and absolute characteristics, depending upon the relative and absolute qualities of the stimulus objects it contains. Since the relational characteristic of the configuration presented on test trials in a transposition problem is the same as the relational characteristic of the configuration used during training, there must be perfect generalization between the configurations on the relational characteristic. Therefore a breakdown in transposition must result from a failure of generalization of the absolute characteristics, which are not the same in the training and test configurations.

The major problems of this approach are, first, that the method of assessing the absolute value of a configuration is not specified; and, second, that the meaning of "generalization" is not at all clear in this context, since it refers to transfer of response from one total stimulus situation to another total stimulus situation (see also I. M. L. Hunter, 1953a). It is apparent that the details of this hypothesis must be spelled out before it can qualify as a theoretical explanation of transposition, especially since I. M. L. Hunter (1954) has complicated the hypothesis by suggesting that there may also be a third component to be considered, the absolute quality of the positive stimulus alone.

I. M. L. Hunter (1954) trained children to discriminate between bivariant stimuli differing in size and width, and tested them with stimuli having one dimension neutralized and the other not transposed (retaining the absolute values). At first, the children responded on test trials to neither component, as evidenced by a breakdown of the discrimination; but with further training on the bivariant stimuli, the children responded to size; and with still further training, they could respond to both size and width. Finally, either width or size could be eliminated without disrupting the discrimination. Hunter said that the sequence illustrates the "basic developmental process" of "perceptual articulation" (Werner, 1948, Chapter III), and that the data support his bivariant-stimulus theory of transposition, on the assumption that the absolute and relational variables are analogous to the size and width variables actually manipulated.

CHAPTER 9

Absolute Theories

It is generally conceded that the classical associationistic theories failed to explain adequately the perception of relations and patterns or forms; but it is more than an historical curiosity that the early Gestalt psychologists argued that these theories, which they referred to as "and-sum" theories, were *in principle* incorrect because they ignored certain emergent qualities of wholes. The early Gestalt psychologists were violently anti-sensationistic, reacting mostly against British Associationism but also against German Associationism. Titchener (1909, pp. 22–37) pointed out that the older Associationism was a preconceived theory, and its adherents often molded the facts to conform to it. He also pointed out, however, that "modern sensationalists" were empirically oriented and adopted sensationalism as an heuristic principle in the search for mental elements. The "modern sensationalists" of Titchener's era accepted the Gestalt, or something very similar to it, as an element; but the adherents of the older Associationism would probably have rejected it on theoretical grounds.

The anti-sensationistic bias of the early Gestalters still influences the thinking of at least some of the modern Gestalt psychologists, who continue to argue against a kind of learning theory that has virtually no modern adherents. This is not the main point, though. The point at issue is that the Gestalt psychologists argued and continue to argue that these theories were inadequate not so much because of a failure to account for the data, but because of a failure to include certain kinds of theoretical principles. This kind of argument need be given no serious consideration.

Spence's Theories

Two-Stimulus Problems

Spence (1937b; 1942) attempted to explain two-stimulus transposition without reference to relation perception, using assumptions about the generalization of response tendencies conditioned to absolute stimulus elements. Humphrey (1951, p. 25) called this kind of explanation of transposition "grotesquely ponderous," but offered no better alternative.

According to Razran (1938b, p. 533), there were attempted explanations of transposition in terms of generalization before Spence's (1937b) theory (for example, Usnadze, 1927). However, Razran characterized the earlier attempts as "rudimentary."

Spence's theory was designed to account for transposition in "inarticulate" subjects, to avoid the complicating effects of mediational processes which might occur in "articulate" subjects. According to the theory, the positive stimulus, choice of which is rewarded during the training phase, acquires a tendency to elicit an approach response as a result of conditioning; and the negative stimulus, choice of which is nonrewarded during training, acquires a tendency to inhibit the approach response. As a result of generalization, each stimulus also acquires, in part, the tendency conditioned to the other stimulus. The generalized response tendency is weaker than the conditioned response tendency, as illustrated in Figs. 9-1 and 9-2, which depict the hypothetical gradients relating the strength of the generalized response tendency to the amount of separation between the conditioned stimulus and the "generalized" or test stimulus. (I have modified Spence's symbolism to conform with usage in modern Hull-Spence theory.) Figure 9-1 shows the shape of the gradient in Spence's 1937 theory, and Fig. 9-2 shows the shape of the gradient in Spence's 1942 theory.

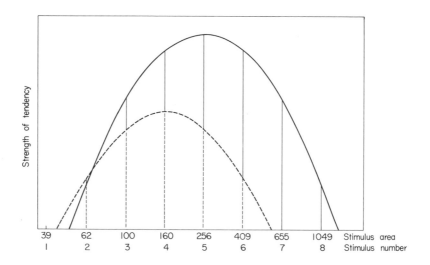

FIG. 9-1. Generalized (- - -) inhibitory and (——) excitatory tendencies after training with stimuli 4 ($-$) and 5 ($+$): Spence's 1937b assumptions. The equation for the generalized approach tendency H is $H = 10 - 20D^2$, and the equation for the generalized inhibitory tendency I is $I = 6 - 20D^2$, where $D = \log S_a - \log S_b$ (see Spence, 1937b, footnote 6). (After Spence, 1937b, Fig. 1, p. 433.)

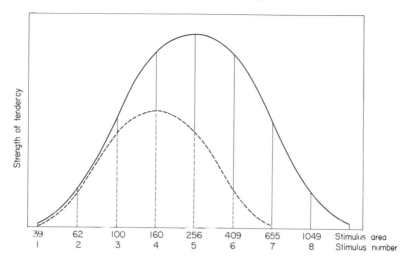

FIG. 9-2. Generalized (- - -) inhibitory and (——) excitatory tendencies after training with stimuli 4 (−) and 5 (+): Spence's 1942 assumptions. $H = 100 \times 10^{-.047D^{2.5}}$, and $I = 60 \times 10^{-.094D^{2.5}}$, where D is the distance in steps (logarithmic units) between the test stimulus and the training stimulus (see Grice, 1953). (After Spence, 1942, Fig. 1, p. 259.)

The net response-evocation potential (E) of a given stimulus is the difference between the approach and inhibitory tendencies associated with the stimulus, including both conditioned and generalized tendencies. The probability that the subject will respond to a given stimulus is determined by the difference between the net response-evocation potential of that stimulus and the net response-evocation potential of the other stimulus. The first two sections of Table 9-1 give values derived from the equations for the curves in Figs. 9-1 and 9-2. The values in the last column represent the differences between the net response-evocation potentials of various pairs of stimuli. These values illustrate the prediction of a greater frequency of transposition in the negative direction than in the positive direction, and illustrate the prediction of a distance effect. If greater distances were included, it could be shown that the predicted gradient relating transposition to distance should begin above the chance level, drop below the chance level at intermediate distances, and finally rise to the chance level at extreme distances.

The theory can predict the drop in performance level from the end of training to the beginning of testing; but as shown in Table 9-1, it can also predict an increase instead of a drop. The prediction depends on the values of the constants of the equations. The theory unequivocally predicts the effect of stimulus similarity.

Although Spence's concept of generalization was very similar to the

TABLE 9-1

HYPOTHETICAL RESPONSE-EVOCATION POTENTIALS AFTER TRAINING WITH
STIMULUS 4 (−) VS STIMULUS 5 (+)

Stimulus pair	Steps[a]	Smaller stimulus			Larger stimulus			Difference[b]
		H	I	E	H	I	E	
Spence (1937b)[c,d]: Concave Downward Gradients								
1 vs 2	−3	0	0	0	0	0	0	0
2 vs 3	−2	0	0	0	67	52	15	15
3 vs 4	−1	67	52	15	92	60	32	17
4 vs 5	0	92	60	32	100	52	48	16
5 vs 6	1	100	52	48	92	27	65	17
6 vs 7	2	92	27	65	67	0	67	2
7 vs 8	3	67	0	67	25	0	25	−42
Spence (1942)[d]: Ogival Gradients								
1 vs 2	−3	3	2	1	19	18	1	0
2 vs 3	−2	19	18	1	54	48	6	5
3 vs 4	−1	54	48	6	90	60	30	24
4 vs 5	0	90	60	30	100	48	52	22
5 vs 6	1	100	48	52	90	18	72	20
6 vs 7	2	90	18	72	54	2	52	−20
7 vs 8	3	54	2	52	19	0	19	−33
Hull (1943): Convex Downward Gradients								
1 vs 2	−3	25	21	4	35	30	5	1
2 vs 3	−2	35	30	5	50	42	8	3
3 vs 4	−1	50	42	8	71	60	11	3
4 vs 5	0	71	60	11	100	42	58	47
5 vs 6	1	100	42	58	71	30	41	−17
6 vs 7	2	71	30	41	50	21	29	−13
7 vs 8	3	50	21	29	35	15	20	−9
Straight Line Gradients[e]								
1 vs 2	−3	60	15	45	70	30	40	−5
2 vs 3	−2	70	30	40	80	45	35	−5
3 vs 4	−1	80	45	35	90	60	30	−5
4 vs 5	0	90	60	30	100	45	55	25
5 vs 6	1	100	45	55	90	30	60	5
6 vs 7	2	90	30	60	80	15	65	5
7 vs 8	3	80	15	65	70	0	70	5

[a] Steps between training pair and test pair.
[b] Difference equals E for larger stimulus minus E for smaller stimulus; $E = H − I$.
[c] Values from equation multiplied by 10.
[d] The values given here do not agree exactly with the values given by Spence.
[e] $H = 100 − 10 D$. $I = 60 − 15 D$, where D symbolizes distance in steps.

concept of "primary stimulus generalization" later elaborated by Hull (1943), an essential difference was that Hull assumed that the generalization gradient is convex downward, as shown in Fig. 9-3, and Spence assumed that the gradient is concave downward (Fig. 9-1) or ogival (Fig. 9-2). Several writers (for example, Bugelski, 1956, p. 412; Lawrence, 1955) have noted

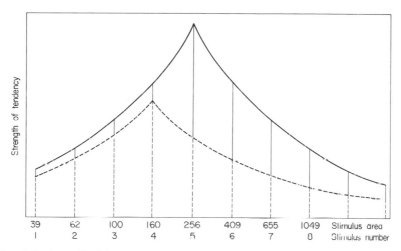

FIG. 9-3. Generalized (- - -) inhibitory und (——) excitatory tendencies after training with stimuli 4 (−) and 5 (+): Hull's 1943 assumptions. $H = 100 \times 10^{-.006d}$, and $I = 60 \times 10^{-.006d}$, where d is the difference in j.n.d.'s between two stimuli (Hull, 1943, p. 199).

that the convex downward gradient cannot yield the same predictions as Spence's gradients, in both of which the drop away from the midpoint is initially positively accelerated. In the Hullian gradient the drop away from the midpoint is negatively accelerated. The third section of Table 9-1 gives net differences derived from Fig. 9-3. As can be seen, transposition would be predicted only in the negative direction. Absolute responses would be predicted in the positive direction, approaching the chance level in frequency as distance increases. The usual distance effect on transposition would be predicted in the negative direction. The last section of Table 9-1 gives predictions derived from straight-line generalization gradients. Transposition is predicted in only one direction, and no distance effect is predictable.

INTERMEDIATE-STIMULUS PROBLEMS

Spence (1942) used the ogival gradients to derive predictions about transposition in the intermediate-stimulus problem. As illustrated in Fig. 9-4 and the first section of Table 9-2, it is predicted that no transposition will occur except at less than one-half step. Absolute responses are predicted at other distances, but the frequency of absolute responses should exhibit a distance effect, decreasing from a high level at one step to the chance level at extreme distances.

The theory predicts the greater difficulty of learning the intermediate-stimulus problem, relative to the two-stimulus problem, because of the two sources of generalized inhibition in the intermediate-stimulus problem.

The last three sections of Table 9-2 give net differences derived from concave generalization gradients, using the equations of Fig. 9-1, from convex gradients, using the equations of Fig. 9-3, and from straight-line gradients. With the curvilinear gradients, absolute responses are predicted. With the straight-line gradients, absolute responses are predicted at one step, and conflict between responses is predicted at more than one step.

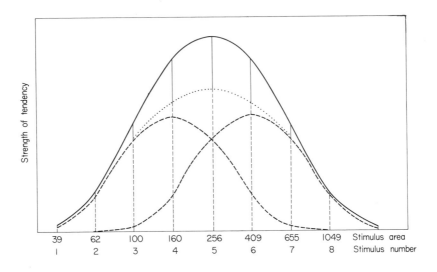

F IG. 9-4. Generalized (- - -) inhibitory and (———) excitatory tendencies after training with stimuli 4 (−), 5 (+), and 6 (−): Spence's 1942 assumptions. (· · ·) Net inhibitory tendency of stimulus $a = \bar{I}_4 + \bar{I}_6 - (\bar{I}_4 \times \bar{I}_6)/\bar{H}_a$, where $\bar{I}_4$ is the inhibition generalized from Stimulus 4 to Stimulus a; $\bar{I}_6$ is the inhibition generalized from Stimulus 6 to Stimulus a; and $\bar{H}_a$ is the excitatory tendency generalized from Stimulus 5 to Stimulus a. (After Spence, 1942, Fig. 2, p. 268.)

THE 1960 THEORY

Spence used a more elaborate model of discrimination learning in his 1960 theory (Spence, 1960, Chapter 22) than he used in the 1937 and 1942 theories, and incorporated assumptions about the functions of observing or orienting responses. It was assumed in the new theory that the subject confronted with

TABLE 9–2

HYPOTHETICAL RESPONSE-EVOCATION POTENTIALS AFTER TRAINING
WITH STIMULI 4, 5, AND 6, WITH 5 POSITIVE

Stimulus set	Steps	Small	Intermediate	Large	Predicted choice[a]
			Stimulus		
		Spence (1942): Ogival Gradients			
1, 2, 3	−3	1	1	6	Large
2, 3, 4	−2	1	6	24	Large
3, 4, 5	−1	6	24	27	Large
4, 5, 6	0	24	27	24	Intermediate
5, 6, 7	1	27	24	6	Small
6, 7, 8	2	24	6	1	Small
		Spence (1937b): Concave Downward Gradients			
1, 2, 3	−3	0	0	15	Large
2, 3, 4	−2	0	15	22	Large
3, 4, 5	−1	15	22	23	Large
4, 5, 6	0	22	23	22	Intermediate
5, 6, 7	1	23	22	15	Small
6, 7, 8	2	22	15	0	Small
		Hull (1943): Convex Downward Gradients			
1, 2, 3	−3	2	3	4	Large
2, 3, 4	−2	3	4	6	Large
3, 4, 5	−1	4	6	33	Large
4, 5, 6	0	6	33	6	Intermediate
5, 6, 7	1	33	6	4	Small
6, 7, 8	2	6	4	3	Small
		Straight Line Gradients			
1, 2, 3	−3	0	15	15	L = M
2, 3, 4	−2	15	15	13	S = M
3, 4, 5	−1	15	13	42	Large
4, 5, 6	0	13	42	13	Intermediate
5, 6, 7	1	42	13	15	Small
6, 7, 8	2	13	15	15	L = M

[a]The predicted choice is to the stimulus with the greatest response evocation potential (E). The Es were derived from the values in Table 9–1, using the equation $E = H - $ net I, where net I is defined as in Fig. 9–4.

two stimulus compounds can orient toward the left, exposing one compound to the sensory receptors, or toward the right, exposing the other compound. Each of these orienting responses has a probability of occurrence, but since the two possible orienting responses are mutually exclusive and, for purposes of the analysis, exhaustive, the sum of the two probabilities is one. Each stimulus compound has some theoretically determinable probability of eliciting an approach response, and each of these probabilities is independent of the other.

The probability of the approach response, given exposure of one stimulus compound, is the same as the probability that the latency of the approach response is shorter than the duration or refractory period of the observing response which exposes the compound. This is because a compound can elicit an approach response only while the subject is oriented toward the compound. (The latency under consideration is the "response-evocation latency," which is the time between the onset of the stimulus and the initiation of the response. The latency as determined by the time required to complete the response, measured from the beginning to the termination of the response, is irrelevant for present purposes [see Spence, 1956, pp. 116–118].) The latency of the approach response is a function of the "momentary superthreshold effective excitatory potential" of the compound.[1] The duration of the observing response must be determined empirically, at least for the present, because the variables that influence it have not yet been identified. (It has generally been found that the introduction of a novel stimulus increases the duration of the observing response [for example, Berlyne, 1958], but not enough quantitative data are available to permit prediction of the *amount* of increase. There are data that could be interpreted as contradictory. Charlesworth [1966] found that the persistence of observing responses over a series of trials in human infants increased with the degree of uncertainty in the locus of the stimulus materials, but the duration of fixation was invariant with uncertainty.)

The probability that a subject will actually respond to a given compound located in a given position is a function of the probability that the subject will orient toward that position and the probability that the compound will, if exposed, elicit a response, corrected for the probability that the subject will orient toward the other position and the probability that the other compound will elicit a response. Using the notational system of Fig. 9-5, which diagrams the model, it can be shown that the probability of responding

---

[1]The momentary superthreshold effective excitatory potential $(\dot{\bar{E}}_L)$ is defined as follows:

$$\dot{E}_L = D(H + \bar{H}) - I - \bar{I} - I_o - L$$

where D is drive strength, H is habit strength, $\bar{H}$ is generalized habit strength, I is inhibition due to nonreinforcement, $\bar{I}$ is generalized inhibition, I_o is oscillatory inhibition, and L is the threshold value that must be obtained before a response will occur (Spence, 1956, Chapter 4). It is not necessary to subtract the excitatory potential of the other stimulus compound, since the observing responses expose only one compound at a time.

to a given compound, say compound W, regardless of its position, is

$$P_W = \frac{P_3(1 - .5P_4)}{P_3 + P_4 - P_3 P_4}$$

(see Spence, 1960, pp. 385–386).[2]

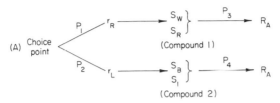

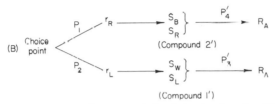

FIG. 9-5. Spence's 1960 model of nonspatial discrimination learning. The positions of the visual stimuli S_W and S_B are interchanged in (A) and (B), representing the configurations confronting the subject on different trials. P_1 and P_2 are the probabilities of the observing responses r_R and r_L; S_R and S_L are kinaesthetic cues; and P_3, P_4, P_3' and P_4' are the probabilities that the compounds will elicit the approach response R_A before the subject's orientation changes. (After Spence, 1960, Fig. 6, p. 384.)

The theory did not deal specifically with the transposition situation, but implications of the theory for transposition can be determined by adding assumptions about generalization. The assumptions about generalization in the 1942 theory could be used, and would generate the prediction that the momentary superthreshold effective excitatory potential of the new stimulus on a one-step test in the positive direction would be greater than

[2] The derivation of this equation requires the assumption that the two observing responses are equally likely to occur (and hence each has a probability of .5, since they sum to unity), and that $P_3 = P_3'$ and $P_4 = P_4'$. The first assumption, needed only to simplify the general equation, seems very likely to be satisfied, especially toward the end of the learning phase. The second assumption is reasonable after position habits have been equalized. The probability of responding to the other compound, regardless of its position is

$$P_B = 1 - P_W = \frac{P_4(1 - .5P_3)}{P_3 + P_4 - P_3 P_4}$$

($P_W + P_B = 1$, because it is assumed that a response will eventually occur).

that of the training stimulus retained on the test. However, there is nothing in the theory which would predict that introducing a new stimulus would affect the excitatory potential of the retained stimulus, and there is nothing that would predict that the duration of orientation would be affected. Therefore, P_3 and P_4 would be the same on the test as they were at the end of the training phase; and on a one-step test in the positive direction, the percentage of transposition responses should equal exactly 50 per cent. When the subject chances to orient first toward the originally positive stimulus, the approach response will be elicited immediately. When the subject chances to orient first toward the new stimulus, the approach response will again be elicited immediately, since the new stimulus has an even greater excitatory potential than the originally positive stimulus. On a one-step test in the negative direction, transposition should be greater than 50 per cent. When the subject orients first toward the originally negative stimulus, no response is elicited, and the subject will orient toward the new stimulus. However, the new stimulus has an even greater inhibitory potential than the originally negative stimulus, and again no response will occur. After a long series of reorientations, the subject will eventually approach one of the stimuli, most probably the one with less inhibitory potential. This one is the originally negative stimulus.

Additional assumptions would obviously be needed to extend the theory to the transposition situation, since the predictions clearly do not agree with the data.

Generalization Theory

In 1926, Margaret Washburn presented a brief review of transposition studies and pointed out that the usual interpretation of the findings was that the subject recognizes the relation involved. She suggested as an alternative that the subject fails to recognize any difference between the two total situations, and added that "Lloyd Morgan's canon would incline us to the latter interpretation" (p. 242).[3] Within a few years, Gundlach and Herington (1933) complained that Washburn's suggestion was being neglected, and they urged its consideration. Nevertheless, it seems to have remained almost forgotten, after Jones discussed it in 1939 (F. N. Jones, 1939a), until Harold Stevenson and his colleagues revived it in 1955 (Stevenson and Bitterman, 1955; Stevenson and Iscoe, 1955; Stevenson *et al.*, 1955b;

---

[3]According to Corbascio (1964), Washburn expressed this idea in the second edition of *The Animal Mind*, published in 1917; but I have been unable to find it before the third edition, published in 1926. Washburn did not discuss relation perception or transposition in the first two editions.

Stevenson and Weiss, 1955). (The suggestion was also discussed by Shirai in 1951 and in 1954, but in unpublished theses.)

Stumpf suggested a similar hypothesis in 1883 in a discussion of difference thresholds. Stumpf pointed out that in psychophysical work three sensations a, b, and c are sometimes judged as follows: $a = b$, $b = c$, and $a \neq c$. He suggested: "Our judgments of equality were based upon our incapacity to notice very small yet actual differences, the consequence of this conclusion being that the difference threshold as measured by our methods appears to be a fact, not of sensation, but of our capacity of perceiving." (Cited from Koffka, 1922, p. 537.) Subjects respond to stimulus situations as though they were equivalent, not because of equivalence of sensations, but because of a failure to perceive the difference between the sensations. Douse (1878) implied the same thing when he said that "transposition" can result from "want of attention" (p. 133), but he was discussing the kind of transposition involved in malapropisms and in Will Honeycomb's blunder with the pebble and watch (*Spectator*, 1711).

All theories assume that the subject responds not to objective or external stimuli but to sensed or perceived stimuli (see, for example, Hull, 1943, pp. 32–33; Köhler, 1928; McCulloch, 1939). Failure to discriminate between two stimuli means that the stimuli are perceptually identical and must arouse the same response. (This assumption can be questioned. Compare the debate about whether sets affect only responses or affect percepts [Haber, 1966].) The failure to discriminate between stimuli has been suggested as one basis for the empirical phenomenon of stimulus generalization. (See Lashley and Wade, 1946; Prokasy and Hall, 1963; Razran, 1949; Stevens, 1965, p. 24. See also the short reviews by J. S. Brown, 1965, pp. 12–16 and 21–22; Mednick and Freedman, 1960.) Therefore, the subject will "transpose" if he fails to discriminate between the training and test sets of stimuli, and transposition can be predicted on the basis of the failure to discriminate in both the two-stimulus problem and the intermediate-stimulus problem.

An illusion yielding an apparent size difference between identical stimuli should also produce transposition. Subjects trained on an actual size discrimination should transpose under the effects of the illusion, responding on the basis of the illusory size relation. Révész (1924) obtained this kind of transposition in hens, using the Jastrow ("ring-segment") illusion and the horizontal-vertical illusion (see Fig. 9-6).[4] Winslow (1933) also obtained

---

[4]Révész (1924, p. 400), Hartmann and Triche (1933), Winslow (1933, p. 8), Koffka (1935, p. 32), and Katz (1937, p. 27) attributed the illusion in Fig. 9-6a to Jastrow; but Titchener (1901) attributed it to Wundt. The figure as depicted by Titchener (Fig. 48B, p. 166) is rotated 180 degrees, but Pillsbury (1934, p. 449) showed it right-side-up with the caption: "Fig. 105.—Illusion due to concentric sectors. (From Titchener, *op. cit.*, after Wundt.)." Ladd and Woodworth (1911, Fig. 143, p. 448) illustrated a different version, which they attributed to Jastrow, with converging instead of parallel arcs in each segment. Jastrow (1892) illustrated

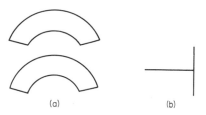

(a)   (b)

FIG. 9-6. (a) The Jastrow illusion: The upper figure appears to be smaller than the lower figure, but they are actually identical in size. (b) The horizontal–vertical illusion: The horizontal line appears to be longer than the vertical line, but they are actually equal in length.

it in chicks with the horizontal-vertical illusion, and with various other illusions of size. C. J. Warden and Baar (1929) obtained it in the ring dove with the Müller-Lyer illusion. Révész (1924) also tested four- to six-year-old children and obtained inconclusive results. Dixon (1949) obtained the illusion in almost all of the five- and six-year-olds he tested, and in at least half of the three- and four-year-olds; but none of the two-year-olds tested gave any evidence that they saw the illusion (however, although the design of the study made it unlikely that there were any false positives, there were possibly a large number of false negatives, and the strength of the illusion was therefore probably underestimated). Huang (1930) tested 20 children ranging in age from about five to eight and one-half years, and obtained the Jastrow illusion in every child, although he found that the horizontal–vertical illusion "did not work well with the children" (p. 164). Piaget has also studied illusions in children (see Wohlwill, 1960b, pp. 252–258; Flavell, 1963, pp. 350–356).

Any variable that increases the probability of discriminating between two sets of stimuli should decrease the probability of transposition responses. The similarity of the stimuli affects the probability of recognizing the change in stimuli, since for any given number of steps separating the training and test sets of stimuli, the absolute change is smaller when the stimuli are similar than when they are distinctively different. Assuming that a small absolute change is less likely to be recognized than a larger absolute change, the probability of recognizing the change increases, and the probability of transposing decreases, as the stimulus differences are increased. (See, however, the discussion of the D. E. Gould [1963] study in the section entitled "Delay," Chapter 4.)

Increasing the number of steps separating the training and test sets of stimuli also increases stimulus differences, and should increase the probability of making the discrimination, reducing transposition. A distance

this last version (Fig. 28, p. 398) and another version with trapezoids (Fig. 27, p. 397), and illustrated a form with open figures (Fig. 26, p. 396). I did not find any illustration of the illusion in the half-dozen or so works by Wundt which I examined.

effect is therefore predicted for both the two-stimulus problem and the intermediate-stimulus problem.

Since the set of stimuli used during training is not present on test trials, the test set must be compared with a memory trace of the training set. Assuming that the memory trace "fades," or becomes less precise with respect to absolute and relative stimulus properties, as the time between the end of training and the beginning of testing increases, delay between the training and test phases should reduce the probability of discriminating the test set of stimuli from the training set, and therefore increase the frequency of transposition.

The three variables—stimulus similarity, distance, and delay—are not independently related to the probability of recognizing the change in stimulus sets. On a Near Test, delay should increase transposition only if the stimuli are so distinctively different from each other that the subjects are likely to discriminate between the training and test sets when the test is given immediately after the end of training. Delay can provide little if any further facilitation of transposition if the stimuli are so similar that the probability of making the discrimination is low when the test is given immediately. On a Far Test, the stimuli may be so discriminably different from the training stimuli that delay has relatively little effect on the ability of the subject to recognize the change; therefore, it seems reasonable to expect delay to facilitate Far Test transposition only if the stimuli in the series are highly similar to one another. The transition points cannot yet be specified exactly, because of the paucity of relevant data, and therefore precise quantitative predictions are impossible; but general directions of effects can be predicted, as illustrated in Fig. 9-7.

If the subject discriminates between the situations, it is not altogether clear whether the response expected would be random or absolute. If the hypothesis were added to Spence's absolute theory, the response could be either, depending on the distance at which the discrimination occurred.

Zeiler (1963d) categorized the hypothesis as one of the "contemporary versions of relational theory" (p. 1), probably because some of its advocates (Stevenson and Bitterman, 1955; Stevenson and Weiss, 1955) seemed to favor a relational interpretation of transposition. However, the hypothesis was actually set forth as one ignored in both relational and absolute theory (Stevenson and Weiss, 1955, p. 288) and as consistent with both kinds of theory (Stevenson and Bitterman, 1955, pp. 278–279; and perhaps Wohlwill, 1957). Furthermore, Washburn (1926) clearly advanced the hypothesis as an alternative to a relational interpretation and therefore as a postulate of some kind of absolute theory. Riley (1958) and Mowrer (1960b, p. 245), who seem to favor an absolute type of theory, have also suggested the hypothesis, apparently independently of the earlier investigators; and I have previously implied that it should be added to absolute

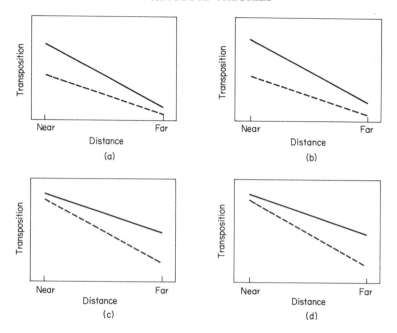

Fig. 9-7. Hypothetical joint effects of stimulus similarity, distance, and delay, predicted on the basis of apparent probability of recognizing change in stimuli. (a) (——) Delayed test and (- - -) immediate test with distinctive stimuli; (b) (——) similar stimuli and (- - -) distinctive stimuli on immediate test; (c) (——) delayed test and (- - -) immediate test with similar stimuli; and (d) (——) similar stimuli and (- - -) distinctive stimuli on delayed test.

theory (Reese, 1961; Reese, 1962a).

Data from studies of verbal mediation in children suggest that young children who possess potential mediators may fail to use them, whereas older children tend to make use of available mediators (see Reese, 1962b; Reese, 1963a). Extending the principle to the intermediate-size transposition problem generates the prediction that young "verbal" children, who possess the concept of middle-sizedness, will behave like "nonverbal" children, who lack the concept; and both of these groups will transpose less than older verbal children, because of mediation of the transposition response in the last group. On the basis of the Washburn hypothesis, transposition should occur on the Near Test, but it should occur on a Far Test only under conditions yielding a low probability of discriminating the change in stimuli from training to test trials. On the basis of Spence's absolute theory, absolute responses should predominate when the discrimination occurs and when mediation does not occur. These predictions have been confirmed experimentally (Reese, 1962a; Reese, 1964b).

Neural Theories

LASHLEY

Lashley (1929a, pp. 168–170) suggested a kind of "neural field theory" of transposition. It was assumed that two stimuli arouse two different centers or neural aggregates, and the "potential difference" between the centers conditions the action of a nerve cell capable of arousing a left (or a right) response, and therefore determines which response is aroused. (Approach and avoidance would have worked as well as left and right responses in the theory.) "The common elements in transfer are not common neurons, but common ratios of excitation in different neuronic systems" (Lashley, 1929b, p. 545).

The polarization of the field was assumed to remain essentially invariant with respect to this function with variations in the stimuli, leading to relational responses. The theory can predict the distance effect and probably the occurrence of random responses when transposition fails to occur, but Lashley did not discuss these phenomena.

GUTHRIE

Guthrie (1935, pp. 196–201) believed that transposition reflects responses to stimulus patterns. According to Guthrie, all stimuli are relations, in the sense that the stimulus is a change in a physical force or a chemical state. Furthermore, neural activity in any one neural tract is dependent on the relative difference between two stimuli, and this difference constitutes a stimulus pattern. The notion is quite similar to Hull's principle of "afferent neural interaction" (Hull, 1943, pp. 216–217), and seems to be related to Klüver's (1933) analysis in terms of "equivalent stimuli." The subject learns to give a certain response to a particular aspect of a stimulus pattern, and whenever this aspect is reproduced by a new situation, the learned response occurs (see Maier and Schneirla, 1935, pp. 436–437).

HEBB

Hebb (1949, pp. 41–44) has also outlined a neurophysiological theory of two-stimulus transposition. The subject looks at and adapts to one stimulus, according to this theory, then looks at and adapts to the other. The change in adaptation in one direction or the other is the conditioned stimulus for the response. (Compare this with the sensationistic theories discussed below.)

It was also assumed that the "whole visual system . . . must act to damp strong stimulations, amplify weak ones" (p. 43). "In one part of the system, the same central neurons might thus be active in the perception of 'brighter,' regardless of absolute stimulus values" (p. 44), accounting for transposition; but in other parts of the system, "the cells that are aroused would still correspond partly to the absolute intensity . . . " (p. 44), accounting for the fact that absolute values have some effect on performance. The hypothesis does not specifically predict a distance effect, nor does it predict what response will occur when transposition fails; and it deals only with two-stimulus brightness discriminations. However, Hebb admitted that the hypothesis is sketchy and probably oversimplifies the problem.

There is some physiological evidence to support this kind of theory. The firing rates of certain cells in the lateral geniculate nucleus in macaque monkeys have been reported to change with relative shifts of brightness and wave length of light. The change in firing rate depends more on the change in stimulation relative to the adaptation level than on the absolute qualities of the light, although both have an effect (DeValois, Jacobs, and Abramov, 1964; DeValois, Jacobs, and Jones, 1962). It can be argued, however, that the neurological basis for relation perception (or sensation) is peripheral, rather than central as Hebb's theory suggests. Although there are several synapses separating cells of the retina from cells of the lateral geniculate nucleus, there is evidence that in the frog, at least, pattern or relation perception takes place at the retinal level (Maturana, Lettvin, McCulloch, and Pitts, 1960).

HOUSEHOLDER

Householder (1947) developed a theory that predicted transposition on the basis of excitatory and inhibitory connections among neurons (the theory was not mathematical, as Campbell [1954] asserted, but neural). Directional responses (left versus right) were assumed to be elicited by intermediary elements that could be excited or inhibited by receptor elements, as shown in Fig. 9-8. Stimulus B (in the figure) has greater magnitude than Stimulus A. Responses to Stimulus B are rewarded, and responses to Stimulus A are nonrewarded. If A were presented on the left and B on the right, A would activate L_1, sending an excitatory impulse to L_1'; and B would activate R_1 and R_2, sending excitatory impulses to R_1' and R_2' and sending inhibitory impulses to L_1'. The right response (response to B) would be activated by R_1' and R_2', but the left response would not be activated since L_1' was inhibited. Since the analogous processes would occur when the positions of A and B were reversed, correct responses during training would be predicted.

If Stimuli B and C were presented (C having greater magnitude than B), with B on the left and C on the right, B would activate L_1 and L_2, sending excitatory impulses to L_1' and L_2' and sending inhibitory impulses to R_1'.

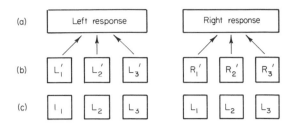

| (a) | Left response | Right response |

| (b) | L_1' L_2' L_3' | R_1' R_2' R_3' |

| (c) | I_1 L_2 L_3 | L_1 L_2 L_3 |

Stimulus	Location of Stimulus	Receptor Activated	Intermediary Excited	Intermediary Inhibited
A	L	L_1	L_1'	None
B	L	L_1, L_2	L_1', L_2'	R_1'
C	L	L_1, L_2, L_3	L_1', L_2', L_3'	R_1', R_2'
A	R	R_1	R_1'	None
B	R	R_1, R_2	R_1', R_2'	L_1'
C	R	R_1, R_2, R_3	R_1', R_2', R_3'	L_1', L_2'

FIG. 9-8. Outline of Householder's theory of transposition; (a) motor element, (b) intermediary element, and (c) receptor element (see text for explanation). (After Householder, 1947, Fig. 4, p. 175.)

Stimulus C would activate R_1, R_2, and R_3, exciting R_1', R_2', and R_3' and inhibiting L_1' and L_2'. The impulses that would have aroused the left response would be inhibited by impulses arising from C. Impulses arising from B would inhibit R_1', but R_2' and R_3' would not be inhibited, and would arouse the right response (response to C). Since the analogous processes would occur when the positions of B and C were reversed, transposition would be predicted.

The theory predicts transposition in the positive, upward direction and the negative, downward direction. In order to predict learning when the stimulus of lesser magnitude is positive, and to predict transposition in the positive, downward direction and in the negative, upward direction, it would be necessary to rearrange the inhibitory connections, as shown in Table 9-3. It is perhaps reasonable to assume that with B positive and C negative, the inhibitory connections shown in Table 9-3 might be acquired through learning; but it is not reasonable to suppose that the inhibitory connections of A would be any different from those shown in Fig. 9-8 since this stimulus is not presented during the learning stage.

Nissen (1950) criticized the theory on the ground that the treatment of responses was not internally consistent. Left and right responses were

TABLE 9–3

CONNECTIONS REQUIRED WHEN THE STIMULUS OF LESSER MAGNITUDE IS POSITIVE[a]

Stimulus	Location of stimulus	Receptor activated	Intermediary excited	Intermediary inhibited
A	L	L_1	L'_1	R'_1, R'_2
B	L	L_1, L_2	L'_1, L'_2	R'_2, R'_3
C	L	L_1, L_2, L_3	L'_1, L'_2, L'_3	None
A	R	R_1	R'_1	L'_1, L'_2
B	R	R_1, R_2	R'_1, R'_2	L'_2, L'_3
C	R	R_1, R_2, R_3	R'_1, R'_2, R'_3	None

[a] $A < B < C$.

assumed in the section on transposition, but approach and avoidance were assumed in a section dealing with discrimination learning. The example Householder used in the exposition of his treatment of discrimination learning was a discrimination between two degrees of warmth. This is usually a successive discrimination, and it would have been easy to substitute "response to left" for "approach" and "response to right" for "avoidance" in this example without changing any of the rest of the exposition. However, Nissen was obviously correct in assuming that for a simultaneous discrimination involving directional responses, the theory would require ten neural cells, instead of the four required for the successive discrimination.

The theory dealt only with transposition on the Near Test, and therefore did not predict a distance effect. However, the theory could be extended to account for the distance effect by assuming the existence of two additional receptor elements L_4 and R_4 and by assuming that L_3, R_3, L_4, and R_4 inhibit all of the opposite intermediary elements. Then when Stimuli C and D were presented, with C on the left and D on the right, C would activate L_1, L_2, and L_3, exciting L'_1, L'_2, and L'_3 and inhibiting R'_1, R'_2, R'_3, and R'_4; and D would activate R_1, R_2, R_3, and R_4, exciting R'_1, R'_2, R'_3, and R'_4 and inhibiting L'_1, L'_2, and L'_3. Random responses would occur, since all intermediary elements would be inhibited. The changed assumption about the inhibitory effects of L_3 and R_3 would not change the prediction of transposition on the Near Test. However, one must arbitrarily decide which particular pair of "receptors" is to have this enhanced inhibitory power, and it would obviously be possible to predict transposition at two steps or at any other number of steps. Furthermore, the transition resulting from the decision is abrupt, and the resulting transposition gradient would be high and flat until it suddenly dropped to the chance level.

The theory did not deal with transposition in the intermediate-stimulus problem, and it seems doubtful that it would be fruitful to try to extend it.

Sensationistic Theories

Washburn (1929) asserted that "motor" psychology "can explain the various form elements and relational elements which are independent of sensory content as due to kinaesthetic processes" (p. 470). She did not indicate the details of the explanation (at least not in the available report, which is an abstract of an oral presentation), but she was probably referring to the kinds of explanations of relational judgments that she had discussed earlier (Washburn, 1906), and that were discussed by Hodgson (1885), Titchener (1909, pp. 184–188 and 286–287), and Ladd and Woodworth (1911, pp. 600–603), among others.

Relational judgments need not be based on a comparison of the stimuli, or even on a comparison of memory traces of the stimuli, according to evidence from introspective reports. Pikler seems to have demonstrated this kind of phenomenon in 1913, and Gleason reported corroborative evidence in 1919. Gleason was unable to find evidence of a "relational element," even though she tested trained introspectors. Theoretically, the first stimulus arouses some kind of "adjustment," "preparation," "expectation," or "set," which can be peripheral or central; and when the second stimulus fails to conform to the adjustment, by deviating in one or the other direction, an "absolute impression" of the quality of the second stimulus is conveyed. The absolute impression is the basis for the relational judgment (see Ladd and Woodworth, 1911, pp. 600–603; Lindworsky, 1931, pp. 239–240; Vernon, 1952, pp. 149–153; Woodworth, 1938, pp. 440–441).

A peripheral muscular adjustment could account for Klüver's (1933) finding that after learning a weight discrimination by direct comparison of the stimuli, monkeys could then respond on the basis of "absolute feel." As a central neural process, the adjustment seems to be very similar to the mechanism suggested by Hebb (discussed above). It can be argued, however, that there is still necessary a comparison between the expected muscular or neural response and the response that actually occurs. (See also the discussion of comparison behavior in the section entitled "Opportunity for Comparison," Chapter 3.)

Jaensch (1920) developed a theory of relations based on the concept of the "transitional experience" or "transitional sensation" (*Übergang-serlebnis*). This concept and similar ones formulated by Lindworsky (1922) and Bühler (1930a) seem to have been based on Schumann's concept of "secondary impressions" or "accompanying impressions" (Lindworsky, 1931, p. 238; Shirai, 1951, p. 9). Unfortunately, the relevant works of these four theorists have apparently never been translated into English. (Lindworsky's *Experimentelle Psychologie* has been translated [Lindworsky, 1931], but it contains only a sketch of the theory of relations and omits too many details to be helpful. Similarly, the *Mental Development of the Child*

[Bühler, 1930b] summarizes Bühler's [1930a] *Die geistige Entwicklung des Kindes*, but omits the details of interest here.) Koffka (1925, pp. 221–230) discussed the concepts at some length, but he was highly critical, and it would probably be unwise to use his treatment as a secondary source.

The transitional experience is more easily illustrated than defined. Examples are the sensation of expansion which emerges when the eyes shift from a small to a large object, and the sensation of brightening which emerges when the eyes shift from a dark to a bright object.

According to Wertheimer (1959), subjects may experience a relation as a "transition phenomenon," such as a raising of the eyes when shifting from observation of a small figure to observation of a large one, and adjustments of the eyes in the transition from dark to bright; or the subject might experience a "whole-quality" without necessarily shifting from one figure to the other. The transition phenomenon might explain how a relation is sensed, but further assumptions would be required to explain transposition. The transition phenomenon is not the same as the "transitional experience," because the transition phenomenon is a peripheral event, and the transitional experience is central. It might also be noted that the transition phenomenon and the transitional experience are not the same as the "transitive state" that William James discussed. The transitive state is a "feeling of relation" (W. James, 1890, Vol. I, pp. 243–248).

Other Solutions

FRANK

According to L. K. Frank (1926), transposition results from learning a response to a "sequence or order of stimuli" (p. 346), analogous to discriminating different words on the basis of the ordering of the letters (p. 347). (Compare with Spence's explanation of transverse patterning, discussed in the section entitled "Opportunity for Comparison," Chapter 3.) The hypothesis does not account for transposition if it is the absolute stimulus qualities that are ordered; and if it is the relative qualities that are ordered, then the explanation is not really an alternative to the Gestalt explanation (as Frank believed it to be).

SKINNER

Skinner (1953), discussing stimulus generalization or "induction," said: "Stimulus induction on the basis of a 'relation' presents no difficulty in a natural science if the relation can be described in physical terms. Where this appears not to be the case, we have to turn to other possibilities—for example, . . . mediating behavior . . ." (p. 138). However, as shown in Chapter 10, not all of the transposition data can be explained on the basis of generalization of stimulus relations even with mediation added.

CHAPTER 10

Summary of Findings and Evaluation of Theories

The data on transposition are summarized in this chapter, and the theories of transposition are evaluated by assessing their ability to account for the empirical findings. Most of the theories are too limited in scope to merit detailed evaluation; and of the others, the theory of Gulliksen and Wolfle contains a basic assumption that is untenable (the one about directional responses), Gestalt theory is too loose to generate exact predictions, and Spence's 1937b theory is outmoded even with the modifications made in 1942. (Spence never extended his 1960 theory of discrimination learning to the transposition situation.) Nevertheless, noting the successes and failures of these theories might aid the development of a new theory by indicating what kinds of assumptions must be included to account for specific findings.

Two-Stimulus versus Intermediate-Stimulus Problems

SPEED OF LEARNING

The two-stimulus discrimination problem is solved more rapidly than the intermediate-stimulus discrimination problem. The finding is consistent with Spence's theory, since in the intermediate-stimulus problem there is generalization of inhibition to the positive stimulus from two negative stimuli instead of from only one negative stimulus. Gulliksen and Wolfle's theory could also predict the finding.

In Gestalt theory, it is assumed that the solution of the intermediate-stimulus problem requires learning about two two-stimulus relations. Since the two-stimulus problem requires learning about only one two-stimulus relation, the two-stimulus problem should be easier to solve than the intermediate-stimulus problem. Even without this assumption, Gestalt theory could predict the greater ease of solving the two-stimulus problem. One of the consequences of presenting three stimuli on a trial in the standard intermediate-stimulus problem is that except when the stimulus that is intermediate on the cue dimension chances to occur in the middle spatial position, the spatial ordering of the stimuli does not correspond with the ordering on the cue dimension. In the standard two-stimulus problem, with only two stimuli presented on a trial, these two kinds of ordering necessarily correspond perfectly. Therefore, stimulus comparison on the cue dimension should be considerably easier in the two-stimulus problem than in the intermediate-stimulus problem, and since there is known to be a relation between comparison behavior and discrimination learning, as shown in Chapter 3, the two-stimulus problem should be easier to solve than the intermediate-stimulus problem. Presumably the ease of comparison determines the probability of relation perception.

Mediation theory could predict the finding, since the two-stimulus relation should be easier to perceive and label than the intermediate-stimulus relation.

The finding is also consistent with "hypothesis" models of learning (for example, Bowman, 1961; Bowman, 1963; Krechevsky, 1932a; Krechevsky, 1932b; Krechevsky, 1932c; Levine, 1959). Because of the difference between the two-stimulus problem and the intermediate-stimulus problem in the number of stimuli presented on a trial, when standard methods of simultaneous presentation are used, there is a difference in the number of response possibilities on a trial. Therefore, according to the "hypothesis" models, there are more possible "hypotheses" in the intermediate-stimulus problem than in the two-stimulus problem, and therefore a reward is more likely to reinforce an incorrect hypothesis in the intermediate-stimulus problem than in the two-stimulus problem. Furthermore, the elimination of any one incorrect hypothesis through nonreinforcement is relatively less important in the intermediate-stimulus problem than in the two-stimulus problem, because of the greater number of alternative incorrect hypotheses in the intermediate-stimulus problem. The intermediate-stimulus problem, then, should be more difficult to solve than the two-stimulus problem.

The other theories seem to generate no prediction about this effect.

AMOUNT OF TRANSPOSITION

There is more transposition in the two-stimulus problem than in the intermediate-stimulus problem. (Compare, for example, Tables 4-6 and 4-8.) Furthermore, Baumeister *et al.* (1964) and Zeiler (1965b) obtained more transposition in children on three-stimulus problems with an extreme stimulus positive than with the intermediate stimulus positive, and Stevenson and Weiss (1955) obtained the same effect in college students on a four-stimulus problem (but only when the transposition test was given twenty-four hours after the end of training).

Spence's theory predicts transposition in two-stimulus problems and in problems with more than two stimuli provided an extreme stimulus is positive. His theory predicts that transposition will not occur in intermediate-stimulus problems. Since intermediate-stimulus transposition occurs, the theory predicts the direction of the obtained difference but not the obtained level of transposition.

Gestalt theory can predict the obtained effects, in the same way that it can predict the difference in speed of learning the initial discriminations. The probability of perceiving the two-stimulus relation and extreme-stimulus relation is greater than the probability of perceiving the intermediate-stimulus relation, and therefore relational responses are more probable on the two-stimulus and extreme-stimulus transposition tests than on the intermediate-stimulus transposition test.

The hypothesis models have no direct implications about the amounts of transposition to be expected in the two kinds of problems.

Washburn's "generalization" hypothesis suggests that there should be more intermediate-stimulus transposition than two-stimulus transposition on the Near Test. On the Near Test in the intermediate-stimulus problem, two of the three training stimuli are retained and one new stimulus is introduced, representing only a 33 per cent change in the total situation. On the Near Test in the two-stimulus problem, only one training stimulus is retained and one new stimulus is introduced, representing a 50 per cent change in the total situation. The relatively smaller change in the intermediate-stimulus problem should be less readily noticeable than the change in the two-stimulus problem, producing more transposition in the intermediate-stimulus problem. The obtained effect is directly opposite to this expectation.

There is another possible explanation of the finding. In the two-stimulus transposition test, there are two possible choices, and random responding would yield 50 per cent transposition. In the intermediate-stimulus trans-postion test, there are three possible choices, and random responding would yield 33 per cent transposition. Random responding would therefore spuriously inflate two-stimulus transposition scores more than intermediate-stimulus transposition scores. This source of the difference may be a relatively important one, because subjects who do not transpose in the two-stimulus problem usually shift to random responses, but subjects who do not transpose in the intermediate-stimulus problem usually shift to absolute responses (see below). (Responding at random with respect to the relevant cues results from responding consistently to some irrelevant cue such as position, as several theorists have pointed out [for example, Krechevsky, 1932a; Krechevsky, 1932b; Krechevsky, 1932c; Lashley, 1929a].)

Absolute Responses

In general, absolute responses do not predominate over transposition responses at any distance in the two-stimulus problem, except under unusual conditions. However, absolute responses are usually predominant in the intermediate-stimulus problem when transposition fails to occur. Spence's theory incorrectly predicts that absolute responses will be predominant at intermediate distances in two-stimulus problems, and incorrectly predicts absolute responses at all distances, even at one step, in intermediate-stimulus problems. Gulliksen and Wolfle's theory correctly predicts that absolute responses will not predominate in the two-stimulus problem. Whether or not the same prediction would be made in the intermediate-stimulus problem has not been determined, because the theory has not been extended to the intermediate-stimulus problem. The theories of Householder and James also predict random responses in the two-stimulus problem when transposition fails to occur and do not deal with the intermediate-stimulus problem. Lashley's theory could probably predict the same effect, although Lashley did not discuss the phenomenon.

The finding for the two-stimulus problem may be inconsistent with Gestalt theory. Köhler said that when the absolute habit is lost, the relative habit replaces it; if the converse is true, then when the relative habit is lost, the absolute habit will replace it. However, if the absolute habit has already been lost, random responses would presumably be expected. The finding for the intermediate-stimulus problem would be consistent with Gestalt theory if the absolute habit is assumed to replace the relative habit, but a single set of assumptions cannot account for the findings of both problems.

Zeiler's theory predicts the obtained effect in the intermediate-stimulus problem but did not deal with two-stimulus transposition.

Measurement

(a) "Consistent" and "predominant" transposition are less than mean transposition. Presumably mean transposition scores are inflated by "chance" transposition responses.

(b) The trends relating intermediate-stimulus transposition to independent variables are essentially the same when different measures of transposition are used. However, the trends in two-stimulus problems may be different when different measures are used.

(c) When only transposition responses are rewarded, there is more transposition on combined test trials than on the first test trial, except when there is a ceiling effect. This finding is not particularly interesting, because it obviously results from relearning.

(d) When all test-trial responses are rewarded, there is usually more transposition on combined test trials than on the first test trial, and more on later trials than on early ones, but the difference is sometimes reversed (at least in two-stimulus problems). Whether an increase or decrease occurs is not a function of problem difficulty, but what it is a function of is as yet unknown. Only James's theory explains the increase, and only for two-stimulus problems. The theory does not explain why there is sometimes a decrease.

(e) Individual differences tend to be relatively small, except when intermittent reinforcement is given (instead of continuous reinforcement), when the successive discrimination procedure is used (instead of the simultaneous discrimination procedure), when verbal pretraining is given (instead of no pretraining), and when multidimensional stimuli are used (instead of unidimensional stimuli).

Stimulus Similarity

Increasing stimulus similarity increases transposition, especially on the Near Test. Washburn's hypothesis can explain the increase in transposition with increasing stimulus similarity, since the change in absolute characteristics of the stimuli is smaller, the more similar the stimuli are, and the change should therefore be more likely to be unnoticed by the subject, the more similar the stimuli are.

Gestalt theory could explain the effect of stimulus similarity by extending somewhat Koffka's "crickets and sixteen-inch guns" analogy, but the Gestalt theorists never explicitly made the extension. Koffka was undoubtedly correct in saying that two stimuli can be so different from one another that the relation between them is not readily perceptible. By extension, it might be expected that as the difference between two stimuli is reduced (to some limit), the likelihood of perceiving the relation increases.

Spence's theory can predict the effect of stimulus similarity obtained in the two-stimulus problem, but it can also predict the opposite effect by making appropriate changes in the values of the constants in the generalization equations. The theory predicts no transposition in the intermediate-stimulus problem, and therefore the effect obtained in this problem contradicts the prediction.

The theory of Gulliksen and Wolfle specifically predicts the effect obtained in the two-stimulus problem, and apparently would predict the same effect in the intermediate-stimulus problem, although Gulliksen and Wolfle did not present the equations required for the latter prediction and I have not considered it worth while to derive them (because of the necessary assumption of directional responses, which is untenable).

Riley's theory predicts the effects, because the ratio of each stimulus to the ground changes less in the shift from training to test when the stimuli are similar than when they are distinctive, and the amount of change in the ratio is inversely related to transposition.

James's theory, which dealt only with the two-stimulus problem, could predict the effect by selectively changing the equations, but the effect was not specifically predicted. Zeiler's theory of intermediate-stimulus transposition can also predict the effect by making appropriate adjustments in the parameters of the equations, but with other adjustments it could predict the opposite result.

Hunter's bivariant-stimulus theory can account for the effect in the two-stimulus problem, since it can be assumed that there would be more generalization of the absolute component when the stimuli are more similar. Whether or not the effect in the intermediate-stimulus problem would be predicted cannot be determined.

None of the other theories provides any basis for predicting the obtained effect.

Asymmetrical Stimulus Sets

It is possible to obtain any desired response on test trials in the intermediate-stimulus problem by selecting appropriate asymmetrical stimulus sets for the training and testing phases. Zeiler's (1963c) adaptation level theory of transposition provides the basis for selecting the stimulus sets (see Chapter 8), but for any given set of stimuli the theory may fail to predict accurately. It may be that the inaccurate predictions are for sets in which the subject ignores the extreme stimulus.

Effect of Absolute Stimulus Components

Absolute stimulus components can affect the performance of animal and human subjects, whether or not relational components have an effect.

Amount of Original Training

(a) In animals, two-stimulus transposition increases with overtraining. In children, two-stimulus transposition increases with moderate overtraining, but is reduced by prolonged overtraining. (b) Moderate overtraining has no effect on intermediate-size transposition in children.

Köhler (1929, p. 293) assumed that continued training fixes the learned habit more firmly in memory; therefore, if a relational habit is learned, the assumption implies that overtraining should increase transposition. The effect of moderate overtraining on two-stimulus transposition is consistent with this implication, but the effect of prolonged overtraining on two-stimulus transposition and the lack of an effect of moderate overtraining on intermediate-stimulus transposition contradict the implication.

Spence's theory predicts an effect of overtraining in the two-stimulus problem, but not the obtained effect. Provided that overtraining is assumed to increase habit strength and to have a negligible effect on inhibition, which is reasonable since few errors occur during overtraining, the theory predicts that transposition in the negative direction will increase with overtraining, but that transposition in the positive direction will decrease with overtraining. This prediction is not confirmed. The theory predicts that overtraining will have no effect on intermediate-stimulus transposition, because it predicts that no intermediate-stimulus transposition will occur.

Jackson suggested modifications of Spence's theory to account for the effects of overtraining in the two-stimulus problem, assuming that overtraining affects the generalization gradients. These modifications provide an explanation of the effects in the two-stimulus problem, but do not help explain the occurrence of intermediate-stimulus transposition. (See p. 63.)

None of the other theories dealt with the possible effects of overtraining. However, another possible explanation of the effects could be derived from a suggestion made by Rudel (1957, p. 295). Extending Klüver's (1933, p. 345) statement that "Every 'generalization' is at the same time a 'differentiation' . . . ," she proposed that "As differentiation proceeds, the identification of a stimulus is more firmly established, but this permits classification of the stimulus according to an ever-increasing number of attributes." The relevant material from Klüver's monograph is in a discussion of the Pavlovian concepts of "generalization" and "differentiation" (Klüver, pp. 344–349), but it appears that both Klüver and Rudel misinterpreted these concepts. Pavlov considered generalization to be a transitory phenomenon resulting from the "irradiation" of nervous impulses, diminishing with the passage of time as a result of "concentration," an active process antagonistic to irradiation. "Differentiation" results from differential conditioning ("go–no-go" successive discrimination), in which one stimulus, which is always associated with reinforcement, acquires excitatory strength, and another stimulus, always associated with nonreinforcement, acquires inhibitory strength. (Pavlov believed that the method of presenting the conditioned stimulus a great number of times, always with reinforcement, and never presenting the negative stimulus, is inefficacious as a technique of obtaining differentiation.) (See Pavlov, 1927, Lectures 7, 9, 10; pp. 110–130 and 152–187.) The decrease in the strength of the generalized response with increasing separation on the stimulus continuum between the conditioned stimulus and the test stimulus, and the eventual limit of generalization, are therefore not necessarily products of differentiation, contrary to Klüver's apparent assumption; and generalization does not refer to the identification of more stimulus attributes, contrary to the implication of Rudel's suggestion.

The foregoing analysis cannot be used as a basis for rejecting Rudel's suggestion, nor its possible application to the problem of explaining the effect of overtraining on transposition, but only for rejecting the implication that the processes she suggested are related to generalization and differentiation in the Pavlovian senses. However, the hypothesis requires elaboration to explain why classification on the basis of irrelevant attributes, which are inevitably present in the stimuli, does not occur and disrupt transposition.

Reward

Two-stimulus discrimination learning is faster and transposition is greater in children when candy is used as the reward than when nonconsumables are used. Candy appears to have a greater incentive value for children than nonconsumables, although Brackbill and Jack (1958) found equal preferences for candy, marbles, and plastic trinkets in kindergarten children, and Screven (1959, footnote 3, p. 464) referred to pilot work showing candy and marbles to be equally effective incentives. Witryol and Fischer (1960) found that bubble gum was preferred over nonconsumables, but they mentioned further data, "not completely analyzed," showing bubble gum to be displaced by charms and money (p. 473). If consumables are the preferred incentives, then it appears that their use facilitates learning and transposition. There appears to be a positive but weak relation between speed of learning and amount of transposition (see section entitled "Speed of Original Learning," Chapter 5), which could explain the apparent effect of the incentive on transposition; but alternatively, the effect might be more indirect. The minimum age of the subjects in the relevant studies was four years, and since by this age children generally possess the required concepts for the two-stimulus problem (see section entitled "Concept Knowledge," Chapter 5), it is possible that increased incentive motivation produced by preferred rewards increases the likelihood that the subject will verbalize the solution of the problem, yielding faster learning and greater transposition (and more rewards, as the subject probably believes). There is also evidence (Witryol, Lowden, and Fagan, 1966) that the probability of attending to a cue is related to the incentive value of the reward associated with the cue. High incentive values more quickly direct the subject's attention to the relevant cues than do low incentive values, and might lead more quickly to the discovery of the relevant relational cues.

Spence's theory has no direct implications about how varying the incentive-value of rewards should affect transposition, but the K variable, which is a function of incentive magnitude, might be added to his transposition theory. The K variable combines with other motives to determine drive level, and drive multiplies the differences between excitatory potentials. Assume that for S_A, the stimulus more similar to the positive training stimulus, habit strength is 80 units and inhibition is 40 units; and

TABLE 10–1

PREDICTED EFFECT OF INCENTIVE MAGNITUDE ON TWO-STIMULUS TRANSPOSITION[a]

	Values of E	
Item	With small K	With large K
S_A	80	120
S_T	100	150
$\bar{E}$	$+20$	$+30$

[a] $E = (D + K)H - I.$ $\bar{E} = E_T - E_A.$ If $\bar{E} > 0$, transposition occurs; if $\bar{E} < 0$, absolute responses occur. See text for other assumptions.

for S_T, the transposition stimulus, habit is 70 units and inhibition is 20 units. Then if general drive level is one unit, and for a small incentive value K is one unit, and for a large incentive value K is two units, the effective excitatory potential, E, would take the values shown in Table 10–1. With increasing K, transposition is predicted to increase.

Multiple-Problem Training

(a) Multiple-problem training generally enhances transposition. (b) The effect is greater when the stimulus sets used in the training problems are widely separated on the stimulus continuum (Gonzalez-Ross procedure) than when they are close together (Johnson-Zara procedure). (c) The effect is greater when the set of test stimuli falls between the sets of training stimuli on the stimulus continuum than when it does not. These generalizations are stated somewhat too broadly, since limitations are ignored. The limitations are discussed in the section entitled "Multiple-Problem Training," Chapter 3.

It might be thought that the Washburn (1926) generalization hypothesis accounts for the Gonzalez and Ross data, since it can explain the published results; but unpublished data obtained by these investigators are inconsistent with this interpretation. According to Washburn, transposition results from a failure to recognize the change in stimuli between the training and test phases. Training was continued in the Gonzalez and Ross study until the subject gave 10 consecutive correct responses, including 5 to each set of training stimuli. The distance between the last training set experienced and the test set was great (five steps), but it could be assumed that the subject would not discriminate between the test set and the penultimate training set.[1] In the experimental group, in which the middle-sized stimulus was correct in each training set, the response would be a "transposition" response. In the control group, in which the largest stimulus was correct in one training set and the smallest one was correct in the other training set, the test response would be to the stimulus having a relative size the same as the relative size of the correct stimulus in the penultimate training set. Eleven of fifteen subjects in the experimental group transposed, and only three subjects in the control group gave the transposition response (both results contradict absolute theory). Six of the control subjects gave the response predicted by the Washburn hypothesis, and the other seven gave the other response. The Washburn interpretation is clearly not supported by these additional data.

The control condition used by Gonzalez and Ross required the subject to learn to choose the smallest stimulus in one three-stimulus set and then to choose the largest stimulus in the second set. The subjects were three to five years old, and could be assumed to have the concepts of "small" and "large" (see section entitled "Concept Knowledge," Chapter 5). The training sets were separated by a distance of 10 steps, but if the basis of solution of the first training problem were verbal, the second problem would be a reversal problem. If verbalization had no effect, the learning of the second problem would not be affected by stimulus generalization from the first problem, since the distance was so great, but it would be facilitated by learning-set formation. (Reese [1965a] has shown that the learning set can be acquired in one problem learned to criterion.) The saving in learning speed on Problem 2 in the control subjects was only 6 per cent, but the saving in the experimental group, for which both problems required choice of the middle-sized stimulus, was 56 per cent, indicating that Problem 2 was a reversal problem for the control group and implying that the subjects possessed the two relevant concepts and used them. If the subjects possessed these concepts, the experimental subjects, who were selected for lacking the concept of middle-sizedness, could nevertheless have had a verbal basis of responding, since "not big and not little" can replace "middle-sized" (Reese, 1966). It is suggested, then, that the subjects had a verbal basis of responding, and that they recognized that the test set of stimuli was different from both training sets. However, the experimental group had

---

[1] I obtained an effect like this with preschool children in an unpublished study of two-stimulus successive discrimination learning, varying the frequency of presentation of the two stimuli (2 to 1 area ratio of stimuli, 2 to 1 ratio of stimulus presentations). On test trials with a stimulus intermediate in area, the response appropriate for the more frequently presented training stimulus was predicted, but the subjects tended to give the response appropriate for the training stimulus penultimate to the test stimulus. When the predicted response and the "alternation" response were identical, 71 per cent of the responses were of the kind predicted, but when the predicted response and the alternation response conflicted, only 40 per cent of the responses were as predicted.

learned to give the same response to two sets of stimuli during training, and would be expected to transfer this response to the new set; but the control group had learned to respond differently to the two training sets, and might well give a new response to the new set, responding at random on the test. The previously unreported data of the study, given in Table 10–2, support this interpretation only if it is assumed that there was also a preference for the smallest test stimulus. The source of such a preference, if it exists, is unknown.

TABLE 10–2

TEST-TRIAL DATA OF THE CONTROL GROUPS OF THE GONZALEZ AND ROSS STUDY[a,b]

| Group | Positive stimuli in training sets | | Penultimate training set | Frequency of choice on first test trial | | |
	1, 2, 3	11, 12, 13		Small	Middle	Large
A	3	11	11, 12, 13	2[c]	1	1
			1, 2, 3	2	1	1[c]
B	1	13	11, 12, 13	3	0	1[c]
			1, 2, 3	2[c]	1	1

[a]Previously unpublished data, kindly provided by Dr. Gonzalez.
[b]The italicized numbers 1 through 13 designate the stimuli in order of increasing size. The test stimuli were 6, 7, and 8 (small, middle, and large).
[c]Response predicted by interpretation based on Washburn hypothesis.

Opportunity for Comparison

Restriction of the opportunity to compare stimuli during training reduces transposition, presumably because it reduces the probability of relation perception.

Disruptive Effects of the Tests

Giving transposition tests has a disruptive effect on performance. This effect is manifested on retraining trials given after the tests, and on the tests themselves. Performance on the retraining trials and on the tests, including Near Tests, is below the criterional level attained by the end of the training phase. If it is assumed that at least some of the subjects notice the change in stimuli, then Washburn's hypothesis can account for the drop in the performance level. Perkins and Wheeler (1930, p. 47) suggested a similar explanation, and although it was not taken up by other Gestalt psychologists, it can be counted as part of Gestalt theory.

Spence's theory can predict that the performance level will drop, but it can also predict an increase by selecting appropriate values for the constants in the prediction equations. It predicts too large a drop for the intermediate-stimulus problem.

Delay

(a) Short delays between the end of the training phase and the beginning of the testing phase increase transposition. The effect is more pronounced when the probability of transposition is low with immediate testing. (b) Long delays may reduce transposition, probably because of forgetting.

Washburn's hypothesis explains the effect of delay between the end of training and the beginning of testing, since the delay should make the change in stimuli less noticeable, increasing transposition. Furthermore, the effect of delay is greater when other factors tend to make the change more noticeable on immediate tests.

Gestalt theory specifically dealt with the effect of delay, and explained it as a result of greater retention of the relational habit than of the absolute habit.

Spence's theory did not deal with this kind of delay, nor did any of the other theories.

Distance

(a) Two-stimulus transposition decreases with increasing distance, except that it increases again at extreme distances. Absolute responses do not predominate at any distance in the two-stimulus problem, except under unusual conditions. (b) Intermediate-stimulus transposition does not occur beyond one-half step in infrahuman subjects, except under unusual conditions, and does not occur beyond one step in children, except at extreme distances, as a result of mediation, and under unusual conditions. Absolute responses predominate when transposition does not occur.

Since the number of subjects who notice the change in stimuli should increase with increasing distance, Washburn's hypothesis predicts the distance effect in both kinds of problem (excluding tests at extreme distances).

The Gestalt theorists never explicitly predicted the distance effect, but as pointed out in Chapter 8, Köhler made assumptions from which the prediction can be derived. However, the distance effect in the inter-mediate-stimulus problem seems to be too precipitous to be considered consistent with these assumptions.

Spence's theory predicts the shape of the gradient relating two-stimulus transposition to distance, but not the obtained levels of transposition; and the occurrence of intermediate-stimulus transposition on tests even one-half step from the training stimuli contradicts Spence's theory.

Gulliksen and Wolfle, Riley, James, and Zeiler all predicted the distance effect; and as indicated in Chapter 9, the theories of Lashley, Hebb, and

Householder could easily be extended to predict it in the two-stimulus problem. The other theories did not deal with it.

Only mediation theory dealt systematically with human subjects who know the verbal concepts required for mediation, compared with human subjects lacking these concepts. The theoretical explanation of the distance effect in "verbal" subjects is discussed in Chapter 8 (section entitled "Mediation Theory"), and need not be repeated here.

The increase in two-stimulus transposition at extreme distances was predicted by Spence's theory, although the levels of transposition obtained at extreme distances are greater than Spence's theory predicted. The obtained trend contradicts all of the other theories that predicted a distance effect. The increase in intermediate-stimulus transposition at extreme distances is inconsistent with all of the theories.

Effect of Direction of Transposition Test

(a) There is more two-stimulus transposition upward than downward, especially when both tests are in the positive direction, but also when both are in the negative direction.

(b) When both tests in the two-stimulus problem are in the upward direction, there is no consistent difference between negative and positive transposition; but when both tests are in the downward direction, there is more negative than positive transposition.

(c) There is more two-stimulus transposition in the negative direction upward than in the positive direction downward, and more negative downward than positive upward.

(d) There is more intermediate-stimulus transposition downward than upward.

Neither Washburn nor the Gestalt theorists dealt with the effects of testing in the positive and negative directions; but since there seems to be no good reason to assume that the change in one direction would be any more noticeable than the change in the other, the obtained effect is not consistent with Washburn's hypothesis; and since there seems to be no good reason to assume that the direction of testing should affect the probability of relation perception, the effect also contradicts Gestalt theory. Spence's theory predicts the direction of the obtained effect, but not necessarily the obtained amounts of transposition. James's theory seems to predict more positive transposition than negative transposition. None of the other theories has any implications about the positive–negative direction of testing.

Neither Washburn nor the Gestalt theorists dealt with the effects of shifting the stimuli upward and downward on the stimulus continuum; but there is no reason to assume any effect in these theories, and the obtained effect therefore is inconsistent with these theories. Spence's theory can predict the effect obtained in the two-stimulus problem, on the basis of Hull's stimulus intensity dynamism; but the apparent effect on intermediate-stimulus transposition is inconsistent with the theory. No other theory dealt with the effect of this variable.

Multiple Tests

Transposition tends to increase over a series of tests. When only trans-position responses are rewarded on a series of tests, the increase in trans-position that is obtained can be explained in the same way as the effect of multiple-problem training. Even when all responses on the tests are rewarded, the same explanations could be used if it were assumed that there is some source of differential reinforcement of the absolute and relative cues. This source might be, for example, the intrinsic reward in discovering that one kind of cue occurs consistently.

Effect of Noticing Change in Stimuli from Training to Test

Transposition usually occurs when the subject does not recognize the change in stimuli, but it often occurs even when some change is apparently noticed.

All psychological theories assume that behavior may be directly in-fluenced by sensed or "effective" stimuli, but can be influenced by external or "potential" stimuli only to the extent that they determine the effective stimuli. If two situations are objectively different, but produce the same effective cues, the situations are psychologically identical and must arouse the same response, not as a result of generalization on the basis of stimulus similarity or identical elements or any other basis, and not as a result of any other kind of transfer. The equivalence of the situations is a result of a kind of illusion, which may be a product of inattentiveness to the dif-ferences between the situations or of limited sensory analyzing capacities. Therefore, the finding that transposition occurs in subjects who fail to notice the change in the situations, or to "see," "recognize," "perceive," or "discriminate" the change, is consistent with all of the theories.

However, transposition sometimes occurs in subjects who apparently do recognize some change in the situation, and this finding contradicts Washburn's hypothesis. It is consistent with Gestalt theory, which predicts transposition on the basis of relative cues even when the change in absolute cues is recognized. It is consistent with Spence's theory, which predicts two-stimulus transposition on the basis of generalization of responses to absolute cues, and which predicts no intermediate-stimulus transposition. The closeness of agreement between expected and obtained levels of intermediate-stimulus transposition is better for Spence's theory than for

Gestalt theory, since this kind of transposition does not normally occur beyond one step.

Speed of Original Learning

There is a positive relation between learning speed and transposition, but it appears to be possible to reverse the relation. No theory ever predicted that the speed of solving the initial discrimination would influence the amount of transposition obtained, but no theorist ever considered the possibility that it might.

Concept Knowledge

(a) Concept knowledge facilitates two-stimulus transposition in older children, but sometimes has no effect in younger children. (b) Concept knowledge generally facilitates intermediate-stimulus transposition, but sometimes the effect is weak. Only mediation theory dealt with these effects; and the theory is discussed at length in Chapter 8 (section entitled "Mediation Theory").

Age

Older children transpose somewhat more than younger children. Only Köhler, among the transposition theorists, speculated about the effect of age on transposition, and his speculation has not been supported. Increasing age appears to have either no effect or a slight enhancing effect on transposition, but Köhler suggested that older human subjects would transpose less, and give more absolute responses, because of their better powers of discrimination and retention.

Intelligence

There is a positive relation between intelligence and transposition, but it is probably a weak relation. The only investigators who expected an effect of intelligence on transposition based the expectation on the assumption that mentally retarded subjects would be deficient in verbal skills or concept knowledge, and would therefore transpose less than normal subjects. The underlying assumption seems to be supported.

Sex Differences

(a) After single-problem training, preschool girls transpose somewhat more than preschool boys on the Near Test, but transpose somewhat less than boys on Far Tests. (b) After multiple-problem training, girls transpose more than boys on Far Tests. Only Caron dealt theoretically with sex differences, and he predicted differences on the basis of differences in concept knowledge. The data do not seem to be attributable to sex differences in the use of available mediators.

Phylogenetic Comparisons

Two-stimulus transposition has been obtained in every species tested, but intermediate-stimulus transposition is rarely obtained. The Gestalt theorists believed that relation perception is fundamental and primitive, and therefore the lack of any demonstrated phylogenetic differences in transposition agrees with the theory. No other theory has implications about possible phylogenetic differences below the human level.

Absolute versus Relative Discrimination Problems

(a) The absolute discrimination problem is harder to solve than the relative discrimination problem; but it can be solved, and the solution is apparently based on absolute stimulus properties and not on combinations of relative properties. (b) Even on the relative discrimination problem, absolute properties have an effect on performance. The difference in difficulty is attributable to the occurrence of transposition between the stimulus sets; transposition facilitates performance on the relative discrimination problem and interferes with performance on the absolute discrimination problem. The relative discrimination is harder to learn than the standard simultaneous discrimination, presumably because transposition in the relative discrimination problem is less than perfect and interfering absolute responses sometimes transfer between the stimulus sets.

Form Transposition

The studies of form transposition suggest that (a) subjects tend to respond to stimulus elements rather than to wholes; (b) even young children can respond to relations, but are likely to ignore relational cues; (c) perceptual training can increase the probability of responding to relational cues; and (d) transfer can be mediated by nonverbal cues in addition to verbal cues.

CHAPTER 11

Outline of a New Theory of Transposition

Assumptions and Basic Deductions

TWO-STIMULUS PROBLEMS

(1) If stimulus differences are not too small or too large, the stimulus relations are potential cues. (Transition points may depend on such subject variables as visual acuity, age level, and motivation, and on such stimulus variables as dimension—for example, differences on "prothetic" dimensions are more likely to be sensed as relations than are differences on "metathetic" dimensions [see section entitled "Stimulus Similarity," Chapter 3]—sensory modality affected, and absolute intensity levels.)

(2) A potential relative cue can be an effective cue if and only if comparison occurs in a vigilant or attentive subject.

(3) The orienting reflex occurs during the learning phase. It includes vigilance or attention and comparison behavior or scanning.[1]

(4) When the orienting reflex occurs, the approach response is inhibited until the total situation has been scanned. Therefore, the potential relative cue becomes an effective cue whenever the orienting reflex occurs.

(5) An "absolute" cue is only "more or less definite" (Köhler, 1929, pp. 303–304); it is also absolute relative to the surround or adaptation level.

(6) Absolute cues can always become effective cues.

(7) (a) Subjects learn to respond to any effective cue that is frequently associated with reward, and learn to inhibit response to any effective cue that is consistently associated with nonreward, in accordance with Hull-Spence theory. (b) Generalization of excitatory and inhibitory tendencies may occur between absolute cues and between relative cues.

Deduction (1). Given potential relative cues, it follows from Assumptions (2) through (7) that learning is based on absolute and relative cues.

(8) By the end of the learning phase, the orienting reflex has usually become adapted or inhibited.

Deduction (2). It follows from Assumptions (2) and (8) and Deduction

---

[1] Pavlov wrote of a "reaction of orientation" or "investigatory reflex," which is now called an "orienting reflex." It consists of physiological reactions and overt observing responses, and may include some kind of selective attention mechanism (Berlyne, 1960, Ch. 4; Berlyne, 1963, pp. 177–178; Milerian, 1954; Sokolov, 1955; Zaporozhets, 1955).

(1) that subjects usually respond only to absolute cues by the end of training.

(9) A change in the effective stimulating situation disinhibits the orienting reflex unless the change is smaller than some as yet unspecifiable threshold value.

(10) The magnitude of change in the effective stimulating situation increases with increasing magnitude of change in the objective situation. In the transposition situation, the magnitude of the objective change is greater on Far Tests than on the Near Test, and is greater with distinctive stimuli than with similar stimuli.

(11) If the change in the objective situation is not too great, the magnitude of the change in the effective situation is reduced by a delay between the original situation and the objectively changed situation. The effect may result from an effect of time on the adaptation level. After a delay, the adaptation level of the training situation is modified, and a new adaptation level is established in the test situation. Since the absolute cues are related to the adaptation level [by Assumption (5)], there must be less effect of a delayed change than of an immediate change.

(12) If the change in the effective situation is so small that there is no disinhibition of the orienting reflex, the effective absolute cues are the same as during training. (This is similar to the conclusion of Lashley and Wade [1946].)

The term "effective situation" in Assumptions (9) through (12) is not synonymous with "effective absolute cue." The effective situation is a compound in which elements are undifferentiated. [Therefore, Assumption (9) can be interpreted to mean that when the subject notices that the situation has changed in some unidentified way, he becomes vigilant or attentive.] Assumption (10) means that the perception of the "situation" is influenced by a compound of objective or potential absolute cues. However, a potential absolute cue is a relation, specifically a relation to the adaptation level [Assumption (5)]. The adaptation level is presumably determined by physical values of objective stimuli, in accordance with Zeiler's equation (see section entitled "Adaptation Level Theories," Chapter 8). Therefore, with greater changes in the adaptation level, changes in the physical values of the objective stimuli have less effect on the potential absolute cues, hence less effect on the objective situation, and finally less effect on the effective situation. Assumption (11) states that the adaptation level changes more when testing is delayed than when it is immediate. In terms of Zeiler's equation, the assumption is that x is reduced by delays.

Since effective absolute cues, in addition to the effective situation, are influenced by the potential absolute cues, Assumption (12) states in effect that if the compound of potential absolute cues does not change enough to bring about a noticeable change in the effective situation, then the individual potential absolute cues do not change enough to bring about noticeable changes in the individual effective absolute cues.

Deduction (*3*). It follows from Assumptions (9) through (12) and Deduction (2) that subjects may respond to a set of transposed stimuli as though it were identical to the set of training stimuli.

(13) If the orienting reflex is disinhibited, "primary stimulus generalization" occurs between the original absolute cues and the new absolute cues. The generalization gradients are assumed to be ogival. There are trial-to-trial variations in the effective absolute cues during training (see, for example, Guthrie, 1952, pp. 82–83; Hull, 1943, pp. 194–197; Spence, 1956, p. 40). The fluctuations of the absolute cue presumably result from variations in the environmental context in which the physical stimulus is presented, variations in the physical stimulus itself, and variations in the organismic variables affecting perception. However, the perceived absolute values should fluctuate around some mean value corresponding to an ideal absolute value. Then even if the theoretically correct generalization gradient were negatively accelerated downward (as shown in Fig. 9-3), the gradient obtained in practice would be ogival (as shown in Fig. 9-2). The extent of the initial positively accelerated decreasing section in the ogival gradient would depend on the extent of the trial-to-trial fluctuations.

(14) A modified form of Spence's (1960, Chapter 22) model of nonspatial discrimination is adopted. The model adopted is illustrated in Fig. 11-1. It is assumed that (a) receptor-orienting responses (r_L and r_R) expose one stimulus at a time. (b) If no response occurs during the refractory period of the receptor-orienting response, the subject will re-orient, exposing the other stimulus. (c) When the orienting reflex has been inhibited the probability, P_i, that the subject will respond while oriented toward compound i is the same as the probability that the latency of the approach response is shorter than the duration of the observing response which exposes the compound. Symbolically:

$$P_i = P[R_{L_i} < R_{o_i}] \tag{1}$$

where R_{L_i} is the response-evocation latency of compound i, and R_{o_i} is the duration of orientation to compound i. The latency of the approach response is a function of the momentary superthreshold effective excitatory potential $\dot{E}_L$; and although the function is not linear, the reciprocal of R_L is linearly related to $\dot{E}_L$, at least in the later stages of learning (Spence, 1956, p. 117). (d) When the orienting reflex has not been inhibited or has been disinhibited, the probability in Eq. (1) is assumed to be zero until both receptor-orienting responses have occurred.

The probability that the subject will eventually respond to compound *a*,

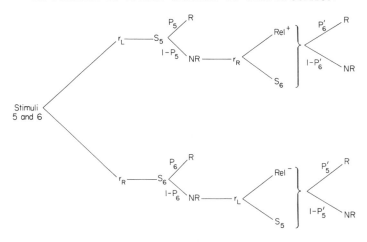

FIG. 11-1. Model of discriminative performance (one-step transposition test in positive direction): S_5 and S_6 are absolute cues; P_5 is the probability that S_5 will evoke a response before orientation changes; and P_6 is the analogous probability for S_6; P_5' and P_6' are the analogous probabilities when a relative cue is combined with an absolute cue. (Compare with Fig. 9-5, showing Spence's 1960 model.)

when compounds a and b are presented, is:

$$P_{R_a} = \frac{P_a(1 - .5P_b)}{P_a + P_b - P_a P_b} \qquad \text{(see Spence, 1960, Eq. 8, p. 386)} \qquad (2)$$

where P_a and P_b are defined as in Eq. (1).

The value of P_i in Eq. (1) is the probability that the $\overline{E}_L$ of compound i will exceed the value of E that will just elicit a response before orientation changes. This threshold value of E can be taken into account in the equation for $\overline{E}_L$:

$$\dot{\overline{E}}_{L_i} = \overline{E}_i - L - I_o$$

where $\overline{E}_i = D(H + \overline{H}) - I - \overline{I}$, L is the threshold value, and I_o is "oscillatory inhibition." (The other symbols represent drive level and conditioned and generalized habit or inhibition.) The value of I_o varies from moment to moment, following a normal distribution with a range of ± 2.5 standard errors; and the other values are constant. If the fixed values could be estimated, and a value of the standard error of I_o were assumed, it would be possible to compute P_i. Since $\overline{E}_L$ is assumed to be normally distributed (because I_o is normally distributed), values of $\dot{\overline{E}}_L$ could be transformed into unit normal deviates, and corresponding probabilities could be obtained from the normal-distribution table. Since, furthermore, $\overline{E}_L$ is linearly related to response speed, these probabilities would correspond to the values of P_i. The equation for transforming the $\bar{E}_L$ values into z values is:

$$z_i = \frac{\bar{E}_i - L - 2.5\sigma_{I_o}}{\sigma_{I_o}} \ . \tag{3}$$

When the stimulus compound includes both absolute and relative cues, it is necessary to make some assumption about the way the elements combine in determining the excitatory potential of the compound. One could assume Hull's (1943) principle of "afferent neural interaction," which stated: "All afferent neural impulses (s) active in the nervous system at any given instant, interact with each other in such a way as to change into something partially different ($\check{s}$) in a manner that varies with every concurrent associated afferent impulse or combination of impulses" (p. 47). This assumption would be consistent with the Gestalt principle that the nature of the relation affects the perception of the absolute elements.

Spiker (1963a) noted that the principle of afferent neural interaction had stimulated little research and had not been utilized theoretically—Spence, for example, never utilized the principle in his theorizing—and Spiker suggested that this neglect is largely attributable to the quasi-physiological form in which Hull stated the principle. Osgood (1953, pp. 211–212) considered the major problem to be the lack of a quantitative expression of the principle. Spiker proposed a mathematically formulated principle, designated the "stimulus interaction hypothesis," to account for the kinds of phenomena which the principle of afferent neural interaction was designed to explain.

I found that when I used Spiker's equations to derive predictions from my theory, the predictions were essentially the same as when I simply added the E values of the absolute and relative components without assuming stimulus interaction. Therefore, in the deductions that follow, I have used the less complicated equations, assuming in effect that stimulus interaction is negligible in the transposition situation.

Deductions about Transposition

Deduction (4). *Near Test in the Positive Direction.* If the orienting reflex is not disinhibited, perfect transposition occurs. If the orienting reflex is disinhibited, both absolute cues will usually tend to evoke the approach response, but the negative relative cue will reduce the probability of the response to the positive training stimulus (the absolute response) and the positive relative cue will increase the probability of the transposition response. Therefore, transposition will usually occur. "Usually" refers to the usual transposition experiment, in which the stimulus differences are not extreme. If the differences are extreme, the originally positive stimulus will tend to evoke the approach response, and the new stimulus will be beyond the range of stimulus generalization and will therefore have no tendency to evoke the approach response. There will be no relative cues, by Assumption (1), and therefore only absolute responses should occur.

Deduction (5). Near Test in the Negative Direction. If the orienting reflex is not disinhibited, perfect transposition occurs. If the orienting reflex is disinhibited, the probability that the originally negative stimulus will evoke the approach response will be low. The new stimulus will also have a low probability of evoking the response; therefore, the response will be determined primarily by the relative cues, and a high level of transposition should be obtained. There should, therefore, be more negative transposition than positive transposition on the Near Test.

Deduction (6). Far Tests in the Positive Direction. Let the absolute cues on a Far Test be designated S_N and S_F; S_N is the absolute cue that is more similar to the positive absolute cue of the training phase, and S_F is the more extreme absolute cue. The orienting reflex will usually be disinhibited on Far Tests. At two or three steps, the response-evocation potential of S_N will be greater than the response-evocation potential of S_F. (The constants of the generalization equation can be adjusted to generate this effect.) The probability of the absolute response will be reduced by the effect of the negative relative cue, and the probability of the transposition response will be increased by the effect of the positive relative cue. The probability of the transposition response will be greater than the probability of the absolute response, but will be less than on the Near Test. As distance increases, a point is reached at which the probabilities of the two kinds of responses are equal, and random responses occur. At this point, the response-evocation potential of S_N combined with the negative relative cue is equal to the response-evocation potential of S_F and the positive relative cue, and the response-evocation potential of S_F alone is near zero. At greater distances, the response-evocation potential of S_N also diminishes to zero, and transposition increases because only the relative cues affect behavior. Therefore, transposition should decrease from the Near Test to moderately Far Tests, reach the "chance" level, then increase again with further increase in distance.

Deduction (7). Far Tests in the Negative Direction. As shown in Table 11-1 it is possible to generate generalization gradients such that the net response-evocation potentials of the absolute cues on negative transposition tests are negative in value (that is, such that there is more generalized inhibitory potential than generalized excitatory potential). Furthermore, on Far Tests, the net "inhibitory" potential of S_N is greater than the net "inhibitory" potential of S_F. The combined response-evocation potential of S_F and the negative

TABLE 11–1
HYPOTHETICAL VALUES OF GENERALIZED HABIT AND
INHIBITION AND NET RESPONSE-EVOCATION POTENTIAL[a]

Stimulus	Habit	Inhibition	Net response-evocation potential
1	0	2	−2
2	0	18	−18
3	3	48	−45
4 (−)	54	60	−6
5 (+)	100	48	52
6	54	18	36
7	3	2	1
8	0	0	0
9	0	0	0

[a] Net response-evocation potential equals habit minus inhibition. Values derived from Spence's (1942) equations with modified constants.

relative cue and the combined response-evocation potential of S_N and the positive relative cue are both negative at some distance, as illustrated in Table 11-2; and at that distance, random responses should occur. (In deriving the values given in Table 11-2, it was assumed that the habit and inhibitory strengths of the relative cues were half as great as the strengths of the absolute cues, because the absolute cues are effective throughout training, but the relative cues are effective in only part of the training phase.) Beyond that distance, the net "inhibitory" potentials diminish, and

TABLE 11–2
HYPOTHETICAL NET RESPONSE-EVOCATION POTENTIALS ON
TWO-STIMULUS TRANSPOSITION TESTS[a]

Stimuli	Distance (steps)	Direction	Smaller stimulus	Larger stimulus	Predicted response
8, 9	4	Positive	−3	26	Larger
7, 8	3	Positive	−2	26	Larger
6, 7	2	Positive	33	27	Random
5, 6	1	Positive	49	62	Larger
4, 5	0	(Training)	—	—	—
3, 4	1	Negative	−48	20	Larger
2, 3	2	Negative	−21	−19	Random
1, 2	3	Negative	−5	8	Larger

[a] Values from Table 11–1. Assumed that net response-evocation potential of negative relative cue is half as great as for S_4, and net response-evocation potential of positive relative cue is half as great as for S_5; and assumed that net potential of combined absolute cue and relative cue is sum of individual potentials.

the frequency of transposition responses should increase. When the absolute cues exert less effect on the net response-evocation potential, the relative cues exert relatively more influence. Therefore, transposition should decrease from the Near Test to moderately Far Tests, reach the chance level, then increase with further increase in distance.

INTERMEDIATE-STIMULUS PROBLEMS

(15) The probability that an intermediate-stimulus relation will become an effective cue is usually low.

(16) This probability can be increased by increasing the probability that the subject will attend to the potential relative cue. The latter probability can be increased by (a) making the relation a type-*a* cue, in Restle's (1958) sense (see section entitled "Multiple-Problem Training," this chapter), or (b) verbalizing about the relation—either spontaneously by the subject or in instructions by the experimenter.

(17) Multiple-problem training makes the relation a type-*a* cue, and also maintains the orienting reflex. It might be assumed that the frequent changes in the stimulus sets prevent the inhibition or adaptation of the orienting reflex or keep disinhibiting the orienting reflex.

Deduction (8). In the usual intermediate-stimulus transposition problem, transposition occurs only if the orienting reflex is not disinhibited by the change in stimulating situations. The subject responds to the transposed stimuli as though they were the training stimuli in this case, and transposes. If the orienting reflex is disinhibited, then absolute responses must occur, because only absolute cues control behavior.

COMMENT

Although the predicted effects seem to correspond fairly well with the obtained effects,[2] it does not seem to be worth while to attempt to derive precise predictions from the model, because so many arbitrary decisions are required. For example, (a) are the excitatory and inhibitory potentials of the relative cues equal to those of the absolute cues? (b) Is generalization between relative cues described by the same equations as generalization between absolute cues? (c) Is the difference between the relative cues equal to the difference between the absolute cues?

Furthermore, the occurrence of selective attention would modify the predictions, through at least two effects. First, attention theory assumes that selective attention affects the amount of habit and inhibition acquired

---

[2] The theory as outlined so far predicts somewhat too much Near Test transposition in the negative direction and somewhat too little in the positive direction. A mechanism that corrects these errors is discussed later, in the section entitled "Disruptive Effects of the Tests."

by the elements during the training phase.[3] Presumably, the absolute and relative cues could acquire quite different excitatory potentials as a result of selective attention to one or the other component of the stimuli. Second, selective attention would presumably affect the relative contribution of each kind of cue to the net response-evocation potentials. The first effect can be taken into account in the theory outlined above by adjusting the assumed values of habit and inhibition in the equations. The second effect can be taken into account by using a weighted sum of the component excitatory potentials instead of an unweighted sum. The less effective cue would add less to the net response-evocation potential than the more effective cue.

In the derivations discussed above, the probability that the orienting reflex would be disinhibited was assumed to be zero or one. If it is assumed to be continuous, then the mathematics of the theory become enormously complicated; and the theory could be made to generate any desired prediction by appropriate selection of various combinations of assumptions. The test of the theory, therefore, is to determine whether one set of assumptions that generates the desired prediction of one effect also generates the desired predictions of other effects.

The theory ignores the possibility that at extreme distances the relative cue may change. For example, the effective relation between stimuli that are one and two square inches in area may well be different from the effective relation between stimuli that are 1024 and 2048 square inches in area (a distance of 10 steps between the stimulus pairs). The implications of assuming that a change in the relative cue occurs at extreme distances is discussed later, in the section entitled "Multiple-Problem Training."

Other Deductions

EFFECT OF STIMULUS SIMILARITY

It follows from Assumption (10) that Near Test transposition should increase with increasing stimulus similarity, because of the reduction in the probability of disinhibiting the orienting reflex. It follows from the assumptions about generalization that when the orienting reflex is disinhibited, two-stimulus transposition at moderate distances should increase with increasing stimulus similarity, and intermediate-stimulus transposition

[3]Attentional mechanisms have been proposed by several theorists (for example, Berlyne, 1960, Ch. 3; Berlyne, 1965, pp. 43–44; Goodwin and Lawrence, 1955; Hebb, 1949, p. 4, etc.; House and Zeaman, 1962; House and Zeaman, 1963; Luria, 1961; Mackintosh, 1965a; McNamara and Fisch, 1964; Simon and Newell, 1962; Sutherland, 1964a; Sutherland, 1964b; Sutherland et al., 1963; Zeaman, 1959). See Spearman (1937a, pp. 133–147) for a brief history of the concept of attention in psychology.

should not be affected (since it is assumed that intermediate-stimulus relations are usually not effective cues).

EFFECT OF OVERTRAINING

Moderate overtraining may increase generalization, and prolonged overtraining may reduce generalization (see Kimble, 1961, pp. 335–337). If so, then the effect of moderate overtraining would be like the effect of increasing stimulus similarity, and the effect of prolonged overtraining would be like the effect of reducing stimulus similarity. The obtained effect of overtraining is consistent with this generalization. It may be that the effect of prolonged overtraining is further enhanced by strengthening the inhibition of the orienting reflex, making disinhibition less likely even on Far Tests. However, research on the orienting reflex indicates that repeatedly presenting a stimulus can increase the speed of habituation of the orienting reflex to a novel stimulus, but does not affect the probability that the novel stimulus will disinhibit the orienting reflex (Sokolov, 1960).

EFFECT OF INCENTIVE VALUE

In Spence's 1956 theory, incentives affect the motivational variable K through the conditioning of fractional anticipatory goal responses (r_g's) to the positive cues. The K variable affects excitatory potential by multiplying the habit strengths of the cues. The absolute cues present on a transposition test presumably have a generalized tendency to elicit fractional anticipatory goal responses; but without further assumptions about the nature of the generalization gradient, it would be impossible to determine what effect K would have on the excitatory potentials of these cues in the 1960 model. However, the positive relative cue would be associated with a much greater value of K than would the negative relative cue, and therefore the excitatory potential of the positive relative cue would be increased more by increasing incentive motivation than the excitatory potential of the negative relative cue would be. If the difference in the increase were great enough, then increasing incentive motivation would always increase two-stimulus transposition.

It may be that when highly valued incentives are used, subjects attend more closely to the cues, including both absolute and relative cues. Closer attention to the absolute cues might increase the probability that the novel stimulus introduced on a Near Test will disinhibit the orienting reflex, and therefore might reduce Near Test transposition. However, the effect should be small, because even when the orienting reflex is disinhibited, transposition is predicted at one step. On Far Tests there would be little effect, because the probability that the orienting reflex will be disinhibited is already high on Far Tests. In intermediate-stimulus problems, disinhibition of the orienting reflex on the Near Test would reduce transposition unless the closer attention to the cues resulted in relation perception. If the inter-mediate-stimulus relation became an effective cue during training with highly valued incentives, then transposition would occur on the Near Test and on Far Tests; and the effect on Far Test transposition would be greater than the effect on Near Test transposition, because Near Test transposition in a group trained with incentives of low value might occur as a result of failure to disinhibit the orienting reflex.

Opportunity for Comparison

It follows from Assumption (2) that facilitating the ease of stimulus comparisons should increase transposition by increasing the probability of relation perception.

Disruptive Effects of the Tests

It is known that both human and animal subjects have a tendency to approach novel stimuli (see Reese, 1963b; Reese, 1964a). This tendency would facilitate one-step transposition in the positive direction and interfere with one-step transposition in the negative direction. These effects would be obtained only if the orienting reflex were disinhibited, because otherwise it is assumed that there is no effective novel stimulus. As already noted in footnote 2 of this chapter, the equations seem to predict too much negative transposition at one step and too little positive transposition at one step. Adding the effect of the novel stimulus would increase the accuracy of the predictions, and would explain why the performance level tends to drop in the shift from the training phase to the one-step test phase. In the shift back to the training phase, the generalized effects of learning in the test phase would interfere with the originally learned discrimination.

Change in Transposition over Test Trials

H. James's (1953) theory of transposition predicted an increase in transposition over test trials because of a gradual change in the adaptation level. In effect, the change in adaptation level reduces the distance between the training and test sets of stimuli. If the initial level of transposition is low, then the reduction in distance should increase transposition; but if the initial level is high, a reduction in distance could be expected to increase transposition or to reduce it. If the initial level of transposition is high because there is initially little separation between the training and test sets, transposition should increase over test trials (unless there is a ceiling effect). However, because of the upswing in transposition at extreme distances, the initial level of transposition could be high because the separation between the training and test sets is large. In that case, reducing the distance would reduce transposition. It is known that there are individual differences in the direction of change in transposition over test trials, even when all subjects are exposed to the same experimental conditions (see section entitled "Empirical Considerations," Chapter 2). Therefore, the direction of change would directly depend not upon the extent of the objective distance between the training and test sets, but upon the effective distance, which is assumed to depend partly upon subject variables, as implied in Assumption (1). Until these subject variables are identified, it will not be possible to predict with any confidence the direction of change; but it might be noted that the level of transposition should be more likely to increase when the objective distance is moderate, and more likely to decrease when the objective distance is extreme.

EFFECT OF DELAY

The effect of delay on transposition is explained by Assumptions (11) and (12). There is experimental support for the assumptions. W. R. McAllister *et al.* (1965) required college students serving as subjects to compare the lengths of successively presented lines, with either a one-half-minute or an eight-minute delay between the presentation of the standard stimulus and the presentation of the comparison stimulus. The longer delay did not affect judgments of equality when the stimuli were actually equal, but it increased the proportion of judgments of equality when the stimuli were unequal. Lipsitt and Engen (1961) obtained a similar effect with a five-second delay.

EFFECT OF DIRECTION OF TRANSPOSITION TEST

As shown in the section on deductions about the distance effect, the theory predicts the occurrence of more two-stimulus transposition in the negative direction than in the positive direction. If Hull's (1949) "stimulus intensity dynamism" is added to the theory, the occurrence of more two-stimulus transposition upward than downward can be explained.

The upward–downward direction of the test should have no effect on intermediate-stimulus transposition, which usually occurs only when the subject does not respond to the change in the stimulus situation. When the intermediate-stimulus relation is an effective cue, and when its excitatory potential is great enough to balance the excitatory potential of the absolute cue that is most similar to the positive absolute cue of the training phase, transposition occurs. In the upward direction, the stimulus intensity dynamism would not affect transposition; but in the downward direction, it would increase the excitatory potential of the absolute cue, and would interfere with transposition. The data contradict this prediction, since there seems to be somewhat more intermediate-stimulus transposition downward than upward. However, the effect is weak, and if it is assumed to result from sampling errors, the prediction of no effect in the usual transposition situation would be confirmed.

Effect of Noticing Change in Stimuli from Training to Test

The behavior that is taken to indicate that animal subjects recognize the change from training to test is interpretable as comparison behavior. The occurrence of comparison behavior indicates that the orienting reflex has been disinhibited, and therefore is expected to be associated with a reduced level of transposition (on Near Tests).

Effect of Speed of Original Learning

It may be that when learning in the initial training phase is rapid, the excitatory potentials of the relative cues are greater than the excitatory potentials of the absolute cues. If so, rapid learning should be associated with a relatively high level of transposition.

Effect of Concept Knowledge

The effect of verbalization is presumably essentially the same as the effect of multiple-problem training. Verbalization insures that the relations become effective cues (see section entitled "Mediation Theory," Chapter 8).

Effects of Age Level and Intelligence

The effects of age level and intelligence on transposition can be explained by assuming that older and more intelligent children are more likely to verbalize the relations than younger and less intelligent children, or that because older and more intelligent children tend to learn the initial discrimination more rapidly than younger and less intelligent children, the relational cues are relatively more potent determinants of behavior in older and more intelligent children than in younger and less intelligent children.

Multiple-Problem Training

Gonzalez and Ross (1958) interpreted the multiple-problem training phenomenon as "extending the range of stimulus equivalence," but this seems to be more descriptive than explanatory, and anyway it is not entirely consistent with Caron's (1966) findings.

Stevenson and Iscoe (1954) explained the effect of multiple-problem training by assuming that the subject learns in one problem which kind of stimulus is correct, and learns in the second problem that this kind of stimulus is always correct. Similarly, in a discussion of the "ordinary transposition problem," Mowrer (1960b, p. 246) suggested that if the subject has or quickly forms a concept of larger–smaller, and if he notices that all stimulus pairs are alike in that one stimulus is larger and one smaller, and that the smaller is correct, he should transpose on all tests. Concept identification, which is what Mowrer is suggesting, should be facilitated by presenting more examples of the concept, and transposition should therefore be more likely with multiple-problem training than with single-problem training.

In "concept identification" the subject must discover which of the concepts he already possesses is relevant; in "concept formation" a new concept is acquired (see Vinacke, 1951). A study by Kreezer and Dallenbach (1929) seems to be an example of the need for the distinction. Young children who failed to respond appropriately when asked to give the opposites of words were given a training session in which they were told what the opposites were. The children were then tested with another set of words. About 37 per cent of the children responded appropriately to the test series after the training session. Kreezer and Dallenbach interpreted the results to indicate that the successful children learned the concept of opposition in the training session. It seems more likely that they learned only to apply the label "opposite" to a previously acquired nonverbal concept, especially since all performance curves that changed at all, changed from a perfectly inaccurate level to a perfectly accurate level (comparing the performance before and after the training session). It was not required that the subject give antonyms; for example, "not smooth" and "un-smooth" were accepted as correct opposites of "smooth"; but it is inconceivable that the subjects would have given such responses unless they already knew that "wet" is "not dry," "fast" is "not slow," and so on for other words in the training list.

Concept identification can be very rapid even when the task does not specifically require it, as in "perceptual set" studies, in which the presentation of a single example of a conceptual class can lead to the identification of the concept by college students (Bugelski and Alampay, 1961). Children require more presentations, and the effectiveness of presenting six examples increases with increasing age level in young children (Reese, 1963c), but the identification of a concept from six examples is fast learning. The flaw in this interpretation of the effect of multiple-problem training is that the effect has been obtained in infrahuman subjects, which are generally presumed to lack the required concepts.

Spence (1942) suggested that multiple-problem training (or "reversal training," as he called it) "might lead to a tendency on the part of the organism to adopt a different basis of response than an absolute one" (p. 270). He noted further: "The data of two subjects, Lia and Cuba [chimpanzees which had been given multiple-problem training], suggest that response might have been on the basis of configurational or relational properties of the stimulus complexes" (p. 270). Harlow (1959, p. 511) quoted the latter statement, and suggested that an attack on transposition problems by means of learning-set methods might prove to be fruitful. (However, Spence concluded on the basis of further testing that Lia and Cuba exhibited an "absence of any widely generalized configuration response" [p. 271].)

R. C. Johnson and Zara (1960) suggested that multiple-problem training may facilitate transposition by emphasizing the relational aspect of the learning problem, as analogously learning-set training emphasizes the principle of solution common to learning-set problems. Zeiler (1963c, p. 520) also spoke of a "relational learning set," which he believed involved a shift from learning on the basis of percepts to learning on the basis of concepts.

According to Restle (1958), learning-set formation involves the conditioning of "valid" cues to the correct response, and the adaptation or suppression of invalid cues ("type-c" cues). Within any one problem, there are two kinds of valid cues: "type-a" cues are valid (consistently reinforced) and common to all problems of the series, and "type-b" cues are valid in a given problem, but not valid across all problems. In the learning-set situation, the type-b cues are those associated with the specific stimulus used in a single problem, and the type-a cue is "the object which has been reinforced" (on the informational trial of a problem). As Restle noted, the type-a cue is abstract. The theory assumes that over a series of problems, the type-c cues become adapted, because they are invalid, and the type-b cues become adapted, because they are not as valid as the type-a cues. "When this process is nearly completed, the animal is responding in terms of the abstract type-a cues only" (p. 79).

Marsh (in press) pointed out that in transposition studies in which multiple-problem training is given, the absolute stimulus qualities are type-b cues, and the relative qualities are type-a cues, since the absolute cues are valid only within problems and the relative cues are valid across problems as well as within problems. (Sherman [1966] has proposed the same extension of Restle's theory.) Applying Restle's theory, then, leads to the expectation that multiple-problem training, with the same relative cue valid in all problems, should increase the probability of relational learning, and therefore increase the probability of transposition. Wohlwill proposed essentially the same hypothesis in 1957, in his doctoral dissertation, and attempted to test its implications in a series of experiments. The results did not conform very closely with expectations, but were too ambiguous to allow firm conclusions to be drawn. Training designed to make the relative quality a type-a cue produced more transposition than training designed to make the absolute quality a type-a cue, but did not interfere with performance on a transfer task requiring response to the absolute cue.

M. S. Scott (1966) obtained data that appear to support this kind of explanation. The training given to her Group *B* (see Table 3-16) was designed to make the type-*b* cue constant, and to provide reinforcement of the type-*b* cue and the type-*a* cue equally often. The extension of Restle's theory predicts that this group should transpose less than her Group *A*, which was given the Johnson-Zara type of multiple-problem training. This prediction was confirmed, but further data complicate the interpretation. Groups *A* and *B* differed not only in whether or not the type-*b* cue was constant but also in the within-pair similarity of the training stimuli. Both pairs of stimuli in Group *A* had ratios of 2 to 1, but in Group *B* one pair had a ratio of 2 to 1 and the other pair had a ratio of 8 to 1. To insure that any difference in transposition in Groups *A* and *B* could not be attributed to variability of within-pair ratios, Group *C* was also trained with one pair having a 2 to 1 ratio and another pair having an 8 to 1 ratio, but the type-*b* cue was not constant. This group should have transposed as much as Group *A*, but actually transposed no more than Group *B*. Therefore, it appears that the inferiority of Group *B* was not attributable to having the type-*b* cue constant, but to having a variable within-pair ratio. Since Groups *B* and *C* did not transpose any more than the single-problem groups, it can be concluded that the training given to Groups *B* and *C* was in effect single-problem training, at least with respect to the type-*a* cue. This conclusion is reasonable on the assumption that the stimulus difference in the pair with the 8 to 1 ratio was so great that no relation was perceptible. In Restle's terms, Group *B* had a constant type-*b* cue, and Group *C* had a variable type-*b* cue; but both groups had a type-*a* cue in only one of the two training problems. (Presumably the reason Group *B* did not give more absolute responses than Group *C*, as a result of having had a constant type-*b* cue, is that the groups were highly overtrained.)

A possible objection to the learning-set type of explanation is that learning sets are acquired too slowly to permit application of learning-set theory to the effect of multiple-problem training in the transposition situation. However, two considerations make the extension of the theory plausible. First, although the object-quality discrimination learning set is acquired very slowly in subhuman primates, which generally require well over a hundred problems to acquire the learning set (see Reese, 1964a), children can acquire this kind of learning set more rapidly (Levinson and Reese, 1963; Reese, 1963b), and may even acquire it by the second problem if the first problem is learned to criterion (Reese, 1965a). Second, in the object-quality discrimination learning-set problems, the type-*a* cue is abstract and should be much less likely to be an effective cue in the early problems than the type-*a* cue in the transposition situation, in which the type-*a* cue (the relation) is as concrete as the type-*b* cues (the absolute cues).

Sherman (1966) pointed out that in multiple-problem training, the subject experiences more different values on the relevant stimulus dimension than in single-problem training. She suggested that this additional experience may focus attention on the relevant dimension, and this may enhance the probability that the subject will spontaneously label the dimension, providing himself with an appropriate mediator. As an alternative, she suggested that the subject given multiple-problem training might learn a "win-stay, lose-shift" hypothesis (see, for example, Levinson and Reese, 1963), and therefore might exhibit less variability on the test trials since he would continue to choose the same stimulus throughout testing. However, this would not explain the enhanced transposition resulting from multiple-problem training, because the data indicate that there is usually more transposition on combined test trials than on the first test trial (see Chapter 2). Furthermore, the phenomenon to be explained is not reduced variability but increased transposition. She suggested as a third alternative the extension of Restle's theory which has already been discussed.

On the basis of the series of experiments she conducted, Sherman concluded that only the last alternative is tenable. However, the data obtained by Caron and by Beaty (Table 3-21) require the addition of two further assumptions. As already indicated (section entitled "Multiple-Problem Training," Chapter 3), Caron and Beaty both found that the kind of multiple-problem training used by Gonzalez and Ross (1958) produces more transposition than the kind used by R. C. Johnson and Zara (1960); and Caron found that the effect of the Johnson-Zara procedure depends upon the amount of separation between the sets of stimuli used in the two training problems. (The Gonzalez-Ross procedure is to train subjects on two extremely different sets of stimuli and to test on an intermediate set. The Johnson-Zara procedure is to train subjects on two sets and to test on a set of stimuli not included in the range of training stimuli. For example, in Caron's studies the subjects were trained on 1, 2, 3 and 7, 8, 9 and tested on 4, 5, 6, using the Gonzalez-Ross procedure; and they were trained on 1, 2, 3 and 4, 5, 6 and tested on 7, 8, 9 or were trained on 1, 2, 3 and 7, 8, 9 and tested on 10, 11, 12, using the Johnson-Zara procedure.)

The first assumption, which Caron (personal communication, 1966) suggested, is that as the disparity between the two training sets is increased, the tendency to transfer between problems on an absolute basis is weakened, and therefore the likelihood of attending to the relational attribute is increased. This assumption appears to be inconsistent with the findings of Zeiler and Paalberg (1964a) because their group that had similar training sets (separated by one-half step) transposed between the training problems, and their group that had more disparate training sets (separated by a full step) transferred absolute responses between the training problems, yet the latter group gave more transposition responses on the test than the first group, and the first group transposed on the test no more than a group given single-problem training. However, I have already suggested that Zeiler and Paalberg's group trained with the more similar stimulus sets failed to notice the difference between the sets and therefore received, in effect, single-problem training.

Caron used training sets three steps apart and six steps apart (with the Johnson-Zara procedure). The multiple-problem training with the three-step separation between sets may have produced no facilitation of transposition. The group given this training averaged 26 per cent transposition on the first test trial and 40 per cent on 10 test trials. The test set of stimuli was three steps from the nearest training set; and Zeiler (1965b) obtained 17 per cent transposition on Trial 1 and 43 per cent on 10 trials at three steps, after single-problem training. There were two major procedural differences between the studies. Zeiler rewarded all test-trial responses, and Caron rewarded none, promising the subject that the accumulated rewards would be given at the end of the test series; Zeiler used a 1.4 to 1 ratio of stimulus areas, and Caron used a 1.8 to 1 ratio of areas. Stimulus similarity has little effect on Far Tests of intermediate-stimulus transposition (see section entitled "Distance," Chapter 4); but the effect of the difference in reward contingencies is unknown. In my own studies in which all test-trial responses were rewarded and a 2 to 1 ratio of areas was used (Reese, 1961; Reese, 1964b; Reese and Fiero, 1964), three-step transposition after single-problem training averaged 13 per cent on the first test trial and 17 per cent on six trials. A new experiment is obviously needed to test the suggestion that Caron's three-step separation did not facilitate transposition, since the cross-study comparisons are of doubtful validity because of the many details of method that varied. (For example, Caron used as stimuli paper squares; Zeiler used quarter-inch-thick Masonite squares; and I used three-quarter-inch-thick wooden squares. Caron structured the task as a game called "Find the Magic Box," but I did not tell the children that the task was a game. Zeiler did not report how he structured the task. Zeiler and I hid the reward under the stimulus object, but Caron used a marble delivery mechanism that separated the locus of reward from the locus of response. Caron used marbles as rewards, Zeiler used plastic chips, and I used marbles in the 1961 study and raisins in the 1964b study and the study with Fiero.)

Since Zeiler and Paalberg obtained the multiple-problem training effect in adult subjects with the one-step separation between training sets, it is important to determine whether the three-step separation yields the effect in children, but only to provide evidence about a possible developmental trend in the relation between the magnitude of the multiple-problem training effect and the amount of separation between the training sets.

One further assumption is required to explain why the amount of transposition in Caron's two groups trained with the six-step separation between sets depended upon the location of the test set. When the test stimuli fell within the range of training stimuli, there was more transposition than when they were located beyond the range of training stimuli. According to the first assumption, both groups should have learned during training to attend to the relational attribute, and therefore the second assumption must deal with the probability of transferring the relational basis of responding to the test situation. The assumption can be that the use of a test set within the range of the training sets enhances the likelihood of this kind of transfer, but there are at least two objections to this assumption. One is that it is little more than a restatement of the empirical finding, and the other is that it suggests no basis for the effect on transfer.

An alternative possibility is that the effect is related to the total range of stimuli. In Caron's condition in which the test stimuli were beyond the range of training stimuli, the total range was 12 steps, from the smallest stimulus to the largest one; and in the condition in which the test stimuli were within the range of training stimuli, the total range was 9 steps. (The total ranges in terms of steps between stimulus *sets* were 9 and 6 steps.) It may be that the larger range is so great that the perception of the relation is affected and the basis of responding is therefore necessarily altered. Gonzalez and Ross used a total range of 13 steps (10 steps between the extreme sets), and obtained the multiple-problem training effect, but their stimuli varied by a ratio of 1.3 to 1 and Caron's stimuli varied by a ratio of 1.8 to 1. The ratio between the largest stimulus and the smallest stimulus in the series used by Gonzalez and Ross would be 1.3^{12} to 1 (about 23 to 1), and the ratio in the series used by Caron would be 1.8^{11} to 1 (about 643 to 1). Therefore, the range of *sizes* used by Gonzalez and Ross was not as wide as the range used by Caron, although the range in steps was wider than Caron's. Like Gonzalez and Ross, Beaty used a 1.3 to 1 ratio and a 13-step range in the Gonzalez-Ross condition, and obtained facilitation of transposition.

On the basis of these considerations, it seems well to modify somewhat the two assumptions used to explain Caron's data. The first assumption should be that as the number of steps separating the stimulus sets used in training is increased, the tendency to transfer between the sets on an absolute basis is weakened, and therefore the likelihood of attending to the relational attribute is increased. The second assumption is that as the difference between the absolute magnitudes of the least and most intense stimuli in the series is increased, the likelihood that the same relation will be perceived in the extreme stimulus sets is reduced, and therefore the likelihood that multiple-problem training will influence transposition is reduced. The first assumption deals only with the difference between sets of training stimuli; and the second assumption deals with the total range of stimuli used, including both training and test sets. The first assumption explains why Beaty's group given the Johnson-Zara procedure, with a one-step separation between the two training sets, transposed little more than the single-problem group; and it explains why Caron's group given the Johnson-Zara procedure with a three-step separation between the training sets transposed less than the group given this procedure with a six-step separation between the training sets. The second assumption explains why the last group transposed less than Caron's group given the Gonzalez-Ross procedure.

The experimental design illustrated in Table 11-3 could be used to test predictions derived from these assumptions. Group G is given the Gonzalez-Ross procedure, with a 10-step separation between the training sets and with a test set 5 steps from each training set. Group J is given the Johnson-Zara procedure, with a 5-step separation between the training sets, and with a test set 5 steps from one training set and 10 steps from the other training set. Group S is given single-problem training and a 5-step transposition test. Stimuli with a small ratio of magnitudes, such as a 1.3 to 1 area ratio, are used with one third of each group; stimuli with a moderate ratio, such as 1.5 or 1.6 to 1, are used with another third; and stimuli with a larger ratio, such as 1.8 to 1, are used with the other third of each group. (If the analysis of Caron's data is correct, then his 12-step total range, with a 1.8 to 1 series, is wide enough to produce a noticeable reduction in the likelihood that the same relation will be perceived at both extremes. In the suggested experiment, a 13-step total range is used to enhance the expected effect. Gonzalez and Ross [1958] and Beaty [1966] have already shown that the 13-step range with a 1.3 to 1 series is narrow enough to leave this likelihood relatively constant.)

TABLE 11–3
DESIGN OF SUGGESTED STUDY

Group	Procedure	Training stimuli	Test stimuli
G	Gonzalez-Ross	1,2,3; 11,12,13	6,7,8
J	Johnson-Zara	1,2,3; 6,7,8	11,12,13
S	Single problem	1,2,3	6,7,8

The predictions are that with the 1.3 to 1 series, Group G will transpose more than Group J, and Group J will transpose more than Group S. According to the second assumption, the same relation should be perceptible in the extreme sets even in Group G when the 1.3 to 1 series is used. According to the first assumption, the probability of attending to the relation during learning should be greater in Group G than in Group J; and according to the extension of Restle's theory, it should be greater in both of these groups than in Group *S*. As the stimulus ratio increases, the prediction is that the three groups will converge in frequency of transposition. When the range is wide enough, the multiple-problem training given to Group *G* should not influence transposition, because according to the second assumption, different relations should be perceived in the two training sets; and the multiple-problem training given to Group *J* should also have no influence on transposition, again according to the second assumption, because the relation perceived in the test set should not be the same as the relation perceived in the training sets.

MULTIPLE TESTS

It seems reasonable to extend the explanation of the effect of multiple-problem training to the effect of multiple testing. Multiple testing usually increases two-stimulus transposition, but often has no effect on intermediate-stimulus transposition. With training on a single two-stimulus problem, the relative cue should acquire excitatory potential (Deduction 1 at beginning of this chapter); but with training on a single intermediate-stimulus problem, the relative cue should acquire little excitatory potential (Assumption 15 in section entitled "Intermediate-Stimulus Problems," this chapter). Therefore, if multiple testing increased attention to the relative cue during the testing phase, transposition would be increased in the two-stimulus situation but would be little affected in the intermediate-stimulus situation.

Summary and Concluding Remarks

The theory outlined in this chapter can account for most of the data on transposition, but many of the predictions are imprecise. The precision of most of the predictions could be increased by manipulating the constants in the equations; but as already noted, it does not seem to be worth while to attempt precise fits at this stage of development of the theory. First, many of the important findings were obtained incidentally and consequently require more careful study. Second, the theory generates several predictions that have never been adequately tested, and modification of the theory will be required if these predictions are eventually disconfirmed. Third, there appear to be some as yet unidentified variables that affect transposition and that must be included in the theory to account for all of the data. It is possible that the introduction of these variables would affect some of the predictions that have already been made. Finally, data are needed to check some of the basic assumptions, especially the assumptions about the effects of the orienting reflex and the effects of selective attention.

It must also be emphasized that the theoretical approach suggested in this chapter consists essentially of adding to an already existing theory the assumption that relations can be effective cues and other assumptions that generate predictions about the conditions under which relations actually become effective cues and how they affect behavior. The basic theory used in this chapter is Spence's—with important modifications adapted from Zeiler's theory—but it might be fruitful to examine the consequences of using the approach with other theories as well.

Bibliography and Author Index

Works cited from secondary sources are included in the Bibliography and Author Index. Secondary sources were used for untranslated works and works published in English but unavailable to the author. In each case, the secondary sources used are given in the reference. Reports of data on unidimensional transposition are identified with asterisks. The pages on which citations occur are given in brackets.

Aarons, L., Halasz, H. K., and Riesen, A. H. Interocular transfer of visual intensity discrimination after ablation of striate cortex in dark-reared kittens. *Journal of Comparative and Physiological Psychology*, 1963, **56**, 196–199. [216]

Abbott, Edwina. See Washburn and Abbott, 1912.

Abramov, I. See DeValois, Jacobs, and Abramov, 1964.

*Adams, D. K. Weight discrimination in rats. *Psychological Bulletin*, 1933, **30**, 703. (Abstract) [176]

*Adams, D. K. Recherches sur la comparaison successive avec grandes différences chez les rats. (Researches on successive comparisons with great differences in the rat.) *Journal de Psychologie Normale et Pathologique*, 1937, **34**, 532–553. (Source: *Psychological Abstracts*, 1938, **12**, 437.) [103, 104, 126, 176]

Alampay, Delia A. See Bugelski and Alampay, 1961.

*Alberts, Elizabeth, and Ehrenfreund, D. Transposition in children as a function of age. *Journal of Experimental Psychology*, 1951, **41**, 30–38. [25, 26, 28, 30, 31, 110–113, 137–138, 142, 148, 151, 160, 162, 163]

Alverdes, F. *The psychology of animals in relation to human psychology.* (Translated by H. S. Hatfield.) New York: Harcourt, Brace, 1932. [231]

Ananiev, B. G. The basis of spatial discrimination. (Translated by H. Milne.) In B. Simon (Ed.), *Psychology in the Soviet Union.* Stanford, Calif.: Stanford University Press, 1957. Pp. 131–151. [82]

Angell, J. R. *Psychology. An introductory study of the structure and function of human consciousness.* New York: Holt, 1908. [81]

Aristotle. (See Strong, 1891, pp. 195–196.) [223]

Baar, J. See C. J. Warden and Baar, 1929.

Babb, H. Transfer between habits based on shock and thirst. *Journal of Comparative and Physiological Psychology*, 1963, **56**, 318–323. [185]

Bachem, A. Time factors in relative and absolute pitch determination. *Journal of the Acoustical Society of America*, 1954, **26**, 751–753. [83–84]

Baer, D. M. See Bijou and Baer, 1965.

*Bagshaw, Muriel H., and Pribram, K. H. Effect of amygdalectomy on transfer of training in monkeys. *Journal of Comparative and Physiological Psychology*, 1965, **59**, 118–121. [133, 141, 142, 177, 186–187]

Bailey, D. E. See P. Johnson and Bailey, 1966.

*Baker, R. A., and Lawrence, D. H. The differential effects of simultaneous and successive stimuli presentation on transposition. *Journal of Comparative and Physiological Psychology*, 1951, **44**, 378–382. [24, 25, 28, 31, 86–87, 89–94, 176]

*Balla, D., and Zigler, E. Discrimination and switching learning in normal, familial retarded, and organic retarded children. *Journal of Abnormal and Social Psychology*, 1964, **69**, 664–669. [126, 165–166]

Barclay, A. (Abstract of Okamoto, 1962.) *Psychological Abstracts,* 1964, 38, 66. [8]

Barnett, C. D., and Cantor, G. N. Discrimination set in defectives. *American Journal of Mental Deficiency,* 1957, 62, 334–337. [75]

Bartholinus. (See Hartmann, 1942, p. 179.) [223]

Baudelaire. (See Bertocci, 1964.) [222]

Baumeister, A. A. Personal communication. 1965. [115]

*Baumeister, A. A., Beedle, R., and Hawkins, W. F. Transposition in normals and retardates under varying conditions of training and test. *American Journal of Mental Deficiency,* 1964, 69, 432–437. [34, 115, 118, 166, 229, 294]

Beach, D. R. See Flavell, Beach, and Chinsky, 1966.

*Beaty, W. E. A comparison of "stimulus-equivalence" and "learning set" explanations of children's performance on the intermediate-size transposition problem. Unpublished master's thesis, University of Illinois, 1966. [34, 76–77, 148, 197–198, 199, 325–328]

Becher, E. *Gehirn und Seele.* Heidelberg: C. Winter, 1911. (Sources: Hartmann, 1942, p. 182; Koffka, 1925, pp. 235 and 357; Köhler, 1929, pp. 346 and 348; Parsons, 1927, pp. 53–54. Parsons also listed "*Arch. f. Psychol.* XXXV, 125, 1916.") [212]

Bedrosian, P. Effects of stimulus change and intermittent reinforcement on reversal and nonreversal shifts. Paper read at meeting of Eastern Psychological Association, New York, April, 1966. [266]

Bee, Helen L., and Brandt, Linda J. Children's drawings and their perceptions of them. An investigation of the lag between perceiving and performing. Paper read at meeting of Society for Research in Child Development, Minneapolis, March, 1965. [205, 207]

Beedle, R. See Baumeister, Beedle, and Hawkins, 1964.

Beiswenger, H. A. Age effects in the internalization of the verbal control of motor behavior. Report No. 10, Development of Language Functions, A Research Program-Project (Study F: Motivation and Control in the Development of Language Functions). Center for Human Growth and Development, University of Michigan, March, 1966. [262]

Bell, Donna D. See Riley, McKee, Bell, and Schwartz, 1967.

Bentley, I. M. The psychology of mental arrangement. *American Journal of Psychology,* 1902, 13, 269–293. [339]

Bentley, I. M. See Washburn and Bentley, 1906.

Bergmann, G. The problem of relations in classical psychology. *Philosophical Quarterly,* 1952, 2, 140–152. [3–5]

Bergmann, G. Some remarks on the ontology of Ockham. *Philosophical Review,* 1954, 63, 560–571. (Reprinted in G. Bergmann, *Meaning and existence.* Madison, Wisc.: University of Wisconsin Press, 1960. Pp. 144–154.) [3]

Bergmann, G. Intentionality. *Semantica (Archivo di Filosofia,* Roma: Bocca, 1955). Pp. 177–216. (Reprinted in G. Bergmann, *Meaning and existence.* Madison, Wisc.: University of Wisconsin Press, 1960. Pp. 3–38.) [3]

Bergmann, G. Some remarks on the philosophy of Malebranche. *Review of Metaphysics,* 1956, 10, 207–226. (Reprinted in G. Bergmann, *Meaning and existence.* Madison, Wisc.: University of Wisconsin Press, 1960. Pp. 189–204.) [3]

Bergmann, G. *Philosophy of science.* Madison, Wisc.: University of Wisconsin Press, 1957. [1, 2, 5, 7, 10]

*Beritoff, J. S., and Topurin, S. Physiology of behavior to complex stimuli: Individual reactions to two successive stimuli. *Russkii Fiziologicheskii Zhurnal,* 1929, 12, 545–569. (Source: Razran, 1939, pp. 318 and 329.) [177, 186]

Berlyne, D. E. The influence of complexity and novelty in visual figures on orienting responses. *Journal of Experimental Psychology,* 1958, 55, 289–296. [280]

Berlyne, D. E. *Conflict, arousal, and curiosity.* New York: McGraw-Hill, 1960. [309, 317]

Berlyne, D. E. Soviet research on intellectual processes in children. In J. C. Wright and J. Kagan (Eds.), Basic cognitive processes in children. *Monographs of the Society for Research in Child Development,* 1963, 28, No. 2. Pp. 165–183. [309]

Berlyne, D. E. *Structure and direction in thinking.* New York: Wiley, 1965. [1–3, 153, 317]

Berlyne, D. E. Curiosity and exploration. *Science,* 1966, 153, 25–33. [62]

Berman, Phyllis W. Learning of relative and absolute size discriminations by preschool children. Unpublished doctoral dissertation, University of Wisconsin, 1963. [61–62, 161, 162, 192, 199, 229]

Berman, Phyllis W., and Graham, Frances K. Children's response to relative, absolute, and position cues in a two-trial size discrimination. *Journal of Comparative and Physiological Psychology,* 1964, 57, 393–397. (Also: Children's response to relative and absolute cues in a two-trial discrimination. *American Psychologist,* 1963, 18, 346. [Abstract]) [61]

Berman, Phyllis W. See F. K. Graham, Ernhart, Craft, and Berman, 1964.

Bernstein, Lilly. See Ghent and Bernstein, 1961.

Bertocci, A. P. *From symbolism to Baudelaire.* Carbondale, Ill.: Southern Illinois University Press, 1964. [222]

Best, C. H., and Taylor, N. B. *The physiological basis of medical practice.* (6th ed.) Baltimore, Md.: Williams & Wilkins, 1955. [223]

Betz. (See Katz, 1937, p. 253.) [233]

Bichowsky, F. R. The consciousness of relations. *American Journal of Psychology,* 1923, 34, 231–243. [9]

Bichowsky, F. R. The mechanism of consciousness: The percept arc. *American Journal of Psychology,* 1926, 37, 382–390. [9]

Biederman, G. B. Reversal in tactile and visual learning. *Science,* 1966, 154, 677. [220]

*Bierens de Haan, J. A. Über Wahl nach relativen und absoluten Merkmalen (Versuche an Affen und Bienen). *Zeitschrift für wissenschaftliche Biologie. Abteilung C, Zeitschrift für vergleichende Physiologie,* 1928, 7, 462–478. (Sources: Katz, 1937, p. 69; C. J. Warden et al., 1940, pp. 679 and 936; Wohlwill, personal communications, 1965, 1966.) [128, 173, 174, 177, 186]

Bijou, S. W., and Baer, D. M. *Child development.* Vol. two. *Universal stage of infancy.* New York: Appleton-Century-Crofts, 1965. [231]

Bindra, D., Williams, Judith A., and Wise, J. S. Judgments of sameness and difference: Experiments on decision time. *Science,* 1965, 150, 1625–1627. [205]

*Bingham, H. C. Size and form perception in *Gallus domesticus. Journal of Animal Behavior,* 1913, 3, 65–113. [174, 180]

*Bingham, H. C. Visual perception of the chick. *Behavior Monographs,* 1922, 4, No. 4 (Serial No. 20). [124, 132, 141, 142, 174, 180–181, 214]

Birch, H. G., and Lefford, A. Intersensory development in children. *Monographs of the Society for Research in Child Development,* 1963, 28, No. 5. [219]

Bitterman, M. E. Approach and avoidance in discriminative learning. *Psychological Review,* 1952, 59, 172–175. [244]

Bitterman, M. E., and McConnell, J. V. The role of set in successive discrimination. *American Journal of Psychology,* 1954, 67, 129–132. [271]

Bitterman, M. E. See Gonzalez, Gentry, and Bitterman, 1954; Stevenson and Bitterman, 1955; Weise and Bitterman, 1951.

Blakeslee, Pat, and Gunter, R. Cross-modal transfer of discrimination learning in cebus monkeys. *Behaviour*, 1966, **26**, 76–90. [220]

Blank, Marion. Use of the deaf in language studies: A reply to Furth. *Psychological Bulletin*, 1965, **63**, 442–444. [153]

Blank, Marion, and Bridger, W. H. Cross-modal transfer in nursery-school children. *Journal of Comparative and Physiological Psychology*, 1964, **58**, 277–282. [164, 218–219, 221]

Blank, Marion, and Bridger, W. H. The use of concepts in problems across sensory modalities in deaf and hearing nursery school children. Paper read at meeting of Society for Research in Child Development, Minneapolis, March, 1965. [221]

Blank, Marion, and Bridger, W. H. Conceptual cross-modal transfer in deaf and hearing children. *Child Development*, 1966, **37**, 29–38. [221]

Blazek, Nancy C. See Mason, Blazek, and Harlow, 1956.

*Blue, S., and Hegge, F. W. Transposition of a stimulus generalization gradient along an auditory intensity continuum. *Psychonomic Science*, 1965, **3**, 201–202. [176, 185]

Blum, A. See Martin and Blum, 1961.

Blum, Josephine S. See Blum and Blum, 1949.

Blum, R. A., and Blum, Josephine S. Factual issues in the "continuity" controversy. *Psychological Review*, 1949, **56**, 33–50. [137]

Boat, Barbara M. Verbal mediation in four-year-old children. Unpublished master's thesis, State University of Iowa, 1966. [263]

Bolles, M. Marjorie. See Rowley and Bolles, 1935.

Boring, E. G. The problem or originality in science. *American Journal of Psychology*, 1927, **39**, 70–90. [5, 231]

Boring, E. G. The *Gestalt* psychology and *Gestalt* movement. *American Journal of Psychology*, 1930, **42**, 308–315. [5, 231]

Boring, E. G. *The physical dimensions of consciousness.* New York: Century, 1933. [11, 80, 81, 221, 222]

Boring, E. G. *A history of experimental psychology.* (2nd ed.) New York: Appleton-Century-Crofts, 1950. [3, 4, 140, 223, 231, 339]

Borisova, M. N. See Teplov and Borisova, 1957.

Börnstein, W. On the functional relations of the sense organs to one another and to the organism as a whole. *Journal of General Psychology*, 1936, **15**, 117–131. [223]

*Borovski, V. M. The problem of transposition in birds. *Instinkty, Navyki, i Refleksy*, 1936, **2**, 39–44. (Source: Razran, 1938b, pp. 535 and 537.) [175, 181]

Bowman, R. E. Discrimination learning set under intermittent and secondary reinforcement. Paper read at meeting of American Psychological Association, New York, September, 1961. [294]

Bowman, R. E. Discrimination learning-set performance under intermittent and secondary reinforcement. *Journal of Comparative and Physiological Psychology*, 1963, **56**, 429–434. [294]

Brackbill, Yvonne, and Jack, D. Discrimination learning in children as a function of reinforcement value. *Child Development*, 1958, **29**, 185–190. [162, 300]

Braine, Lila Ghent. Age changes in the mode of perceiving geometric forms. *Psychonomic Science*, 1965, **2**, 155–156. [204–205]

Brandt, Linda J. See Bee and Brandt, 1965.

*Breed, F. S. Reactions of chicks to optical stimuli. *Journal of Animal Behavior,* 1912, **2**, 280–295. [174, 181, 195]

*Bregadze, A. The formation of individual reactions to a complex of musical tones in dogs. *Trudy Institut Beritashvili,* 1937, **3**, 415–430. (Sources: *Psychological Abstracts,* 1938, **12**, 134; Razran, 1939, pp. 318 and 329.) [177, 186]

Bridger, W. H. See Blank and Bridger, 1964; Blank and Bridger, 1965; Blank and Bridger, 1966.

Brooks, R. M., and Goldstein, A. G. Recognition by children of inverted photographs of faces. *Child Development,* 1963, **34**, 1033–1040. [210]

Brown, J. S. Generalization and discrimination. In D. I. Mostofsky (Ed.), *Stimulus generalization.* Stanford, Calif.: Stanford University Press, 1965. Pp. 7–23. [283]

Brown, T. *Lectures on the philosophy of the human mind.* (20th ed.) London: William Tegg, 1860. [3–4, 5, 80]

Brown, W., and Whittell, Florence. Yerkes' multiple choice method with human adults. *Journal of Comparative Psychology,* 1923, **3**, 305–318. [67, 194, 199]

Brown, W. See Wong and Brown, 1923.

*Brown, W. L., Overall, J. E., and Gentry, G. V. "Absolute" vs. "relational" discrimination of intermediate size in the rhesus monkey. *American Journal of Psychology,* 1959, **72**, 593–596. [39, 75, 99–100, 115, 126, 177, 187]

Brown, W. L. See Gentry, Overall, and Brown, 1959.

Bryant, P. [E.] The effect of a verbal instruction on transfer in normal and severely subnormal children. *Journal of Mental Deficiency Research,* 1964, **8**, 35–43. [268–270]

Bryant, P. E. The transfer of positive and negative learning by normal and severely subnormal children. *British Journal of Psychology,* 1965, **56**, 81–86. (a) [268–270]

Bryant, P. E. The transfer of sorting concepts by moderately retarded children. *American Journal of Mental Deficiency,* 1965, **70**, 291–300. (b) [270]

Buckhout, R. (No title.) *Science,* 1966, **152**, 1109–1110. [223]

Bucy, P. C. See Klüver and Bucy, 1939.

Bugelski, B. R. *The psychology of learning.* New York: Holt, 1956. [245, 277]

Bugelski, B. R. *An introduction to the principles of psychology.* New York: Holt, 1960. [223]

Bugelski, B. R., and Alampay, Delia A. The role of frequency in developing perceptual sets. *Canadian Journal of Psychology,* 1961, **15**, 205–211. [322]

Bugelski, B. R., and Scharlock, D. P. An experimental demonstration of unconscious mediated association. *Journal of Experimental Psychology,* 1952, **44**, 334–338. [95, 218]

Bühler, K. *Die geistige Entwicklung des Kindes.* (6th ed.) Jena: Fischer, 1930. (a) (Source: Shirai, 1951, pp. 9 and *i.*) [291–292]

Bühler, K. *The mental development of the child. A summary of modern psychological theory.* (Translated from the 5th German ed. by O. Oeser.) New York: Harcourt, 1930. (b) [150, 291–292]

*Burkamp, W. Versuche über das Farbenwiedererkennen der Fische. *Zeitschrift für Psychologie und Physiologie der Sinnesorgane. II Abteilung, Zeitschrift für Sinnesphysiologie,* 1923, **55**, 133–170. (Sources: Gelb, 1929, p. 203; Katz, 1937, p. 77; Tolman, 1927, pp. 15 and 30; C. J. Warden *et al.,* 1936, pp. 51 and 443; Woodworth, 1938, pp. 606–607 and 829.) [174, 179, 246–248]

Burton, D., and Ettlinger, G. Cross-modal transfer of training in monkeys. *Nature,* 1960, **186**, 1071–1072. [221]

*Buss, A. H. Rigidity as a function of absolute and relational shifts in the learning of successive discriminations. *Journal of Experimental Psychology,* 1953, **45,** 153–156. [97]

Butter, C. M., and Gekoski, W. L. Alterations in pattern equivalence following inferotemporal and lateral striate lesions in rhesus monkeys. *Journal of Comparative and Physiological Psychology,* 1966, **61,** 309–312. [204, 208]

Calkins, Mary W. *An introduction to psychology.* (2nd ed.) New York: Macmillan, 1916. [4, 222]

Calkins, Mary W. Critical comments on the '*Gestalt-Theorie.*' *Psychological Review,* 1926, 33, 135–158. [5]

Calvin, A. D. Configurational learning in children. *Journal of Educational Psychology,* 1955, **46,** 117–120. [84]

Campbell, D. T. Operational delineation of 'what is learned' via the transposition experiment. *Psychological Review,* 1954, **61,** 167–174. [288]

*Campbell, D. T., and Kral, T. P. Transposition away from a rewarded stimulus card to a nonrewarded one as a function of a shift in background. *Journal of Comparative and Physiological Psychology,* 1958, **51,** 592–595. [26, 27, 28, 29, 31, 175, 181, 189, 246–248]

Campbell, D. T., Miller, N., and Diamond, A. L. Predisposition to identify instigating and guiding stimulus as revealed in transfer. *Journal of General Psychology,* 1960, **63,** 69–74. [8, 225]

Campione, J., Hyman, L., and Zeaman, D. Dimensional shifts and reversals in retardate discrimination learning. *Journal of Experimental Child Psychology,* 1965, **2,** 255–263. [267]

Cantor, G. N. Basic learning research and mental retardation. In E. P. Trapp and P. Himelstein (Eds.), *Readings on the exceptional child.* New York: Appleton-Century-Crofts, 1962. Pp. 170–180. [75]

Cantor, G. N., and Spiker, C. C. Effects of nonreinforced trials on discrimination learning in children. *Journal of Experimental Psychology,* 1954, **47,** 256–258. [162]

Cantor, G. N. See Barnett and Cantor, 1957; Rabinowitz and Cantor, 1966.

Cantor, Joan H. Transfer of stimulus pretraining to motor paired-associate and discrimination learning tasks. In L. P. Lipsitt and C. C. Spiker (Eds.), *Advances in child development and behavior.* Vol. 2. New York: Academic Press, 1965. Pp. 19–58. [261, 264]

Caron, A. J. Distribution of the middle-size concept among suburban nursery school children. Unpublished manuscript, National Institute of Mental Health, 1965. [148, 167]

*Caron, A. J. Far transposition of intermediate-size in preverbal children. *Journal of Experimental Child Psychology,* 1966, 3, 296–311. [34, 76–77, 78, 142, 144, 155, 162, 164, 165, 167–168, 170–171, 307–308, 321, 325–328]

Caron, A. J. Personal communication. 1966. [77, 325]

*Caron, A. J. Intermediate-size transposition at an extreme distance in preschool children. *Journal of Experimental Child Psychology,* 1967, **5,** 186–207. [34, 100, 101, 115, 116, 120, 133, 155, 164, 165, 166, 167]

Carr, A. E. See Sutherland and Carr, 1963; Sutherland and Carr, 1964.

Carter, J. W., Jr. An experimental study of the stimulus-function. *Psychological Record,* 1937, **1,** 35–48. [v, 215]

*Casteel, D. B. The discriminative ability of the painted turtle. *Journal of Animal Behavior,* 1911, **1,** 1–28. [174, 179]

*Chang, M. Transposition of size and pattern discrimination in the white rat. *Scientific Report of the National Tsing Hua University,* 1936, **2**, No. 2, 89–110. (Sources: *Psychological Abstracts,* 1937, **11**, 69; Shirai, 1951, pp. 13, 16–17, and *i.*) [176]

Charlesworth, W. R. Persistence of orienting and attending behavior in infants as a function of stimulus-locus uncertainty. *Child Development,* 1966, **37**, 473–491. [280]

Chinsky, J. M. See Flavell, Beach, and Chinsky, 1966.

*Chisum, Gloria T. Transposition as a function of the number of test trials. *Journal of Comparative and Physiological Psychology,* 1965, **59**, 419–421. [27, 30, 31, 176]

Chorover, S. L. See M. Cole, Chorover, and Ettlinger, 1961.

Clark, G. See Goldberg and Clark, 1955.

*Coburn, C. A. The behavior of the crow, *Corvus Americanus, Aud. Journal of Animal Behavior,* 1914, **4**, 185–201. [68, 99, 175, 181–182, 183, 195, 214]

*Cohen, D. H. Transposition in pigeons as a function of the temporal delay between training and testing. Unpublished doctoral dissertation, University of California, 1963. [87, 89–90, 94, 102, 104, 108, 109, 132, 175, 182, 229, 235]

Cohen, M. R., and Nagel, E. *An introduction to logic and scientific method.* New York: Harcourt, 1934. [10]

Cohen, N. E. Equivalence of brightness across modalities. *American Journal of Psychology,* 1934, **46**, 117–119. [221, 347]

Cole, L. W. The relation of strength of stimulus to rate of learning in the chick. *Journal of Animal Behavior,* 1911, **1**, 111–124. [195]

Cole, M., Chorover, S. L., and Ettlinger, G. Cross-modal transfer in man. *Nature,* 1961, **191**, 1225–1226. [219]

*Cole, R. E., Dent, H. E., Eguchi, Pauleia E., Fujii, K. K., and Johnson, R. C. Transposition with minimal errors during training trials. *Journal of Experimental Child Psychology,* 1964, **1**, 355–359. [33, 65, 66, 94–95, 98, 148]

Contract Bridge Bulletin, 1966, **32**, No. 7, 10. [8]

*Corbascio, Anna M. Factors determining size transposition in young children. Unpublished doctoral dissertation, University of California, Berkeley, 1964. [25, 26, 124, 130, 138, 139, 148, 248, 249, 282]

Cordeau, J. P. See Stepien and Cordeau, 1960.

Cornelius, P. (See Mach, 1914, p. 286.) [225]

Craft, M. See F. K. Graham, Ernhart, Craft, and Berman, 1964.

Croxall, S. *Fables of Aseop, and others: Translated into English; with instructive applications, by Samuel Croxall.* Edinburgh: William P. Nimmo, [1866]. [140]

Culbertson, J. T. *The minds of robots.* Urbana, Ill.: University of Illinois Press, 1963. [9]

Cumming, W. W., Siegel, I. M., and Johnson, D. F. Mirror-image reversal in pigeons. *Science,* 1965, **149**, 1518–1519. [216]

*Cutsforth, Margery G. A study of successive discrimination of brightness in chicks. *Psychological Monographs,* 1933, **44**, 57–87. [96, 113, 174]

Dallenbach, K. M. See Kreezer and Dallenbach, 1929.

D'Amato, M. R. Transfer of an early-acquired brightness discrimination from bar-pressing to a Y maze. *Journal of Comparative and Physiological Psychology,* 1961, **54**, 548–551. [244]

Davenport, J. W. Choice behavior and differential response strength in discrimination reversal learning. *Journal of Comparative and Physiological Psychology,* 1959, **52**, 349–352. [83]

Davenport, J. W. The interaction of magnitude and delay of reinforcement in spatial discrimination. *Journal of Comparative and Physiological Psychology,* 1962, **55**, 267–273. [83]

Davenport, J. W. Spatial discrimination and reversal learning based upon differential percentage of reinforcement. *Journal of Comparative and Physiological Psychology,* 1963, **56**, 1038–1043. [83]

Davidson, Helen P. A study of reversals in young children. *Journal of Genetic Psychology,* 1934, **45**, 452–465. [209]

Davidson, Helen P. A study of the confusing letters b, d, p, and q. *Journal of Genetic Psychology,* 1935, **47**, 458–468. [209, 210]

Dearborn, G. V. N. Recognition under objective reversal. *Psychological Review,* 1899, **6**, 395–406. [208]

DeBold, R., and Mayland, E. J. Verbal labels and memory for form. Unpublished manuscript. 1965. (Based on paper entitled "Verbal labels and recognition memory for form," by R. C. DeBold, read at meeting of Eastern Psychological Association, Atlantic City, April, 1965.) [235]

Dees, Valerie, and Grindley, G. C. The transposition of visual patterns. *British Journal of Psychology,* 1947, **37**, 152–163. [137, 211–212]

Dennis, W. A study of learning in the white rat. *Journal of Genetic Psychology,* 1930, **37**, 294–308. [82]

Dennis, W., and Russell, R. W. Comments on recent studies of VTE. *Journal of Genetic Psychology,* 1939, **54**, 217–221. [82]

Dent, H. E. See R. E. Cole, Dent, Eguchi, Fujii, and Johnson, 1964.

DeRivera, J. See Lawrence and DeRivera, 1954.

Deutsch, J. A. See Trabasso, Deutsch, and Gelman, 1966.

DeValois, R. L., Jacobs, G. H., and Abramov, I. Responses of single cells in visual system to shifts in the wavelength of light. *Science,* 1964, **146**, 1184–1186. [288]

DeValois, R. L., Jacobs, G. H., and Jones, A. E. Effects of increments and decrements of light on neural discharge rate. *Science,* 1962, **136**, 986–988. [288]

Diamond, A. L. See Campbell, Miller, and Diamond, 1960.

Dixon, J. C. Concept formation and emergence of contradictory relations. *Journal of Experimental Psychology,* 1949, **39**, 144–149. [284]

Doan, Helen. See Eimas and Doan, 1965.

Dollard, J., and Miller, N. E. *Personality and psychotherapy.* New York: McGraw-Hill, 1950. [260–261]

Dominguez, K. See Jackson and Dominguez, 1939; Jackson, Stonex, Lane, and Dominguez, 1938.

Douse, T. le M. "Transposition of traces of experience." *Mind,* 1878, **3**, 132–134. [8, 283]

Draper, W. A. See Riopelle, Rahm, Itoigawa, and Draper, 1964.

Dunn, Dorothy. See H. E. Jones and Dunn, 1932.

Durkin, K. See Terrell, Durkin, and Wiesley, 1959.

*Ebel, H. C., and Werboff, J. Transposition of intermediate size in dogs. Paper read at meeting of Eastern Psychological Association, New York, April, 1966. [74 103, 105, 126, 177]

Ebenholtz, S. See Rock and Ebenholtz, 1959.

Eckerman, Carol. See Salzinger and Eckerman, 1965.

Eckhardt, M. E. See Jackson and Eckhardt, 1940.

Eguchi, P. E. See R. E. Cole, Dent, Eguchi, Fujii, and Johnson, 1964.

Ehrenfels, C. von. Über Gestaltqualitäten. *Vierteljahresschrift für wissenschaftlich*

Philosophie, 1890, **14**, 249–292. (Numerous secondary sources, e.g., Bentley, 1902, pp. 272–275; Boring, 1950, pp. 442–444, 453, etc.; Heidbreder, 1933, pp. 336–337; Parsons, 1927, pp. 47 and 49.) [5, 9, 80, 231]

Ehrenfels, C. von. On Gestalt-qualities. (Translated by Mildred Focht.) *Psychological Review*, 1937, **44**, 521–524. [5, 231, 240]

*Ehrenfreund, D. A study of the transposition gradient. *Journal of Experimental Psychology*, 1952, **43**, 81–87. [29, 30, 107, 108, 124, 130, 176]

Ehrenfreund, D. See Alberts and Ehrenfreund, 1951.

Eimas, P. D. Personal communication. 1965. [85]

Eimas, P. D., and Doan, Helen. Stimulus compounding and conditional discrimination learning in rats. Paper read at meeting of Eastern Psychological Association, Atlantic City, April, 1965. [85]

Eisenberg, A. M. See Yerkes and Eisenberg, 1915.

Eisenberg, P. See Wesman and Eisenberg, 1941.

Elkind, D. Discrimination, seriation, and numeration of size and dimensional differences in young children: Piaget replication study VI. *Journal of Genetic Psychology*, 1964, **104**, 275–296. [149]

Ellis, W. D. (Ed.), *A source book of Gestalt psychology*. London: Routledge & Kegan Paul, 1938. [346]

Engen, T. See Lipsitt and Engen, 1961.

Ernhart, C. B. See F. K. Graham, Ernhart, Craft, and Berman, 1964.

Ettlinger, G. Cross-modal transfer of training in monkeys. *Behaviour*, 1960, **16**, 56–65. (a) [220]

Ettlinger, G. Discrimination learning theory: Excitatory vs. inhibitory tendencies in monkeys. *Quarterly Journal of Experimental Psychology*, 1960, **12**, 41–44. (b) [83]

Ettlinger, G. Learning in two sense-modalities. *Nature*, 1961, **191**, 308. [220]

Ettlinger, G. See Burton and Ettlinger, 1960; M. Cole, Chorover, and Ettlinger, 1961; Moffett and Ettlinger, 1966a; Moffett and Ettlinger, 1966b.

Fagan, J. F. See Witryol, Lowden, and Fagan, 1966.

Fantz, R. L. Visual experience in infants: Decreased attention to familiar patterns relative to novel ones. *Science*, 1964, **146**, 668–670. [62]

Farber, I. E. The things people say to themselves. *American Psychologist*, 1963, **18**, 185–197. [219]

Fehrer, Elizabeth V. See Helson and Fehrer, 1932.

Fernberger, S. W. Possible effects of the imaginal type of the subject on aphasic disturbances. *American Journal of Psychology*, 1919, **30**, 327–336. [256]

Fiero, Patricia G. See Reese and Fiero, 1964.

Fisch, R. I. See McNamara and Fisch, 1964.

Fischer, W. F. See Witryol and Fischer, 1960.

Flavell, J. H. *The developmental psychology of Jean Piaget*. Princeton, N. J.: Van Nostrand, 1963. [284]

Flavell, J. H. The function of private speech in children's thinking. Paper read at meeting of Society for Research in Child Development, Minneapolis, March, 1965. [257]

Flavell, J. H., Beach, D. R., and Chinsky, J. M. Spontaneous verbal rehearsal in a memory task as a function of age. *Child Development*, 1966, **37**, 283–299. [257]

*Flory, R. M. A study of the factors determining discrimination of size by the white rat. Unpublished master's thesis, University of Virginia, 1938. [42–43, 47, 103, 104, 107, 109, 124, 130, 133, 176]

* Flory, R. M. A study of the factors determining discrimination of size by the white rat. *Psychological Bulletin,* 1939, **36**, 607. (Abstract) [47, 109, 176]

Forsman, R. See Munsinger and Forsman, 1966.

Franchina, J. J. See McAllister, McAllister, and Franchina, 1965.

*Frank, H. Untersuchung über Sehgrössenkonstanz bei Kindern. *Psychologische Forschung,* 1926, **7**, 137. (Source: Klüver, 1933, pp. 321 and 370.) [135]

*Frank, H. Die Sehgrössenkonstanz bei Kindern. *Psychologische Forschung,* 1928, **10**, 102. (Source: Klüver, 1933, pp. 321 and 370.) [135]

Frank, L. K. The problem of learning. *Psychological Review,* 1926, **33**, 329–351. [8, 292]

Franz, S. I. Visual cross education and cerebral function. *Psychological Bulletin,* 1931, **28**, 206. (Abstract) [v]

Fraser, D. C. Humphrey's paradox: A further investigation. *British Journal of Psychology,* 1948, **38**, 227–233. [11]

Freedman, J. L. See Mednick and Freedman, 1960.

Freeman, R. B., Jr. Bibliography of transposition research in animals and humans. Research Bull. No. 30, Department of Psychology, Pennsylvania State University, University Park, Pennsylvania, February, 1966. [vi, 367]

Fröbes, J. *Lehrbuch der Experimentelle Psychologie.* Freiberg: Herder, 1923. (Sources: Lindworsky, 1931, p. *v*; Spearman, 1937a, p. 220; Spearman, 1937b, p. 303; Woodworth, 1938, p. 834.) [80]

Fujii, K. K. See R. E. Cole, Dent, Eguchi, Fujii, and Johnson, 1964.

Furth, H. G. Research with the deaf: Implications for language and cognition. *Psychological Bulletin,* 1964, **62**, 145–164. [153, 361]

Furth, H. G. Clarification on language and thinking: A reply to Marion Blank. Unpublished manuscript. 1965. [153]

Furth, H. G., and Youniss, J. The influence of language and experience on discovery and use of logical symbols. *British Journal of Psychology,* 1965, **56**, 381–390. [153]

Furth, H. G. See Youniss and Furth, 1963.

Galt, W. E. The capacity of the rhesus and cebus monkey and the gibbon to acquire differential response to complex visual stimuli. *Genetic Psychology Monographs,* 1939, **21**, 387–457. [82]

Gamble, Eleanor A. McC. A study in memorizing various materials by the reconstruction method. *Psychological Monographs,* 1909, **10**, No. 4 (Whole No. 43). [8, 222]

Gardner, Ann M. See Zeiler and Gardner, 1966a; Zeiler and Gardner, 1966b.

Gardner, D. B., and Judisch, J. M. Transfer effects of discrimination learning across sensory modalities. Paper read at meeting of Society for Research in Child Development, Berkeley, April, 1963. [221]

Gardner, D. B., and Judisch, J. M. Intersensory transfer of training in young children. *Perceptual and Motor Skills,* 1965, **20**, 802. [221]

Gardner, D. B. See Houck, Gardner, and Ruhl, 1965.

Gardner, M. Dermo-optical perception: A peek down the nose. *Science,* 1966, **151**, 654–657. [223]

Gaydos, H. F. Intersensory transfer in the discrimination of form. *American Journal of Psychology,* 1956, **69**, 107–110. [220]

*Gayton, A. H. The discrimination of relative and absolute stimuli by albino rats. *Journal of Comparative Psychology,* 1927, **7**, 93–105. [11, 24, 29, 30, 47, 99, 100, 102–103, 104, 132, 176, 256]

Geier, F. M., Levin, M., and Tolman, E. C. Individual differences in emotionality, hypothesis formation, vicarious trial and error, and visual discrimination learning in rats. *Comparative Psychology Monographs*, 1941, 17, No. 3 (Whole No. 87). [82]

Gekoski, W. L. See Butter and Gekoski, 1966.

Gelb, A. Colour constancy. (Die 'Farbenkonstanz' der Sehdlinge. *Handbuch der normalen und pathologischen Physiologie*, 1929, 12, 594–678.) In W. D. Ellis (Ed.), *A source book of Gestalt psychology*. London: Routledge & Kegan Paul, 1938. Pp. 196–209. (Hsia, 1943, gave the volume number as 121, and the pages as 594–777.) [335, 350, 352]

Gellermann, L. W. Form discrimination in chimpanzees and two-year-old children: I. Form (triangularity) *per se. Journal of Genetic Psychology*, 1933, 42, 3–27. (a) [82, 208, 212]

Gellermann, L. W. Form discrimination in chimpanzees and two-year-old children: II. Form versus background. *Journal of Genetic Psychology*, 1933, 42, 28–50. (b) [82, 208, 212–213]

Gellert, Elizabeth. The transition from mirror-image to diagonal sets in children's lateralizations of human figures. Paper read at meeting of Society for Research in Child Development, Minneapolis, March, 1965. [8]

Gelman, Rochel. See Trabasso, Deutsch, and Gelman, 1966.

*Gentry, G., Overall, J., and Brown, W. Transpositional responses of rhesus monkeys to stimulus-objects of intermediate size. *American Journal of Psychology*, 1959, 72, 453–455. [39, 74–75, 99, 126, 177, 187]

Gentry, G. V. See W. L. Brown, Overall, and Gentry, 1959; Gonzalez, Gentry, and Bitterman, 1954.

Gerben, M. J., and Wischner, G. J. A comparison of the effects of motor and verbal pretraining on the learning of a single Weigl discrimination by normal and retarded children. Paper read at meeting of Eastern Psychological Association, Atlantic City, April, 1965. [258–260]

Gerjuoy, Irma R. See Spiker, Gerjuoy, and Shepard, 1956.

Ghent, Lila. Recognition by children of realistic figures presented in various orientations. *Canadian Journal of Psychology*, 1960, 14, 249–256. [204–205, 210]

Ghent, Lila. Stimulus orientation as a factor in the recognition of geometric forms by school-age children. Paper read at meeting of Eastern Psychological Association, New York, April, 1963. [204–205]

Ghent, Lila, and Bernstein, Lilly. Influence of the orientation of geometric forms on their recognition by children. *Perceptual and Motor Skills*, 1961, 12, 95–101. [204–205, 210]

Gibson, Eleanor J. Development of perception: Discrimination of depth compared with discrimination of graphic symbols. In J. C. Wright and J. Kagan (Eds.), Basic cognitive processes in children. *Monographs of the Society for Research in Child Development*, 1963, 28, No. 2. Pp. 5–24. [206]

Gibson, Eleanor J., Gibson, J. J., Pick, Anne D., and Osser, H. A developmental study of the discrimination of letter-like forms. *Journal of Comparative and Physiological Psychology*, 1962, 55, 897–906. [206–207, 208]

Gibson, Eleanor J., Walk, R. D., Pick, H. L., Jr., and Tighe, T. J. The effect of prolonged exposure to visual patterns on learning to discriminate similar and different patterns. *Journal of Comparative and Physiological Psychology*, 1958, 51, 584–587. [206]

Gibson, Eleanor J. See J. J. Gibson and Gibson, 1955.

Gibson, J. J., and Gibson, Eleanor J. Perceptual learning: Differentiation or enrichment? *Psychological Review*, 1955, 62, 32–41. [206]

Gibson, J. J. See E. J. Gibson, Gibson, Pick, and Osser, 1962.

Gleason, Josephine M. An experimental study of 'feelings of relation.' *American Journal of Psychology*, 1919, 30, 1–26. [291]

Goggin, Judith P. See Riley, Goggin, and Wright, 1963.

Goldberg, S. E., and Clark, G. "Relational" vs. "specific stimulus" learning in discrimination. *Journal of Genetic Psychology*, 1955, 86, 187–190. [87]

Goldstein, A. G. See Brooks and Goldstein, 1963.

Gollin, E. S. Reversal learning and conditional discrimination in children. *Journal of Comparative and Physiological Psychology*, 1964, 58, 441–445. [213–214]

*Gonzalez, R. C. Personal communication. 1964. [301–303]

*Gonzalez, R. C., Gentry, G. V., and Bitterman, M. E. Relational discrimination of intermediate size in the chimpanzee. *Journal of Comparative and Physiological Psychology*, 1954, 47, 385–388. [39, 75, 99, 126, 132, 142, 143, 178, 187, 229, 233]

*Gonzalez, R. C., and Ross, S. The basis of solution by preverbal children of the intermediate-size problem. *American Journal of Psychology*, 1958, 71, 742–746. [34, 76, 148, 155, 236–237, 301–303, 321, 325–329]

Goodwin, W. R., and Lawrence, D. H. The functional independence of two discrimination habits associated with a constant stimulus situation. *Journal of Comparative and Physiological Psychology*, 1955, 48, 437–443. [317]

Goss, A. E. Early behaviorism and verbal mediating responses. *American Psychologist*, 1961, 16, 285–298. (a) [256]

Goss, A. E. Verbal mediating responses and concept formation. *Psychological Review*, 1961, 68, 248–274. (b) [260–261]

Goss, A. E., and Wischner, G. J. Vicarious trial and error and related behavior. *Psychological Bulletin*, 1956, 53, 35–54. [83]

Götz, W. Vergleichende Untersuchungen zur Psychologie der optischen Wahrnehmungsvorgänge. I. Experimentelle Untersuchungen zum Problem der Sehgrössenkonstanz beim Haushuhn. *Zeitschrift für Psychologie und Physiologie der Sinnesorgane. I Abteilung. Zeitschrift für Psychologie*, 1926, 99, 247–260. (Sources: Gulliksen, 1932a, pp. 38 and 49; Katz, 1937, p. 79.) [181]

Götz, W. See Kroh, 1927.

*Gould, Donna E. Pitch transposition and discrimination in adult humans as a function of stimulus ratio and inter-pair interval. Unpublished doctoral dissertation, University of California, Berkeley, 1963. [25, 26, 31, 48, 51, 103, 104, 106–107, 284]

Gould, J. D., and Schaffer, Amy. Eye-movement patterns in scanning numeric displays. *Perceptual and Motor Skills*, 1965, 20, 521–535. [207]

Gould, J. D., and Schaffer, Amy. Eye-movement parameters in pattern perception. Paper read at meeting of Eastern Psychological Association, New York, April, 1966. [206, 231]

Gould, J. D. See Schaffer and Gould, 1964.

Graber, V. *Grundlinien zur Erforschung des Helligkeits- und Farbensinnes der Tiere.* Prag: Tempsky, 1884. (Sources: C. J. Warden *et al.*, 1936, pp. 38–39 and 446; Washburn and Bentley, 1906, pp. 113–114.) [194]

Graham, Frances K., Ernhart, Claire B., Craft, Marguerite, and Berman, Phyllis W. Learning of relative and absolute size concepts in preschool children. *Journal of Experimental Child Psychology*, 1964, 1, 26–36. [192, 199]

Graham, Frances K. See Berman and Graham, 1964.

*Graham, V., Jackson, T. A., Long, L., and Welch, L. Generalization of the concept of middleness. *Journal of Genetic Psychology*, 1944, **65**, 227–237. [149, 154, 162, 164, 165]

Greene, Frances M. Effect of novelty on choices made by preschool children in a simple discrimination task. *Child Development*, 1964, **35**, 1257–1264. [123]

*Grether, W. F., and Wolfle, D. L. The relative efficiency of constant and varied stimulation during learning. II. White rats on a brightness discrimination problem. *Journal of Comparative Psychology*, 1936, **22**, 365–374. [12, 176, 194–195, 199]

Grice, G. R. The acquisition of a visual discrimination habit following response to a single stimulus. *Journal of Experimental Psychology*, 1948, **38**, 633–642. [55, 56, 93]

Grice, G. R. Visual discrimination learning with simultaneous and successive presentation of stimuli. *Journal of Comparative and Physiological Psychology*, 1949, **42**, 365–373. [86, 87]

Grice, G. R. The acquisition of a visual discrimination habit following extinction of response to one stimulus. *Journal of Comparative and Physiological Psychology*, 1951, **44**, 149–153. [55, 56, 93]

Grice, G. R. Hunter's test of the absolute and relative theories of transposition. *British Journal of Psychology*, 1953, **44**, 257–260. [152, 275]

Grindley, G. C. See Dees and Grindley, 1947.

*Gulliksen, H. Studies of transfer of response: I. Relative vs. absolute factors in the discrimination of size by the white rat. *Journal of Genetic Psychology*, 1932, **40**, 37–51. (a) [12, 29, 30, 99, 108, 124, 133, 176, 342]

Gulliksen, H. Transfer of response in human subjects. *Journal of Experimental Psychology*, 1932, **15**, 496–516. (b) [29, 135]

*Gulliksen, H. The relationship between degree of original learning and degree of transfer. *Psychometrika*, 1936, **1**, 37–43. [63, 64, 176]

Gulliksen, H., and Wolfle, D. L. A theory of learning and transfer: I. and II. *Psychometrika*, 1938, **3**, 127–149 and 225–251. [239–245, 271, 293–308 passim]

Gulliksen, H., and Wolfle, D. L. Correction of an error in "A theory of learning and transfer." *Psychometrika*, 1939, **4**, 178. [239]

Gundlach, R. H., and Herington, G. B., Jr. The problem of relative and absolute transfer of discrimination. *Journal of Comparative Psychology*, 1933, **16**, 199–206. [46, 234, 282]

Gunter, R. See Blakeslee and Gunter, 1966.

Guthrie, E. R. *The psychology of learning.* New York: Harper, 1935. [287, 311]

Haber, R. N. Nature of the effect of set on perception. *Psychological Review*, 1966, **73**, 335–351. [283]

*Hadley, C. V. D. Transfer experiments with guinea-pigs. *British Journal of Psychology*, 1927, **18**, 189–224. [24, 25, 26, 27, 28, 30, 31, 83, 99, 100, 175, 184]

Hadley, R. W. See Riley, McKee, and Hadley, 1964.

Halasz, H. K. See Aarons, Halasz, and Riesen, 1963.

Hall, J. F. See Prokasy and Hall, 1963.

Hamilton, W. *Lectures on metaphysics.* Boston, Mass.: Gould & Lincoln, 1859. [231]

Hanfmann, Eugenia. Some experiments on spacial position as a factor in children's perception and reproduction of simple figures. *Psychologische Forschung*, 1933,

17, 319–329. (Sources: Ling, 1941, pp. 2 and 65; Sekuler and Rosenblith, 1964, pp. 143 and 144.) [209]

Hanson, H. M. Stimulus generalization following three-stimulus discrimination training. *Journal of Comparative and Physiological Psychology,* 1961, **54,** 181–185. [86, 114]

Hara, K., and Warren, J. M. Equivalence reactions by normal and brain-injured cats. *Journal of Comparative and Physiological Psychology,* 1961, **54,** 91–93. [215]

Harlow, H. F. Learning set and error factor theory. In S. Koch (Ed.), *Psychology: A study of a science.* Vol. 2. New York: McGraw-Hill, 1959. Pp. 492–537. [22, 323]

Harlow, H. F., Harlow, Margaret K., Rueping, R. R., and Mason, W. A. Performance of infant rhesus monkeys on discrimination learning, delayed response, and discrimination learning set. *Journal of Comparative and Physiological Psychology,* 1960, **53,** 113–121. [161]

Harlow, H. F. See Mason, Blazek, and Harlow, 1956.

Harlow, Margaret K. See Harlow, Harlow, Rueping, and Mason, 1960.

*Harrison, R., and Nissen, H. W. The response of chimpanzees to relative and absolute positions in delayed response problems. *Journal of Comparative Psychology,* 1941, **31,** 447–455. [47, 178, 187]

Hartmann, G. W. The field theory of learning and its educational consequences. In N. B. Henry (Ed.), *The forty-first yearbook of the National Society for the Study of Education.* Part II. *The psychology of learning.* Chicago, Ill.: University of Chicago Press, 1942. Pp. 165–214. [140, 217, 219, 220–221, 222, 223, 233, 332, 353]

Hartmann, G. W., and Triche, A. Differential susceptibility of children and adults to standard illusions. *Journal of Genetic Psychology,* 1933, **42,** 493–498. [283]

Hawkins, W. F. See Baumeister, Beedle, and Hawkins, 1964.

Hazlitt, Victoria. Children's thinking. *British Journal of Psychology,* 1930, **20,** 354–361. [219]

Head, H. Aphasia and kindred disorders of speech. *Brain,* 1920, **43,** 87–165. [256–257]

Hearst, E., and Pribram, K. H. Appetitive and aversive generalization gradients in amygdalectomized monkeys. *Journal of Comparative and Physiological Psychology,* 1964, **58,** 296–298. [186]

Hebb, D. O. The innate organization of visual activity: I. Perception of figures by rats reared in total darkness. *Journal of Genetic Psychology,* 1937, **51,** 101–126. (a) [213]

*Hebb, D. O. The innate organization of visual activity. II. Transfer of response in the discrimination of brightness and size by rats reared in total darkness. *Journal of Comparative Psychology,* 1937, **24,** 277–299. (b) [42, 99, 100, 137, 176, 185]

*Hebb, D. O. The innate organization of visual activity. III. Discrimination of brightness after removal of the striate cortex in the rat. *Journal of Comparative Psychology,* 1938, **25,** 427–437. [99, 124, 176, 185]

Hebb, D. O. *The organization of behavior.* New York: Wiley, 1949. [153, 287–288, 291, 293–308 *passim,* 317]

*Hebert, J. A., and Krantz, D. L. Transposition: A reevaluation. *Psychological Bulletin,* 1965, **63,** 244–257. [229, 237]

Hegge, F. W. See Blue and Hegge, 1965.

Heidbreder, Edna. *Seven psychologies.* (*Student's Edition.*) New York: Appleton-Century, 1933. [339]

Helmholtz, H. von. *Helmholtz's treatise on physiological optics.* (Translated by J. P. C. Southall from *Handbuch der Physiologischen Optik.* Dritte Auflage, Dritter Band. Orig. publ. 1910.) The Optical Society of America, 1925. [6, 7]

Helson, H. The psychology of *Gestalt. American Journal of Psychology,* 1925, **36**, 342–370. [353]

*Helson, H. "Insight" in the white rat. *Journal of Experimental Psychology,* 1927, **10**, 378–396. [126, 133, 176, 214, 233]

Helson, H. (Abstract of Rignano, 1928.) *Psychological Abstracts,* 1928, **2**, 532. [6]

Helson, H. *Adaptation-level theory. An experimental and systematic approach to behavior.* New York: Harper, 1964. [31, 234, 249, 251, 350]

Helson, H., and Fehrer, Elizabeth V. The role of form in perception. *American Journal of Psychology,* 1932, **44**, 79–102. [231]

Helson, H. See Kaplan and Helson, 1950.

Hempel, C. G., and Oppenheim, P. Studies in the logic of explanation. *Philosophy of Science,* 1948, **15**, 135–175. (Reprinted in H. Feigl and May Brodbeck [Eds.], *Readings in the philosophy of science.* New York: Appleton-Century-Crofts, 1953. Pp. 319–352.) [5]

Herington, G. B., Jr. See Gundlach and Herington, 1933.

Hermelin, B. See O'Connor and Hermelin, 1959.

Herrnstein, R. J., and Loveland, D. H. Complex visual concept in the pigeon. *Science,* 1964, **146**, 549–551. [215]

Hershenson, M. Visual discrimination in the human newborn. *Journal of Comparative and Physiological Psychology,* 1964, **58**, 270–276. [191]

Hershenson, M. Form perception in the human newborn. Paper read at 2nd Annual Symposium, Center for Visual Science, University of Rochester, New York, June, 1965. [191, 204]

Hershenson, M., Munsinger, H., and Kessen, W. Preference for shapes of intermediate variability in the newborn human. *Science,* 1965, **147**, 630–631. [191]

*Herter, K. Weiter Dressurversuche an Fischen. *Zeitschrift für wissenschaftliche Biologie. Abteilung C, Zeitschrift für vergleichende Physiologie,* 1929, **11**, 730–748. (Source: Shirai, 1951, pp. 13, 15, 21, and *iii.*) [174, 179, 246]

*Herter, K. Dressurversuche mit Igeln. *Zeitschrift für wissenschaftliche Biologie. Abteilung C, Zeitschrift für vergleichende Physiologie,* 1932, **18**. (Source: Katz, 1937, p. 69.) [175, 182]

*Herter, K. Dressurversuche mit Igeln, i. Orts-, Helligkeits-, und Farbendressuren. *Zeitschrift für wissenschaftliche Biologie. Abteilung C, Zeitschrift für vergleichende Physiologie,* 1933, **18**, 481–515. (Source: Shirai, 1951, pp. 14–16 and *iii.*) [175, 179]

*Herter, K. Dressurversuche mit ogeln, ii. Form- und Helligkeitsdressuren, Farbenunterscheidung, Labyrinthversuche, Rhythmus- und Selbstdressuren. *Zeitschrift für wissenchaftliche Biologie. Abteilung C, Zeitschrift für vergleichende Physiologie,* 1934, **21**, 450–462. (Source: Shirai, 1951, pp. 14–16 and *iii.* [175, 179]

*Hertz, Mathilde. Wahrnehmungspsychologische Untersuchungen am Eichelhäher. I. *Zeitschrift für wissenschaftliche Biologie. Abteilung C, Zeitschrift für vergleichende Physiologie,* 1928, **7**, 144–194. (a) (Source: Shirai, 1951, pp. 13 and *iii.*) [179]

Hertz, Mathilde. Wahrnehmungspsychologische Untersuchungen am Eichelhäher. II. *Zeitschrift für wissenschaftliche Biologie. Abteilung C, Zeitschrift für ver-*

gleichende Physiologie, 1928, **7**, 617–656. (b) (Source: Ellis, 1938, footnote 1, p. 252.) [195]

*Hertz, Mathilde. Weitere Versuche an der Rabenkrähe. *Psychologische Forschung*, 1928, **10**, 111–141. (c) (Source: Shirai, 1951, pp. 13 and *iii.*) [179]

*Hertz, Mathilde. Figural perception in bees. (Translated from Die Organisation des optischen Feldes bei der Biene. I. *Zeitschrift für wissenschaftliche Biologie. Abteilung C, Zeitschrift für vergleichende Physiologie*, 1929, **8**, 693–748.) In W. D. Ellis (Ed.), *A source book of Gestalt psychology*. London: Routledge & Kegan Paul, 1938. Pp. 253–263. [173, 174, 212]

Hertz, Mathilde. (See Warden *et al.*, 1940, p. 695.) [173, 174, 179]

Hetherington, Mavis. See Ross, Hetherington, and Wray, 1965.

*Heyman, M. N. An investigation of hypothetical generalization gradients in a visual transposition situation. Unpublished master's thesis, State University of Iowa, 1951. [26, 27, 29, 30, 31, 42–43, 99, 100, 108, 133, 141, 142, 176]

*Hicks, J. A., and Stewart, Florence D. The learning of abstract concepts of size. *Child Development*, 1930, **1**, 195–203. [162, 164, 165, 229]

Hilgard, E. R. *Theories of learning*. (2nd ed.) New York: Appleton-Century-Crofts, 1956. [229, 240]

Hill, Suzanne D. Chronological age levels at which children solve three problems varying in complexity. *Perceptual and Motor Skills*, 1962, **14**, 254. [162]

Hiss, R. H., and Thomas, D. R. Stimulus generalization as a function of testing procedure and response measure. *Journal of Experimental Psychology*, 1963, **65**, 587–592. [12]

Hodgson, R. Feelings of relation. *Mind*, 1885, **10**, 250–256. [291]

Hodgson, R. See Sidgwick and Hodgson, 1884.

Hofstaetter, P. R. The changing composition of "intelligence": A study in *T*-technique. *Journal of Genetic Psychology*, 1954, **85**, 159–164. [262]

Hoge, Mildred A., and Stocking, Ruth J. A note on the relative value of punishment and reward as motives. *Journal of Animal Behavior*, 1912, **2**, 43–50. [82]

Holland, M. K., and Wertheimer, M. Some physiognomic aspects of naming, or, maluma and takete revisited. *Perceptual and Motor Skills*, 1964, **19**, 111–117. [217]

*Honig, W. K. Prediction of preference, transposition, and transposition-reversal from the generalization gradient. *Journal of Experimental Psychology*, 1962, **64**, 239–248. [86, 93–94, 98, 107, 109–110, 127–128, 175, 182]

Honig, W. K. Discrimination, generalization, and transfer on the basis of stimulus differences. In D. I. Mostofsky (Ed.), *Stimulus generalizaton*. Stanford, Calif.: Stanford University Press, 1965. Pp. 218–254. [182, 198]

*Hopkins, A. E. Experiments on color vision in mice in relation to the duplicity theory. *Zeitschrift für wissenschaftliche Biologie. Abteilung C, Zeitschrift für vergleichende Physiologie*, 1927, **6**, 299–344. (Sources: *Psychological Abstracts*, 1928, **2**, 411; Shirai, 1951, pp. 13, 15, and *iv.*) [175, 184]

*Hörmann, M. Über den Helligkeitssinn der Bienen. *Zeitschrift für wissenschaftliche Biologie. Abteilung C, Zeitschrift für vergleichende Physiologie*, 1934, **21**, 188–249. (Sources: Katz, 1937, p. 69; Shirai, 1951, pp. 12, 15, 21, and *iii*; C. J. Warden *et al.*, 1940, pp. 679 and 972.) [173, 174, 246]

Hornbostel, E. M. von. The unity of the senses. (Translated by Elizabeth Koffka and W. Vinton from Die Einheit der Sinne. *Melos, Zeitschrift für Musik*, 1925, **4**, 290–297.) In W. D. Ellis (Ed.), *A source book of Gestalt psychology*. London:

Routledge & Kegan Paul, 1938. Pp. 210–216. (Reprinted from *Psyche,* 1927, 7, 83–89.) [217–218, 222]

Hornbostel, E. M. von. Über Geruchschelligkeit. *Pflügers Archiv für die gesamte Physiologie des Menschen und der Tiere,* 1931, 227, 517–538. (Sources: N. E. Cohen, 1934, p. 117; von Schiller, 1935, pp. 465–466 and 469.) [221]

Horton, D. L. See Kjeldergaard and Horton, 1960.

Houck, Elaine V., Gardner, D. B., and Ruhl, Donna. Effects of auditory and visual pretraining on performance in a tactile discrimination task. *Perceptual and Motor Skills,* 1965, 20, 1057–1063. [221]

House, Betty, and Zeaman, D. Reversal and nonreversal shifts in discrimination learning in retardates. *Journal of Experimental Psychology,* 1962, 63, 444–451. [317]

House, Betty J., and Zeaman, D. Miniature experiments in the discrimination learning of retardates. In L. P. Lipsitt and C. C. Spiker (Eds.), *Advances in child development and behavior.* Vol. 1. New York: Academic Press, 1963. Pp. 313–374. [317]

Householder, A. S. Neural structure in perception and response. *Psychological Review,* 1947, 54, 169–176. [288–290, 293–308 *passim*]

Hsia, Yun. Whiteness constancy as a function of difference in illumination. *Archives of Psychology,* 1943, No. 284. [341]

Huang, I. Children's explanations of strange phenomena. *Smith College Studies in Psychology, Northampton, Massachusetts,* 1930, No. 1. [284]

Hughes, C. See North, Maller, and Hughes, 1958.

Hull, C. L. The problem of stimulus equivalence in behavior theory. *Psychological Review,* 1939, 46, 9–30. [11]

Hull, C. L. Conditioning: Outline of a systematic theory of learning. In N. B. Henry (Ed.), *The forty-first yearbook of the National Society for the Study of Education.* Part II. *The psychology of learning.* Chicago, Ill.: University of Chicago Press, 1942. Pp. 61–95. [11]

Hull, C. L. *Principles of behavior.* New York: Appleton-Century-Crofts, 1943. [11, 276, 277, 279, 283, 287, 311, 313]

Hull, C. L. Stimulus intensity dynamism (V) and stimulus generalization. *Psychological Review,* 1949, 56, 67–76. [123, 246, 306, 320]

Hull, C. L. *A behavior system.* New Haven, Conn.: Yale University Press, 1952. [83, 123, 193–194]

Humphrey, G. The theory of Einstein and the *Gestalt-Psychologie:* A parallel. *American Journal of Psychology,* 1924, 35, 353–359. [362]

Humphrey, G. The effect of sequences of indifferent stimuli on a reaction of the conditioned response type. *Journal of Abnormal and Social Psychology,* 1927, 22, 194–212. [11]

Humphrey, G. *Thinking. An introduction to its experimental psychology.* New York: Wiley, 1951. [273]

*Hunter, I. M. L. An experimental investigation of the absolute and relative theories of transposition behavior in children. *British Journal of Psychology,* 1952, 43, 113–128. (a) [25, 26, 31, 32, 65–66, 71, 95, 112, 125, 133, 148, 152, 229]

*Hunter, I. M. L. Discrimination learning and transposition behavior of rats in a water tank apparatus. *Quarterly Journal of Experimental Psychology,* 1952, 4, 91–100. (b) [63, 83–84, 176]

Hunter, I. M. L. Reply to Professor Grice. *British Journal of Psychology,* 1953, 44, 261–262. (a) [272]

*Hunter, I. M. L. The absolute and relative theories of transposition behavior in rats. *Journal of Comparative and Physiological Psychology,* 1953, **46,** 493–497. (b) [58–59, 63, 64, 83–84, 95, 176]

*Hunter, I. M. L. Children's reactions to bivariant stimuli. *British Journal of Psychology,* 1954, **45,** 288–293. [229, 271–272, 293–308 *passim*]

Hunter, I. M. L. *Memory.* (Revised ed.) Baltimore: Penguin, 1964. [235]

Hunter, W. S. Some notes on the auditory sensitivity of the white rat. *Psychobiology,* 1918, **1,** 339–351. [222]

Hunter, W. S. Learning: II. Experimental studies of learning. In C. Murchison (Ed.), *The foundations of experimental psychology.* Worcester, Mass.: Clark University Press, 1929. Pp. 564–627. [141]

Hunton, Vera D. The recognition of inverted pictures by children. *Journal of Genetic Psychology,* 1955, **86,** 281–288. [210, 211]

Huysmans, J.-K. *A Rebours.* (Orig. publ. 1889.) In *Oeuvres complètes de J.-K. Huysmans.* Vol. VII. Paris: Les Éditions G. Crès et Cie., [No Date]. [222]

Hyman, L. See Campione, Hyman, and Zeaman, 1965.

Ingle, D. J. Interocular transfer in goldfish: Color easier than pattern. *Science,* 1965, **149,** 1000–1002. [216]

Inhelder, Bärbel, and Piaget, J. *The early growth of logic in the child.* New York: Harper, 1964. [153]

Inhelder, Bärbel. See Piaget and Inhelder, 1956; Piaget, Inhelder, and Szeminska, 1960.

Irion, A. L. See McGeoch and Irion, 1952.

Iscoe, I. See Stevenson and Iscoe, 1954; Stevenson and Iscoe, 1955; Stevenson, Iscoe, and McConnell, 1955a.

Itoigawa, N. See Riopelle, Rahm, Itoigawa, and Draper, 1964.

Ivashchenko, F. I. An experimental study of the relationships between words heard, seen and pronounced. *Pavlov Journal of Higher Nervous Activity,* 1958, **8,** 168–174. [153]

Jack, D. See Brackbill and Jack, 1958.

*Jackson, T. A. Studies in transposition learning by children: III. Transpositional response as a function of the number of transposed dimensions. *Journal of Experimental Psychology,* 1939, **25,** 116–124. [12, 42, 136–138]

*Jackson, T. A., and Dominguez, K. Studies in the transposition of learning by children: II. Relative vs. absolute choice with multi-dimensional stimuli. *Journal of Experimental Psychology,* 1939, 24, 630–639. [12, 26, 27, 31, 42, 63–64, 66, 137–138]

Jackson, T. A., and Eckhardt, M. E. Studies in the transposition of learning by children: V. The number of stimuli in the training series as a factor in generalization. *Journal of Experimental Psychology,* 1940, **27,** 303–312. [129–131]

*Jackson, T. A., and Jerome, E. Studies in the transposition of learning by children: IV. A preliminary study of patternedness in discrimination learning. *Journal of Experimental Psychology,* 1940, **26,** 432–439. [13, 41–42, 63–64, 65, 97–98, 107]

*Jackson, T. A., and Jerome, E. A. Studies in the transposition of learning by children. VI. Simultaneous vs. successive presentation of stimuli to bright and dull children. *Journal of Experimental Psychology,* 1943, **33,** 431–439. [40–41, 43, 63–64, 65, 97–98, 165]

*Jackson, T. A., Stonex, E., Lane, E., and Dominguez, K. Studies in the transposition of learning by children. I. Relative vs. absolute choice as a function of the amount of training. *Journal of Experimental Psychology*, 1938, **23**, 578–599. [12, 26, 27, 31, 48, 63–64, 112, 137–138, 150, 160, 299]

Jackson, T. A. See V. Graham, Jackson, Long, and Welch, 1944.

Jacobs, G. H. See DeValois, Jacobs, and Abramov, 1964; DeValois, Jacobs, and Jones, 1962.

*Jaensch, E. R. *Einige allgemeine Fragen der Psychologie und Biologie des Denkens.* Leipzig: Barth, 1920. (Sources: Koffka, 1925, pp. 221 and 368; Shirai, 1951, pp. 8b–9, 13–16, and *v*; Shirai, 1954, pp. 13 and 60; Tolman, 1927, pp. 14 and 31; C. J. Warden *et al.*, 1936, pp. 225 and 482. In Shirai, 1954, the reference is given as: Einige allgemeinere Fragen der Psychologie und Biologie des Denkens, erlautert an der Lehre vom Vergleich. *Arbeiten zur Psychologie und Philosophie*, 1–31. Leipzig: Joh. Ambr. Barth, 1920.) [140, 174, 180–181, 291–292]

Jakobovits, L. A. Mediation theory and the "single-stage" S-R model: Different? *Psychological Review*, 1966, **73**, 376–381. [265]

James, H. An application of Helson's theory of adaptation level to the problem of transposition. *Psychological Review*, 1953, **60**, 345–351. [31, 234–235, 249–250, 254, 293–308 *passim*, 319–320]

James, W. *The principles of psychology.* (Orig. publ. 1890.) [New York]: Dover, 1950. [3, 5, 14, 82, 222, 231, 245, 292]

Jasper, Kathleen. See Zeiler and Jasper, 1966.

Jastrow, J. The perception of space by disparate senses. *Mind*, 1886, **11**, 539–554. [219]

Jastrow, J. Studies from the laboratory of experimental psychology of the University of Wisconsin.—II. A study of Zollner's figures and other related illusions. *American Journal of Psychology*, 1892, **4**, 381–398. (Whole report, pp. 381–428.) [783–784]

Jeeves, M. See North and Jeeves, 1956.

Jefferson, T. *Notes on Virginia.* (Orig. publ. 1782.) In A. E. Bergh (Ed.), *The writings of Thomas Jefferson.* Vol. II. Washington, D. C.: Thomas Jefferson Memorial Association, 1907. [81]

Jeffrey, W. E. Variables in early discrimination learning: I. Motor responses in the training of a left-right discrimination. *Child Development*, 1958, **29**, 269–275. (a) [259–260]

Jeffrey, W. E. Variables in early discrimination learning: II. Mode of response and stimulus difference in the discrimination of tonal frequencies. *Child Development*, 1958, **29**, 531–538. (b) [259–260]

Jeffrey, W. E. Variables affecting reversal-shifts in young children. *American Journal of Psychology*, 1965, **78**, 589–595. [260, 264]

Jenkins, T. N. See C. J. Warden, Jenkins, and Warner, 1936; C. J. Warden, Jenkins, and Warner, 1940.

Jerome, E. A. See Jackson and Jerome, 1940; Jackson and Jerome, 1943.

Johnsgard, K. W. The role of contrast in stimulus intensity dynamism (*V*). *Journal of Experimental Psychology*, 1957, **53**, 173–179. [246]

Johnson, D. F. See Cumming, Siegel, and Johnson, 1965.

*Johnson, H. M. Visual pattern-discrimination in the vertebrates—III. Effective differences in width of visible striae for the monkey and the chick. *Journal of Animal Behavior*, 1916, **6**, 169–188. [68, 99, 100, 102, 104, 175, 177, 180, 181, 186]

*Johnson, P., and Bailey, D. E. Some determinants of the use of relationships in discrimination learning. *Journal of Experimental Psychology,* 1966, **71**, 365–372. [31, 60–61, 69]

*Johnson, R. C., and Zara, R. C. Relational learning in young children. *Journal of Comparative and Physiological Psychology,* 1960, **53**, 594–597. [50, 51, 70, 71, 76, 110–112, 148, 196, 197, 199, 301, 323, 324, 325–329]

Johnson, R. C. See R. E. Cole, Dent, Eguchi, Fujii, and Johnson, 1964.

Jones, A. E. See DeValois, Jacobs, and Jones, 1962.

Jones, C. G. See Thomas and Jones, 1962.

Jones, F. N. The stepwise phenomenon. *American Journal of Psychology,* 1939, **52**, 125–127. (a) [8, 12, 229, 282]

*Jones, F. N. The "stepwise phenomenon" in rats. *Journal of Comparative Psychology,* 1939, **27**, 39–44. (b) [8, 42, 63, 64, 99, 100, 176]

*Jones, H. E., and Dunn, Dorothy. The configural factor in children's learning. *Journal of Genetic Psychology,* 1932, **41**, 3–15. [32, 66, 73–74, 124, 125, 160, 161, 162, 165]

Judisch, J. M. See D. B. Gardner and Judisch, 1963; D. B. Gardner and Judisch, 1965.

*Kafka, H. Beitrag zur Psychologie eines niederen Affen: Grössenuntershiedung bei cercocebus fuliginosus. *Zeitschrift für wissenschaftliche Biologie. Abteilung C, Zeitschrift für vergleichende Physiologie,* 1931, **15**, 71–120. (Source: Shirai, 1951, pp. 14, 16, 21, and *v.*) [63, 177, 186]

Kagan, J. The role of cognition in developmental theory: Theory and research. Lecture given at the State University of New York at Buffalo, November, 1965. [263]

Kagan, J., Moss, H. A., and Sigel, I. E. Psychological significance of styles of conceptualization. In J. C. Wright and J. Kagan (Eds.), Basic cognitive processes in children. *Monographs of the Society for Research in Child Development,* 1963, **28**, No. 2. Pp. 73–112. [263]

Kaplan, S., and Helson, H. A study of judgment in pre- and post-lobotomized patients. Unpublished study. 1950. (Source: Helson, 1964, pp. 411 and 688.) [246]

Karn, H. W., and Munn, N. L. Visual pattern discrimination in the dog. *Journal of Genetic Psychology,* 1932, **40**, 363–374. [208]

Kasianova, A. (See Zaporozhets, 1965, pp. 90–91.) [160, 161–163, 263]

Katz, D. *Animals and men. Studies in comparative psychology.* London: Longmans, Green, 1937. [15, 217, 233, 283, 333, 335, 342, 345, 346, 350, 352, 368]

Katz, D. *Psychologischer Atlas, Orbis Pictus Psychologicus.* Basel: Benno Schwabe, 1945. [7]

Katz, D. *Gestalt psychology.* (Translated by R. Tyson.) New York: Ronald Press, 1950. [224–225]

*Katz, D., and Révész, G. Experimentelle Studien zur vergleichenden Psychologie. Versuche mit Hühnern. *Zeitschrift für angewandte Psychologie,* 1921, **18**, 307–320. (Sources: Gelb, 1929, p. 203; Katz, 1937, p. 76; Tolman, 1927, pp. 15 and 32; C. J. Warden *et al.,* 1936, pp. 255 and 482.) [174, 247–248]

*Katz, D., and Toll, A. Die Messung von Charakter- und Begabungsunterscheiden bei Tieren (Versuche mit Hühnern). *Zeitschrift für Psychologie und Physiologie der Sinnesorgane. I Abteilung. Zeitschrift für Psychologie,* 1923, **93**, 287–311. (Sources: Katz, 1937, p. 228; Tolman, 1927, pp. 14 and 32; C. J. Warden *et al.,* 1936, pp. 255 and 482.) [174]

*Keller, H., and Takemasa, T. Farben im Wechsel-Umfeld. *Zeitschrift für Psychologie und Physiologie der Sinnesorgane. I Abteilung. Zeitschrift für Psychologie,* 1933,

129, 121–134. (Sources: *Psychological Abstracts,* 1933, **7,** 610; Shirai, 1951, pp. 13, 15–16, 21, and *v.*) [63, 174, 246]

Kellogg, W. N., and Rice, C. E. Visual discrimination in a bottlenose porpoise. *Psychological Record,* 1963, **13,** 483–498. [82]

Kellogg, W. N., and Rice, C. E. Visual problem-solving in a bottlenose dolphin. *Science,* 1964, **143,** 1052–1055. [82]

Kelvin, R. P. Discrimination of size by sight and touch. *Quarterly Journal of Experimental Psychology,* 1954, **6,** 23–34. [219]

Kelvin, R. P., and Mulik, A. Discrimination of length by sight and touch. *Quarterly Journal of Experimental Psychology,* 1958, **10,** 187–192. [219]

Kendler, H. H. See T. S. Kendler, Kendler, and Learnard, 1962; T. S. Kendler, Kendler, and Wells, 1960.

*Kendler, Sylvia Tracy S. Experimental investigation of the effect of difference between training and test stimuli on the amount of transposition. Unpublished doctoral dissertation, State University of Iowa, 1943. [13, 176]

*Kendler, Tracy S. An experimental investigation of transposition as a function of the difference between training and test stimuli. *Journal of Experimental Psychology,* 1950, **40,** 552–562. [26, 27, 28–29, 30, 31, 108, 109, 113, 124, 130, 176, 242]

Kendler, Tracy S. Development of mediating responses in children. In J. C. Wright and J. Kagan (Eds.), Basic cognitive processes in children. *Monographs of the Society for Research in Child Development,* 1963, **28,** No. 2. Pp. 33–48. [266]

Kendler, Tracy S. Verbalization and optional reversal shifts among kindergarten children. *Journal of Verbal Learning and Verbal Behavior,* 1964, **3,** 428–436. [264]

Kendler, Tracy S., Kendler, H. H., and Learnard, Beulah. Mediated responses to size and brightness as a function of age. *American Journal of Psychology,* 1962, **75,** 571–586. [146, 161]

Kendler, Tracy S., Kendler, H. H., and Wells, Doris. Reversal and nonreversal shifts in nursery school children. *Journal of Comparative and Physiological Psychology,* 1960, **53,** 83–88. [263, 266]

Kennedy, W. A. See Terrell and Kennedy, 1957.

Kerpelman, L. C., and Pollack, R. H. Developmental changes in the location of form discrimination cues. *Perceptual and Motor Skills,* 1964, **19,** 375–382. [204]

Kessen, W. See Hershenson, Munsinger, and Kessen, 1965; Salapatek and Kessen, 1966.

Key, Cora B. Recall as a function of perceived relations. *Archives of Psychology,* 1926, **13,** No. 83. [236]

Kimble, G. A. *Hilgard and Marquis' conditioning and learning.* (2nd ed.) New York: Appleton-Century-Crofts, 1961. [318]

*Kinnaman, A. J. Mental life of two *Macacus rhesus* monkeys in captivity. I and II. *American Journal of Psychology,* 1902, **13,** 98–148 and 173–218. [124, 177, 186, 229]

Kitagawa, Yoshiko. See Sato and Kitagawa, 1951.

Kjeldergaard, P. M., and Horton, D. L. An experimental analysis of associative factors in stimulus equivalence, response equivalence and chaining paradigms. Studies in Verbal Behavior, Report No. 3, University of Minnesota, August, 1960. [11]

*Kleshchov, S. V. The relations of tones as conditioned stimuli. *Trudy Fiziologicheskikh Laboratorii Imeni I. P. Pavlova,* 1933, **5,** 213–218. (Sources: *Psychological Abstracts,* 1933, **7,** 698; Razran, 1938a, pp. 370 and 376; Razran, 1939, pp. 312, 318, and 329. In 1938, Razran gave the author as "Klestchov," and gave the title as "Sound ratios as conditioned reflex stimuli.") [107, 108, 177, 186]

*Klüver, H. Relational thinking in monkeys. *Psychological Bulletin*, 1929, 26, 168–169. (Abstract) (a) [186]

*Klüver, H. The equivalence of stimuli in monkeys. *Ninth International Congress of Psychology, Proceedings and Papers*, 1929. Pp. 263–264. (Abstract) (b) [186]

*Klüver, H. Some of the functions underlying the responses of monkeys to stimuli in different sense fields. *Psychological Bulletin*, 1930, 27, 647–648. (Abstract) [186]

*Klüver, H. The equivalence of stimuli in the behavior of monkeys. *Journal of Genetic Psychology*, 1931, 39, 3–27. [186]

*Klüver, H. *Behavior mechanisms in monkeys*. Chicago, Ill.: University of Chicago Press, 1933. [1, 6, 7, 10–12, 68, 82, 83, 100, 107, 108, 124, 125, 126, 132, 135, 137, 177, 186, 214, 215, 229, 237, 287, 291, 299, 340, 353]

Klüver, H., and Bucy, P. C. Preliminary analysis of functions of the temporal lobes in monkeys. *Archives of Neurology and Psychiatry*, 1939, 42, 979–1000. [215]

Knox, G. W. Where is the confusion? *Journal of Psychology*, 1939, 7, 17–27. [237]

Koffka, K. Reply to V. Benussi. (Zur Grundlegung der Wahrnehmungspsychologie. Eine Auseinandersetzung mit V. Benussi. *Zeitschift für Psychologie und Physiologie der Sinnesorgane. I Abteilung. Zeitschift für Psychologie*, 1915, 73, 11–90.) In W. D. Ellis (Ed.), *A source book of Gestalt psychology*. London: Routledge & Kegan Paul, 1938. Pp. 371–378. [6]

Koffka, K. Perception: An introduction to the *Gestalt-Theorie*. *Psychological Bulletin*, 1922, 19, 531–585. [5, 8, 13, 80, 233, 283, 297, 372]

Koffka, K. The perception of movement in the region of the blind spot. *British Journal of Psychology, General Section*, 1924, 14, 269–273. [140]

Koffka, K. *The growth of the mind. An introduction to child-psychology*. (Translated by R. M. Ogden.) New York: Harcourt, 1925. [138, 159, 231, 237, 292, 332, 349, 352, 353, 355]

Koffka, K. *Principles of Gestalt psychology*. New York: Harcourt, 1935. [13, 283, 353]

*Köhler, W. Aus der Anthropoidenstation auf Teneriffa. II. Optische Untersuchungen am Schimpansen und am Haushuhn. *Abhandlungen der Königlich preussische Akademie der Wissenschaften. Physikalisch-mathematische Klasse*, 1915, No. 3. (Sources: Katz, 1937, p. 75; Koffka, 1925, *passim;* Tolman, 1927, pp. 16 and 32; Vernon, 1952, pp. 74–75 and 275; C. J. Warden *et al.*, 1936, pp. 255 and 483.) [174, 178, 181, 187, 231, 247–248]

*Köhler, W. Die Farben der Sehdinge beim Schimpansen und beim Haushuhn. *Zeitschrift für Psychologie und Physiologie der Sinnesorgane. I Abteilung. Zeitschrift für Psychologie*, 1917, 77, 248–255. (Sources: Gelb, 1929, p. 203; Vernon, 1952, pp. 74–75 and 275; C. J. Warden *et al.*, 1936, pp. 255 and 483.) [174, 178, 187, 247–248]

*Köhler, W. Simple structural functions in the chimpanzee and in the chicken. (Translated excerpts from Aus der Anthropoidenstation auf Teneriffa. IV. Nachweis einfacher Strukturfunktionen beim Schimpansen und beim Haushuhn. Über eine neue Methode zur Untersuchung des bunten Farbensystems. *Abhandlungen der Königlich preussische Akademie der Wissenschaften. Physikalisch-mathematische Klasse*, 1918, No. 2.) In W. D. Ellis (Ed.), *A source book of Gestalt psychology*. London: Routledge & Kegan Paul, 1938. Pp. 217–227. (Maier and Schneirla, 1935, pp. 352–354, were used as source for data omitted from the translated portion.) [46, 102, 104, 124, 132, 135, 153, 159, 174, 178, 187, 232–239, 293–308 *passim*]

Köhler, W. Physical Gestalten. (*Die physischen Gestalten in Ruhe und im stationären Zustand, eine naturphilosophische Untersuchung.* Ehrlangen: Philosophischen Akademie, 1920.) In W. D. Ellis (Ed.), *A source book of Gestalt psychology.* London: Routledge & Kegan Paul, 1938. Pp. 17–54. [6, 9, 232]

Köhler, W. The mentality of apes. (Translated from the 2nd revised ed. by Ella Winter.) New York: Harcourt, 1925. [233]

Köhler, W. Reply to Eugenio Rignano. (Bemerkungen zur Gestalttheorie (in Anschluss an Rignanos Kritik). *Psychologische Forschung*, 1928, 11, 188–234.) In W. D. Ellis (Ed.), *A source book of Gestalt psychology.* London: Routledge & Kegan Paul, 1938. Pp. 389–396. [6, 283]

Köhler, W. Gestalt psychology. New York: Liveright, 1929. [7, 217, 218, 220–221, 222, 229, 232–239, 245, 293–308 *passim*, 309, 332, 353]

Köhler, W. Relational determination in perception. In L. A. Jeffress (Ed.), *Cerebral mechanisms in behavior.* New York: Wiley, 1951. Pp. 200–230. [245]

Kohlrausch, A. Tagessehen, Dämmersehen, Adaptation. *Handbuch der normalen und pathologischen Physiologie mit Berücksichtung der experimentellen Pharmakologie*, 1931, 12, No. 2, Receptionsorgane II, 1499–1594. (Source: Klüver, 1933, pp. 314 and 375.) [245]

*Kol'tsova, M. M. The interaction of different kinds of temporary connections in the process of forming conditioned reflexes to the relationship of stimuli. *Pavlov Journal of Higher Nervous Activities*, 1961, 11, No. 4, 43–44. [152–153]

Kral, T. P. See Campbell and Kral, 1958.

Krantz, D. L. See Hebert and Krantz, 1965.

Krauthamer, G. M. Form perception across sensory modalities. *American Psychologist*, 1959, 14, 396. (Abstract) [220]

Krechevsky, I. "Hypotheses" in rats. *Psychological Review*, 1932, 39, 516–532. (a) [236, 294, 295]

Krechevsky, I. "Hypotheses" versus "chance" in the pre-solution period in sensory discrimination-learning. *University of California Publications in Psychology*, 1932, 6, No. 3, 27–44. (b) [294, 295]

Krechevsky, I. The genesis of "hypotheses" in rats. *University of California Publications in Psychology*, 1932, 6, No. 4, 45–64. (c) [294, 295]

Kreezer, G., and Dallenbach, K. M. Learning the relation of opposition. *American Journal of Psychology*, 1929, 41, 432–441. [237–238, 322]

Kries, J. A. von. *Über die materiellen Grundlagen der Bewusstseinserscheinungen. Programm der Universität Freiburg* i. *B.*, 1898. (Sources: Hartmann, 1942, p. 182; Helson, 1925, p. 345; Koffka, 1925, pp. 235 and 370; Koffka, 1935, pp. 463 and 696; Köhler, 1929, pp. 343–347 and 348; Parsons, 1927, pp. 53–54. The reference given here is from Helson and Parsons. Hartmann cited no reference. In 1925, Koffka gave the reference as ". . . Bewusstseins-Erscheinungen, Tübingen und Leipzig, 1901." In 1935, Koffka omitted the hyphen. Köhler omitted "Über" and "Tübingen und Leipzig," but gave the date as 1901.) [212]

*Kroh, O. (in Gemeinschaft mit W. Götz, R. Scholl und W. Ziegler.) Weitere Beiträge zur Psychologie des Haushuhns. (Further contributions to the psychology of the hen.) *Zeitschrift für Psychologie und Physiologie der Sinnesorgane. I Abteilung. Zeitschrift für Psychologie*, 1927, 103, 203–227. (Source: *Psychological Abstracts*, 1928, 2, 24–25.) [132, 174, 180, 204, 208, 213, 214]

*Kuenne, Margaret R. Experimental investigation of the relation of language to transposition behavior in young children. *Journal of Experimental Psychology*, 1946, 36, 471–490. [13, 40, 41, 42, 110–113, 126, 133, 141–142, 148, 150–151, 160, 162, 163, 166, 229, 242, 255, 263]

*Kuenne, Margaret R. Transfer of response in young children on the intermediate size problem. *American Psychologist*, 1948, 3, 361. (Abstract) [119]

Külke, E. (See Mach, 1914, p. 286.) [225]

Külpe, O. *Outlines of psychology. Based upon the results of experimental investigation.* (Translated by E. B. Titchener.) London: Swan Sonnenschein, 1909. [81]

Künnapas, T. M. Influence of frame size on apparent length of a line. *Journal of Experimental Psychology*, 1955, 50, 168–170. [248]

Kurke, M. I. See Riesen, Kurke, and Mellinger, 1953.

*Kuroda, R. Studies on visual discrimination in the tortoise *Clemmys japonica. Acta Psychologica Keijo*, 1933, 2, 31–59. (Sources: *Psychological Abstracts*, 1934, 8, 168–169; Shirai, 1951, pp. 13, 15–16, 20–21, and *vi.*) [47, 63, 174, 180]

Kurtz, K. H. *Foundations of psychological research. Statistics, methodology, and measurement.* Boston, Mass.: Allyn & Bacon, 1965. [83]

Lachman, R. The model in theory construction. *Psychological Review*, 1960, 67, 113–129. [265]

*Lachman, S. J. Absolute and relational stimulus training in discrimination learning. *Psychological Monographs*, 1956, 70, No. 5 (Whole No. 412). [87–89, 93, 98, 124, 176, 245]

Lachman, S. J., and Taylor, D. H. Brightness discrimination learning under conditions of simultaneous and successive presentation of stimuli with punishment. *Psychological Reports*, 1963, 13, 127–132. [88–89, 93, 98]

Ladd, G. T. *Psychology. Descriptive and explanatory.* New York: Charles Scribner's Sons, 1894. [7, 80]

Ladd, G. T., and Woodworth, R. S. *Elements of physiological psychology.* (Revised ed.) New York: Charles Scribner's Sons, 1911. [223, 283, 291]

Landau, J. S. A developmental investigation of stimulus generalization. Paper read at meeting of Eastern Psychological Association, New York, April, 1966. [42]

Lane, E. See Jackson, Stonex, Lane, and Dominguez, 1938.

*Lang, J. The effect of delay in test and intra-set differences on the solution of the intermediate size problem by children. Unpublished manuscript, 1965. (Cited by Zeiler, 1967. See Zeiler and Lang, 1966b.) [381]

Lang, Jo. See Zeiler and Lang, 1966a; Zeiler and Lang, 1966b.

Langford, T. See Stevenson and Langford, 1957; Stevenson, Langford, and Reese, 1955b.

*Lashley, K. S. Visual discrimination of size and form in the albino rat. *Journal of Animal Behavior*, 1912, 2, 310–331. [82, 176]

Lashley, K. S. The color vision of birds. I. The spectrum of the domestic fowl. *Journal of Animal Behavior*, 1916, 6, 1–26. [181, 195]

Lashley, K. S. Studies of cerebral function in learning. *Psychobiology*, 1920, 2, 55–135. [82]

Lashley, K. S. Studies of cerebral function in learning. VI. The theory that synaptic resistance is reduced by the passage of the nerve impulse. *Psychological Review,* 1924, 31, 369–375. [v, 225]

Lashley, K. S. Studies of cerebral function in learning. VII. The relation between cerebral mass, learning, and retention. *Journal of Comparative Neurology*, 1926, 41, 1–58. [80, 82, 256]

Lashley, K. S. *Brain mechanisms and intelligence.* Chicago, Ill.: University of Chicago Press, 1929. (a) [225–226, 229, 236, 287, 293–308 *passim*]

Lashley, K. S. Learning: I. Nervous mechanisms in learning. In C. Murchison (Ed.), *The foundations of experimental psychology.* Worcester, Mass.: Clark University Press, 1929. Pp. 524–563. (b) [213, 215, 255–256, 287]

Lashley, K. S. Conditional reactions in the rat. *Journal of Psychology,* 1938, **6,** 311–324. (a) [213]

*Lashley, K. S. The mechanism of vision. XV. Preliminary studies of the rat's capacity for detailed vision. *Journal of General Psychology,* 1938, **18,** 123–193. (b) [93, 108, 137, 176, 184, 233, 244–245]

Lashley, K. S. An examination of the "continuity theory" of discriminative learning. *Journal of General Psychology,* 1942, **26,** 241–265. [82, 212, 244–245]

Lashley, K. S., and Wade, Marjorie. The Pavlovian theory of generalization. *Psychological Review,* 1946, **53,** 72–87. [82, 237, 238, 283, 310]

Lawrence, D. H. The applicability of generalization gradients to the transfer of a discrimination. *Journal of General Psychology,* 1955, **52,** 37–48. [277]

*Lawrence, D. H., and DeRivera, J. Evidence for relational transposition. *Journal of Comparative and Physiological Psychology,* 1954, **47,** 465–471. [59–60, 68–69, 99, 100, 107, 176, 237]

Lawrence, D. H. See Baker and Lawrence, 1951; Goodwin and Lawrence, 1955.

Learnard, Beulah. See T. S. Kendler, Kendler, and Learnard, 1962.

Leeper, Dorothy O. See R. Leeper and Leeper, 1932.

Leeper, R., and Leeper, Dorothy O. An experimental study of equivalent stimulation in human learning. *Journal of General Psychology,* 1932, **6,** 344–376. [195, 199]

Lefford, A. See Birch and Lefford, 1963.

Leonard, Sister M. John Catherine. Verbal mediation in children. Paper read at meeting of Midwestern Psychological Association, Chicago, May, 1966. [263]

L'Estrange, R. *Fables, of Aesop and other eminent mythologists: With morals and reflexions. By Sir Roger L'Estrange.* (5th ed.) London: R. Sare, A. and F. Churchil, D. Brown, T. Goodwin, M. Wotton, F. Nicholson, G. Sawbridge, B. Tooke, and G. Strahan, 1708. [140]

Lettvin, J. Y. See Maturana, Lettvin, McCulloch, and Pitts, 1960.

Levin, M. See Geier, Levin, and Tolman, 1941.

Levine, M. A model of hypothesis behavior in discrimination learning set. *Psychological Review,* 1959, **66,** 353–366. [294]

Levinson, Billey, and Reese, H. W. Patterns of discrimination learning set in preschool children, fifth graders, college freshmen, and the aged. Final Report, Cooperative Research Project No. 1059, Office of Education, U. S. Department of Health, Education, and Welfare, 1963. (Also: *Monographs of the Society for Research in Child Development,* 1967, **32,** No. 7 [Whole No. 115].) [324, 325]

Levinson, Billey. See Nissen, Levinson, and Nichols, 1953.

Lewis, C. S. Transposition. In C. S. Lewis, *Transposition and Other Addresses.* London: Geoffrey Bles, 1949. Pp. 9–20. [217]

Lewis, D. J. *Scientific principles of psychology.* Englewood Cliffs, N. J.: Prentice-Hall, 1963. [60]

*Lewis, M. H. Elemental versus configural response in the chick. *Journal of Experimental Psychology,* 1930, **13,** 61–75. [12, 114, 174, 180, 195, 199, 215, 245]

Lindworsky, J. (Review of Köhler's *Nachweis einfacher Strukturfunktionen . . .* [1918].) *Stimmen der Zeit,* 1919, **97,** 62ff. (Sources: Koffka, 1925, pp. 216–230 and 368–369; Lindworsky, 1931, p. *x,* footnote *.) [231]

*Lindworsky, J. Umrifsskizze zu einer theoretischen Psychologie. *Zeitschrift für Psychologie und Physiologie der Sinnesorgane. I Abteilung. Zeitschrift für Psychologie,* 1922, **89,** 313–357. (Source: Shirai, 1951, pp. 9 and *vii.*) [291–292]

Lindworsky, J. *Experimental psychology.* [4th ed.] (Translated by H. R. DeSilva.) New York: Macmillan, 1931. [9, 49, 81, 138, 223, 291, 340, 355]

*Line, W. The growth of visual perception in children. *British Journal of Psychology Monograph Supplements,* 1931, **5,** No. 15. [48, 95, 103, 104, 192–193, 199, 205, 213, 231, 246]

Ling, B.-C. Form discrimination as a learning cue in infants. *Comparative Psychology Monographs,* 1941, **17,** No. 2 (Whole No. 86). [344]

Lipsitt, L. P., and Engen, T. Effects of presentation of paired and single-stimulus on discrimination of length. *American Journal of Psychology,* 1961, **74,** 274–277. [320]

Liublinskaya, A. A. The development of children's speech and thought. (Translated by N. Parsons.) In B. Simon (Ed.), *Psychology in the Soviet Union.* Stanford, Calif.: Stanford University Press, 1957. Pp. 197–204. [146]

Locke, J. *Essay concerning human understanding.* (Orig. publ. 1690.) Reprinted in *The works of John Locke* Vol. 1. London: Thomas Tegg; W. Sharpe and Son; G. Offor; G. and J. Robinson; J. Evans and Co.: Also R. Griffin and Co. Glasgow; and J. Cumming, Dublin, 1823. [2, 3, 5, 80–81]

Loewenberg, J. Are relations effable? *Journal of Philosophy,* 1930, **27,** 309–319. [1–2]

Long, L. Size discrimination in children. *Child Development,* 1941, **12,** 247–254. [212]

Long, L. See V. Graham, Jackson, Long, and Welch, 1944.

Lotze, H. *Outlines of psychology.* Dictated portions of the lectures of Herman Lotze. (Translated by G. T. Ladd from the 3rd German ed.) Boston, Mass.: Ginn, 1886. [80, 223]

Lovaas, O. I. Cue properties of words: The control of operant responding by rate and content of verbal operants. *Child Development,* 1964, **35,** 245–256. [146, 263]

Loveland, D. H. See Herrnstein and Loveland, 1964.

Lowden, Lynn M. See Witryol, Lowden, and Fagan, 1966.

Lund, E. J. The relations of Bursaria to food. I. Selection in feeding and in extrusion. *Journal of Experimental Zoology,* 1914, **16,** 1–52. [191, 224]

Luria, A. R. The role of language in the formation of temporary connections. In B. Simon (Ed.), *Psychology in the Soviet Union.* Stanford, Calif.: Stanford University Press, 1957. Pp. 115–129. [263]

Luria, A. R. *The role of speech in the regulation of normal and abnormal behaviour.* New York: Liveright, 1961. (Also Bethesda: U. S. Department of Health, Education, and Welfare: Russian Scientific Translation Program, 1960.) [146, 263, 317]

Lyon, D. O. The relation of quickness of learning to retentiveness. *Archives of Psychology,* 1916, **5** (Whole No. 34). (*Columbia University Contributions to Philosophy and Psychology,* 1916, **24,** No. 3.) (Also in D. O. Lyon, *Memory and the learning process.* Baltimore, Md.: Warwick & York, 1917. Ch. IV, pp. 76–154.) [141]

McAllister, Dorothy E. The effects of various kinds of relevant verbal pretraining on subsequent motor performance. *Journal of Experimental Psychology,* 1953, **46,** 329–336. [260]

McAllister, Dorothy E. See W. R. McAllister, McAllister, and Franchina, 1965.

McAllister, W. R., McAllister, Dorothy E., and Franchina, J. J. Dependence of equality judgments upon the temporal interval between stimulus presentations. *Journal of Experimental Psychology*, 1965, **70**, 602–605. [205–206, 320]

McBee, G. See Stevenson and McBee, 1958.

MacCaslin, E. F. Successive and simultaneous discrimination as a function of stimulus-similarity. *American Journal of Psychology*, 1954, **67**, 308–314. [86]

McCleary, R. A. See Meyers and McCleary, 1964.

McConnell, Claudia. See Stevenson, Iscoe, and McConnell, 1955a.

McConnell, J. V. See Bitterman and McConnell, 1954.

McCosh, J. *Psychology: The cognitive powers*. New York: Charles Scribner's Sons, 1886. [4]

*McCulloch, T. L. The selection of the intermediate of a series of weights by the white rat. *Journal of Comparative Psychology*, 1935, **20**, 1–11. [74, 99, 100, 177, 189–190]

McCulloch, T. L. Comment on the formation of discrimination habits. *Psychological Review*, 1939, **46**, 75–85. [283]

McCulloch, W. S. See Maturana, Lettvin, McCulloch, and Pitts, 1960.

McGeoch, J. A., and Irion, A. L. *The psychology of human learning*. (2nd ed.) New York: Longmans, Green, 1952. [141]

*McGrade, Betty Jo. A comparison of transposition learning in sighted and blind children. Unpublished master's thesis, University of Texas, 1958. [24, 25, 31, 32, 51, 136]

Mach, E. *The analysis of sensations and the relation of the physical to the psychical*. (Translated by C. M. Williams from the 1st ed. of *Die Analyse der Empfindungen und das Verhältnis des Psychischen zum Physischen*, orig. publ. 1886; revised and supplemented by S. Waterlow from the 5th ed., orig. publ. 1907.) Chicago, Ill.: Open Court, 1914. (Reprinted, with a new introduction by T. S. Szasz. New York: Dover, 1959.) [5, 16, 81, 208–211, 217, 225, 235, 245]

*McKee, J. P., and Riley, D. A. Auditory transposition in six-year-old children. *Child Development*, 1962, **33**, 469–476. [25, 26, 31, 48–50, 125, 131–132, 150]

McKee, J. P. See Riley and McKee, 1963; Riley, McKee, Bell, and Schwartz, 1967; Riley, McKee, and Hadley, 1964; Riley, Sherman, and McKee, 1966.

Mackintosh, Janet. See Sutherland, Mackintosh, and Mackintosh, 1963.

Mackintosh, N. J. Selective attention in animal discrimination learning. *Psychological Bulletin*, 1965, **64**, 124–150. (a) [29, 55, 317]

*Mackintosh, N. J. Transposition after 'single-stimulus' training. *American Journal of Psychology*, 1965, **78**, 116–119. (b) [55, 56, 93, 176]

Mackintosh, N. J. See Sutherland, Mackintosh, and Mackintosh, 1963.

McNamara, H. J., and Fisch, R. I. Effect of high and low motivation on two aspects of attention. *Perceptual and Motor Skills*, 1964, **19**, 571–578. [317]

*Maekawa, T. An experimental study on the law of development of the transposition behavior. *Proceedings of the 19th Meeting of the Japanese Psychological Association*, 1955. Abstract No. 374. (Source: Shirai, 1963, pp. 70–73 and 143.) [160, 161]

*Maier, N. R. F. Qualitative differences in the learning of rats in a discrimination situation. *Journal of Comparative Psychology*, 1939, **27**, 289–332. [60, 99, 100, 108, 124–125, 176]

Maier, N. R. F. The effect of cortical injury on equivalence reactions in rats. *Journal of Comparative Psychology*, 1941, **32**, 165–189. [205]

Maier, N. R. F., and Schneirla, T. C. *Principles of animal psychology.* New York: McGraw-Hill, 1935. [232, 287, 352]

Makous, W. L. Cutaneous color sensitivity: Explanation and demonstration. *Psychological Review,* 1966, 73, 280–294. (a) [223]

Makous, W. L. (No title.) *Science,* 1966, 152, 1109. (b) [223]

Maller, O. See North, Maller, and Hughes, 1958.

*Maltzman, I. M. Discrimination and transposition under single and paired stimulus presentation. Unpublished doctoral dissertation, State University of Iowa, 1949. [26, 27, 28–29, 30, 31, 86, 89, 124, 177, 184]

Marsh, G. Effect of overtraining on reversal and nonreversal shifts in nursery school children. *Child Development,* 1964, 35, 1367–1372. [264]

*Marsh, G. Relational learning set in the pigeon. *Journal of Comparative and Physiological Psychology,* in press. (Also read at meeting of Western Psychological Association, Honolulu, June, 1965.) [192–193, 195–196, 199, 323]

*Marsh, G., and Sherman, Marian. Verbal mediation of transposition as a function of age level. *Journal of Experimental Child Psychology,* 1966, 4, 90–98. [25, 26, 31, 126, 151, 160, 161, 162, 257–258, 259]

*Marshall, Helen R. Transposition in children as a function of age and knowledge. *Journal of Genetic Psychology,* 1966, 108, 65–69. [148, 149, 155, 162, 164, 165, 167]

*Martin, W. E., and Blum, A. Intertest generalization and learning in mentally normal and subnormal children. *Journal of Comparative and Physiological Psychology,* 1961, 54, 28–32. [34, 126, 162, 164, 165, 166]

Mason, W. A., Blazek, Nancy C., and Harlow, H. F. Learning capacities of the infant rhesus monkey. *Journal of Comparative and Physiological Psychology,* 1956, 49, 449–453. [161]

Mason, W. A. See Harlow, Harlow, Rueping, and Mason, 1960.

Maturana, H. R., Lettvin, J. Y., McCulloch, W. S., and Pitts, W. H. Anatomy and physiology of vision in the frog (*Rana pipiens*). *Journal of General Physiology,* 1960, 43, 129–175. [288]

Mayland, E. J. See DeBold and Mayland, 1965.

Medlicott, H. B. *The evolution of mind in man.* London: Kegan Paul, Trench, Trübner, 1892. [3]

Mednick, S. A., and Freedman, J. L. Stimulus generalization. *Psychological Bulletin,* 1960, 57, 169–200. [283]

Mellinger, Jeanne C. See Riesen, Kurke, and Mellinger, 1953.

Mello, Nancy K. Interhemispheric reversal of mirror-image oblique lines after monocular training in pigeons. *Science,* 1965, 148, 252–254. (a) [216]

Mello, Nancy K. (No Title.) *Science,* 1965, 149, 1519–1520. (b) [216]

Menaker, Shirley L. Heteromodal facilitation in perceptual development. Paper read at meeting of American Psychological Association, New York, September, 1966. (Also: *American Psychologist,* 1966, 21, 649–650. [Abstract]) [223]

Mendel, Gisela. Children's preferences for differing degrees of novelty. *Child Development,* 1965, 36, 453–465. [123]

Menkhaus, Irmgard. Versuche über einäugiges Lernen und Transponieren beim Haushuhn. *Zeitschrift für Tierpsychologie,* 1957, 14, 210–230. (English summary: pp. 228–229.) [216]

Meumann, E. *The psychology of learning. An experimental investigation of the economy and technique of memory.* (Translated by J. W. Baird from the 3rd ed. of *Ökonomie und Technik des Lernens.*) New York: Appleton, 1913. [140, 231]

Meyer, Merle E. Discriminative learning under various combinations of discriminanda. *Journal of Comparative and Physiological Psychology*, 1964, **58**, 146–147. (a) [185, 193–194, 199]

*Meyer, Merle E. Transposition under various combinations of discriminanda. *Psychonomic Science*, 1964, **1**, 243–244. (b) [99, 107, 108, 177, 185]

Meyers, B., and McCleary, R. A. Interocular transfer of a pattern discrimination in pattern deprived cats. *Journal of Comparative and Physiological Psychology*, 1964, **57**, 16–21. [216]

Michels, K. M., and Zusne, L. Metrics of visual form. *Psychological Bulletin*, 1965, **63**, 74–86. [204]

Milerian, E. A. Involuntary and voluntary attention. (Translated by J. and M. Ellis from *Sovetskaya Pedagogika*, 1954, **2**, 55–67.) In B. Simon (Ed.), *Psychology in the Soviet Union*. Stanford, Calif.: Stanford University Press, 1957. Pp. 84–91. [309]

Mill, James. *Analysis of the phenomena of the human mind.* (Orig. publ. 1829.) Revised and annotated ed. London: Longmans, Green, Reoder & Dyer, 1869. (Ch. III, "The association of ideas," reprinted in W. Dennis [Ed.], *Readings in the history of psychology*. New York: Appleton-Century-Crofts, 1948. Pp. 140–154. Also in B. Rand [Ed.], *The classical psychologists; Selections illustrating psychology from Anaxagoras to Wundt*. Boston, Mass.: Houghton Mifflin, 1912. Pp. 463–482.) [3, 231]

Miller, N. See Campbell, Miller, and Diamond, 1960.

Miller, N. E. Liberalization of basic S-R concepts: Extensions to conflict behavior, motivation, and social learning. In S. Koch (Ed.), *Psychology: A study of a science. Study I. Conceptual and systematic. Vol. 2. General systematic formulations, learning, and special processes*. New York: McGraw-Hill, 1959. Pp. 196–292. [229]

Miller, N. E. See Dollard and Miller, 1950.

Miller, R. E. See Murphy and Miller, 1959.

Moffett, A., and Ettlinger, G. Opposite responding in two sense modalities. *Science*, 1966, **153**, 205–206. (a) [220]

Moffett, A., and Ettlinger, G. Reversal in tactile and visual learning. *Science*, 1966, **154**, 799. (b) [220]

*Moody, P. A. Brightness vision in the deer-mouse, Peromyscus maniculatus gracilis. *Journal of Experimental Zoology*, 1929, **52**, 367–405. [86, 175, 184]

Morgan, C. L. *An introduction to comparative psychology.* (Revised ed.) London: Walter Scott, [1903]. [4, 17, 81]

Morgulis, S. See Yerkes and Morgulis, 1909.

Moss, H. A. See Kagan, Moss, and Sigel, 1963.

*Motoyoshi, Y. The problem of attitude in absolute and relative responses. *Psukhe*, 1948, **3**, 63–73. (Source: Shirai, 1951, pp. 14–15, 17, 20, 23, 31, and vii.) [48, 128, 167]

Mowrer, O. H. *Learning theory and behavior.* New York: Wiley, 1960. (a) [109]

Mowrer, O. H. *Learning theory and the symbolic processes.* New York: Wiley, 1960. (b) [83, 285, 322]

Muenzinger, K. F. Vicarious trial and error at a point of choice: I. A general survey of its relation to learning efficiency. *Journal of Genetic Psychology*, 1938, **53**, 75–86. [82, 83]

Mulik, A. See Kelvin and Mulik, 1958.

Munn, N. L., and Stiening, Beryl R. The relative efficacy of form and background in a child's discrimination of visual patterns. *Journal of Genetic Psychology,* 1931, 39, 73–90. [208, 213]

Munn, N. L. See Karn and Munn, 1932.

Munsinger, H., and Forsman, R. Symmetry, development, and tachistoscopic recognition. *Journal of Experimental Child Psychology,* 1966, 3, 168–176. [207]

Munsinger, H. See Hershenson, Munsinger, and Kessen, 1965.

Murdock, B. B., Jr. Effects of task difficulty, stimulus similarity, and type of response on stimulus predifferentiation. *Journal of Experimental Psychology,* 1958, 55, 167–172. [259–260]

Murphy, J. V., and Miller, R. E. Spatial contiguity of cue, reward, and response in discrimination learning by children. *Journal of Experimental Psychology,* 1959, 58, 485–489. [162]

Nagel, E. See M. R. Cohen and Nagel, 1934.

*Nahinsky, I. D. The transfer of a drive intensity discrimination between two drives. *Journal of Comparative and Physiological Psychology,* 1960, 53, 598–602. [177, 185]

Newell, A. See Simon and Newell, 1962.

Newhall, S. M. Identification by young children of differently oriented visual forms. *Child Development,* 1937, 8, 105–111. [208–209]

Newson, E. The development of line figure discrimination in pre-school children. Unpublished doctoral dissertation, University of Nottingham, 1955. (Source: Vernon, 1957, pp. 17–19 and 214.) [210, 211]

Nichols, J. W. See Nissen, Levinson, and Nichols, 1953.

Nishijima, Y. See Sato and Nishijima, 1955.

*Nissen, H. W. Ambivalent cues in discriminative behavior of chimpanzees. *Journal of Psychology,* 1942, 14, 3–33. [58, 99, 178, 187]

Nissen, H. W. Description of the learned response in discrimination behavior. *Psychological Review,* 1950, 57, 121–131. [84, 244, 289–290]

Nissen, H. W. Approach and avoidance; a reply. *Psychological Review,* 1952, 59, 237–238. (a) [244]

Nissen, H. W. Further comment on approach-avoidance as categories of response. *Psychological Review,* 1952, 59, 161–167. (b) [244]

Nissen, H. W. Sensory patterning versus central organization. *Journal of Psychology,* 1953, 36, 271–287. [82, 187]

Nissen, H. W., Levinson, Billey, and Nichols, J. W. Reinforcement and "hypothesis" in the discrimination behavior of chimpanzees. *Journal of Experimental Psychology,* 1953, 45, 334–340. [229]

Nissen, H. W. See Harrison and Nissen, 1941.

North, A. J., and Jeeves, M. Interrelationships of successive and simultaneous discrimination. *Journal of Experimental Psychology,* 1956, 51, 54–58. [86, 87]

North, A. J., Maller, O., and Hughes, C. Conditional discrimination and stimulus patterning. *Journal of Comparative and Physiological Psychology,* 1958, 51, 711–715. [82]

O'Connor, N. Speech and thought in severe subnormality. In P. H. Mussen (Ed.), European research in cognitive development. *Monographs of the Society for Research in Child Development,* 1965, 30, No. 2. Pp. 68–81. [165, 220, 266–268]

O'Connor, N. Personal communication. 1965. [165, 166]

O'Connor, N., and Hermelin, B. Discrimination and reversal learning in imbeciles.

Journal of Abnormal and Social Psychology, 1959, **59**, 409–413. [165, 166, 266–268]

*Odani, S. An experimental study of brain mechanism in learning. *Japanese Journal of Experimental Psychology*, 1934, **1**, 143–209. (Source: Shirai, 1951, pp. 13, 15, and *ix*.) [179]

*Ohtsuka, N. Über die absolute und relative Wahl beim Affen *Cercopithecus* sp. (On absolute and relative choice in the monkey *Cercopithecus* sp.) *Acta Psychologica Keijo*, 1937, **3**, 33–44. (Sources: *Psychological Abstracts*, 1938, **12**, 74; Shirai, 1951, pp. 14–15, 17, 20–21, and *ix*; Wohlwill, personal communications, 1965, 1966. Shirai spelled the name "Otsuka.") [46–47, 63, 103, 104, 178, 186, 221]

*Ohtsuka, N. Ein Beitrag zur Wahl der Mitte mit dem Vielfach-Wahl-apparat bei Affen. *Acta Psychologica Keijo*, 1939, **3**, 86–94. (Sources: *Psychological Abstracts*, 1939, **13**, 525; Shirai, 1951, pp. 14–15, 17, 20–21, and *ix*. Shirai spelled the name "Otsuka.") [47, 63, 178, 187]

*Ohtsuka, N. A further study of absolute and relative choice in the monkey. *Japanese Journal of Psychology*, 1942, **17**, 74–80. (Source: Shirai, 1951, pp. 14–15, 17, 20–21, and *ix*. Shirai spelled the name "Otsuka.") [47, 63, 178, 186]

Okamoto, N. Verbalization process in infancy (I)—Transpositive use of sounds in development of symbolic activity—*Psychologia, Kyoto*, 1962, **5**, 32–40. [7–8]

*Okamoto, N., and Okuno, S. Transposition with multidimensional stimuli in young children. *Japanese Psychological Research*, 1958, **5**, 28–37. (Source: *Psychological Abstracts*, 1959, **33**, 763.) [137, 141, 142, 160, 161]

*Okano, T, (An experimental study of Spence's theory of transposition of discrimination learning: Studies of transposition II.) *Japanese Journal of Psychology*, 1957, **27**, 285–295. (English summary: pp. 320–321.) (Source: *Psychological Abstracts*, 1958, **32**, 233.) [109, 113, 126, 177]

Okuno, S. See Okamoto and Okuno, 1958.

*Oléron, P. *Recherches sur le développement mental des sourds-muets*. [Paris]: Centre National de la Recherche Scientifique, 1957. (Sources: Furth, 1964, pp. 152 and 164; Wohlwill, personal communication, 1965; Youniss, 1965, pp. 3 and 8.) [152, 160, 163]

*Oléron, P. The role of language in intellectual and cognitive functions. Seminar at Department of Psychology, University of Rochester, July, 1963. [152]

Oppenheim, P. See Hempel and Oppenheim, 1948.

Orbeli, L. A. Visual conditioned reflexes in the dog. Thesis, Petrograd, 1908. (Sources: Pavlov, 1927, pp. 133–134; C. J. Warden *et al.*, 1936, pp. 307–308 and 512; Yerkes and Morgulis, 1909, pp. 267–269 and 272. In the last source, the reference is given as: "Conditioned reflexes resulting from optical stimulation of the dog. Dissertation. St. Petersburg.") [215]

Osgood, C. E. *Method and theory in experimental psychology*. New York: Oxford University Press, 1953. [223, 245, 313]

Osgood, C. E., Suci, G. J., and Tannenbaum, P. H. *The measurement of meaning*. Urbana, Ill.: University of Illinois Press, 1957. [147, 217, 220–221, 223, 256]

Osser, H. See Gibson, Gibson, Pick, and Osser, 1962.

Osterreith, P. A. *Archives de Psychologie*, 1945, **30**, 205. (Sources: Vernon, 1952, pp. 35–36, 250, and 273; Vernon, 1957, pp. 14–15 and 215.) [205]

Overall, J. E. See W. L. Brown, Overall, and Gentry, 1959; Gentry, Overall, and Brown, 1959.

Paalberg, Juta. See Zeiler and Paalberg, 1964a; Zeiler and Paalberg, 1964b.

Parsons, Sir J. H. *An introduction to the theory of perception.* New York: Macmillan, 1927. [6, 231–232, 332, 339, 353]

*Pattie, F. A., Jr., and Stavsky, W. H. Die Struktur-Funktion und das Geschwindigkeitsunterscheidungsvermögen des Huhnes. *Psychologische Forschung,* 1932, 16, 166–170. (Sources: *Psychological Abstracts,* 1932, 6, 276; Shirai, 1951, pp. 13, 16, and *ix.*) [174, 181]

Pattie, F. A., Jr. See Stavsky and Pattie, 1930.

Patton, E. K. The problem of insightful behavior. *Psychological Monographs,* 1933, 44, 98–124. [198]

Pavlov, I. P. *Conditioned reflexes. An investigation of the physiological activity of the cerebral cortex.* (Translated and Edited by G. V. Anrep.) [London]: Oxford University Press, 1927. [11, 75, 225, 232, 299–300, 309, 361]

Peckham, Elizabeth G. See G. W. Peckham and Peckham, 1898.

Peckham, G. W., and Peckham, Elizabeth G. On the instincts and habits of the solitary wasps. *Bulletin, Wisconsin Geological and Natural History Survey,* 1898, 2, 1–245. [179]

Peckham, R. H. Visual discrimination in pre-school children. *Child Development,* 1933, 4, 292–297. [209]

Penney, R. K. Excitatory vs inhibitory tendencies in children's discrimination performance. *Perceptual and Motor Skills,* 1963, 17, 909–910. [82, 83]

Penney, R. K. Personal communication. 1965. [82]

*Perkins, F. T. A further study of configurational learning in the goldfish. *Journal of Experimental Psychology,* 1931, 14, 508–538. [114, 174, 179, 194, 199, 245]

*Perkins, F. T., and Wheeler, R. H. Configurational learning in the goldfish. *Comparative Psychology Monographs,* 1930, 7, No. 1, 1–50. [v, 22, 43, 99, 100, 102, 114, 133, 135, 174, 179, 181, 190, 194–195, 199, 215, 245, 303]

Perkins, F. T. See Wheeler and Perkins, 1929.

Piaget, J., and Inhelder, Bärbel. *The child's conception of space.* (Translated by F. J. Langdon and J. L. Lunzer.) London: Routledge & Kegan Paul, 1956. [205]

Piaget, J., Inhelder, Bärbel, and Szeminska, Alina. *The child's conception of geometry.* (Translated by E. A. Lunzer.) London: Routledge & Kegan Paul, 1960. [205]

Piaget, J. See Inhelder and Piaget, 1964.

Pick, Anne D., Pick, H. L., Jr., and Thomas, Margaret L. Cross-modal transfer and improvement of form discrimination. *Journal of Experimental Child Psychology,* 1966, 3, 279–288. [220]

Pick, Anne D. See Gibson, Gibson, Pick, and Osser, 1962.

Pick, H. Some Soviet research on learning and perception in children. In J. C. Wright and J. Kagan (Eds.), Basic cognitive processes in children. *Monographs of the Society for Research in Child Development,* 1963, 28, No. 2. Pp. 185–190. [380]

Pick, H. L., Jr. See E. J. Gibson, Walk, Pick, and Tighe, 1958; A. D. Pick, Pick, and Thomas, 1966.

Pikler, J. Empfindung und Vergleich. I. *Zeitschrift für Psychologie und Physiologie der Sinnesorgane. I Abteilung. Zeitschrift für Psychologie,* 1913, 67, 277–288. (Source: Humphrey, 1924, p. 358.) [291]

Pikler, J. *Sinnesphysiologische Untersuchungen.* Leipzig: Ambrosius Barth., 1917. (Source: Review by H. J. Watt in *Mind,* 1920, 29, 490–492.) [138]

Pillsbury, W. B. *The fundamentals of psychology.* (3rd ed.) New York: Macmillan, 1934. [222, 223, 231, 283]

Pitts, W. H. See Maturana, Lettvin, McCulloch, and Pitts, 1960.

Plum, G. E. See White and Plum, 1964.

Pollack, R. H. See Kerpelman and Pollack, 1964.

Polosina, L. V. The investigation of conditioned reflexes to synthetic stimuli and their differentiation. *Na Putyakh k Izuch. Vysshykh Form Neirodin. Reb.,* 1934, **4**, 117–130. (Sources: *Psychological Abstracts,* 1935, **9**, 129; Razran, 1939, pp. 317 and 330.) [154]

Pribram, K. H. Interrelations of psychology and the neurological disciplines. In S. Koch (Ed.), *Psychology: A study of a science. Study II. Empirical substructure and relations with other sciences.* Vol. 4. *Biologically oriented fields: Their place in psychology and in biological science.* New York: McGraw-Hill, 1962. Pp. 119–157. [186]

Pribram, K. H. See Bagshaw and Pribram, 1965; Hearst and Pribram, 1964; Schwartzbaum and Pribram, 1960.

Price, Aida E. See Zeiler and Price, 1965.

*Price, L. E. The effect of type of verbal pretraining on transposition in children. Unpublished doctoral dissertation, State University of Iowa, 1960. [34, 115, 116, 118, 126, 130, 155, 242]

Prokasy, W. F., and Hall, J. F. Primary stimulus generalization. *Psychological Review,* 1963, **70**, 310–322. [12, 283]

Pyles, Marjorie K. Verbalization as a factor in learning. *Child Development,* 1932, **3**, 108–113. [146]

Rabinowitz, F. M., and Cantor, G. N. Children's stimulus alternation, response repetition, and circular behavior as a function of age and stimulus conditions. Paper read at meeting of American Psychological Association, New York, September, 1966. [161]

Rahm, U. See Riopelle, Rahm, Itoigawa, and Draper, 1964.

Rayner, Rosalie. See Watson and Rayner, 1920.

*Razran, G. H. S. Studies in configural conditioning VII. Ratios and elements in salivary conditioning to various musical intervals. *Psychological Record,* 1938, **2**, 370–376. (a) [113, 114, 132, 186, 351]

Razran, G. H. S. Transposition of relational responses and generalization of conditioned responses. *Psychological Review,* 1938, **45**, 532–538. (b) [237, 274, 334, 375]

Razran, G. H. S. Studies in configural conditioning: I. Historical and preliminary experimentation. *Journal of General Psychology,* 1939, **21**, 307–330. [154, 186, 332, 335, 351, 362, 375]

*Razran, G. H. S. Studies in configurational conditioning: V. Generalization and transposition. *Journal of Genetic Psychology,* 1940, **56**, 3–11. [13, 64–65]

Razran, G. Stimulus generalization of conditioned responses. *Psychological Bulletin,* 1949, **46**, 337–365. [283]

Reese, H. W. Discrimination learning as a function of amount of stimulus pretraining with motor responses. Unpublished manuscript, State University of Iowa, 1958. [259–260]

*Reese, H. W. Transposition in the intermediate-size problem by preschool children. *Child Development,* 1961, **32**, 311–314. [35, 36, 37–38, 39, 43, 115, 116, 118–120, 121, 134, 144, 145, 148, 155, 167–171, 286, 326]

*Reese, H. W. The distance effect in transposition in the intermediate size problem. *Journal of Comparative and Physiological Psychology,* 1962, **55**, 528–531. (a)

[35, 36, 37–38, 43, 52, 79, 115, 116, 118–120, 121, 134, 144, 145, 149, 155, 162, 164, 165, 167–171, 286]

Reese, H. W. Verbal mediation as a function of age level. *Psychological Bulletin,* 1962, **59,** 502–509. (b) [49, 146, 155, 224, 257, 259, 260–261, 263, 266, 267, 286]

Reese, H. W. A reply to Youniss and Furth. *Psychological Bulletin,* 1963, **60,** 503–504. (a) [49, 155, 260–261, 286]

Reese, H. W. Discrimination learning set in children. In L. P. Lipsitt and C. C. Spiker (Eds.), *Advances in child development and behavior.* Vol. 1. New York: Academic Press, 1963. Pp. 115–145. (b) [62, 123, 319, 324]

Reese, H. W. "Perceptual set" in young children. *Child Development,* 1963, **34,** 151–159. (c) [322]

Reese, H. W. Discrimination learning set in rhesus monkeys. *Psychological Bulletin,* 1964, **61,** 321–340. (a) [62, 84, 123, 319, 324]

*Reese, H. W. Mediation in young children in the intermediate-size problem. Paper read at meeting of Eastern Psychological Association, Philadelphia, April, 1964. (b) [35, 36, 37–38, 43, 52, 115, 116, 118–120, 121, 133–134, 144, 145, 152, 155, 162, 164, 165, 167–171, 286, 326]

Reese, H. W. Discrimination learning set and perceptual set in young children. *Child Development,* 1965, **36,** 153–161. (a) [79, 260, 302, 324]

Reese, H. W. Imagery in paired-associate learning in children. *Journal of Experimental Child Psychology,* 1965, **2,** 290–296. (b) [153–154, 235, 236]

*Reese, H. W. Intermediate-size transposition in young children. *Journal of Comparative and Physiological Psychology,* 1965, **59,** 413–415. (c) [119–120, 251–253]

*Reese, H. W. Verbal effects in the intermediate-size transposition problem. *Journal of Experimental Child Psychology,* 1966, **3,** 123–130. (In the title as originally published, "transportation" was substituted for "transposition." The error was corrected in a notice on p. 107 of Vol. 4 of the journal.) [35, 36, 37–38, 43, 115, 116, 118–120, 121, 156–158, 167–171, 172, 257, 260, 263, 302]

Reese, H. W. Unpublished studies. [157–158, 167–171, 173, 217, 302]

*Reese, H. W., and Fiero, Patricia G. Overlearning and transposition. *Child Development,* 1964, **35,** 1361–1365. [35, 36, 37–38, 43, 66, 101, 115, 116, 118–120, 121, 133–134, 144, 145, 149, 167–171, 326]

Reese, H. W. See Levinson and Reese, 1963; Stevenson, Langford, and Reese, 1955b.

Restle, F. Toward a quantitative description of learning set data. *Psychological Review,* 1958, **65,** 77–91. [316, 323–329]

*Révész, G. Experiments on animal space perception. *British Journal of Psychology (General Section),* 1924, **14,** 387–414. [175, 180, 212, 283–284]

Révész, G. See Katz and Révész, 1921.

Rexroad, C. N. Verbalization in multiple choice reactions. *Psychological Review,* 1926, **33,** 451–458. [153–154]

Ricciuti, H. N. Object grouping and selective ordering behavior in infants 12 to 24 months old. *Merrill-Palmer Quarterly of Behavior and Development,* 1965, **11,** 129–148. [163]

Rice, Charlotte. The orientation of plane figures as a factor in their perception by children. *Child Development,* 1930, **1,** 111–143. [205, 209]

Rice, C. E. See Kellogg and Rice, 1963; Kellogg and Rice, 1964.

Rieber, M. An analysis of simultaneous vs. successive stimulus presentation in children's discrimination learning. Paper read at meeting of Society for Research in Child Development, Minneapolis, March, 1965. [82, 97]

*Riekel, A. Psychologische Untersuchungen an Hühnern. *Zeitschrift für Psychologie und Physiologie der Sinnesorgane. I Abteilung. Zeitschrift für Psychologie,* 1922, **89**, 81–115. (Sources: Shirai, 1951, pp. 1, 8b–9, 14–16, 23, and *xi*; Shirai, 1954, pp. 13–14 and 62; Tolman, 1927, pp. 14–15 and 34; C. J. Warden *et al.*, 1936, pp. 255 and 487; Washburn, 1926, pp. 242 and 404; Washburn, 1936, pp. 258 and 487.) [87, 159, 160, 175, 180–181, 256]

Riesen, A. H., Kurke, M. I., and Mellinger, Jeanne C. Interocular transfer of habits learned monocularly in visually naive and visually experienced cats. *Journal of Comparative and Physiological Psychology,* 1953, **46**, 166–172. [216]

Riesen, A. H. See Aarons, Halasz, and Riesen, 1963; P. D. Wilson and Riesen, 1966.

Rignano, E. The psychological theory of form. *Psychological Review,* 1928, **35**, 118–135. [6]

*Riley, D. A. The nature of the effective stimulus in animal discrimination learning: Transposition reconsidered. *Psychological Review,* 1958, **65**, 1–7. [99, 108, 109, 177, 213, 245–248, 251, 285, 293–308 *passim*]

*Riley, D. A. Experiments on the development of pitch and loudness as psychological dimensions. *Tijdschrift voor Psychologie (Tijdschrift van de Psychologische Kring aan de Nijmeegse Universiteit),* 1965, **13**, 312–318. (a) [50]

*Riley, D. A. Stimulus generalization and transposition. *Tijdschrift voor Psychologie (Tijdschrift van de Psychologische Kring aan de Nijmeegse Universiteit),* 1965, **13**, 301–311. (b) [94, 178, 182]

*Riley, D. A., and McKee, J. P. Pitch and loudness transposition in children and adults. *Child Development,* 1963, **34**, 471–482. [25, 26, 31, 48–50, 63, 64, 86, 92–93, 125, 131–132, 160, 177]

*Riley, D. A., Goggin, Judith P., and Wright, D. C. Training level and cue separation as determiners of transposition and retention in rats. *Journal of Comparative and Physiological Psychology,* 1963, **56**, 1044–1049. [26, 27, 28, 29–31]

*Riley, D. A., McKee, J. P., Bell, Donna D., and Schwartz, Carolyn R. Auditory discrimination in children: The effect of relative and absolute instructions on retention and transfer. Unpublished manuscript, University of California (Berkeley), 1967. [49]

*Riley, D. A., McKee, J. P., and Hadley, R. W. Prediction of auditory discrimination learning and transposition from children's auditory ordering ability. *Journal of Experimental Psychology,* 1964, **67**, 324–329. [25, 26, 31, 48–50, 126]

*Riley, D. A., Ring, K., and Thomas, J. The effect of stimulus comparison on discrimination learning and transposition. *Journal of Comparative and Physiological Psychology,* 1960, **53**, 415–421. [26, 27, 28, 29–31, 47–48, 86, 87, 90–91, 92, 177]

*Riley, D. A., Sherman, Marian, and McKee, J. P. A comment on intermediate size discrimination and adaptation-level theory. *Psychological Review,* 1966, **73**, 252–256. [54, 156, 254]

Riley, D. A. See McKee and Riley, 1962.

Ring, K. See Riley, Ring, and Thomas, 1960.

Riopelle, A. J., Rahm, U., Itoigawa, N., and Draper, W. A. Discrimination of mirror-image patterns by rhesus monkeys. *Perceptual and Motor Skills,* 1964, **19**, 383–389. [208]

Roberts, Katherine E. The ability of pre-school children to solve problems in which a simple principle of relationship is kept constant. *Journal of Genetic Psychology*, 1932, **40**, 118–135. [162]

Robinson, E. J. The influence of photometric brightness on judgments of size. *American Journal of Psychology*, 1954, **67**, 464–474. [248]

Robinson, J. S. The sameness-difference discrimination problem in chimpanzee. *Journal of Comparative and Physiological Psychology*, 1955, **48**, 195–197. [187]

Robinson, J. S. The conceptual basis of the chimpanzee's performance on the sameness-difference discrimination problem. *Journal of Comparative and Physiological Psychology*, 1960, **53**, 368–370. [187]

Rock, I., and Ebenholtz, S. The relational determination of perceived size. *Psychological Review*, 1959, **66**, 387–401. [248]

Romanes, G. J. *Animal intelligence.* New York: Appleton, 1883. [233]

Romanes, G. J. *Mental evolution in animals.* New York: Appleton, 1884. [233]

Rose, E. L. The establishment by rats of two contrary discrimination habits. *University of California Publications in Psychology*, 1931, **4**, 335–345. [96]

Rose, E. L. Spatial and temporal bases for the establishment by rats of contrary discrimination habits. *University of California Publications in Psychology*, 1939, **6**, 189–218. [96]

Rosenblith, Judy F. Perceptual discrimination in children. Paper read at meeting of Society for Research in Child Development, University Park, Pennsylvania, March, 1961. [210]

Rosenblith, Judy F. Perceptual discrimination in children II. Paper read at meeting of Society for Research in Child Development, Berkeley, April, 1963. [210]

Rosenblith, Judy F. Judgments of simple geometric figures by children. *Perceptual and Motor Skills*, 1965, **21**, 947–990. Monograph Supplement 2-V21. [210]

Rosenblith, Judy F. See Sekuler and Rosenblith, 1964.

*Ross, L. E. Personal communication. 1965. [33, 125]

*Ross, L. E., Hetherington, Mavis, and Wray, Nancy P. Delay of reward and the learning of a size problem by normal and retarded children. *Child Development*, 1965, **36**, 509–517. [33, 52, 125, 141, 142, 166]

Ross, S. See Gonzalez and Ross, 1958.

Rowley, Jean B., and Bolles, M. Marjorie. Form discrimination in white mice. *Journal of Comparative Psychology*, 1935, **20**, 205–210. [100, 101, 184]

Rowley, Jean B. See Warden and Rowley, 1929.

Ruckmick, C. A. The fifth annual meeting of the Midwestern Psychological Association. *American Journal of Psychology*, 1930, **42**, 650–653. [96]

*Rudel, Rita G. A re-evaluation of the dichotomy of absolute and relative responses in transposition. *American Psychologist*, 1954, **9**, 461–462. (Abstract) [31, 34]

*Rudel, Rita G. Transposition of response by children trained in intermediate-size problems. *Journal of Comparative and Physiological Psychology*, 1957, **50**, 292–295. [34–35, 52, 103, 105–106, 135, 149, 155, 189, 229, 234, 238, 299–300]

*Rudel, Rita G. Transposition of response to size in children. *Journal of Comparative and Physiological Psychology*, 1958, **51**, 386–390. [28, 30, 31, 96, 111, 113, 115, 125, 128–129, 148, 150–151, 160, 162, 163, 229, 234]

Rudel, Rita G. The absolute response in tests of generalization in normal and retarded children. *American Journal of Psychology*, 1959, **72**, 401–408. [81, 129–131, 166]

*Rudel, Rita G. The transposition of intermediate size by brain-damaged and mongoloid children. *Journal of Comparative and Physiological Psychology*, 1960, **53**, 89–94. [22, 34–35, 52, 104–106, 144, 149, 155, 166, 229, 234]

Rudel, Rita G. Cross-modal transfer effects in children and adults. Paper read at meeting of American Psychological Association, Philadelphia, August, 1963. [219]

Rudel, Rita G., and Teuber, H.-L. Decrement of visual and haptic Müller-Lyer illusion on repeated trials: A study of crossmodal transfer. *Quarterly Journal of Experimental Psychology*, 1963, 15, 125–131. (a) [219, 220]

Rudel, Rita G., and Teuber, H.-L. Discrimination of direction of line in children. *Journal of Comparative and Physiological Psychology*, 1963, 56, 892–898. (b) [210, 212]

Rudel, Rita G., and Teuber, H.-L. Crossmodal transfer of shape discrimination by children. *Neuropsychologia*, 1964, 2, 1–8. [219, 220]

Rudolph, R. (See Riley, 1965b, pp. 308–310.) [94, 175, 182]

Rueping, R. R. See Harlow, Harlow, Rueping, and Mason, 1960.

Ruhl, Donna. See Houck, Gardner, and Ruhl, 1965.

*Rüssel, A. Über Formauffassung zwei- bis fünfjäriger Kinder. *Neue Psychologische Studien*, 1931, 7, 1–108. (Sources: *Psychological Abstracts*, 1932, 6, 57; Shirai, 1951, pp. 14, 16, and xi; Vernon, 1952, pp. 76 and 275.) [229]

Russell, R. W. See Dennis and Russell, 1939.

Sackett, L. W. The Canada Porcupine: A study of the learning process. *Behavior Monographs*, 1913, 2, No. 2. [204]

*Sadovinkova, Mary P. A study of the behavior of birds by the multiple choice method. *Journal of Comparative Psychology*, 1923, 3, 249–282. [67, 175, 181]

Salapatek, P. H. Visual scanning of geometric forms by the human newborn. Paper read at meeting of American Psychological Association, New York, September, 1966. [207]

Salapatek, P., und Kessen, W. Visual scanning of triangles by the human newborn. *Journal of Experimental Child Psychology*, 1966, 3, 155–167. [207]

Salten, C. S. See Zeiler and Salten, 1966.

Salzinger, K., and Eckerman, Carol. Grammar and the recall of chains of verbal responses. Unpublished manuscript. 1965. (Part of the data were reported in K. Salzinger and C. Eckerman, The effect of different sequence structures on the acquisition of chains of verbal responses. Paper read at meeting of Eastern Psychological Association, Atlantic City, April, 1965.) [236]

*Sato, K. Studies of the perception of relation. I. i. An experimental and theoretical study of the problem of transitional experience. *Japanese Journal of Experimental Psychology*, 1934, 1, 99–125. (Sources: *Psychological Abstracts*, 1936, 10, 426; Shirai, 1951, pp. 14, 15, and xi.) [vi]

*Sato, K. Studies of the perception of relation. I. ii. Manifestation process in successive comparison and its meaning. *Japanese Journal of Experimental Psychology*, 1935, 2, 13–26. (Source: Shirai, 1951, pp. 14, 15, and xi.) [vi]

*Sato, K. Studies of the perception of relation; II. i. An experimental analysis of the problem of transfer of selective response. *Japanese Journal of Experimental Psychology*, 1936, 3, 219–261. (Source: Shirai, 1951, pp. 14–15, 20, 22–23, 31, and xi.) [48, 65, 103, 104, 128, 167]

*Sato, K. A genetic study of how an impression of relation is built up. *Japanese Psychological Monographs*, 1938, 6, 205–210. (Source: Shirai, 1951, pp. 14, 15, and xi.) [vi]

*Sato, K. Japanese studies on the transposition problem. *Psychologia*, 1957, 1, 22–29. (Source: Freeman, 1966.) [vi]

*Sato, K., and Kitagawa, Yoshiko. The alternation of attitude in apprehension of relations. *Psukhe*, 1947, **1**, 44–52. (Sources: Shirai, 1951, pp. 14, 15, and *xi*; Shirai, 1963, pp. 70–73 and 147. Cited in the latter source as "Versatility of the attitude in the apprehension of relation—Studies on the apprehension of relation: II, ii.") [160, 161]

*Sato, K., and Nishijima, Y. The basis of solution by children of the intermediate size problem. *American Psychologist*, 1955, **10**, 406. (Abstract) [43, 119]

Schabtach, Gretchen. Interocular and interhemispheric transfer of nonmirror-image and of mirror-image stimuli in the domestic chick. Paper read at meeting of Eastern Psychological Association, New York, April, 1966. [216]

Schaeffer, M. See Shepard and Schaeffer, 1956.

Schaffer, Amy, and Gould, J. D. Eye movement patterns as a function of previous tachistoscopic practice. *Perceptual and Motor Skills*, 1964, **19**, 701–702. [207]

Schaffer, Amy. See Gould and Schaffer, 1965; Gould and Schaffer, 1966.

*Schaller, A. Sinnesphysiologische und psychologische Untersuchungen an Wasserkäfern und Fischen. *Zeitschrift für wissenschaftliche Biologie. Abteilung C, Zeitschrift für vergleichende Physiologie*, 1926, **4**, 370–464. (Source: Shirai, 1951, pp. 13, 16, and *xi–xii*.) [179]

Scharlock, D. P. See Bugelski and Scharlock, 1952.

Schiller, P. von. Intersensorielle Transposition bei Fischen. *Zeitschrift für wissenschaftliche Biologie. Abteilung C, Zeitschrift für vergleichende Physiologie*, 1933, **19**. (Sources: Katz, 1937, pp. 72–73; von Schiller, 1935, p. 469.) [217, 218, 222, 224]

Schiller, P. [von]. Interrelation of different senses in perception. *British Journal of Psychology (General Section)*, 1935, **25**, 465–469. [221, 222, 224, 347, 368]

Schlosberg, H. See Woodworth and Schlosberg, 1954.

Schmerler, Susan. Visual discrimination of orientation by pigeons. Paper read at meeting of Eastern Psychological Association, Atlantic City, April, 1965. [87, 208]

Schneirla, T. C. See Maier and Schneirla, 1935.

Scholl, R. See Kroh, 1927.

Schusterman, R. J. Orienting responses and underwater visual discrimination in the California sea lion. *Proceedings of the 73rd Annual Convention of the American Psychological Association*. New York: American Psychological Association, 1965. Pp. 139–140. [82, 83]

Schwartz, Carolyn R. See Riley, McKee, Bell, and Schwartz, 1967.

*Schwartzbaum, J. S., and Pribram, K. H. The effects of amygdalectomy in monkeys on transposition along a brightness continuum. *Journal of Comparative and Physiological Psychology*, 1960, **53**, 396–399. [178, 186, 191]

Scott, K. G. A comparison of similarity and oddity. *Journal of Experimental Child Psychology*, 1964, **1**, 123–134. [264]

*Scott, Marcia S. Some observations of transposition behavior in retardates under different double-discrimination training procedures. Unpublished master's thesis, George Peabody College for Teachers, 1966. [25, 26, 48, 50–51, 65, 70–71, 99, 111, 112, 129, 130, 133, 148, 150, 196, 197, 199, 324]

Screven, C. G. Research on running time and physical work of children under various reinforcement conditions. *Child Development*, 1959, **30**, 461–470. [300]

Sekuler, R. W., and Rosenblith, Judy F. Discrimination of direction of line and the effect of stimulus alignment. *Psychonomic Science*, 1964, **1**, 143–144. [210, 344]

Shaffer, Olivia C. See W. A. Wilson and Shaffer, 1963.

Shepard, Winifred O. The effect of verbal training on initial generalization tendencies. *Child Development,* 1956, **27,** 311–316. [157]

Shepard, Winifred O. Learning set in preschool children. *Journal of Comparative and Physiological Psychology,* 1957, **50,** 15–17. [22]

Shepard, Winifred O., and Schaeffer, M. The effect of concept knowledge on discrimination learning. *Child Development,* 1956, **27,** 173–178. [146]

Shepard, Winifred O. See Spiker, Gerjuoy, and Shepard, 1956.

Shepp, B. E. Some cue properties of anticipated rewards in discrimination learning of retardates. *Journal of Comparative and Physiological Psychology,* 1962, **55,** 856–859. [86]

Shepp, B. E., and Turrisi, F. D. Learning and transfer of mediating responses in discriminative learning. In N. R. Ellis (Ed.), *International review of research in mental retardation.* Vol. 2. New York: Academic Press, in press [1966]. [264]

Sheridan, C. L. Interocular transfer of brightness and pattern discriminations in normal and corpus callosum-sectioned rats. *Journal of Comparative and Physiological Psychology,* 1965, **59,** 292–294. [216]

*Sherman, Marian B. The effect of variations in size of training stimuli on relational responding in young children. Unpublished doctoral dissertation, University of California, Berkeley, 1966. [25, 26, 31, 50, 51, 70, 95, 110, 111, 140, 142, 148, 150, 160, 162, 167, 196, 197, 198, 199, 323, 325]

Sherman, Marian B. Personal communication. 1966. [70]

*Sherman, Marian, and Strunk, Jacqueline. Transposition as a function of single versus double discrimination training. *Journal of Comparative and Physiological Psychology,* 1964, **58,** 449–450. [26, 27, 31, 50, 51, 70, 110–112, 196, 197, 199]

Sherman, Marian. See Marsh and Sherman, 1966; Riley, Sherman, and McKee, 1966.

*Shirai, Tsune. An experiment on apprehension of relation. *Japanese Journal of Educational Psychology,* 1939, **14,** 882–904. (Sources: *Psychological Abstracts,* 1940, **14,** 298; Shirai, 1951, pp. 14–16, 23–24, and *xii*; Shirai, 1954, pp. 18, 20, 50, and 62. In 1954 Shirai gave the title as "An experiment on relational judgment.") [159, 160]

*Shirai, Tsune. A study of development of the apprehension of relation. *Japanese Educational Psychology Monographs,* 1941, **1,** 74–129. (Sources: Shirai, 1951, pp. 14–16, 23–24, and *xii*; Shirai, 1954, pp. 18, 20, 50, and 62. In 1954 Shirai gave the title as "A study of development of relational judgment.") [159, 160]

*Shirai, Tsune. Developmental variation in the visual discrimination of cube size by children 2 to 13 years of age. Unpublished master's thesis, University of Toronto, 1951. [26, 27, 31, 32–33, 47, 48, 63, 65, 159–161, 162, 172, 179, 246, 283, 291, 335, 337, 345, 346, 349, 350, 351, 354, 356, 359, 361, 362, 365, 367, 368, 369, 373, 376, 380]

*Shirai, Tsune. Relationship between type of visual discrimination of size and accuracy of memory of size. Unpublished doctoral dissertation, University of Toronto, 1954. [25, 113–114, 137, 283, 349, 365, 369]

*Shirai, Tsune. Developmental and methodological study of the problem of transposition behavior in visual discrimination learning. Tokyo: *Academic Society of Tokyo Woman's Christian College,* 1963 (Monograph Series No. 2). [125, 136, 159, 162, 357, 368]

Sidgwick, Eleanor M., and Hodgson, R. On vision with sealed and bandaged eyes. *Journal of the Society for Psychical Research,* 1884, **1,** 84–86. [223]

Siegel, I. M. See Cumming, Siegel, and Johnson, 1965.

Sigel, I. E. See Kagan, Moss, and Sigel, 1963.

Silverman, I. W. Effect of verbalization on reversal shifts in children: Additional data. *Journal of Experimental Child Psychology,* 1966, **4**, 1–8. [260, 263]

Simon, H. A., and Newell, A. Computer simulation of human thinking and problem solving. In W. Kessen and Clementine Kuhlman (Eds.), Thought in the young child. *Monographs of the Society for Research in Child Development,* 1962, **27**, No. 2. Pp. 137–150. [317]

Skinner, B. F. *Science and human behavior.* New York: Macmillan, 1953. [292]

*Smith, C. B. Background effects on learning and transposition of lightness-discriminations. Unpublished doctoral dissertation, University of Texas, 1956. [214, 249]

Smith, K. U. Visual discrimination in the cat: II. A further study of the capacity of the cat for visual figure discrimination. *Journal of Genetic Psychology,* 1934, **45**, 336–357. [208, 214]

Sokolov, E. N. Higher nervous activity and the problem of perception. (Translated in the U.S.S.R. from *Voprosy Psikhologii,* 1955, **1**, 58–66.) In B. Simon (Ed.), *Psychology in the Soviet Union.* Stanford, Calif.: Stanford University Press, 1957. Pp. 92–99. [309]

Sokolov, E. N. Neuronal models and the orienting reflex. In Mary A. B. Brazier (Ed.), *The central nervous system and behavior. Transactions of the third conference.* New York: Josiah Macy, Jr. Foundation, 1960. Pp. 187–276. [318]

Spearman, C. E. *The nature of 'intelligence' and the principles of cognition.* London: Macmillan, 1923. [80]

Spearman, C. E. *Psychology down the ages.* Vol. 1. London: Macmillan, 1937. (a) [3, 5, 10, 80, 231, 237, 317, 340]

Spearman, C. E. The confusion that is Gestalt-psychology. *American Journal of Psychology,* 1937, **50**, 369–383. (b) [5, 231, 237, 340]

Spectator, No. 77, May 29, 1711. (Pp. 329–333 in *The Spectator,* Vol. I. Edited with introduction and notes by D. F. Bond. London and New York: Oxford University Press, 1965.) [283]

Spence, K. W. The nature of discrimination learning in animals. *Psychological Review,* 1936, **43**, 427–449. (a) [255]

*Spence, K. W. The response of chimpanzees to size relationships. *Psychological Bulletin,* 1936, **33**, 729–730. (Abstract) (b) [178, 187]

Spence, K. W. Analysis of the formation of visual discrimination habits in chimpanzee. *Journal of Comparative Psychology,* 1937, **23**, 77–100. (a) [254–255]

*Spence, K. W. The differential response in animals to stimuli varying within a single dimension. *Psychological Review,* 1937, **44**, 430–444. (b) [9, 46, 94, 95, 99, 107, 108, 109, 125, 130, 132, 178, 182, 187, 229–230, 234–235, 237, 239, 245, 273–277, 278, 279, 285, 293–308 *passim*]

*Spence, K. W. "Relative" vs. "absolute" size discrimination by chimpanzees. *Psychological Bulletin,* 1938, **35**, 505. (Abstract) [46, 178, 187]

Spence, K. W. A reply to Dr. Razran on the transposition of response in discrimination experiments. *Psychological Review,* 1939, **46**, 88–91. (a) [237]

*Spence, K. W. The solution of multiple choice problems by chimpanzees. *Comparative Psychology Monographs,* 1939, **15**, No. 3. (b) [35, 67–68, 142, 143–144, 163–164, 178, 187]

*Spence, K. W. Failure of transposition in size-discrimination in chimpanzees. *American Journal of Psychology,* 1941, **54**, 223–229. [55–58, 129, 178, 187]

*Spence, K. W. The basis of solution by chimpanzees of the intermediate size problem. *Journal of Experimental Psychology,* 1942, **31**, 257–271. [7, 74, 95,

103, 105, 115, 123, 126, 129, 132, 152, 178, 185, 187, 189, 233, 234–235, 240, 245, 271, 273–278, 279, 281, 285, 286, 293–308 *passim,* 315, 322–323, 330]

Spence, K. W. The nature of the response in discrimination learning. *Psychological Review,* 1952, **59,** 89–93. [84–85, 240, 244, 292]

Spence, K. W. *Behavior theory and conditioning.* New Haven: Yale University Press, 1956. [21, 280, 311]

Spence, K. W. *Behavior theory and learning. Selected papers.* Englewood Cliffs, N. J.: Prentice-Hall, 1960. [83, 278–282, 293, 311–312, 330]

Spencer, H. *A system of synthetic philosophy.* Vol. IV. *The principles of psychology.* Vol. 1. New York: Appleton, 1883. [4]

Spencer, H. *A system of synthetic philosophy.* Vol. V. *The principles of psychology.* Vol. II. New York: Appleton, 1887. [190]

*Spigel, I. M. Running speed and intermediate brightness discrimination in the fresh water turtle (*Chrysemys*). *Journal of Comparative and Physiological Psychology,* 1963, **56,** 924–928. [47, 174, 179–180]

Spiker, C. C. Experiments with children on the hypothesis of acquired distinctiveness and equivalence of cues. *Child Development,* 1956, **27,** 253–263. (a) [224]

Spiker, C. C. Stimulus pretraining and subsequent performance in the delayed reaction experiment. *Journal of Experimental Psychology,* 1956, **52,** 107–111. (b) [264, 318]

Spiker, C. C. Performance on a difficult discrimination following pretraining with distinctive stimuli. *Child Development,* 1959, **30,** 513–521. [75, 236]

Spiker, C. C. The hypothesis of stimulus interaction and an explanation of stimulus compounding. In L. P. Lipsitt and C. C. Spiker (Eds.), *Advances in child development and behavior.* Vol. 1. New York: Academic Press, 1963. Pp. 233–264. (a) [11, 313]

Spiker, C. C. Verbal factors in the discrimination learning of children. In J. C. Wright and J. Kagan (Eds.), Basic cognitive processes in children. *Monographs of the Society for Research in Child Development,* 1963, **28,** No. 2, Pp. 53–69. (b) [260–261, 264]

*Spiker, C. C., and Terrell, G., Jr. Factors associated with transposition behavior of preschool children. *Journal of Genetic Psychology,* 1955, **86,** 143–158. [135–136, 148, 155]

*Spiker, C. C., Gerjuoy, Irma R., and Shepard, Winifred O. Children's concept of middle-sizedness and performance on the intermediate size problem. *Journal of Comparative and Physiological Psychology,* 1956, **49,** 416–419. [148, 155, 156, 162, 192, 194–195, 199]

Spiker, C. C. See G. N. Cantor and Spiker, 1954.

Squires, P. C. A criticism of the configurationist's interpretation of 'Structuralism.' *American Journal of Psychology,* 1930, **42,** 134–140. [5, 231]

Stavsky, W. H., and Pattie, F. A., Jr. Discrimination of direction of moving stimuli by chickens. *Journal of Comparative Psychology,* 1930, **10,** 317–323. [87]

Stavsky, W. H. See Pattie and Stavsky, 1932.

Stephens, W. E. A comparison of the performance of normal and subnormal boys on structured categorization tasks. *Exceptional Children,* 1964, **30,** 311–315. [267]

Stephens, W. E. Category usage by normal and mentally retarded boys. *Child Development,* 1966, **37,** 355–361. [267]

Stepien, L. S., and Cordeau, J. P. Memory in monkeys for compound stimuli. *American Journal of Psychology,* 1960, **73,** 388–395. [221]

Stevens, S. S. Mathematics, measurement, and psychophysics. In S. S. Stevens (Ed.), *Handbook of experimental psychology*. New York: Wiley, 1951. Pp. 1–49. [10, 49, 54, 191]

Stevens, S. S. On the psychophysical law. *Psychological Review*, 1957, 64, 153–181. [49]

Stevens, S. S. On the uses of poikilitic functions. In D. I. Mostofsky (Ed.), *Stimulus generalization*. Stanford, Calif.: Stanford University Press, 1965. Pp. 24–29. [283]

*Stevenson, H. W., and Bitterman, M. E. The distance-effect in the transposition of intermediate size by children. *American Journal of Psychology*, 1955, 68, 274–279. [34, 76, 77–78, 79, 115, 116, 118, 126, 134, 149, 229, 232, 234, 237, 282, 285]

*Stevenson, H. W., and Iscoe, I. Overtraining and transposition in children. *Journal of Experimental Psychology*, 1954, 47, 251–255. [32, 34, 65, 66, 72–73, 125, 133, 148, 150–151, 162, 321–322]

*Stevenson, H. W., and Iscoe, I. Transposition in the feebleminded. *Journal of Experimental Psychology*, 1955, 49, 11–15. [22, 24, 25, 31, 32–34, 111, 112–113, 148, 162, 282]

*Stevenson, H. W., and Langford, T. Time as a variable in transposition in children. *Child Development*, 1957, 28, 365–369. [24, 25, 31, 103, 104, 110–113]

Stevenson, H. W., and McBee, G. The learning of object and pattern discriminations by children. *Journal of Comparative and Physiological Psychology*, 1958, 51, 752–754. [156, 162]

*Stevenson, H. W., and Weiss, E. S. Time as a variable in transposition. *American Journal of Psychology*, 1955, 68, 285–288. [24, 25, 31, 105, 117, 122, 126, 136, 283, 285, 294]

*Stevenson, H. W., Iscoe, I., and McConnell, Claudia. A developmental study of transposition. *Journal of Experimental Psychology*, 1955, 49, 278–280. (a) [24, 25, 31, 32–34, 112, 126, 141, 142, 148, 150, 160, 161, 162]

*Stevenson, H. W., Langford, T., and Reese, H. Transposition in preverbal children. *American Psychologist*, 1955, 10, 406. (Abstract) (b) [103, 104, 110–112, 137, 282]

Stevenson, H. W. See Weir and Stevenson, 1959.

Stewart, Florence D. See Hicks and Stewart, 1930.

Stiening, B. See Munn and Stiening, 1931.

Stocking, Ruth J. See Hoge and Stocking, 1912.

Stollnitz, F. Personal communication. 1965. [101]

Stonex, E. See Jackson, Stonex, Lane, and Dominguez, 1938.

Stout, G. F. *Analytic psychology*. (4th ed.) Vol. I. London: Allen & Unwin, 1918. (a) [16, 230, 232, 233]

Stout, G. F. *Analytic psychology*. (4th ed.) Vol. II. London: Allen & Unwin, 1918. (b) [81, 217, 232]

Strong, C. A. A sketch of the history of psychology among the Greeks. *American Journal of Psychology*, 1891, 4, 177–197. [223]

Strunk, Jacqueline. See Sherman and Strunk, 1964.

Stumpf, C. *Tonpsychologie*. I. Leipzig: Hirzel, 1883. (Source: Koffka, 1922, p. 537.) [283]

Suci, G. J. See Osgood, Suci, and Tannenbaum, 1957.

Sully, J. *Outlines of psychology*. New York: Appleton, 1891. [205, 222]

Suppes, P. Mathematical concept formation in children. *American Psychologist*, 1966, 21, 139–150. [211]

Sutherland, N. S. Discrimination of horizontal and vertical extents by *Octopus*. *Journal of Comparative and Physiological Psychology*, 1961, 54, 43–48. (a) [212]

Sutherland, N. S. The methods and findings of experiments on the visual discrimination of shape by animals. *Experimental Psychology Society Monograph*, [1961?], No. 1. (b) [204–214]

Sutherland, N. S. Visual discrimination of shape by *Octopus:* Squares and crosses. *Journal of Comparative and Physiological Psychology*, 1962, 55, 939–943. [212]

Sutherland, N. S. Shape discrimination and receptive fields. *Nature*, 1963, 197, 118–122. [212]

Sutherland, N. S. The learning of discriminations by animals. *Endeavour*, 1964, 23, 148–152. (a) [75, 317]

Sutherland, N. S. Visual discrimination in animals. *British Medical Bulletin*, 1964, 20, 54–59. (b) [317]

Sutherland, N. S., and Carr, A. E. The visual discrimination of shape by *Octopus:* The effects of stimulus size. *Quarterly Journal of Experimental Psychology*, 1963, 15, 225–235. [214]

Sutherland, N. S., and Carr, A. E. Shape discrimination by rats: Squares and rectangles. *British Journal of Psychology*, 1964, 55, 39–48. [208]

Sutherland, N. S., Mackintosh, N. J., and Mackintosh, Janet. Simultaneous discrimination of *Octopus* and transfer of discrimination along a continuum. *Journal of Comparative and Physiological Psychology*, 1963, 56, 150–156. [86, 317]

Szeminska, Alina. See Piaget, Inhelder, and Szeminska, 1960.

*Takagi, S. Influence of background on transfer of selective response to brightness. *Japanese Psychological Monographs*, 1935, 5, 85–100. (a) (Source: Shirai, 1951, pp. 13, 15, 18, 21–23, and *xiii.*) [65, 128, 175, 181, 246]

*Takagi, S. The influence of immediate backgrounds upon the transposition of selective responses for brightness in the varied tit, *Sittiparus varius varius*. *Japanese Journal of Psychology*, 1935, 10, 789–805. (b) (Sources: *Psychological Abstracts*, 1936, 10, 329–330; Shirai, 1951, pp. 13, 15, 18, 21–23, and *viii.*) [65, 128, 175, 181, 246]

*Takagi, S. Absolute and relative factors in brightness discrimination by the varied tit, *Sittiparus varius*. *Psychological Monographs in Memory of Dr. Hayami*, 1937, pp. 165–181. (Source: Shirai, 1951, pp. 13, 15, 18, 21–23, and *xiii.*) [65, 128, 175, 181, 246]

*Takei, K. On visual discrimination and its learning with chickens. *Japanese Journal of Psychology*, 1927, 2, 32–87. (Source: *Psychological Abstracts*, 1928, 2, 552–553.) [47, 68, 175, 180–181, 195, 208]

*Takemasa, T. An experiment on learning in the chick—selective learning of color. *Japanese Journal of Educational Psychology*, 1934, 9, 78–93. (Source: Shirai, 1951, pp. 13, 15, 21–22, and *xiv.*) [63, 102, 104, 175, 246]

Takemasa, T. See Keller and Takemasa, 1933.

*Talland, G. A. Criteria in conceptual transposition. *American Journal of Psychology*, 1957, 70, 263–267. [97–98]

Tannenbaum, P. H. See Osgood, Suci, and Tannenbaum, 1957.

Taylor, D. H. See S. J. Lachman and Taylor, 1963.

*Taylor, H. A study of configuration learning. *Journal of Comparative Psychology*, 1932, 13, 19–26. (a) [47, 126, 135, 141, 142, 175, 180]

Taylor, H. The method of Gestalt psychology. *American Journal of Psychology*, 1932, 44, 356–361. (b) [237]

Taylor, N. B. See Best and Taylor, 1955.

Teplov, B. M., and Borisova, M. N. Discriminative sensitivity and sensory memory. (Translated by R. Kisch from *Voprosy Psikhologii,* 1957, 1, 61–77.) In N. O'Connor (Ed.), *Recent Soviet psychology.* New York: Liveright, 1961. Pp. 141–164. [83–84]

Ternus, J. The problem of phenomenal identity. (Experimentelle Untersuchung über phänomenale Identität. *Psychologische Forschung,* 1926, 7, 81–136.) In W. D. Ellis (Ed.), *A source book of Gestalt psychology.* London: Routledge & Kegan Paul, 1938. Pp. 149–160. [138, 140]

Terrace, H. S. Wavelength generalization after discrimination learning with and without errors. *Science,* 1964, 144, 78–80. [94, 98]

*Terrell, G., Jr. The role of incentive in discrimination learning in children. *Child Development,* 1958, 29, 231–236. [32–33, 67, 71, 112, 142, 160, 162]

*Terrell, G., Jr. Manipulatory motivation in children. *Journal of Comparative and Physiological Psychology,* 1959, 52, 705–709. [24, 25, 31, 67, 71, 112, 142, 160, 162]

*Terrell, G., Jr., and Kennedy, W. A. Discrimination learning and transposition in children as a function of the nature of the reward. *Journal of Experimental Psychology,* 1957, 53, 257–260. [67, 71, 112, 142, 160, 162]

*Terrell, G., Jr., Durkin, Kathryn, and Wiesley, M. Social class and the nature of the incentive in discrimination learning. *Journal of Abnormal and Social Psychology,* 1959, 59, 270–272. [24, 25, 31, 67, 71, 112, 142, 160, 162]

Terrell, G., Jr. See Spiker and Terrell, 1955.

Teuber, H.-L. See Rudel and Teuber, 1963a; Rudel and Teuber, 1963b; Rudel and Teuber, 1964.

Thomas, D. R., and Jones, C. G. Stimulus generalization as a function of the frame of reference. *Journal of Experimental Psychology,* 1962, 64, 77–80. [250]

Thomas, D. R. See Hiss and Thomas, 1963.

Thomas, J. See Riley, Ring, and Thomas, 1960.

Thomas, Margaret L. See A. D. Pick, Pick, and Thomas, 1966.

*Thompson, G. R. Effects of number of relevant stimulus dimensions and kind of verbal pretraining on transposition in retardates. Unpublished doctoral dissertation, University of Minnesota, 1965. [23, 28, 30, 31, 100, 101, 111, 112, 136, 160, 163, 166, 260]

Thompson, Helen. Adaptive behavior. In A. Gesell *et al., The first five years of life.* New York: Harper, 1940. Pp. 108–188. [150]

Thompson, R. Approach-avoidance in an ambivalent object discrimination problem. *Journal of Experimental Psychology,* 1953, 45, 341–344. [244]

*Thompson, R. Transposition in the white rat as a function of stimulus comparison. *Journal of Experimental Psychology,* 1955, 50, 185–190. [24, 25, 31, 47, 90, 92, 102, 104, 177, 229]

Thrum, Martha E. The development of concepts of magnitude. *Child Development,* 1935, 6, 120–140. [148, 149]

Tibout, P. H. C. See Wissenburgh and Tibout, 1921.

Tighe, Louise S. Effect of perceptual pretraining on reversal and nonreversal shifts. *Journal of Experimental Psychology,* 1965, 70, 379–385. [264]

Tighe, T. J. See G. J. Gibson, Walk, Pick, and Tighe, 1958.

Titchener, E. B. *Lectures on the experimental psychology of the thought-processes.* New York: Macmillan, 1909. [2, 3, 11, 273, 291]

Titchener, E. B. *Experimental psychology. A manual of laboratory practice.* Vol. I.

Qualitative experiments: Part I. *Student's manual.* New York: Macmillan, 1927 (orig. publ. 1901). [7, 283]

Toll, A. See Katz and Toll, 1923.

Tolman, E. C. A behavioristic theory of ideas. *Psychological Review,* 1926, 33, 352–369. [82]

Tolman, E. C. Habit formation and higher mental processes in animals. *Psychological Bulletin,* 1927, **24**, 1–35. [9, 335, 349, 350, 352, 365, 378]

Tolman, E. C. Backward elimination of errors in two successive discrimination habits. *University of California Publications in Psychology,* 1934, **6**, 145–152. [96]

Tolman, E. C. The determiners of behavior at a choice point. *Psychological Review,* 1938, **45**, 1–41. [11, 82, 83]

Tolman, E. C. Prediction of vicarious trial and error by means of the schematic sowbug. *Psychological Review,* 1939, **46**, 318–336. [82, 83]

Tolman, E. C. See Geier, Levin, and Tolman, 1941.

Topurin, S. See Beritoff and Topurin, 1929.

*Towe, A. L. A study of figural equivalence in the pigeon. *Journal of Comparative and Physiological Psychology,* 1954, **47**, 283–287. [99, 175, 182]

Trabasso, T., Deutsch, J. A., and Gelman, Rochel. Attention in discrimination learning of young children. *Journal of Experimental Child Psychology,* 1966, **4**, 9–19. [162]

Triche, A. See Hartmann and Triche, 1933.

Tugman, Eupha F. Light discrimination in the English sparrow. *Journal of Animal Behavior,* 1914, **4**, 79–109. [195]

Turrisi, F. D. See Shepp and Turrisi, in press.

Underwood, B. J. *Experimental psychology. An introduction.* New York: Appleton-Century-Crofts, 1949. [13]

Underwood, B. J. Speed of learning and amount retained: A consideration of methodology. *Psychological Bulletin,* 1954, **51**, 276–282. [141]

*Usnadze, D. Zum Problem der Relationserfassung beim Tier. (The apprehension of relations by the animal.) *Archiv für die gesamte Psychologie,* 1927, **60**, 361–390. (Sources: *Psychological Abstracts,* 1928, **2**, 698–699; Razran, 1938b, pp. 533 and 538; Razran, 1939, pp. 318 and 330; C. J. Warden *et al.,* 1936, pp. 289 and 521.) [177, 185–186, 274]

Van De Moortel, R. Immediate memory span in children: A review of the literature. Report No. 1, Development of Language Functions (Study E: Recognition and Recall, Dr. Edwin Martin), University of Michigan Center for Human Growth and Development. National Institute for Child Health and Human Development Grant No. 1 PO1 HDO1368-01, May 1965. [171]

*Vatzuro, E. G. (A comparative study of the relation response in normal and mentally retarded children.) *Voprosy Psikhologii,* 1959, No. 4, 140–145. (Sources: *Child Development Abstracts and Bibliography,* 1960, **34**, 39; *Psychological Abstracts,* 1960, **34**, 450–451. In the latter source, the author is given as "Vatsuro, E. G.," and the title is given as "Sravnitel'noe izuchenie refleska na otnoshenie u normal'nykh detei i oligofrenov. [Comparative study of the reflex to relation in normal children and oligophrenics].") [160, 161, 164]

Verdon, R. Forgetfulness. *Mind,* 1877, **2**, 437–452. [8]

*Verlaine, L. L'instinct et l'intelligence chez les hyménoptères; vii. L'abstraction. *Annales Société royale zoologique de Belgique,* 1927, **58**, 137–140. (Source,

Shirai, 1951, pp. 12, 15, and *xiv*. See also C. J. Warden *et al.*, 1940, pp. 801 and 1012.) [179]

*Verlaine, L. Le relatif et l'absolu chez le macaque; La grandeur moyenne. *Bulletin de la Société Royale des sciences de Liége*, 1935, **4**, No. 2, 90–96. (Sources: *Psychological Abstracts*, 1937, **11**, 72–73; Shirai, 1951, pp. 14–15 and *xiv*.) [178]

Verlaine, L. (See Warden *et al.*, 1940, p. 801.) [204]

Vernon, M. D. *A further study of visual perception*. London and New York: Cambridge University Press, 1952. [229, 291, 352, 361, 367]

Vernon, M. D. *Backwardness in reading. A study of its nature and origin*. London and New York: Cambridge University Press, 1957. [205, 208, 211, 360, 361]

Vinacke, W. E. The investigation of concept formation. *Psychological Bulletin*, 1951, **48**, 1–31. [v, 322]

Wade, Marjorie. See Lashley and Wade, 1946.

Walk, R. D. See Gibson, Walk, Pick, and Tighe, 1958.

Wapner, S. The differential effects of cortical injury and retesting on equivalence reactions in the rat. *Psychological Monographs*, 1944, **57**, No. 2 (Whole No. 262). [213, 233]

Warden, Cree. A study in the recall of perceived relations. *Psychological Monographs*, 1933, **44**, 195–206. [1, 236]

Warden, C. J., and Baar, J. The Müller-Lyer illusion in the ring dove, Turtur Risorius. *Journal of Comparative Psychology*, 1929, **9**, 275–292. [15, 212, 284]

Warden, C. J., and Rowley, Jean B. The discrimination of absolute versus relative brightness in the ring dove, Turtur Risorius. *Journal of Comparative Psychology*, 1929, **9**, 317–337. [v, 22, 114, 189, 190, 195]

Warden, C. J., and Winslow, C. N. The discrimination of absolute versus relative size in the ring dove, *Turtur Risorius*. *Journal of Genetic Psychology*, 1931, **39**, 328–341. [v, 114, 189]

Warden, C. J., Jenkins, T. N., and Warner, L. H. *Comparative psychology*. [Vol. III.] *Vertebrates*. New York: Ronald Press, 1936. [186, 194, 214, 335, 342, 349, 350, 352, 361, 365, 375, 378]

Warden, C. J., Jenkins, T. N., and Warner, L. H. *Comparative psychology*. Vol. II. *Plants and invertebrates*. New York: Ronald Press, 1940. [173, 178, 179, 204, 333, 346, 376, 382]

Warner, L. H. See C. J. Warden, Jenkins, and Warner, 1936; C. J. Warden, Jenkins, and Warner, 1940.

Warren, J. M. Solution of sign-differentiated object and positional discriminations by rhesus monkeys. *Journal of Genetic Psychology*, 1960, **96**, 365–369. [84, 85–86]

*Warren, J. M. Functions of association cortex in cats and monkeys. Progress Report, Research Grant M-4726, National Institute of Mental Health, U. S. Public Health Service, 1964. [103, 104, 105, 177, 185]

Warren, J. M. See Hara and Warren, 1961.

Washburn, Margaret F. The term 'feeling.' *Journal of Philosophy Psychology and Scientific Methods*, 1906, **3**, 62–63. [291]

Washburn, Margaret F. *The animal mind*. New York: Macmillan, 1917 (2nd ed.), 1926 (3rd ed.), 1936 (4th ed.). [135, 282–283, 285–286, 293–308 *passim*, 365, 378]

Washburn, Margaret F. Köhler's discussion of association. *Ninth International Congress of Psychology, Proceedings and Papers*, 1929. P. 470. (Abstract) [291]

*Washburn, Margaret F., and Abbott, Edwina. Experiments on the brightness value of red for the light-adapted eye of the rabbit. *Journal of Animal Behavior*, 1912, **2**, 145–180. [30–31, 99, 100, 137, 175, 182]

Washburn, Margaret F., and Bentley, I. M. The establishment of an association involving color-discrimination in the creek chub, Semotilus antromaculatus. *Journal of Comparative Neurology and Psychology,* 1906, **16,** 113–125. [342]

Watson, J. B. *Behavior. An introduction to comparative psychology.* New York: Holt, 1914. [180]

Watson, J. B., and Rayner, Rosalie. Conditioned emotional reactions. *Journal of Experimental Psychology,* 1920, 3, 1–14. [v]

Watson, J. B., and Watson, Rosalie R. Studies in infant psychology. *Scientific Monthly,* 1921, **13,** 493–515. [v]

Watson, Rosalie R. See Watson and Watson, 1921.

Webb, Wilse B. A test of "relational" vs. "specific stimulus" learning in discrimination problems. *Journal of Comparative and Physiological Psychology,* 1950, 43, 70–72. [87]

Webster's New Collegiate Dictionary. Springfield, Mass.: Merriam, 1953. [203]

Wegener, J. G. Cross-modal transfer in monkeys. *Journal of Comparative and Physiological Psychology,* 1965, **59,** 450–452. [221]

Weintraub, D. J. (No title.) *Science,* 1966, **152,** 1108–1109. [223]

Weir, M. W., and Stevenson, H. W. The effect of verbalization in children's learning as a function of chronological age. *Child Development,* 1959, **30,** 143–149. [146]

Weise, P., and Bitterman, M. E. Response-selection in discrimination learning. *Psychological Review,* 1951, **58,** 185–195. [244–245]

Weiss, A. P. *A theoretical basis of human behavior.* Columbus, Ohio: Adams, 1925. [153]

Weiss, E. S. See Stevenson and Weiss, 1955.

Weiss, G. Discrimination learning in preschool children under three levels of instruction. Unpublished master's thesis, State University of Iowa, 1954. [162]

Welch, L. The development of size discrimination between the ages of 12 and 40 months. *Journal of Genetic Psychology,* 1939, **55,** 243–268. [150, 214]

Welch, L. See V. Graham, Jackson, Long, and Welch, 1944.

Wells, Doris. See T. S. Kendler, Kendler, and Wells, 1960.

Wells, F. L. Symbolism and synaesthesia. *American Journal of Insanity,* 1919, **75,** 481–488. [222]

Werboff, J. See Ebel and Werboff, 1966.

Werner, H. *Comparative psychology of mental development.* (Revised ed.) Chicago, Ill.: Follett, 1948. [4, 138, 140, 222–224, 232, 272]

Wertheimer, M. Gestalt theory. (*Über Gestalttheorie.* Erlangen: Verlag der Philosophischen Adademie, 1925.) In W. D. Ellis (Ed.), *A source book of Gestalt psychology.* London: Routledge & Kegan Paul, 1938. Pp. 1–11. [135]

Wertheimer, M. On discrimination experiments: I. Two logical structures. *Psychological Review,* 1959, **66,** 252–266. [229, 234–236, 292]

Wertheimer, Michael. See Holland and Wertheimer, 1964.

*Wesman, A. G., and Eisenberg, P. The perception of relationship in human adults. *Journal of Experimental Psychology,* 1941, **28,** 63–76. [47, 71–72, 73, 154, 180]

Wheeler, R. H. *The science of psychology. An introductory study.* New York: Crowell, 1929. (2nd ed., 1940.) [5, 6, 13, 141, 233]

*Wheeler, R. H., and Perkins, [F.] T. Learned and unlearned responses in the goldfish. *Ninth International Congress of Psychology, Proceedings and Papers,* 1929. Pp. 484–485. (Abstract) [179]

Wheeler, R. H. See Perkins and Wheeler, 1930.

White, S. H. Evidence for a hierarchical arrangement of learning processes. In L. P.

Lipsitt and C. C. Spiker (Eds.), *Advances in child development and behavior.* Vol. 2. New York: Academic Press, 1965. Pp. 187–220. [261–263]

White, S. H. Personal communication. 1965. [261]

White, S. H., and Plum, G. E. Eye movement photography during children's discrimination learning. *Journal of Experimental Child Psychology,* 1964, **1,** 327–338. [82, 83]

*Whitman, T. L. Transposition in children under three treatment conditions. Unpublished master's thesis, University of Illinois, 1965. [34, 38–39, 40, 43, 78–79, 115, 117, 118, 134, 150, 151, 155, 162, 164, 165, 264]

Whittell, Florence. See W. Brown and Whittell, 1923.

Wiener, M. See Wohlwill and Wiener, 1964.

Wiesley, M. See Terrell, Durkin, and Wiesley, 1959.

Williams, J. A. Experiments with form perception and learning in dogs. *Comparative Psychology Monographs,* 1926, **4,** No. 18. [212]

Williams, Judith A. See Bindra, Williams, and Wise, 1965.

Willmann, R. R. An experimental investigation of the creative process in music. The transposability of visual design stimuli to musical themes. *Psychological Monographs,* 1944, **57,** No. 1 (Whole No. 261). [217, 220–221]

Wilson, Martha. Further analysis of intersensory facilitation of learning sets in monkeys. *Perceptual and Motor Skills,* 1964, **18,** 917–920. [51, 220]

Wilson, Martha. Learning and cross-modal transfer in monkeys with posterior association-cortex lesions. *Proceedings of the 73rd Annual Convention of the American Psychological Association.* New York: American Psychological Association, 1965. Pp. 95–96. (Abstract) [220]

Wilson, Martha. Strategies and cross-modal transfer in monkeys. *Psychonomic Science,* 1966, **4,** 321–322. [220]

Wilson, Martha, and Wilson, W. A., Jr. Intersensory facilitation of learning sets in normal and brain operated monkeys. *Journal of Comparative and Physiological Psychology,* 1962, **55,** 931–934. [220]

Wilson, P. D., and Riesen, A. H. Visual development in rhesus monkeys neonatally deprived of patterned light. *Journal of Comparative and Physiological Psychology,* 1966, **61,** 87–95. [208, 215–216, 236]

Wilson, W. A., Jr., and Shaffer, Olivia C. Intermodality transfer of specific discriminations in the monkey. *Nature,* 1963, **197,** 107. [220]

Wilson, W. A., Jr. See M. Wilson and Wilson, 1962.

Winslow, C. N. Visual illusions in the chick. *Archives of Psychology,* 1933, **23,** (Whole No. 153). [204, 283–284]

Winslow, C. N. See Warden and Winslow, 1931.

Wischner, G. J. See Gerben and Wischner, 1965; Goss and Wischner, 1956.

Wise, J. S. See Bindra, Williams, and Wise, 1965.

*Wissenburgh, J. C., and Tibout, P. H. C. Choix basé sur l'aperception complexe chez les cobayes. *Archives néerlandaises de physiologie de l'homme et des animaux,* 1921, **6,** 149–162. (Sources: Tolman, 1927, pp. 14 and 35; C. J. Warden *et al.,* 1936, pp. 351–352 and 524; Washburn, 1926, pp. 242 and 415; Washburn, 1936, pp. 258 and 508–509.) [175, 184]

Witryol, S. L., and Fischer, W. F. Scaling children's incentives by the method of paired comparisons. *Psychological Reports,* 1960, **7,** 471–474. [300]

Witryol, S. L., Lowden, Lynn M., and Fagan, J. F. Incentive effects upon attention in children's discrimination learning. Paper read at meeting of Eastern Psychological Association, New York, April, 1966. [300]

*Wohlwill, J. F. Perceptual determinants of the response to absolute and relative size. Unpublished doctoral dissertation, University of California, 1957. [103, 104, 136, 191–192, 199, 229, 285, 323–324]

*Wohlwill, J. F. Absolute vs. relational discrimination on the dimension of number. *Journal of Genetic Psychology,* 1960, 96, 353–363. (a) [126, 159, 162, 191–192, 199]

Wohlwill, J. F. Developmental studies of perception. *Psychological Bulletin,* 1960, 57, 249–288. (b) [205, 210, 284]

Wohlwill, J. F. The perspective illusion: Perceived size and distance in fields varying in suggested depth, in children and adults. *Journal of Experimental Psychology,* 1962, 64, 300–310. [248]

Wohlwill, J. F. The learning of absolute and relational number discriminations by children. *Journal of Genetic Psychology,* 1963, 101, 217–228. [191–192, 199]

Wohlwill, J. F. Personal communication. 1965. [333, 361]

Wohlwill, J. F. Personal communication. 1966. [333, 361]

Wohlwill, J. F., and Wiener, M. Discrimination of form orientation in young children. *Child Development,* 1964, 35, 1113–1125. [208, 210, 211]

Wolf, E., and Zerrahn-Wolf, Gertrud. Flicker and the reactions of bees to flowers. *Journal of General Physiology,* 1937, 20, 511–518. [173]

Wolfle, D. L. The relative efficiency of constant and varied stimulation during learning. *Journal of Comparative Psychology,* 1935, 19, 5–27. [195, 199]

Wolfle, D. L. The relative efficiency of constant and varied stimulation during learning. III. The objective extent of stimulus variation. *Journal of Comparative Psychology,* 1936, 22, 375–381. [195, 199]

*Wolfle, D. L. Absolute brightness discrimination in the white rat. *Journal of Comparative Psychology,* 1937, 24, 39–71. [73, 114, 177, 190–191, 199, 215]

Wolfle, D. L. See Grether and Wolfle, 1936; Gulliksen and Wolfle, 1938; Gulliksen and Wolfle, 1939.

Wong, H., and Brown, W. Effects of surroundings upon mental work as measured by Yerkes' multiple choice method. *Journal of Comparative Psychology,* 1923, 3, 318–326. [67, 194, 199]

Woodworth, R. S. The consciousness of relation. In *Essays philosophical and psychological in honor of William James.* New York: Longmans, Green, 1908. Pp. 483–507. [2, 216–217]

Woodworth, R. S. *Dynamic psychology.* New York: Columbia University Press, 1918. [231]

Woodworth, R. S. *Gestalt* psychology and the concept of reaction stages. *American Journal of Psychology,* 1927, 39, 62–69. [6]

Woodworth, R. S. *Experimental psychology.* New York: Holt, 1938. [245, 247, 291, 335, 340]

Woodworth, R. S., and Schlosberg, H. *Experimental psychology.* (Revised ed.) New York: Holt, 1954. [10–11]

Woodworth, R. S. See Ladd and Woodworth, 1911.

Wray, Nancy P. See Ross, Hetherington, and Wray, 1965.

Wright, D. C. See Riley, Goggin, and Wright, 1963.

Wulf, F. Tendencies in figural variation. (Über die Veränderung von Vorstellungen (Gedächtnis und Gestalt). *Psychologische Forschung,* 1922, 1, 333–373.) In W. D. Ellis (Ed.), *A source book of Gestalt psychology.* London: Routledge & Kegan Paul, 1938. Pp. 136–148. [235]

Wundt, W. *Lectures on human and animal psychology.* (Translated from 2nd

German ed. by J. E. Creighton and E. B. Titchener.) London: Swan Sonnenschein, 1896. [245]

Wylie, H. H. Some experiments on transfer of learning. *Psychological Bulletin*, 1916, **13**, 78–79. (Abstract) [222]

*Yerkes, R. M. *The dancing mouse. A study in animal behavior.* New York: Macmillan, 1907. [82, 83, 134, 175, 184, 236]

Yerkes, R. M. A new method of studying ideational and allied forms of behavior in man and other animals. *Proceedings of the National Academy of Sciences of the United States of America*, 1916, **2**, 631–633. (a) [67]

Yerkes, R. M. Ideational behavior of monkeys and apes. *Proceedings of the National Academy of Sciences of the United States of America*, 1916, **2**, 639–642. (b) [67]

Yerkes, R. M. Modes of behavioral adaptation in chimpanzees to multiple-choice problems. *Comparative Psychology Monographs*, 1934, **10**, No. 1. [67]

Yerkes, R. M., and Eisenberg, A. M. Preliminaries to a study of color vision in the ring-dove *Turtur risorius*. *Journal of Animal Behavior*, 1915, **5**, 25–43. [189]

Yerkes, R. M., and Morgulis, S. The method of Pawlow in animal psychology. *Psychological Bulletin*, 1909, **8**, 257–273. [361]

*Yoshida, S. The structure of personality in the feebleminded child. *Japanese Journal of Educational Psychology*, 1939, **14**, 864–881. (Sources: *Psychological Abstracts*, 1940, 14, 530; Shirai, 1951, pp. 14–15 and xv.) [vi]

Youniss, J. Language deficiency and concrete operations. Paper read at meeting of Society for Research in Child Development, Minneapolis, April, 1965. [153, 361]

Youniss, J., and Furth, H. G. Reaction to a placebo: The mediational deficiency hypothesis. *Psychological Bulletin*, 1963, **60**, 499–502. [260–261]

Youniss, J. See Furth and Youniss, 1964; Furth and Youniss, 1965.

Youtz, R. P. (No title.) *Science*, 1966, **152**, 1108. [223]

Zakher, U. Y. (New data concerning the problem of the physiological mechanisms of a conditioned reflex to the relation between stimuli in children.) *Voprosy Psikhologii*, 1963, No. 4, 125–134. (Source: *Child Development Abstracts and Bibliography*, 1964, 38, 177.) [160, 161, 162]

Zaporozhets, A. V. The development of voluntary movements. (Translated in the U.S.S.R. from *Voprosy Psikhologii*, 1955, 1, 42–49.) In B. Simon (Ed.), *Psychology in the Soviet Union.* Stanford, Calif.: Stanford University Press, 1957. Pp. 108–114. [82, 309]

Zaporozhets, A. V. The origin and development of the conscious control of movements in man. (Translated by R. Crawford from *Voprosy Psikhologii*, 1958, 1, 24–36.) In N. O'Connor (Ed.), *Recent Soviet Psychology.* New York: Liveright, 1961. Pp. 273–289. [161, 264]

*Zaporozhets, A. V. The development of perception in the preschool child. In P. H. Mussen (Ed.), European research in cognitive development. *Monographs of the Society for Research in Child Development*, 1965, 30, No. 2. Pp. 82–101. [160, 161–162, 263]

Zaporozhets, A. V. (See H. Pick, 1963, p. 187.) [219]

Zara, R. C. See R. C. Johnson and Zara, 1960.

Zeaman, D. Discrimination learning in retardates. *Training School Bulletin*, 1959, **56**, 62–67. [317]

Zeaman, D. See Campione, Hyman, and Zeaman, 1965; House and Zeaman, 1962; House and Zeaman, 1963.

*Zeiler, M. D. New dimensions of the intermediate size problem: Neither absolute nor relational response. *Journal of Experimental Psychology,* 1963, **66,** 588–595. (a) [54, 149, 155, 234–235]

*Zeiler, M. D. Response to the small, intermediate, or large test stimulus in the intermediate size problem. Paper read at meeting of Eastern Psychological Association, New York, April, 1963. (b) [54, 149, 155]

*Zeiler, M. D. The ratio theory of intermediate size discrimination. *Psychological Review,* 1963, **60,** 516–533. (c) [11, 22–23, 52, 53, 54, 103, 117, 118–120, 236, 237, 248, 250, 251–254, 293–308 *passim,* 310, 323, 330]

*Zeiler, M. D. Transposition, non-relational choice, and non-equivalence in the intermediate size problem. Paper read at meeting of American Psychological Association, Philadelphia, September, 1963. (d) [11, 76, 117, 118–120, 149, 155, 236, 285]

Zeiler, M. D. Component and configurational learning in children. *Journal of Experimental Psychology,* 1964, **68,** 292–296. (a) [271]

*Zeiler, M. D. Transposition in adults with simultaneous and successive stimulus presentation. *Journal of Experimental Psychology,* 1964, **68,** 103–107. (b) [80, 117, 121–122]

*Zeiler, M. D. Solution of the intermediate size problem by pigeons. *Journal of the Experimental Analysis of Behavior,* 1965, **8,** 263–268. (a) [35, 51–52, 114, 175, 182]

*Zeiler, M. D. Transposition after training to the largest, smallest, or middle-sized of three stimuli. Paper read at meeting of Eastern Psychological Association, Atlantic City, April, 1965. (b) [27, 34, 66–67, 100, 101, 117, 120, 121, 125, 126, 129, 134, 143, 149, 151, 155, 294, 326]

Zeiler, M. D. Personal communication. 1966. [76, 94, 175, 182, 381]

*Zeiler, M. D. Solution of the two stimulus transposition problem by four- and five-year-old children. *Journal of Experimental Psychology,* 1966, **71,** 576–579. (a) [26, 27, 28, 30, 31, 48, 50–51, 111, 112, 130]

Zeiler, M. D. The stimulus in the intermediate size problem. *Psychological Review,* 1966, **73,** 257–261. (b) [54, 156, 254]

*Zeiler, M. D. Stimulus definition and choice. In L. P. Lipsitt and C. C. Spiker (Eds.), *Advances in child development and behavior.* Vol. 3. New York: Academic Press, 1967. Pp. 125–156. [21, 23, 54, 76, 257, 381]

*Zeiler, M. D., and Gardner, Ann M. Individual choice gradients after large, small, or middle-sized training. Unpublished manuscript. 1966. (a) (Sources: Zeiler, personal communication, 1966; Zeiler, 1967.) [37, 52, 53, 117, 121]

*Zeiler, M. D., and Gardner, Ann M. Intermediate size discrimination in seven- and eight-year-old children. *Journal of Experimental Psychology,* 1966, **71,** 203–207. (b) [52, 53, 117, 119, 120, 126, 130, 149]

Zeiler, M. D., and Jasper, Kathleen. The effect of double training sets on two- and three-stimulus discrimination problems. Unpublished manuscript, Wellesley College, 1966. [148, 149, 196–197]

*Zeiler, M. D., and Lang, Jo. Adults and the intermediate size problem. *Journal of Experimental Psychology,* 1966, **72,** 312–314. (a) [34, 52–53, 117, 122, 233]

*Zeiler, M. D., and Lang, Jo. The effects of a 24-hour delay between training and testing in the intermediate size problem. Unpublished manuscript, Wellesley College, 1966. (b) (Cited by Zeiler, 1967, as Lang, 1965, *q. v.*) [52, 53, 103–106, 115, 117, 119–120, 149, 155]

*Zeiler, M. D., and Paalberg, Juta. The effect of two training sets on transposition in adults. *Psychonomic Science,* 1964, 1, 85–86. (a) [79–80, 117, 122, 197–198, 199, 325–326]

*Zeiler, M. D., and Paalberg, Juta. Transposition in children with two discriminations in training. Unpublished manuscript, Wellesley College, 1964. (b) [15, 34, 76, 80, 115, 117, 148, 155, 197–198, 199]

*Zeiler, M. D., and Price, Aida E. Discrimination with variable interval and continuous reinforcement schedules. *Psychonomic Science,* 1965, 3, 299–300. [51–52, 100, 101, 114, 126, 175, 182]

*Zeiler, M. D., and Salten, Cynthia S. Individual gradients of transposition and absolute choice. Unpublished manuscript. 1966. (Also, in part: *Journal of Experimental Child Psychology,* 1967, 5, 172–185.) [35, 37, 43, 52, 53, 100, 101, 104–106, 115, 117, 133, 136, 142, 144, 149, 155–156]

Zerrahn, G. Formdressur und Formunterscheidung bei der Honigbiene. *Zeitschrift für wissenschaftliche Biologie. Abteilung C, Zeitschrift für vergleichende Physiologie,* 1933, 2, 117–150. (Source: C. J. Warden *et al.,* 1940, pp. 698 and 1021.) [173]

Zerrahn-Wolf, Gertrud. See Wolf and Zerrahn-Wolfe, 1937.

Ziegler, W. See Kroh, 1927.

Zigler, E. F. See Balla and Zigler, 1964.

Zimmermann, R. R. Form generalization in the infant monkey. *Journal of Comparative and Physiological Psychology,* 1962, 55, 918–923. [213, 215]

Zusne, L. See Michels and Zusne, 1965.

Subject Index

"Absolute" discrimination, *see also* Discrimination learning, 49, 114, 161, 189–198, 244–245, 246–247
comparison of absolute, relative, and standard discrimination problems, 189–198, 308
defined, 189
as learning of two relational responses, 190–191, 238
transposition between stimulus sets, effect of, 192–193
variables affecting, *see* Age level, Brain injury, Concept knowledge
"Absolute feel" (Klüver), *see also* Comparison, 68, 83, 291
Absolute response, defined, 14, 15
Absolute stimulus
defined, 5, 13, 81, 245
preferences, 55, 62, 75, 181–182, 184, 191, 194, 195, 303
qualities
existence of, 5, 7
memory of, 137, 159, 234–236, 237, 239, 298
relation perception, effect on, 232–234, 239, 317
response to, 55–62, 81, 129, 190–191, 198, 273, 298, 309
Absolute theories of transposition, 7, 9–10, 59–60, 69, 123, 129, 152, 196, 229, 237, 245, 273–292, 293–308 *passim*
Acquired distinctiveness of cues, 49, 155, 258–261
Action forms (Katz), transposition of, 224–226
Adaptation level, 31, 54, 234–235, 249–254, 309, 310, 319
delay of test, effect of, 310
Adaptation level theories of transposition, 234–235, 249–254, 293–308 *passim*
Afferent neural interaction (Hull), 11, 287, 313

Age level effect on
absolute and relative discrimination learning, 192
cognitive functions, *see also* Associative-cognitive functions, Mediational deficiency, 261, 266, 267–268
concept knowledge, 150, 151, 321
cross-modal transfer, 219
direction of scanning, 204–205
discrimination learning speed, 161, 192
discrimination shifts, 266
distance effect, 52, 110, 112, 118, 120, 163, 164
form transposition, 204–205, 206–207, 209, 210–211
relation perception, 309
stimulus similarity, effect of, 52, 164
transposition, 69, 75, 78, 141, 144, 159–164, 169, 256, 286, 307, 321
Albedo, transposition as a function of change in, 247–248
Amount of training, effect on
disruptive effect of tests, 101
distance effect, 118
transposition
intermediate-stimulus problems, 66–67, 144, 170, 298–300, 318
motivation, effect of, 63–64
after simultaneous vs successive discrimination training, 63–64
two-stimulus problems, 42, 58, 63–66, 67, 133, 298–300, 318
Aphasia, possible effect on transposition, 256–257
Associationism, 3–5, 9–10, 16, 223, 231, 273
Associative-cognitive functions (White), 261–263
Asymmetrical stimulus sets, 53–54, 298
Attention, *see also* Comparison, Observing response, Orienting reflex, 39, 54, 78–79, 81, 101, 138, 157–158,